Beyond Babar

The European Tradition in Children's Literature

Edited by
Sandra L. Beckett
Maria Nikolajeva

The Children's Literature Association
and
The Scarecrow Press, Inc.
Lanham, Maryland • Toronto • Oxford
2006

SCARECROW PRESS, INC.

Published in the United States of America
by Scarecrow Press, Inc.
A wholly owned subsidiary of
The Rowman & Littlefield Publishing Group, Inc.
4501 Forbes Boulevard, Suite 200, Lanham, Maryland 20706
www.scarecrowpress.com

PO Box 317
Oxford
OX2 9RU, UK

British Library Cataloguing in Publication Information Available

Library of Congress Cataloging-in-Publication Data

Beckett, Sandra L., 1953–
  Beyond Babar : the European tradition in children's literature / edited by
Sandra L. Beckett, Maria Nikolajeva.
      p. cm.
  Includes bibliographical references and index.
  ISBN-13: 978-0-8108-5415-4 (pbk. : alk. paper)
  ISBN-10: 0-8108-5415-5 (pbk. : alk. paper)
  1. Children's literature, European—History and criticism.   I. Nikolajeva,
Maria. II. Title.
PN1009.A1B43   2006
809′.89282094—dc22   2006020838

♾ ™The paper used in this publication meets the minimum requirements of
American National Standard for Information Sciences—Permanence of Paper
for Printed Library Materials, ANSI/NISO Z39.48-1992. Manufactured in the
United States of America.

Contents

Introduction

Sandra L. Beckett

This project began with the intention of devoting a volume to a selection of the best international children's novels, as a complementary work to the three volumes of *Touchstones: Reflections on the Best in Children's Literature* that were edited by Perry Nodelman and published by the Children's Literature Association in 1985–89. The ChLA Canon Committee, which was appointed in 1980 to develop a children's literature "canon," established the list of "touchstones."[1] The traditional literary canon included only one children's book, Lewis Carroll's *Alice in Wonderland*, according to Nodelman (1985, 9), although it should be pointed out that such a canon would apply particularly to the English-speaking world. At the time, there was a perceived need by children's literature scholars, at least in North America, for a canon of children's literature, even though traditional literary canons were already being questioned and criticized, revisited and revised, deconstructed and reconstructed, in an attempt to be inclusive. In his introduction to the first *Touchstones* volume, Nodelman admits that one of the defects of the touchstones list is the fact that the books are "mainly American or British" (8). Of the twenty-eight titles selected for that particular volume, which was devoted to children's novels, there are only two non-English-language works, *Heidi* and *Pinocchio*. *Beyond Babar* was intended to fill the gaps left by the first *Touchstones* volume by adopting a global perspective and providing essays on a corpus of masterpieces for children from around the world, a kind of "International Touchstones."

As members of the ChLA International Committee and former presidents of the International Research Society for Children's Literature, Maria Nikolajeva and I are particularly committed to introducing to English-speaking readers international children's books that are little known in North America or Great Britain. However, the lack of translations into English of important children's books from many parts of the world made it impossible to compile a truly representative international volume. This difficulty led us to revise the project and devote it entirely to European literature, since the majority of the small proportion of international children's books translated into English in North America are from the Western tradition. Children's literature from the so-called developing countries hardly ever reaches American readers. Paradoxically, globalization is only making the problem more acute. Regretfully, one is forced to conclude, as Emer O'Sullivan does in her article on "Internationalism" in Peter Hunt's *International Companion Encyclopedia of Children's Literature*, that a "genuinely international literature" for children is not available (O'Sullivan 2004, 23), at least not in English-speaking countries. It is, however, certainly something that all those working in the field of children's literature studies must strive to achieve. It is our hope that enough translations of important children's novels from Africa, Asia, the Middle East, South America, and other geographical areas will be made available that another volume can be added to the series in the near future.

It is obvious that translations play a key role in the constitution of literary canons that cross languages and cultures. Maria Nikolajeva devotes an entire essay in this volume to the issues involved in the translation of children's novels. As a professor in a Department of Modern Languages, Literatures, and Cultures, I have been deeply troubled for years by the fact that many works that are bestsellers in their country of origin, and often in many other countries as well, have never been translated into English. Even works by major, award-winning authors all too often remain completely unknown in the Anglophone world. In contrast, the works of important English-language authors tend to be translated rapidly into most major European languages. An examination of the global book market reveals an appalling discrepancy in the proportion of translations produced from one country to another. It is not surprising that English-speaking countries translate the smallest percentage of books, but the actual statistics are alarming.

Whereas 80% of the books published in Finland are translations, that figure drops to a mere 3% in Great Britain and only 1% in the United States (O'Sullivan 2004, 22). Although there is a growing interest in international literature among teachers and scholars in North America, it is crucial that publishers be convinced of the importance of issuing translations of foreign books. Even a number of the authors included in this volume have not been translated into English to the extent that their significance in their own country would warrant. For example, only the first two novels in Cecil Bødker's lengthy Silas suite have been translated. Likewise, the sequel to Janusz Korczak's popular *King Matt the First* was never translated. *The Little Prince*, by Antoine de Saint-Exupéry, is unique in that it was written and published first in the United States, and has enjoyed equal success in English and French.

Even when works have the good fortune to be translated, the quality of the translations is often quite poor. In fact, translations often diverge radically from the original work. Nikolajeva attributes Pippi Long-stocking's misadventures in English-speaking countries to inadequate translations. Other books have had similar misfortunes. Dieter Petzold rightly claims that Ralph Manheim's faithful translation of Michael Ende's *The Neverending Story* is "a happy exception to a sad rule." Another fortunate exception is Michel Tournier's *Friday and Robinson: Life on Speranza Island*, which, on the whole, was well translated by Manheim. In this case, however, the excellent translation was not enough to ensure its success in the North American market.

The Mildred L. Batchelder Award is presented, by the American Library Association, to an American publisher for an outstanding translation of a foreign children's book. This award was given to the translations of books by several authors discussed in this volume, including Astrid Lindgren and Cecil Bødker. Even award-winning translations may be problematic, however, as Sabine Fuchs shows in her essay on Christine Nöstlinger's *Konrad*, for which Anthea Bell's American translation won the award in 1978. Several of the works included in this volume underwent radical title changes when they were translated into English, changes that may very well have affected nega-tively their fate in the North American or British markets. Gianni Rodari's *La Freccia Azzurra*, which means "The Blue Arrow," was translated as *The Befana's Toyshop: A Twelfth Night Tale*, a more com-plex, learned title that Ann Lawson Lucas suggests may account for its more limited circulation. Tournier's elevation of Friday to mythic status in his retelling of the story of Robinson Crusoe was undermined by the English translation of the title, which not only reinstated Robinson, but actually gave him first billing.

Tournier's novel was published in the United States in the year following its issue in France. In other cases, however, many years may go by before the first translation even appears in English. Ende's *The Neverending Story* came out four years after its publication in Germany and Lindgren's *Pippi Longstocking* five years after its issue in Sweden. Rodari's novel was not published in English until 1970, although it appeared in Italy in 1954. Even Rodari's groundbreaking theoretical work, *Grammatica della fantasia* (1973), which has influenced writers and educators throughout Europe for several decades, was not made available to English readers until Jack Zipes published his translation, *The Grammar of Fantasy*, with the Teachers & Writers Collaborative in 1996.

In most cases, the circulation of these books in the English-speaking world is quite limited in comparison with sales in the country of origin or even in many other European countries. Although excellent English translations of Tournier's and Ende's novels exist, they have never been widely read in the Anglophone world, nor have they been the object of much discussion by critics and scholars. Some international novels are known to the North American public largely through film versions that frequently distort the original stories and invest them with new meanings. This was the case for two cinematographic adaptations of the 1980s. Nikolajeva discusses some of the shortcomings of the American film based on Lindgren's Pippi stories in 1988. Ende himself lamented the "Americanization" of his book in the 1984 film version of *The Neverending Story*, which deviates so much from the novel that, as Dieter Petzold explains, the author felt obliged to take legal action against it. That did not prevent the production of two sequels, which also take extensive liberties with the book. It is no doubt fortunate that many of these novels have managed to escape both the Disney empire and the Hollywood film industry. They have thus remained somewhat unscathed by the rampant consumerism that has engulfed J. K. Rowling's Harry Potter novels or J. R. R. Tolkien's *Lord of the Rings* series.

The purpose of this volume was never to present as many books as possible from the largest number of countries possible. Several recent publications have already undertaken to provide this information, notably Carl Tomlinson's *Children's Books from Other Countries* (1998), and Susan Stan's companion volume, *The World through Children's Books* (2002), annotated bibliographies of international children's books containing several hundred titles each. In contrast, *Beyond Babar* examines in depth eleven of the most celebrated European children's novels in substantial, critical essays written by well-known international scholars. This approach allows a comprehensive discussion of the selected works from a variety of theoretical perspectives. Each essay offers a critical introduction to the text that can serve as a point of departure for literary scholars, professors of children's literature, primary and secondary school teachers, and librarians who are interested in texts that cross languages and cultures. *Beyond Babar* is especially meant to assist instructors of children's literature who would like to use these texts in the classroom, in order to begin to redress the English-language dominance of many children's literature courses. We also hope that the volume will be of interest to the general public, as its ultimate aim is bring to the attention of all English-speaking readers the literature from other parts of the world, in this case from Europe.

In selecting the works to be included in *Beyond Babar*, we used very similar criteria to those applied for the original *Touchstones* volumes, that is to say, excellence, importance, distinctiveness, and popularity. Like the novels included in the first volume, those we chose are also, to a certain extent, "books that are paradoxically both the most unconventional and the most representative of conventions" (Nodelman 1985, 8). In addition, our selection process involved a number of pragmatic criteria dictated by the fact that we were dealing with texts in languages other than English. Firstly, we included only novels that have been translated into English. Although this is an obvious condition, it made the selection quite difficult because so few foreign books are translated. Many works that are considered classics in their homeland are never made available to English-speaking readers. Even when they have been translated, quite often they do not stay in print for very long. Another practical consideration was, therefore, that the books be easily available in English, that is, in print and preferably in paperback editions. This consideration was to ensure that professors or teachers would have easy access to the books for classroom use. Although this is indeed the case for the majority of the novels, Rodari's *The Befana's Toyshop* is no longer in print. This work is important enough, however, that we felt it was imperative to include it. Further, it is available through libraries and second-hand networks. In their own countries, these books have become modern classics and are regularly reissued in new editions. Tournier's *Friday and Robinson* has sold several million copies in France, where it is one of France's bestselling children's books, surpassed only by *The Little Prince*, but it was more than thirty years after the first translation before it was finally reissued in English in 2003. It is our hope that, as was the case with the European Picture Book Collection, a project carried out with the support of the European Community, other major works will once again be made available if there is enough demand from children's literature mediators. In that particular instance, however, it was a question of keeping books in print in their own countries, a decidedly easier feat than keeping translated books in print, especially in North America.

Beyond Babar includes a selection of the very best European children's books available in translation. For that reason, some countries are represented by more than one essay, whereas other countries are not represented at all. Since this book is devoted only to novels, other genres, such as the fairy tales of Charles Perrault, the Grimm Brothers, and Hans Christian Andersen—undoubtedly the best-known European children's stories—were obviously not included. Further, as the title *Beyond Babar* suggests, books that are widely known in North America were deliberately excluded, in particular *Pinocchio* and *Heidi*, which were selected for the first *Touchstones* volume. All the novels were written in the twentieth-century, and they span much of the century. The earliest novel examined is Korczak's *King Matt the First*, published in Poland in 1923. With the exception of *The Little Prince*, written in 1943, all the other novels are post-World War II, beginning with *Pippi Longstocking*, issued in Sweden in 1945. The most recent is Jostein Gaarder's international bestseller *Sophie's World*, which appeared in 1991.

The books selected have radically marked children's literature and affected significantly its status in their country of origin and, in most cases, far beyond. They are written by some of the most important twentieth-century children's authors, several of whom were awarded the prestigious Andersen Medal: Astrid Lindgren in 1958, Tove Jansson in 1966, Gianni Rodari in 1970, Cecil Bødker in 1976, and Christine Nöstlinger in 1984. However, these authors are generally not as well known as they deserve in the English-speaking world. Rodari, for example, is considered the most significant Italian children's author of the twentieth-century (that is to say, he is surpassed only by Carlo Collodi), and his reputation is well established in many European countries, but he remains virtually unknown by English-speaking readers. Ende became a kind of cult author in Germany, but he is probably better known in Japan than in North America. Very prestigious literary prizes were awarded to many of these novels. *The Neverending Story*, for example, won no less than ten international prizes within the first four years of its publication, that is, before it was even translated into English. Christine Nöstlinger won the very first international Astrid Lindgren Memorial Award in 2003. These books are favorites with young readers, parents, educators, and publishers in their own countries and in many other parts of the world. They are firmly established in school curricula and constitute customary school prizes. Many are highly regarded by critics at home and have engendered a substantial body of highly reputable scholarship and criticism. A few, but far from all, of these works have been the object of serious critical study by the English-speaking scholarly community. The lasting success of these novels attests to their excellence. Many years after their publication, they are still bestsellers in their own countries, and often in many other countries as well, indicating that they are indeed true classics. Ende's bestselling novel offers an excellent example. According to Dieter Petzold, 7.7 million copies of *The Neverending Story* have been sold worldwide, 3.2 million of those in Germany and the rest abroad. It has been translated into a total of thirty-six languages. Tove Jansson's Moomin novels have been translated into thirty-four languages and Astrid Lindgren's into more than eighty. A few of these books nonetheless had a difficult start. Ironically, the manuscripts for Lindgren's first *Pippi* book and for Tournier's *Friday and Robinson*, both still huge bestsellers, were initially turned down by leading Swedish and French publishers, respectively. Some of these highly popular works inspired sequels, as in the case of the Pippi stories and the Moomin books.

The authors of these novels often broke with the conventions of children's book publishing of the time and forged new paths for their successors. Cecil Bødker's writing for children transgressed the notion of children's literature in 1960s Denmark. Although Tove Jansson's Moomin books more or less respected literary conventions in the beginning, they gradually became increasingly experimental. Astrid Lindgren, Michel Tournier, and Peter Pohl, among others, sought to question the status quo and overturn conventional attitudes. Freeing themselves from the rigid moral codes and taboos that had long governed children's literature, many of these authors explore controversial topics, for example, gender issues and child abuse in *Johnny, My*

Friend, racism in *Friday and Robinson*, and war and power in *King Matt the First*. Some authors, notably Ende, came under attack from the extreme religious right, in much the same manner as J. K. Rowling and Philip Pullman in more recent years. There is a great deal of innovative formal experimentation in many of these works. Often they are complex and multilayered books that invite readings on various levels. Ende and Gaarder were by no means certain that their ambitious and challenging novels would meet with success. The metafictional play in *The Neverending Story* and *Sophie's World* is quite sophisticated, as are the narrative strategies of *Johnny, My Friend*. Open endings are a common feature of these novels, and *Johnny, My Friend* and *Moominvalley in November* offer striking examples. Often these authors engage in clever intertextual play, alluding to some of the most beloved works of children's literature. *The Befana's Toyshop* contains intertextual references to *Pinocchio*, *Friday and Robinson* to *Robinson Crusoe*, *The Neverending Story* to *The Lord of the Rings*, *Pippi Longstocking* to *Anne of Green Gables*, *Johnny, My Friend* to *Pippi*, and so forth. Several novels share common traits with traditional tales and other favorite genres for children, but they are generally updated and given a modern twist. *The Befana's Toyshop* is a fairy tale, but it marks a modern evolution of the genre, as Ann Lawson Lucas points out. *The Neverending Story* has been called an educational fairy tale, but it is also a fantasy fiction and, as Petzold demonstrates, a meta-fantasy that reflects on the fantasy genre. These books are often difficult to categorize, defying genre classification. *The Little Prince* has been designated as a fable, a fairy tale, a parable, an allegory, and a philosophical tale. Furthermore, as Claire Malarte-Feldman illustrates in her essay, the graphic element is inseparable from the text in this unique book illustrated by the author. Frequently, the conventions of several genres are blended, as, for example, in the Moomin novels or the Pippi books. *The Befana's Toyshop* is an episodic story that shares some of the characteristics of a short story collection. The limited success of some of these books in English-speaking countries may have something to do with differences in literary traditions. For example, Lucas rightly points out that English literary history does not have the long tradition of linked tales that exists in Italy.

The novels included in *Beyond Babar* are all classics of children literature, even if some have perhaps not achieved that status in the English-speaking world. Further, many are considered masterpieces of literature in Europe and would find their place in the literary canons of certain linguistic areas, just as Carroll's *Alice in Wonderland* does in English-language countries. At least one of these works is actually among the most famous books in the world. As Malarte-Feldman mentions, Saint-Exupéry's *The Little Prince* is said to be the third best-known book after the Bible and *Das Kapital*. A number of these authors wrote for adults as well as children. Jansson published her first novel for adults two years after winning the Andersen Medal. Saint-Exupéry and Tournier are first and foremost novelists for adults, but their most famous works are children's books. Ende considered himself above all a playwright, but his most successful work is also a children's novel. Many of these novels are, in fact, crossover books that are read by a dual audience of adults and children. In the case of *The Neverending Story*, critics don't even agree that it can be considered a children's book. From Korczak's *King Matt the First* to Gaarder's *Sophie's World*, these books offer multiple layers of meaning for readers of all ages. Like *Alice in Wonderland*, many of these works have an important philosophical element, in particular *The Little Prince*, *Friday and Robinson*, and *Sophie's World*, which is subtitled "A Novel About the History of Philosophy." Because these novels transcend and blur the so-called borders between adult and children's literature, Malarte-Feldman calls these works "books without borders." Their success in many countries makes them "books without borders" in another sense. As we have seen, however, children's books do not "cross all the frontiers" with the ease that Paul Hazard suggests in his influential book *Les livres, les enfants et les hommes* (Hazard 1944, 147). Some borders are much more difficult to cross than others. It is our hope that *Beyond Babar* will help to facilitate the border crossings of these European masterpieces of children's literature in the English-speaking world.

NOTE

1. The term "touchstone" is borrowed from the English poet and essayist Matthew Arnold, who had used it to refer to great poetry (see Nodelman 1985, 1).

WORKS CITED

Hazard, Paul. *Les livres, les enfants et les hommes*. Paris: Flammarion, 1932. Translated by Marguerite Mitchell under the title *Books, Children and Men*. Boston: The Horn Book, 1944.

Nodelman, Perry, ed. *Touchstones: Reflections on the Best in Children's Literature*. 3 vols. West Lafayette, Ind: ChLA, 1985–89.

O'Sullivan, Emer. "Internationalism, the universal child and the world of children's literature." Pp. 13–25 in *International Companion Encyclopedia of Children's Literature*. Ed. Peter Hunt. 2nd ed. Volume I. London: Routledge, 2004.

Rodari, Gianni. *Grammatica della fantasia*. Torino: Einaudi, 1973. Translated by Jack Zipes under the title *The Grammar of Fantasy*. New York: Teachers & Writers Collaborative, 1996.

Stan, Susan, ed. *The World through Children's Books*. Lanham, Md: Scarecrow, 2002.

Tomlinson, Carl M., ed. *Children's Books from Other Countries*. Lanham, Md: Scarecrow, 1998.

1

Earth Hanging in Infinity
Janusz Korczak's *King Matt the First*

Lilia Ratcheva-Stratieva

In 1923 a book was published in the Polish language that has continued to appeal to readers and to play an important role in Polish, European, and world literature for children. This book, entitled *Król Maciusz Pierwszy* (translated as *King Matt the First*, 1986), and its sequel *Król Maciusz na wyspie bezludnej* (1923, "King Matt on the Desert Island"[1]), is the story of an orphan child king who wants to change the world. The author, a pediatrician and educator, was already known for other literary works signed with the pen name Janusz Korczak.[2]

When Little Matt's father, the King, dies, the ten-year-old boy is left alone in the world since he had lost his mother earlier. Further, he is obliged to become the king and to rule the country. In the beginning, the little king is treated as a child by the ministers and virtually left to observe what they do. However, little by little, Matt learns how to fight for his rights and how to make the ministers obey. He learns by asking questions, by trying to remember what his father did in similar situations, and by analyzing the facts in his childlike manner, all while discovering truths for himself. When his neighbors declare war on him, he secretly joins the army and fights on the front lines as an ordinary soldier. In this first war Matt is the winner, and he is very generous toward his enemies, the neighboring kings, a fact that does not save

1

him from being wronged later and from nursing a deeper feeling of loneliness. After the victory Matt comes back to his capital enriched with new experience as a warrior and with better knowledge of people. Having met many times with betrayal on the part of the people around him, he is disappointed with their moral values. Back to peace and to his capital, but disillusioned with adults, King Matt decides to reform the country with the children as allies and organizes a children's parliament. Because of their lack of experience and because of bad advice, the children make a mess of the country. Matt is not only betrayed by adults, but also by his best child friend, Felek. Matt's only true friend appears to be the black girl Klu-Klu, daughter of one of the black kings with whom Matt cooperates. Klu-Klu brings black kids to King Matt's capital and makes them study there. Being brave, honest, direct, and spontaneous, she is the only one who is always ready to help Matt and to make sacrifices for him. Inexperienced, betrayed by the adults in his entourage, and disappointed with those whom he has trusted, King Matt fails in his attempt to reform the kingdom. Using the chaos in his country, the same kings to which he has been generous attack him again. This time King Matt is defeated and condemned to exile on a desert island.

The sequel to *King Matt the First, King Matt on the Desert Island*, begins as an adventure story, describing Matt's different adventures while trying to escape exile. Although written according to the conventions of an adventure novel, this part of the book is also a psychological study of the people Matt meets on the way. The second half of the book takes place on the desert island where Matt has lots of time to read, study, and think. He tries to understand the world. Korczak leaves Matt to think over his bitter experience, his reforms, and the reasons that they have failed. The more he knows, the greater is his disappointment. Eventually, it appears that there is no place for him on earth. People like him are not needed; they create only trouble with their ambitions to change the world. The second book ends with Matt's death.

KORCZAK'S CONCERN FOR CHILDREN

Books for children are usually born of love. Korczak's *King Matt the First* is no exception. The child was, for Korczak, a miracle. Before *King Matt the First* was published, the author had already shown his love, care, and respect for children in his pedagogical works[3] and in his activities as a physician. People who knew Korczak often said how important children were for him. In the book of memoirs by the pupils or collaborators of Janusz Korczak, *Wspomnienia o Januszu Korczaku* (Remembrances of Janusz Korczak), the authors state repeatedly that Korczak saw in children the meaning of his life. The following anecdote is only one example of his attitude. A schoolmate once met Korczak in the Saski Park in Warsaw, where he was sitting on a bench, observing children. The friend asked him why he started studying medicine if he wanted to be a writer. He answered:

> In order to write valuable works, one has to be a good diagnostic. In other words it is necessary to know the human being and its diseases. But the human being is up to now a completely unknown creature. . . . The writer in my opinion must not only have the ambition to know but also to cure human souls. (Barszczewska 1981, 225)

Two words are important when addressing Korczak's attitude toward children: love and respect. Even the titles of his pedagogical works alone are sufficient to illustrate this fact: *How to Love a Child* and *Prawo dziecka do szacunku* (1928; *The Child's Right to Respect* 1992). This concern for children was definitively proven by the example of Korczak's life and death. He did not have children of his own. His children were the pupils from the Jewish orphanage in Krochmalna Street in Warsaw. He dedicated his life to organizing and running this orphanage. Not only did he love these children and take care of them, but he also sacrificed his life for them. During World War II the orphanage was forced to become part of the Warsaw Ghetto. Korczak had many opportunities to leave the Ghetto and save his own life, but he refused and stayed with *his children* till the end. During the deportation of the Ghetto, he went to the gas chambers of Treblinka ahead of them. He was last seen in Warsaw on the "Umschlagplatz" on August 6, 1942. Thus Korczak has become an epitome of humanity and care for children. Like *his children* he became "earth hanging in infinity."

What is the origin of Korczak's interest and concern for children and childhood? The turn of the 19th century witnessed a rapid development of pedagogy as a scientific field, as well as the development of biological science, in conjunction with studies of human behavior and psychology. The pedagogical ideas at the time were concerned with developing respect rather than obedience and punishment, which were a common practice in Europe. In the first decades of the twentieth century, Europe produced several reformers of the methods of bringing up children, whose methods are still used. One example was Maria Montessori (1870–1952), whose system was based on belief in children's creative potential, their drive to learn, and their right to be treated as individuals; she created a school for disadvantaged children, and wrote about the need to build inner discipline. Another was the French teacher Celestine Freinet (1896–1996), who, after World War I, devised a system to help children to learn by themselves without depending on classroom instruction. During his stays in Berlin (1907), Paris (1909), and London (1911) Korczak had the opportunity to get acquainted with the new trends in pedagogy, as well as with the educational theories developed in the nineteenth century by Johann Heinrich Pestalozzi in Switzerland and Herbert Spenser in Britain. Serving as an army doctor during World War I, he used his time not only to cure people but also to visit educational institutions using Maria Montessori's program. Later Janusz Korczak developed his own pedagogical views and became one of this group of reformers of European education in the first half of the twentieth century. All these pioneers believed that children have to be treated with respect and their educational systems involved genuine esteem for the child's feelings, for his or her needs and concerns, and deeper knowledge of the child's psychology.

Another source of Korczak's interest in the child was probably his own childhood experience. As a child, the little Henryk Goldszmit—Korczak's name at birth—observed the poor children playing in the yard of his Warsaw home with whom he was not allowed to play. Later Korczak ascribes the same experience to his protagonist King Matt. As early as that time Korczak began to reflect upon the injustice in the world and, like King Matt, the little Henryk dreamed of changing the world. Many years later he wrote in his diary:

> Already at that time I confessed to my granny in a face-to-face conversation my plan to rebuild the world, for example to ban all the money. Where and how, and what to do next I, of course, didn't know. Don't judge me too severely. I was then five years old, and the task was extremely difficult. What to do so that children will no longer be dirty, shabby and hungry, like the ones in the yard with whom I was not allowed to play. ("Pamietnik" 513)

Yet another reason for Korczak's interest in the child was the contemporary manner of bringing up children, which relied heavily on punishment. The main principle of this practice was "Better to cry now than later, for the child's own sake." This practice often led to children feeling miserable, frightened, and mistreated, and living with constant guilt. These principles, or rather the lack thereof, are to be found in many of Korczak's literary works. In *King Matt the First*, for example, Felek, Matt's friend, often shares with Matt his father's threats; on different occasions and for different reasons, the latter promises to beat him until his skin peels off. In one note written to King Matt, Felek mentions that his father had thrashed him severely because, when preparing to go to the front, the boy took his flask, penknife, and bandolier. Felek, of course, never owns up to having taken them. Physical punishment is also mentioned when Felek insists on receiving a certificate for being King Matt's favorite; his father learns about it, and his first reaction is to beat him severely. The attitude toward the child and the pedagogical practice that Korczak witnessed as a child and later as pediatrician and educator, the humiliations he himself suffered as a child, or the humiliations of other children he observed are depicted in his literary works. In another of his works, *Dziecko salonu* (*The Salon Child*, 1906), Korczak gives striking examples of how children were treated at the time in the family, at school, or by society. He depicts a scene in which a child, Stasiek, who had to work from nine in the morning till seven in the evening for the miserable salary of one rouble per week, arrives late to work and gets punished by his father. The narrator describes in a matter-of-fact tone how the father pulled down Stasiek's shorts, tucked up his shirt, put the boy's head between his legs, took off his own belt, and beat him cruelly. And he adds, in the same matter-of-fact tone, that Stasiek was nine years old. The philosophy of the boy's father is that he who beats, loves, whereas the one who kisses does his child wrong.

In *Kiedy znów będę mały* (1925; *When I Am Little Again*, 1992), the protagonist describes the schools of his dreams, probably the schools of the future, with smiling and good-hearted teachers. Assigned the task of drawing a picture in class, the adult-turned-child protagonist makes a so-called triptych, entitled "The Former School," that presents three school scenes from the time when he first was a child. In the middle there is a picture of a break, in which a teacher is holding a pupil by his ear and beating him with a rod, while the pupil cries and tries to get free. The other children are depicted with bent heads, nobody says anything; they are too afraid. The scene on the right side represents a classroom. The teacher is beating a child with a ruler while one boy on the first bench laughs and the others sympathize. The left side depicts the very cruel punishment. The pupil lies on the bench, the warden holds his feet, and the calligraphy teacher is holding up his hand with the rod, ready to strike. This is a real picture of the school the protagonist attended when he was eight years old. Later he confesses that he was terribly frightened at that time. Further, he confides that schools were not good places when he was a child: they were strict and boring; everything was forbidden. It was so alien, cold, and suffocating that, years later, when his school came to him in his dreams, he would wake in a sweat but always happy that it was only a dream.

Children working ten hours a day, seven days a week and earning nearly nothing; children being beaten because the parents blamed them for their misery or simply because they were persuaded children exist to be tormented; frightened children, serious and worried children— the world was not a comfortable place for a child at that time. It was precisely this view of the child and this attitude toward the child that Korczak wanted to change with his writings, with his practice, and with the example of his own life.

SOCIAL CRITICISM

As an educator and writer who respected child readers, Janusz Korczak discussed in his literary works important "adult" issues, such as friendship and fidelity, improving society, the role of the press, discrimination and inclusion, life and death, the divine and the human. He also discussed these problems with younger readers in *King Matt the First*, where he mixed social and political topics with psychological analysis of human character and human behavior. He charged his readers with a greater responsibility to think over these problems and to develop into thinking grownups. This challenge was not common in the children's literature of the time.

In 1912 Korczak created the orphanage for Jewish children in Warsaw, where he started applying his innovative pedagogical ideas— creating a children's parliament and court, giving children the power to make decisions about their everyday lives and about their destiny, to adjudicate, to run their own press, and so forth. The society in the orphanage, organized in conformity with Korczak's ideas and principles, was so different from the reality outside it that when, in the early thirties, the *Circle of the Former Pupils of the Krochmalna Orphanage* was founded, some of the former pupils started criticizing the pedagogical methods of Korczak, accusing him of not preparing them for real life. This complaint must have been a big shock for Korczak.

After World War I, there was a common feeling of disappointment and bitterness in Europe. In Poland these feelings were initially held in check by enthusiasm for newly won freedom. Poland was independent after having been divided up for 150 years among Russia, Prussia, and Austria-Hungary. But the political reality was not at all easy: the new state was slowly creating its political foundation, and it did not always conform to expectations. Korczak had many reasons to be disenchanted with his contemporaries and with reality. Back in the free Poland of the early thirties after the war and feeling disappointment and bitterness with the political and social reality, Korczak started writing his sad novel about *King Matt the First*—the reformer childking whose dream it was to create a society with "good and wise laws" (121) equally valid for everybody, and to reform his kingdom.

Matt decides to be a Reformer King, but his first problem is that he doesn't know what reforms are: "I'll ask him [the sad king] for advice. He must be a good person. I am the Reformer King and I don't know what reforms are. But he says they are very hard" (120). The sad king, the only one who treats Matt as a grownup, tells him how dangerous it is to win a war, as doing so can make you forget what a king is for. When Matt asks what that is, he replies:

"Not just to wear a crown—but to bring happiness to the people of his country. But how can you bring them happiness? What I did was to make various reforms. . . . But reforms are the hardest thing of all, yes, the hardest."

And then the sad king began playing his violin so sadly that it seemed to be weeping. (120)

Later, the sad king explains to Matt:

"Listen, Matt. My grandfather gave his people freedom, but it didn't turn out well. He was assassinated. And people ended up even more unhappy than before. My father built a great monument to freedom. . . . It's beautiful, but what does that matter when there are still wars, still poor people, still unhappy people? I ordered that great parliament building built. And nothing changed. Everything's still the same." (121–22)

This king also gives Matt a very clear explanation of what Parliament means and shows him his Parliament building. "Parliament was a huge and beautiful building whose interior looked a bit like a theatre [the idea of theatre appears often in *King Matt*; the young king loves the theatre and Korczak wrote for the theatre, yet another shared feature between author and protagonist] and a bit like a church," says the narrator (122). The reader is bewildered as to whether this is Matt's voice or just the voice of the adult narrator:

> The members of parliament sat on a sort of stage at a table, just as they did in Matt's palace during conferences. Except that here there were an awful lot of chairs with all sorts of people sitting in them. Speakers would get up, go to a sort of pulpit, and speak as if they were delivering sermon. There was a special section where the ministers sat. To one side, at a large table, sat the people who wrote for the newspapers. The public was up above. (122)

King Matt then attaches to his name the appellation *the Reformer* and starts changes in his kingdom. He changes the etiquette in the court and introduces reforms. It was the sad king who suggested that he start the reforms with the children: "You know, Matt, we always did the wrong thing by making reforms for adults. Try doing it for children, maybe you will succeed . . ." (122). Matt follows the sad king's advice and starts his reforms with the children:

> Matt waited impatiently for the money, because he wished to introduce three reforms:
>   1. To build camps in all the forests, in the mountains, and at the seashore so that poor children could spend the entire summer in nature.
>   2. To supply all schools with seesaws and merry go rounds of the type that play music.
>   3. To construct a zoo in the capital, with cages for wild animals—lions, bears, elephants, monkeys, snakes, and birds.
>   But Matt was soon to meet with disappointment. When the money arrived, it turned out that the ministers couldn't spare any for Matt's reforms, because they had only calculated how much was required for their own needs. (130)

Following the sad king's recommendations, Matt creates a children's parliament, which orders all the grownups to go back to school while children take over their jobs. This change leads to great confusion: the trains stop running, the phones are out of order, shops are closed, factories shut down, military supplies depleted. Taking advantage of the internal chaos, enemy kings invade Matt's country. By the time that Matt sends the adults back to work and the children back to school and rebuilds his armed forces, it is already too late. Yet, it is not the chaos but the cowardice and the betrayal that cause Matt to lose the war.

Korczak's protagonist, the child-king Matt, does not succeed in his reforms and his attempt to give children the power to decide about their world and their destiny. This failure is the sign of the author's disappointment with humankind and the political reality in which he lived. It also explains the reason why Korczak created in his parable *King Matt the First* a world parallel to the real world and equally cruel and unjust.

Analyzing the behavior of the Ministers, Felek, the journalist, or the cowards who betray Matt and the town, both Matt and the adult narrator describe reality and human behavior with bitterness and irony. While irony takes over the voice of the adult narrator, bitterness comes through in King Matt's naïve and sincere narrative voice. Among the many examples in the book are the chapters relating events just after the first war, after Matt's victorious comeback to the capital, when he orders the arrest of his Ministers because they all complain about money shortages and demand that contributions be exacted from the defeated kings.

A PEDAGOGICAL NOVEL

In his literary work Korczak remains an educator. While Matt learns new skills or listens to other people's explanations, the reader is also educated. Matt does not accept the ready-made answers offered by the adult world. He analyses them, trying to find a solution for himself. From the sad king he learns how very little is allowed even to a king. And still he succeeds in making some changes, starting with tradition and etiquette. Tradition itself is not something that has to be respected. For Korczak this notion doesn't have positive connotations only, and he is often critical of traditions, when he perceives them as irrational, unworkable, or inhumane. At the very beginning of his rule, King Matt experiences the meaning of tradition.

> Every day, Matt would get up at seven o'clock in the morning, wash and dress, shine his boots himself, and make his bed. This custom had been established by his great grandfather, the valiant king Paul the Conqueror. After washing and getting dressed, Matt would drink a glass of cod-liver oil and sit down to breakfast, which could not last more than sixteen minutes thirty-five seconds. That was because Matt's grandfather, the good king Julius the Virtuous, had always taken that amount of time for his breakfast. Then Matt would go to the throne room, which was always very cold, and receive the ministers. There was no heat in the throne room because Matt's great-grandmother, the wise Anna the Pious, had nearly been asphyxiated by a faulty stove when she was a little girl, and in memory of her lucky escape she had decreed that the throne room not be heated for five hundred years. (18)

Korczak doesn't make any comments. By simply describing how the little king receives the ministers, "his teeth chattering from the cold," he directs the reader's thoughts toward an analysis of the meaning of the notion *tradition*, and probably toward a critical appreciation of existing traditions. Later in the book, King Matt breaks with this tradition and orders the throne room to be heated, an act that confirms the reader in his or her judgment about traditions. In addition, such notions as etiquette or diplomacy are introduced with irony. For example, explaining etiquette, Korczak writes:

> It may seem strange that so many things were forbidden to the king. And so I must explain that there is a very strict etiquette at royal courts. Etiquette tells how kings have always acted. A new king cannot do otherwise without losing his honor and without everyone ceasing to fear and respect him for not respecting his father, the king, or his grandfather the king, or his great-grandfather the king. If the king wants to do something differently, then he must inquire of the master of ceremonies, who watches over court etiquette and knows what kings have always done. . . . Once in a while a king could make little changes, but then there would be long meetings, as there had been when Matt wanted to take walks. And it was no fun to ask for something and then have to wait and wait. (21)

King Matt is in a worse position than other kings because etiquette has been established for grownup kings and Matt is a child.

The increased role of the press, which Korczak addresses in his work, is a new topic for children's literature. In the beginning of the twentieth century, the press already began to play an increasingly important role in Western society. Korczak saw the influence of the press and its power to manipulate public opinion and influence politics. In the schools where he worked, he organized children's newspapers. The newspaper *Mały przegląd*, in the orphanage for Jewish children, was quite popular. In his fiction, too, Korczak attributed great importance to the press and its double-edged benefits. On the formal level this opinion of the press is reflected by his punctilious description of an editorial office in *King Matt the First*, and, much more importantly, by the frequent expression of his own political and educative ideas through passages presented in the form of quotations from the press. Yet he sees the manipulative danger in modern mass media. It is very often the journalist who tells Matt, Felek, and the other children what to do. In the beginning he succeeds in persuading them of the importance of his own ideas; then he manages to persuade them that these were their own ideas. This duplicitous practice is clearly condemned by the way in which the author portrays the betrayal of the press; initially the press supports King Matt, but little by little it turns against him and contributes to the failure of his reforms.

In his parable, the author combines entertainment, found in the unending adventures of the protagonist, with the process of educating both the protagonist and the reader. Korczak's works are for both child and adult reader, provided the reader thinks, asks questions, looks for the truth, and is not afraid of challenges. The destiny of Korczak's protagonists is often tragic. The most tragic fate of all is that of King Matt. It is striking that such a sad book was written for children. The powerful book moves the reader and, once read, becomes unforgettable. Korczak's works have deep philosophical meaning, with bitter reflections, at the same time enlivened by jokes, irony, and the grotesque.

Bruno Bettelheim, who wrote the foreword to the American translation of *King Matt the First*, claims that this book is a profound study of children's psychology:

> Further, in this work of fiction about a boy king, we are given one of the most penetrating and subtle studies of the psychology of children, a study far superior to the usual scientific and popular studies of child psychology, because most of these are based on considerably less intimate, less intensive, and less prolonged involvement with children, and on an understanding far inferior to that of Korczak. (vi)

There are many occasions in this book when Korczak shows the feelings and concerns of his young protagonist. For example, when Matt and Felek are at the front line and Felek leaves to go into the air force, the narrator writes:

> Matt was a little sad that Felek was gone, but he was a little happy too.
>
> Felek was the only one who knew that Matt was the king. True, Matt had asked him to call him Tomek. But it wasn't right for Felek to treat him as an equal. And he didn't even do that. Matt was younger, and so Felek was disrespectful to him. Felek drank vodka and smoked cigarettes, but whenever someone wanted to treat Matt to some, Felek would say right away: "Don't give him any, he's too little."
>
> Matt didn't like drinking or smoking, but he wanted to say no, thank you, himself, and not have Felek answer for him. (73)

Another example shows him being discriminated against by others because of his age. Although Matt had won the war, he "had been surprised that none of the kings discussed the loan or anything else with him. After all, kings get together to talk about politics and other important things. But not them. He thought they didn't want to talk to him because he was little . . ." (120). Matt is intelligent enough to notice that no matter how clever his words, decisions, or acts, adults usually disregard and neglect him because of his age. When he meets with respect and understanding, when he meets people for whom his opinion is of importance, however, he is happy and confident.

A scene in the children's parliament describes Korczak's comprehension of the desires and concerns of the other children:

> "I want to keep pigeons," one shouted.
> "I want a dog."
> "Every child should have a watch."
> "Children should be allowed to use the telephone."
> "We want kielbasa."
> "And headcheese."
> "We want to go to bed late."
> "Every child should have a bicycle . . ." (248)

Some of the childish wishes provoke particular reflection, for example, "We don't want people kissing us." Other wishes include: "Let them tell us fairy tales," every child should have "his own bookcase," or "Every child should have his own room," but also "Abolish girls and little children," or "Children should have money and be able to buy things," "We want a special day when the grownups have to stay at home and the children can go wherever they want," "Grownups should go to school," and "Every child should be allowed to break a window once a month." Presenting and discussing children's wishes, having them commented on by the journalist, Korczak creates a book that defamiliarizes both child and adult behavior. The desire to abolish girls gives the author the opportunity to introduce Klu-Klu's speech in the children's parliament, where she defends equal rights for girls and boys. It is significant that the author decides to have the black girl Klu-Klu present the progressive idea of equal rights. Bruno Bettelheim comments on Korczak's understanding of the distinct manner in which children perceive things:

> Most do not entertain the idea that children and adults have different perceptions of the same experience, as this book makes clear. For children are delighted if adults show them affection the way they desire to receive it: foremost, by being taken seriously, and second, by being treated and played with on the level they enjoy. (viii)

The most convincing psychological portrait of a child protagonist in Korczak's works is that of the little King Matt. The author not only deeply sympathizes with his child protagonist's feelings, but he really identifies with that protagonist. The extent to which Korczak has identified himself with his protagonist is evident from the beginning of King Matt's story. For the frontispiece of the book, Korczak used his own picture as a child, with the following explanation:

> When I was the little boy you see in the photograph, I wanted to do all the things that are in this book. But I forgot to, and now I'm old. I no longer have the time or the strength to go to war or travel to the land of the cannibals. I have included this photograph because it's important what I looked like when I truly wanted to be a king, and not when I was writing about King Matt. I think it's better to show pictures of what kings, travelers, and writers looked like before they grew up, or grew old, because otherwise it might seem that they knew everything from the start and were never young themselves. And then children will think they can't be statesmen, travelers, and writers, which wouldn't be true. (Korczak 1966, n.p.)

Korczak himself was an introvert and did not like to show his feelings; some of his pupils write that he was very reserved toward them, but his writings show a fine, sensitive empathy that allowed him to identify with the child protagonists. Indeed, Korczak identifies with his protagonist so deeply that he not only gives him his thoughts, not only speaks through his mouth, but he also ascribes to him his deeds. The reforms the child king introduces are the reforms that the child Henryk Goldszmit wanted, reforms that would bring justice to the world, or the reforms Korczak as educator experimented with in the orphanage for Jewish children. If we borrow Flaubert's "Madame Bovary, c'est moi," we may say for Korczak, "King Matt, it's me."

Although Korczak identifies deeply with his child king protagonist, it is important for him as an educator to present not only the child's perspective, but the perspective of the experienced adult as well. In all his important literary works this double perspective appears, presented in different ways. In *King Matt* the double perspective is achieved through the different narrative voices—the voice of the narrator, the voice of King Matt, and also the voices of other children and adults. Two years after *King Matt the First*, Korczak published *When I Am Little Again*. In this book the author finds an original solution for providing this double perspective and mixing different narrative voices: his protagonist, an adult person with adult experience, knowledge, and understanding of the world, turns into a child. Thus, two narrative voices fuse into one through a fantastic plot; this child looks at the world and makes comments and judgments from the perspectives of both a child and an adult. Something similar happens in *King Matt*. Little by little, as the plot develops, the two narrative voices—the child Matt's and the narrator's—come closer to each other in their bitterness and disappointment.

This fusion of narrative perspectives and voices leads to one of the main problems in Korczak's prose: the problem of identity. This is obviously not a new theme for literature, but Korczak discusses it in the new context of twentieth-century history. The issue of changed identity recurs in Korczak's literary works, and doubles and doubling are one of the principles upon which his works are built. The child-adult protagonist of *When I Am Little Again* is one example. The topic of multiple identities culminates in the *King Matt* books. The protagonist constantly changes identity: he is a king, but he is also an ordinary child playing with other children or picking blueberries and wild cherries; further he is a soldier who goes to the front and thus experiences contemporary war.

The story of King Matt the First, unlike other literary works by

Korczak, is not in the first person singular. There is a narrator who, sometimes with the irony of the experienced adult and sometimes with the sincere and naive voice of the child king, accompanies the reader throughout the adventures of the child protagonist. The voice of King Matt is heard throughout the story. A description of the daily routine in the Palace of King Matt shows this hybridization, to use Mikhail Bakhtin's term, of narrator's and character's voices:

> Then Matt would go to the throne room, which was always very cold, and receive the ministers. . . .
>
> Matt would sit on the throne, his teeth chattering from the cold, while his ministers told him what was happening throughout the country. This was very unpleasant because, for some reason, the news was always bad.
>
> The Minister of Foreign Affairs would tell him who was angry at them and who wanted to be their friend. Usually, Matt could not make heads or tails of any of it.
>
> The Minister of War would list how many fortresses were damaged, how many cannons were out of commission and how many soldiers were sick. The Minister of the Railroads would say that they had to buy new locomotives.
>
> The Minister of Education would complain that the children weren't studying, were late to school, that boys were sneaking out to smoke cigarettes and were also tearing pages out of their workbooks. The girls were calling each other names and arguing, the boys were fighting, throwing stones, and breaking windows.
>
> The Minister of Finance was always angry that there was no money, and he didn't want to buy new cannons or new machines because they cost too much.
>
> Then Matt would go to the royal gardens. For an hour he could run and play, but it wasn't very much fun to play alone. (19)

In these reflections the reader distinguishes both the irony of the adult narrator and the naivety of the child king. In his other literary works, Korczak also often connects the viewpoint of the child with the viewpoint of the experienced adult. This connection is especially evident in *When I Am Little Again,* in which the narration is from the perspective of adult-child. Naive at the beginning, King Matt gets wiser and sadder as he gains knowledge and experience, thus coming closer to the adult narrator, so that the two narrative voices nearly fuse at the end. The narrative and dialogues in this book mix different styles: the high, literary style and the ordinary, vulgar language of the soldiers at war or the children in the street; the ironic narrative of an adult dissatisfied with reality, and the naïve and emotional language of children. The adult narrator's voice is sometimes ironic, while King Matt's voice filters through as sincere and full of emotion. When King Matt's voice comes to the fore, there are subtle stylistic changes to signal this: the syntax of the narrative voice changes, the sentences become sometimes elliptic, sometimes repetitive, full of rhetorical questions or exclamations.

The voice of the adult narrator mixes in this book with the voices of the child characters and especially with the inner voice of King Matt himself, who dominates the narration. The sincerity of this voice moves the readers, who can believe in the fortunes and misfortunes of Matt, although they are expressed in the convention of fantasy.

LITERARY ARTISTRY

In formal terms, Korczak is also innovative: he uses various elements from adult literature, subverts traditional genre conventions, and changes narrative perspectives. In introducing themes previously unknown in literature for children, he mixes elements from different styles, thus creating a body of work that anticipates postmodern practices. In *King Matt the First*, we find elements of the literary tradition of the Enlightenment and the nineteenth-century realistic novel, mixed with pre-postmodern elements and fantasy. Korczak blurs genre boundaries in most of his literary works. His works are at once novels, essays on education, and fairy tales. Using his own experience and his observation of children as a starting point, Korczak reveals insights into child psychology that teachers and educators can use as an aid to better understand it.

One of the secrets to the success of *King Matt the First* and its sequel *King Matt on the Desert Island* is the fact that Korczak combines new with familiar, fantasy with contemporary reality, and that these two books are intended for and appeal to both children and adults. One specificity of Korczak's work—the coming together of fiction and documentary—can also be found in *King Matt the First*. The imaginative Matt lives in the reality of the early twentieth century. The Press Office, for instance, is a real press office of Korczak's time, described in a detailed manner. Some descriptions and scenes in *King Matt the First*, as in other Korczak works, have the value of a documentary account. The depiction of war in *King Matt* is like a documentary of the First World War, which Korczak experienced as an army doctor on the front line. The war described in the book, with its long marches, the digging of trenches, the crawling silently on one's belly to the enemy's barbed wire during reconnaissance, the drinking of vodka, the smoking of cigarettes, the long waiting in the trenches, and the use of airplanes for launching bombs, is a realistic account of World War I.

King Matt the First is, at the same time, a realistic novel and a fantasy; Korczak often uses fantastic, fairy-tale elements, such as the idea of a Cap of Invisibility:

> For a long time, a very long time, Matt wondered if it was possible to get ahold of a Cap of Invisibility. Wouldn't that be dandy—Matt would put on the cap, go wherever he liked, and no one would be able to see him. He would say that he had a headache. They would let him spend the day in bed so he could rest. Then at night he would put on the Cap of Invisibility and go into town, walk around his capital, look in all store windows, and go to the theatre. (20)

Korczak's work evokes the stereotype of the orphan as protagonist. Children's literature and fairy tales at the end of the nineteenth and at the beginning of the twentieth century often had orphans as protagonists: indeed this use of orphans may be seen as a typical fairy-tale element. Yet Korczak brings to life the little orphan King Matt. He is not a stereotypical device of children's literature of the time, but a study in loneliness. Being an orphan is part of the author's own childhood experiences. Korczak lost his father when he was very young; this loss led the family to poverty and forced upon him the task of taking care of the whole family: his sisters, his mother, and his grandmother. Obviously, this fact had a great influence on him and on his further development. Taking care of orphan children became one of his preoccupations.

Korczak wrote a great deal for theatre and for the radio, a fact that helped him develop density, persuasiveness, and exactitude in the dialogues and turned him into a master of dialogue. He was also a master in imitating children's speech. Take, for instance, the episode during the war when the trenches of the two hostile armies are so close that the soldiers can hear each other, so they start quarrelling. They shout at each other and call each other names, just as children do. By imitating children's quarrels and teasing, Korczk again shows ironically that the adult world is, in fact, often not grown-up at all, and that adults are not much cleverer than children. Here is an example of the dialogue between the soldiers of the two armies:

"Your king is a snot-nose," shouted the enemy.

"And yours is a good-for-nothing beggar."

"You're beggars. You've got holes in your boots."

"And you're hungry dog-faces. You get slops instead of coffee."

"Come on over here and try it. When we take your soldiers prisoner, they're hungry as wolves."

"And yours are ragged and starving."

"It's a good thing you ran away from us."

"But we'll beat you in the end."

"You don't know how to shoot. You couldn't hit the broad side of a barn." (71–72)

Korczak's style was economical yet sophisticated. The sparing use of words that marked his early works remained to a large extent unchanged: one of his first publications, *Salon Child*, and his last work, published after his death, *Pamiętnik z getta* (1942; *Ghetto Diary* 1978), are written in short, dense sentences, with cool, ironic distance from the described reality (in the latter case it was the terrible everyday life in the Warsaw Ghetto). In his introduction to the American edition of *King Matt*, Bruno Bettelheim describes the formal artistry of Korczak in the following terms:

> So convincingly are King Matt's life, ideas, and adventures presented, so great is the artistry with which his tale is told—a fascinating mixture of down-to-earth realism and flights of fancy—that it keeps us in thrall from the very beginning. The story ends when King Matt's carefully but all too childishly planned reforms collapse as the result of his being nefariously betrayed by the world of adults, and because the children, being but children, all too carelessly and childishly execute his plans. (Bettelheim v–vi)

King Matt the First has not lost its charm at the beginning of the twenty-first century. This parable continues to be equally appealing to children and adults. Themes like friendship, relations between children and parents, behavior to foreigners or those who are different, thoughts about the structure of society, war and peace, racism, prejudices, etc. are eternal themes. In this book they are discussed in a way that is still acceptable today, more than 80 years after its first publication. Reading *King Matt the First* today, the reader understands that when writing his sad, bitter, and desperate book, Korczak did not have illusions that he could change the world. The sequel to *King Matt*, *King Matt on the Desert Island*, ends with the death of Matt, which shows

Korczak's complete pessimism, augmented by the fact that nobody heard his desperate call or heeded his voice predicting catastrophes. What is astonishing in *King Matt the First* is the fact that this very sad book is written with irony and humor, warmth and compassion. The form of a charming parable makes it possible to read it in one sitting. The social critique we find in *King Matt the First* was common in nineteenth-century novels, such as those by Charles Dickens, Hector Malot, and Victor Hugo, who frequently introduced child protagonists. Children also take center-stage in books from the second half of the twentieth century; for example *Lord of the Flies* by William Golding, *1984* by George Orwell, or *Watership Down* by Richard Adams also offer parables of human society. But all of these books were written initially for adults and only later adopted by children. In contrast, *King Matt the First* is a book intended initially for children, although the author had the adult reader in mind as well. This book is based on Korczak's own dreams and ideas, and is as bitter as his own experience. Mixing fantasy with realism, the study of human nature with social critique, the language of the child with the language of the adult, Korczak created a unique book with no predecessors and no successors.

NOTES

1. No English translation available. All translations into English are mine unless otherwise indicated.

2. At the age of twenty, in 1898, the young Henryk Goldszmit entered a play in a literary competition. The name on the envelope was Janusz Korczak. This literary name became the name under which he was known ever after.

3. At this time Korczak had already published his first important theoretical work *Jak kochać dziecko* (1919; Engl. *How to Love a Child* 1995).

WORKS CITED

Barszczewska, Ludwika, and Boleslaw Milewicz (eds). *Wspomnienia o Januszu Korczaku*. Warsaw: Nasza Księgarnia, 1981.

Bettelheim, Bruno. "Introduction." In Korczak, Janusz. *King Matt the First*. New York: Farrar, Strauss and Giroux, 1986.

Korczak, Janusz. *Dziecko salonu* (1906). Kraków: Wydawnice Literackie, 1980.

———. *Ghetto Diary*. New York: Holocaust Library, 1978.

———. *How to Love a Child: The Inspirational Words of Janusz Korczak* edited by Sandra Joseph. Chapel Hill, NC: Algonquin Books of Chapel Hill, 2005.

———. *Jak kochać dziecko*. Warszawa: Towarzystwo wydawnicze w Warszawie. 1919.

———. *Kiedy znów będę mały* (1925). Wroclaw: Ossolineum, 1991.

———. *King Matt the First*. Translated by Richard Lourie. New York: Farrar, Strauss and Giroux, 1986; 2nd edition, Chapel Hill, NC: Algonquin Books, 2004 (also available adapted as *Matthew, the Young King*. New York: Roy Publishers, 1945).

———. *Król Macius Pierwszy* (1923). Warszawa, Nasza Ksiegarnia, 1966.

———. *Król Macius na wyspie bezludnej* (1923. Warszawa: Nasza Ksiegarnia, 1978.

———. "Pamietnik." In his *Wybór pism*, vol IV. Warszawa: Nasza Ksiegarnia, 1958

———. *Prawo dziecka do szacunku* (1928). Krakow: Ksiązka, 1948.

———. *The Warsaw Ghetto Memoirs of Janusz Korczak*. Translated with an introduction and notes by E. P. Kulawiec. Washington, D.C.: University Press of America, 1979.

———. *When I Am Little Again,* and *The Child's Right to Respect*. Translated with introduction by E. P. Kulawiec. Lanham, MD: University Press of America, 1992.

2

The Taming of the Two
Antoine de Saint-Exupéry's *Little Prince*

Claire Malarte-Feldman

"Please . . . draw me a sheep . . ."
And that's how I made the acquaintance of the little prince.

A FRAGILE ROSE

A shroud of mystery has clung to *The Little Prince* (1943), by Antoine de Saint-Exupéry, since it was first published more than six decades ago. This poignant tale of an extraterrestrial boy come to earth and of his love for a beautiful rose is likely never to yield all its secrets. They are part of the book's enduring magic. Speaking of *The Little Prince* in 1956, the scholar Maxwell Smith wrote: "To analyze in detail so lovely and fragile a tale would be like removing the petals of a rose to discover its charm" (199). And any adult who comes near this hallowed text would certainly do well to tread softly. Mindful of Smith's admonition, let us try then, not to remove, but to lift delicately a petal here, a petal there, in hopes of glimpsing the heart of the rose.

Along the way, we shall examine the strikingly meaningful context in which this unique text was composed, underlining the historical, social, and literary circumstances that surrounded its appearance, first in New York in 1943, and then in a recently liberated France three years later. As a deep affection develops between Saint-Exupéry's pilot-narrator and the little boy with the wheat-colored hair, we will listen closely to a complex intermingling of narrative voices. In the process we shall penetrate the world of childhood and measure the distance that separates it from the world of grown-ups, walking the fine line between children's literature and its adult counterpart. Finally, and I hope without taking the last petals off the rose, we shall consider *The Little Prince* as a cultural sign of our time, a "book without borders" par excellence.

All translations from French, unless otherwise specified, are mine.

A WORLD OF TRANSLATIONS
AND EDITIONS

It is said that *The Little Prince* is the third best-known book in the world after the Bible and *Das Kapital*.[1] We know for sure that it has sold more copies in France than any other book (ten million this year, according to Delphine Lacroix)[2] and that it has been translated into more foreign languages.[3] We unveil here a key piece in *The Little Prince*'s puzzle that will guide our reading: the blurring of boundaries, in this case of national borders, but we shall see how this text also blurs the line between adult and children's literature. Against the backdrop of a universe defined by a total absence of national markers since it first was published simultaneously both in French and in English, *The Little Prince* has been rendered in an unprecedented number of diverse languages and dialects, regional and national, throughout the world. The one hundred forty translations mentioned on the official *Petit Prince* website, http://www.lepetitprince.com/en, include recent translations in Urdu, Indonesian, and Khmer, in addition to regional languages such as Occitan from the Piedmont, Franco-Provençal from the Valdôtan region, and Platt, a dialect of northeastern France.

In a curious twist of fate for a book that soon became a French national treasure, *The Little Prince* began its life, on 6 April 1943, not in French but in Katherine Woods's English translation, published in New York by Reynal and Hitchcock. A few days later, *Le Petit Prince* appeared in French at the same publishing house, just about at the same time that Saint-Exupéry would leave the United States for North Africa. Not until three years later, after the end of World War II, did

Gallimard release *Le Petit Prince* in Paris, in 1946. In her review for the *New York Times* of April 11, 1943, Beatrice Sherman, sensitive to the simplicity of Katherine Woods' style, noted that "the translation from the French is admirably done, preserving the surface simplicity of a lovely fable with significant undertones." "Fable" is a word that John Chamberlain also used in "Books of the Times," his review of *The Little Prince* for the *New York Times* of April 6, 1943. Both Sherman and Chamberlain spontaneously asked themselves a question that still nags at a number of readers today. What genre of literature is *The Little Prince*? Is it "a parable for grown people in the guise of a simple story for children" (Sherman) or "a fascinating fable for grown-ups but of conjectural value for boys and girls of 6, 8 and 10" (Chamberlain)? By contrast, Anne Carroll Moore, established close ties between Saint-Exupéry's world and that of Hans Christian Andersen's *Fairy Tales* in her review of *The Little Prince* for the *Horn Book* of May–June 1943. Both works appealed to the imagination, which, in her view, is not the prerogative of any particular age group. Under the spell of the magical pictures created by Saint-Exupéry and their evocative power, she dismissed the question whether *Le Petit Prince* is for adults or children, preferring to "look upon it as a book so fresh and different, so original yet so infused with wisdom as to take a new place among books in general." *The Little Prince* creates meaning in various, interacting ways, both verbal and graphic, and thus can reach a wide and diverse audience. Though its narrative differentiates sharply between grown-ups and children, the book has a unique ability to bring these groups together, an apparent paradox that we intend to investigate further.

In June 2000, fifty-seven years after Katherine Woods's translation was released, Harcourt brought out a new English version of *The Little Prince* by Richard Howard. Well aware of the potential for committing a crime of lèse-majesté, Howard notes that "all translations date; certain works never do" and believes that "a new version of a work fifty-seven years old is entitled and, indeed, is obliged to persist further in the letter of that work." With the clear understanding that *The Little Prince* is one of those works that never become dated, Howard stated that his goal was to confront "the often radical outrage of what the author, in his incomparable originality, ventures to say" in an elusive yet determined attempt to get closer to a "standard version" (translator's note, n.p.). We have chosen to work with Howard's modernized translation here because of its deliberate and commendable intention of reflecting the small changes in contemporary American speech patterns that have occurred since 1943.

THE PUZZLING NATURE
OF *THE LITTLE PRINCE*

We should not allow the multiple translations and editions of *The Little Prince* to distract us for too long from the circumstances that surround the book's creation and release. Rare are the books that, written away from their homeland, find themselves, from the start, on an equal footing in two languages, almost as if the French and English versions were of strictly equal value. Indeed, this mystical tale would never even have been written had it not been for the extraordinary historical circumstances that brought Saint-Exupéry from France to the United States.

In December 1940, several months after France fell to the Germans, Antoine de Saint-Exupéry left his occupied homeland and sailed to America. He was already a best-selling author, known for virile classics such as *Night Flight* (1932) and *Wind, Sand, and Stars* (1939). A stay that was supposed to last only a few weeks ended up lasting over two years. They were years of illness, homesickness, and heartache for the displaced aviator-author. In February 1942, Reynal and Hitchcock brought out Saint-Exupéry's *Flight to Arras*, which by May was number one on the best-seller list (Schiff 1993, 1). Although delighted by this success, Saint-Exupéry despaired of ever being able to return to the land of his birth. He had also been injured a number of times in plane crashes, with the result that his health was very poor.

Saint-Exupéry had long had the habit of sketching a whimsical character in the margins of his manuscripts. It was the wife of one of his publishers, Elizabeth Reynal, who suggested one day that he write a book based on that "petit bonhomme" (Schiff 1993, 1). And so it was that *The Little Prince* was conceived, written, and illustrated in New York. In early April, 1943, as that book was about to come off the presses, Antoine de Saint-Exupéry was boarding the SS *Stirling Castle*, which would take him from New York to North Africa. Before leaving the United States, Saint-Exupéry presented to his friend Silvia Hamilton his old Zeiss Ikon camera and the original French manuscript of *The Little Prince*, which now resides at the Pierpont Morgan Library in New York City (des Vallières 2003, 178).

Upon arriving in Algiers, Saint-Exupéry would rejoin the Allied war effort. Slightly over a year later, the plane in which he was flying a reconnaissance mission disappeared without a trace in the Mediterranean Sea.

SAINT-EXUPÉRY'S ALTER EGOS

The Little Prince is peopled by multiple voices in addition to those of the little prince and the unnamed aviator from whose point of view the tale unfolds. The reader soon becomes overwhelmingly aware of other, extradiegetic presences: those of Antoine de Saint-Exupéry himself and past heroes of his own fiction. These alter egos have the effect of creating what Nicole Biagioli, looking at the narrative of *The Little Prince* as a form of therapy, has called "narrative hypnosis," which in the end enables the aviator in each one of us "to fly . . . on his own wings." In a psychoanalytic sense, the therapeutic dimension of *The Little Prince* belongs to the realm of the Freudian "rêve éveillé," or daydream (Biagioli 2001, 37).[4]

The aviator is the core character in Saint-Exupéry's body of works, as in this passage from Saint-Exupéry's first novel, *Courrier sud* (1929; *Southern Mail*, 1971), which speaks of Bernis, the aviator-hero who, like the little prince and his rose, found a reflection of his lost love in the brilliant night sky:

> One night, in a Sahara peopled with stars, as he was dreaming of these tender friendships, so distant, so warm, and now so covered by the weather and the night, like seeds, he suddenly felt as though he had stepped aside to watch someone sleep. Propped against the stranded plane opposite that curve of sand, this dip in the skyline, he had found himself watching over his past loves like a shepherd. (Exupéry 1971, 25)

After losing Geneviève, his terrestrial love, Bernis, who must have belonged to the same species of migrating wild birds that helped the little prince escape from his planet, found solace in his passion for flying airplanes. It was a passion that allowed him, like Saint-Exupéry, to make his way closer to the stars. "I felt young, as though put down on some star where life begins anew" (26) mused a regretful and sad Bernis about starting a new life without his love.

In *The Little Prince* Saint-Exupéry subtly blended autobiographical elements with fantasy, creating two narrative voices, one linked to reality, the other to fiction. Like the aviator who crashed in the desert of *The Little Prince*, Saint-Exupéry had also crashed his plane several times. Once in late December, 1935, for example, he and his mechanic, André Prévot, were on their way in an attempt to set a record time for a flight from Paris to Saigon. They crashed in the Libyan Desert and were forced to roam for days with hardly any water before eventually being rescued by a caravan of Bedouins. Two of them were sent with a handwritten note from Saint-Exupéry asking for help, addressed to a Swiss national whom Saint-Exupéry knew who lived twelve miles away in Wadi-Natroum (between Alexandria and Cairo). Unable to sit upright on a camel's back, he requested to be rescued by car. After a few more fantastic episodes, he and Prévot were able to go back to civilization, and later on to Paris (Schiff 1995, 256–67).

Saint-Exupéry's literary career is superimposed on his career as an aviator, and the autobiographical threads woven into his fiction become an important piece of the legend of his heroism. With deft and subtle strokes, Saint-Exupéry created a complex interplay of mirrors reflecting aspects of himself as storyteller, aviator, war hero, adventurer, and poet. There are few works in French literature whose mix of autobiography and fiction is so intimate or such a challenge to unravel. Nathalie des Vallières, an art historian and Saint-Exupéry's great-niece, has published a thorough, richly illustrated study of the author's manuscripts. In her book one finds a few sketches and preparatory drawings for the first edition of *The Little Prince* in which Saint-Exupéry had represented the pilot sleeping in the desert, curled up in a fetal position A similar drawing at a more advanced stage would include the image of the crashed plane in the background. Another sketch featured a hand holding a hammer in the foreground with the little prince standing on a sand dune, hands on his hips, his signature scarf flying in the wind as he looked toward the pilot repairing his machine. None of those images of the pilot were chosen for inclusion in *The Little Prince*, as if Saint-Exupéry had wanted to erase any pictorial representation of his own self. "The narrator, that is to say the conscious adult author, has thus been evicted from the image and what we can see unknowingly, is the unconscious image of the author's body, that is to say the little prince," proposes Nicole Biagioli in her psychoanalytic reading of Saint-Exupéry's *The Little Prince* (2001, 30), stressing the intimate mix of identities at play. Indeed, the connection between the little prince and the aviator, the child and the adult, the character and the author is so tight that we must turn once again to the life of Antoine de Saint-Exupéry if we are to fully understand how *The Little Prince* came to be.

THE LIFE OF A PIONEER, THE LEGEND OF A HERO

In 1912 at age twelve, less than a decade after Orville Wright's historic flight on board the *Kitty Hawk*, Saint Exupéry went up in an airplane for the first time. A passion was born. Fourteen years later, he flew his first mail route, Toulouse-Casablanca-Dakar, thus joining the chosen few who ruled the airways before anyone could dare imagine how far aviation would take humankind. In 1929, based in Buenos Aires as the director of the Aeroposta Argentina, he opened the airmail route to Patagonia and was the first to reach Terra del Fuego by plane. As a civilian pilot for more than a decade, Saint-Exupéry led an exciting and dangerous life, the life of an adventurer straight from a book, all dressed in leather, a white silk scarf flying behind him from the cockpit! In 1939 he was mobilized for war. With the fall of France the following year, as we have noted, he went into exile, arriving in New York Harbor on 31 December 1940. Saint-Exupéry would remain in the United States, actively pleading the cause of his occupied country, until April 1943. Living some of the darkest moments of French history, he was overwhelmed with doubts about the future of humanity.

The disappearance of the aviator-narrator's newfound friend at the end of *The Little Prince* connects the book closely to its author, who in Jean Perrot's words, "was undoubtedly responding to the anguish aroused in him in 1943 by the war, and by his meditation on the nature of heroism and the impossible purity of exceptional beings" (Perrot 1999, 186). It was against the painful backdrop of a defeated France and a world at war, a time of metaphysical struggle for this thinking man of action, that *The Little Prince* made its way into the world in April 1943. When Saint-Exupéry left the United States that same month, with the help of the U.S. Navy, he joined his comrades of Reconnaissance Group 2/23 in Morocco. Despite his age of forty-three and his poor health, Saint-Exupéry was once again actively involved in military action, flying missions to gather strategic intelligence that would pave the way for the liberation of Provence and the whole South of France.

On 31 July 1944, he set out in fine weather from Corsica to monitor

German activity in the Rhone valley, just above the Lyonnais region where he was born. In a fashion fitting only for the hero that he was, Saint-Exupéry never returned from that mission. On that fatal day, his amazing career, his adventurous life, and his migratory wanderings all came to an end when Saint-Exupéry and his faithful Lockheed Lightning were lost at sea. No earthly remains of either plane or aviator were found, as if both had vanished into thin air. One cannot help evoking the moment when the little prince disappeared and the pilot could rationalize that his little friend "did get back to his planet because at daybreak, I didn't find his body" (81). The absence of Saint-Exupéry's remains gave little consolation to his countrymen, however, who had lost a beloved national hero. But it gave birth to a legend that endured for over half a century.

On 7 April 2004, two pieces of his plane, a Lockheed Lightning P-38, which had vanished with its pilot in July of 1944, were pulled from the Mediterranean Sea. The serial number on the fuselage, 2734L, matched the ID of Saint-Exupéry's plane. Suddenly, the long-standing legend had acquired a closing chapter, albeit an ambiguous one. As stated by Stacy Schiff in her *New York Times* op-ed piece of 11 April 2004, "some riddles endure." The position of the plane on the seabed was consistent with a vertical dive. Had he been shot down by the German foe? Did his plane malfunction? Or had his dark doubts about the future of mankind driven him to suicide? Some will protest that Saint-Exupéry's underwater gravesite should have been left untouched. The debate had already started in 1998, when a fisherman from Marseilles caught in his net a silver bracelet identified as Saint-Exupéry's because of an engraving on its back with the name of Consuelo, Saint-Exupéry's wife. That new episode in the unfinished life of the aviator inspired Jules Roy, who knew him well, to plead for the respect of his peace: "Legendary heroes are the ones we never find . . . Like Saint-Exupéry, they occupy the lofty heights of myth and cloud to which ordinary mortals have no access" (Roy 1999, 12). The irony of the final chapter in the life of this French writer-hero was nicely underlined in a *Le Monde* editorial of 9 April 2004 by Eric Fottorino, who notes the paradoxical fact that this "man of letters, and such beautiful letters . . . could be identified thanks to some numbers." This irrefutable identification on the fuselage that lay at the bottom of the sea gave a final position to the pilot without compass.

A MIGRATION OF WILD BIRDS

Antoine de Saint-Exupéry, the migratory bird, has now been found in his final resting place at the bottom of the sea. He was a hero in pursuit of himself, questing after something that no reader or scholar may ever be able to determine with certainty, with invisible companions at his side all along: his father who died when Antoine was four years old, his younger brother too early departed, all the dear comrades whose planes did not come back from their missions, and an imaginary child from a world of elves and spirits who has touched the hearts of readers all over the world. The little prince, too, was in pursuit of Saint-Exupéry. He caught the attention of Elizabeth Reynal, who spotted him amid the steady flow of endearing little guys doodled into the corners and margins of the many pages that Saint-Exupéry blackened in the course of his life with his unmistakable penmanship.[5]

Like Saint-Exupéry in his plane, like Bernis in *Southern Mail*, the little prince belongs to the flying breed. A migration of wild birds brings the little prince to planet Earth, where a pilot has crash-landed his plane in the Sahara Desert. That is where the two travelers meet, in a landscape of total isolation blending waves of desert sand with those of the ocean. That is where the tale of their mutual initiation will unfold. Despite the apparent immobility and permanence of the setting in which their encounter takes place, *The Little Prince* is a tale of flight and wide open spaces, a tale of travel and adventure, a tale of searching and discovery. Like all good quest narratives, it starts with a departure: the little prince has left his Asteroid B-612 and the pilot his air base. It fits in the eternal world of folktales, where the weight of history is irrelevant, and time meaningless and where heroes of all kinds, from Tom Thumb to Nils Holgersson and the Hobbit, embark on quests. Lying ahead of them beckon the rites of passage that will reveal to them the secret of life. The migration of the little prince and of the aviator will end where it began, in the mineral world of sand dunes, where they will find knowledge and fulfillment. "There must be rites," said the fox (61). Having grown infinitely richer in wisdom from their mutual contact, both will be able to depart again, like birds, for different migrations. Having each gained a friend, the intimacy that gradually develops between the two characters is marked by their shared knowledge that what matters does not need words to be explained, and is invisible to the eye.

It is on the wings of their shared intimacy that we as readers, along with the pilot who woke up in the desert with a blond-haired boy at his side, shake free of our terrestrial ties to glide between sky and land. We step beyond the looking glass. We penetrate an imaginary world where Alice enters the land of wonder, Mary and Colin find the secret garden, and the little prince discovers the secret of the fox.

THE SECRET OF THE FOX, OR THE
MEANING OF THE TALE

The Little Prince's aviator-narrator, utterly alone, plies a night sky shrouded in mystery, darkness, and danger. In the middle of the desert under millions of stars, he is aware both of the immensity of the universe and of his own insignificance within it: "I was more isolated than a man shipwrecked on a raft in the middle of the ocean" (3). His absolute isolation on the site of the crash places him closer to the mystery of the universe, while setting up the perfect frame for a fairy tale in that space devoid of all temporal markers, an endless desert inhabited by a "petit bonhomme," a fox, a snake, and the spirit of a rose:

> I should have liked to begin this story like a fairy tale. I should have liked to say: "Once upon a time there was a little prince who lived on a planet hardly any bigger than he was, and who needed a friend . . ." For those who understand life, that would sound much truer. (12)

Despite the narrator's clear disclaimer, lots of critics have labeled *The Little Prince* a fairy tale. Anne Carroll Moore, in her *Horn Book* review of 1943, was quick to establish the connection between the styles of Hans Christian Andersen and Saint-Exupéry. For Thérèse Reynal, "this book is situated half-way between nostalgic childhood memories and serious fairy tales." James Higgins, in his 1996 study of *The Little Prince*, remarked that "the uniqueness of Saint-Exupéry's fairy tale lies in his style, the product of his rare combination of imagination and close observation. He is both a dreamer and a doer." Here, Higgins touches on the double discourse that shuttles back and forth between flights of fiction and the depiction of an aviator-narrator who is Saint-Exupéry's alter ego. Unlike Moore, who saw *The Little Prince* as appealing in similar ways to the imaginations of young and old alike, Higgins observed that "for the younger reader it is indeed a fairy tale.

For the more mature reader it may also be an allegorical *conte*, reminiscent of Rabelais or La Fontaine" (Higgins 1996, 90–91). Whether *The Little Prince* is a fairy tale, a fable, an allegory, or a conte is in the end far less important than its capacity to touch the minds and hearts of both children and adults.

We might find it more fruitful to turn toward other French writers who could easily have inspired Saint-Exupéry in cultural and literary ways. Two influential voices, in particular, spoke loudly in the late years of the *ancien régime*. Voltaire and Montesquieu, in keeping with the increasing involvement of literature with politics in a century of Enlightenment, added another dimension to the meaning of the tale by their use of wit and irony. Candide's false naïveté and the Persian's feigned stupefaction in the face of the realities of human behavior in France turn the standard fairy tale into a philosophical reflection on man's weaknesses and failures. Literature of that period became a means to undertake "the criticism of mores and characters" (Reynal 1944, 303). Indeed, the little prince is very much a character in the same vein as Candide and the Persian, embodying their innocence and power. Saint-Exupéry is also a philosopher. Candide and the little prince, who both look forward to tending their garden (Higgins 1996, 62), force us to look at ourselves from the viewpoint of an outsider. We must see, as they do, how strange the world seems, though we still recognize it as normal. We must face the fact that our planet is filled with kings and very vain men, drunkards and businessmen, lamplighters and geographers, some of them looking and acting strangely quite in the same fashion we do. The little prince takes the leading role in Saint-Exupéry's twentieth-century philosophical tale, despite his extreme youth and apparent fragility. Anne-Isabelle Mourier summarized nicely a primary trait in the little prince's character when she wrote:

> The child-hero leads the way for someone older than him, as Antigone guided Oedipus or Tom Thumb his brothers. He is the archetypal innocent or simpleton who succeeds where they all fail because he does not look at the world in the usual way and whose visible weakness hides his moral strength. (Mourier 2001, 31)

The little prince is not naive, nor is he simple in his understanding of the mysteries of life, love, and death. He is innocent, and that innocence is his power and his strength. The snake said to the little prince:

"But you're innocent, and you come from a star . . ." (51).[6] On the faraway planet from which comes this "exceptional being" (Perrot 1999, 186) lives the rose, his one true love. She is needy and insecure. He leaves his planet and his rose, though. He flies with a migration of wild birds away from his unhappy love for the rose, and embarks on a long voyage that takes him to six stations on planets inhabited by rather pathetic specimens of humanity. Finally, the little prince lands on Earth, in a deserted space where he will find clues that help answer his questions and where a fox will reveal to him the most important secret of all. The little prince looks at our world as a pure-hearted, innocent outsider, and in his understanding of how we humans function are integrated both the adult's and the child's perspectives. Though the two may seem mutually exclusive, in the end *The Little Prince* stresses only how blurred are the lines that separate one viewpoint from the other, one genre from the other. One realizes how unimportant is the distance between reality and fiction. The aviator, left behind after the little prince's disappearance, asks himself: "has the sheep eaten the flower or not?" (83). The little prince's worry that the sheep may eat his rose once he goes back to his planet becomes a worry in the pilot's life too. Along with the little prince, he has imagined a planet where baobab growth must be controlled. With the child, the pilot has made the acquaintance of a snake and understood "the sense of something irreparable" (76) that he felt in its presence. He can now see beyond his limited, grown-up frame of vision and touch the heart of what is invisible and essential. And that is the secret of the fox.

HAT? OR BOA?

The little prince does not look at the world as grown-ups do; his concerns and his needs are deeply anchored in the concrete and the heart of things: a sheep and a rose, a fox and a snake, baobabs, the song of the pulley over the well, and the golden color of wheat fields. And yet the little prince knows quite a bit about the ways grown-ups have of doing and looking at things.

The tale opens with the narrator remembering something that happened when he was six years old. He had drawn a picture of a boa constrictor swallowing an elephant. Of course the resulting image looked more or less like a hat, and grown-ups could not readily see that it was anything other than a hat. Even when they were told what the drawing was intended to represent, they could not appreciate it. This memory illustrates Saint-Exupéry's belief that appearances, as well as words, can be the source of all kinds of misunderstanding. And so the little prince has to show patience and understanding toward grown-ups who can only see the hat, where the child is able to see the elephant within the boa constrictor. At first such a smart drawing can be deceiving for an unimaginative observer, particularly if it is an adult: "grown-ups never understand anything by themselves, and it is exhausting for children to have to provide explanations over and over again" (2). The drawing of the boa and the elephant as seen from outside, then from inside illustrates the apparently unbridgeable gap between adults and children that is underlined first in the dedication of *The Little Prince* to Saint-Exupéry's friend Leon Werth, then in the introduction of *The Little Prince*. According to these texts, a firm line seemingly separates the worlds of grown-ups and children. For Saint-Exupéry, grown-ups blindly engross themselves in matters of no consequence at all. In Mourier's analysis, adults, as symbolized by the little prince's encounters on six successive planets, are all seen as slaves to their need for possession and power.

> The very vain man's cult of personality, the drunkard's addiction, the businessman's thirst for possession, the lamplighter's or the geographer's unquestioning adherence to a system or a profession . . . their parts make them all slaves. The grown-ups, whose souls are held captive, often look mythomaniac, masochistic, or absurd, as they are slowly overcome by insanity. Their lack of feelings, a sort of love anemia, leaves them seized by emptiness. (Mourier 2001, 50)

The little prince feels this "love anemia" and, with a "discreet resignation" (Reynal 1944, 303), goes from one grown-up to the next thinking that they all "are certainly quite extraordinary" (40). His incomprehension in the face of adults' failure to grasp what to a child would be immediately obvious reinforces the aviator's childhood observation that "grown-ups never understand anything by themselves" (2). That failure may well be due to the nature of language: in his "Letter to Young Americans," published in the *Scholastic* magazine of 25–30 May 1942, Saint-Exupéry had already warned his young readers that "men's words wear out and lose their meaning." For this man of both action and spirituality, words are not enough to express the invisible, they are just the envelope, the boa, or the sheep crate that contain truth. Only the little prince knows how to use them wisely, sparingly. Words obscure the truth the same way appearances veil what is essential. It is only when the aviator accepts that the little prince has little faith in the power of words and will not answer his questions that communication between the two becomes possible. Both man and child will, in the end, have stepped beyond the limitations of language to speak by way of symbols, signs, and images rather than words. As stated by Le Hir, "the elimination of speech is here again the condition necessary for infinitely more intimate forms of communication" (Le Hir 2002, 239). And yet, paradoxically, Saint-Exupéry is using language, and one must emphasize, in one of its purest forms, to deliver the message that "language is the source of misunderstandings" (60). Language is worn out and cannot be trusted. But *The Little Prince*'s unique ability to touch the hearts of people all over the world may itself be proof that language, like a phoenix, can rise from its own ashes and renew itself again if it is treated with the same care the little prince lavished on his rose.

Saint-Exupéry's luminous illustrations are key aspects of *The Little Prince*'s semiotic code. Their interaction with the text creates a unique system of communication in which the simple silhouette of a planet, star, or tree takes on new meaning, as best illustrated by the last drawing of two simple curved lines and a five-point star with the aviator-narrator's comment across on the last page of the book:

> For me this is the loveliest and the saddest landscape in the world. It's the same landscape as the one on the preceding page [same drawing but with the little prince falling gently], but I have drawn it one more time in order to be sure you see it clearly. It's here that the little prince appeared on Earth, then disappeared. (85)

The playful complicity between text and image reflects the evolving relationship between the pilot and his extraterrestrial friend, thus helping to bridge the very gap between grown-ups and children that *The Little Prince* repeatedly brings to our attention. Our mental image of what the little prince looks like is shaped by Saint-Exupéry's drawing of this character: a beautiful and solitary child, shining like a light. But *The Little Prince* has taught us to be somewhat suspicious of the link between appearances and reality. Could it be that the little prince only *looks like* a child? Beneath his juvenile appearance, Saint-Exupéry's hero is in truth quite an ambiguous and complex character. As Michel

Autrand remarks in La Pléiade edition of Saint-Exupéry's complete works:

> Despite his childlike appearance, his character, because of his life experiences, is ageless. He is closer to the Berber lord in *The Wisdom of the Sands* than to any Tom Thumb. There is nothing specifically juvenile about the world, the objects, and the scenery around him. He is an adult proposition dressed as a child. Leon Werth, as stated in the dedication, was no longer a child. (Autrand 1999, 1354)

In the preface of *The Little Prince*, the tale is initially dedicated "to Leon Werth,"[7] with the opening sentence: "I ask children to forgive me for dedicating this book to a grown-up" (n.p). Then, following the text of the preface, the original dedication is rephrased as follows: "To Leon Werth when he was a little boy" (n.p.). Saint-Exupéry's game of illusions blurs the lines between grown-ups and children. By framing the tale in such a fashion, the author creates an ambiguous narrative space in which adults are distinguished from children while also raising the hope that reconciliation between the two may be possible. Saint-Exupéry's strategy calls to mind the tricks of a talented storyteller, who wraps his audience in a web of connivance, creating an ironic narrative environment for readers of all ages to enjoy. Saint-Exupéry also loved tricks: on top of his many other talents, he was an accomplished prestidigitator who loved to perform card tricks for his guests after dinner!

A TOUCH OF GENIUS

The Little Prince belongs to that generically mixed group of tales that blend children's literature and its adult "other"; or, to borrow Sandra Beckett's terms, *The Little Prince* "crosswrites adults and children." In her book *De grands romanciers écrivent pour les enfants*, Beckett observed that "those who write for children are taking on a big challenge: they must aim very high, because one needs a touch of genius to give children the books they deserve" (Beckett 1997, 250). There can be no doubt that Saint-Exupéry met that challenge when he wrote *The Little Prince*. If Beckett had not purposely chosen to focus her study on the postwar period between 1945 and 1995, she would certainly have added Saint-Exupéry to the likes of Henri Bosco, Jean Giono, Michel

Tournier, Marguerite Yourcenar, and Jean-Marie Le Clézio as writers who all share this "touch of genius."

Saint-Exupéry wrote his first and only children's book at the request of a friend, as if almost against his own will. But, using a deceptively simple and poetic prose, he nonetheless found a way to reach the hearts and minds of adults as well as children. While emphasizing the gulf that separates the two groups, the former focusing only on "matters of no consequence," the latter understanding the secret of the fox: that "one sees clearly only with the heart. Anything essential is invisible to the eyes" (63), *The Little Prince* also brings together readers old and young to share the fox's lesson of life. Along with this teaching, the fox explains the meaning of a new word for the little prince, a word that opens up a linguistic divide between the English and French versions, stressing literally indeed the fox's observation that "language is the source of misunderstandings" (60). When the fox asked the little prince to "tame" him, he asked only to be "apprivoisé." In English there is only that one word, "to tame" which, unfortunately, also means "to control," "to subdue," "to master" or "to overcome," all power-loaded signifiers that would be translated into French with the word "dompter," a term best used to describe, for example, what happens on the circus ring between a lion or a tiger and their breaker. The little prince is asked by the fox to become his friend, not his subordinate. The understanding is that their need for each other will be built on trust and friendship, not on fear and power. The fox is ready to see beyond his total lack of need for wheat because of the unmistakable visual reminder that the little prince has hair the color of those useless fields. Suddenly, they become essential to his life because, as he said to the little prince, "you have hair the color of gold. So it will be wonderful, once you've tamed me! The wheat, which is golden, will remind me of you. And I'll love the sound of the wind in the wheat . . ." (60). The fox and the little prince are only tamed because they choose to and it makes them "apprivoisés."

The uniqueness of their friendship brings together children and adults, and stresses thus the notion, well established by Beckett, that "with the great authors, the categories of fiction for adults and fiction for children seem to fall apart. What is left is only 'literature'" (Beckett 1997, 247). Saint-Exupéry's mastery of language and the power of his evocations place him among this small number of memorable authors whose style and inspiration made it possible to transcend boundaries. No matter how we try to classify or name the literary genre to which it belongs, *The Little Prince* defies our efforts. John Chamberlain, in his review of 1943, failed in his attempt to do so, as he himself wisely admitted: "After all, who am I to say what children will or won't like?" The little prince's world is evoked in a uniquely poetic manner that contributes to the erosion of borders. Even the end of the story becomes a beginning, with a new cycle of migration. In this "quiet tale of innocent tragedy" (Higgins 1996, 37), the little prince, who falls to earth "gently, the way a tree falls" (82), departs from the desert with a heartbreaking lightness. The disappearance of his corpse into thin air is reminiscent of Wang-Fo's mysterious and poetical sail-away in "Comment Wang-Fô fut sauvé" (in *Nouvelles Orientales*, 1938; "How Wang-Fô Was Saved," *Oriental Tales*, 1985) by Marguerite Yourcenar.[8] That Chinese artist from the Kingdom of Han, condemned to death by an embittered emperor, sallies forth upon the surface of the ocean in a boat he has painted on the waves: "its wake disappeared from the deserted surface, and the painter Wang-Fô and his disciple Ling vanished forever on the jade-blue sea that Wang-Fô had just created" (Yoursenar 1985, 20). Yourcenar and Saint-Exupéry, both "great writers," share the art of literary storytellers and the emotion of humanists. Wang-Fô on the ocean and the little prince on his Asteroid B-612 have the flesh of characters, who help us imagine possible bridges between land and space, air and ocean, between the sky and the earth. Only an old man and a frail child, both in their great wisdom, can beckon the readers, any reader, to their world of quiet magic. Imagination, poetry, and timelessness, such is the stuff of which are made a few blessed tales. *The Little Prince* today has become the legend of a mythical hero for millions of readers on this planet.

THE LITTLE PRINCE AS AN ICON

In addition, Saint-Exupéry's literary character has more recently taken on a life of his own, becoming a veritable cultural sign of our times. Such is no doubt the price of his fame. Countless human beings of all races, creeds, and ages are able to identify the little prince by the mere shape of his body, the colors of his clothes, the soft gold of his hair, and his long yellow scarf, just the way Saint-Exupéry created him. We have already observed that the little prince had been nagging at his creator long before Saint-Exupéry gave him a shape and a costume. That "little fellow" who would surreptitiously appear at the corner of a page

or in the margin of a letter was, and remains, first and foremost a drawing. *The Little Prince* is also a tale about drawing pictures and, in the
process, infusing them with the reality of objects, as well as life and
meaning. One may remember the opening sentence of *The Little
Prince*: "Once when I was six I saw a magnificent picture in a book
about the jungle, called *True Stories*. It showed a boa constrictor swallowing a wild beast. Here is a copy of the picture" (1). This memory
from a childhood picture book triggers the narrator's desire to make it
more real by drawing it on the page. For Saint-Exupéry, who mis-
trusted words, illustrations were an intricate form of connection with
his fiction, a medium other than language, yet complementary to it. By
sketching, drawing, and water-coloring the little prince, he created the
perfect symbiosis of a literary character with a visual icon. One of the
two defining representations of the little prince comes from a drawing
made "from memory" by the aviator, who shortly after his encounter
with the little prince, noted: "Here is the best portrait I managed to
make of him later on. But of course my drawing is much less attractive
than my model" (4). This portrait of the little prince, firmly planted in
his high boots, wrapped in his ceremonial cape, his left hand resting on
the hilt of his sword, combines with the tender figure of childhood the
frail yet imperial look of *L'Aiglon*, the Duke of Reichstadt and King of
Rome, son of Napoleon I and Empress Marie-Louise, who disappeared
tragically at the age of 21. Today that particular representation, which
captures the "princely" stature of the child, can be identified everywhere. The second, possibly even more widely familiar representation
of the little prince is a softer, less regal one: his hands in his pockets, a
little boy with a whimsical red bow tie around the neck is standing on
his planet near one of its volcanoes. Both iconic renderings of this
much-loved character have long since transcended the pages of the
book that brought them into the world.

One could say that *The Little Prince*'s Asteroid B-612 is at the heart
of a constellation of planets found in books of all forms and shapes.
There is, in any case, no doubt that Saint-Exupéry's tale has multiplied
and expanded into a variety of satellite versions. With an extensive use
of the little prince's imagery, board books were made available to a new
readership of very young children. In a 2002 Harcourt publication, the
little prince even became the children's voice in *A Guide for Grown-
ups: Essential Wisdom from the Collected Works of Antoine de Saint-
Exupéry*, which gathers a number of aphorisms and quotations from
The Little Prince and other works by Saint-Exupéry as a "way to

explain to a grown-up small parts of my story."[9] A variety of special
editions of *The Little Prince* have also been used as primers for French
language learners, or for literature students (French and foreign), and
provided to them as a package of "Enrichment Workbooks for Explor-
ing Languages and Themes."[10] Along the same lines, because of the
brilliance and clarity of its style, Saint-Exupéry's text generated an
additional flood of exercises and class activities, thus becoming a pedagogical tool for language instructors in many classrooms. Indeed, for a
long time here in the United States, the apparent simplicity of *The Little Prince* gave secondary-school teachers the impression that it would
be a good book to offer students who wanted the quick gratification
of reading a French classic in its original form. But younger students
in their second or third year of studying French as a foreign language
may not always be fully able to grasp the depth of the book. Many of
my own students of French have told me that rereading the tale at a
more mature age has enabled them to learn from its philosophy. In the
long literary tradition of "books without borders," *The Little Prince*
belongs to a larger body of French texts, such as La Fontaine's *Fables*
and Charles Perrault's *Contes*, whose pedagogical function and "civilizing" use, combined with the playful nature of their respective styles,
helped them quickly to find a way into the hands of children reading
for fun as well as pupils reading to learn. Following in the steps of its
illustrious predecessors, *The Little Prince* is nowadays at once a classic
of literature, a core textbook in the French school system, and a model
of excellent French at various levels of instruction in departments of
foreign languages. Finally, *The Little Prince* in its sixty years of existence, because of its undisputed excellence, has been used as a prized
reward for achievements of all kinds. Its guaranteed status as the "perfect children's book" and its universal consecration as a masterpiece of
literature make *The Little Prince* a perfect gift for graduates of all
kinds. Already a pedagogical tool, a coffee table book, an *exemplum*,
The Little Prince will undoubtedly generate many more incarnations
beyond the printed page as the twenty-first century unfolds.

In recent years, the most famous characters in *The Little Prince* have
been reprocessed into "boutique" objects and can be found everywhere, on school satchels and pencil pots, on ties decorated with the
fox or the sheep, on silk scarves (for 120 euros), on the cover of address
books, or in the delicate perfume of an eau de toilette for children. *The
Little Prince* may even accompany you as carry-on luggage; while you
wait to board your plane, the familiar silhouettes of the little prince and

his friends will make your take-off for new adventures more exciting![11] Metamorphoses like these reflect "the changing nature of children's fiction" (Mackey 2000, 37) in a world of constant multimedia stimulation. Today's young readers of *The Little Prince* are increasingly accustomed to seeing his familiar form in places other than the pages of a book. Their expectations driven by the market demand secured for the little prince a prominent place in the pantheon of familiar characters from children's fiction, such as Babar, Curious George, Madeline, Peter Rabbit, and Winnie the Pooh, among other "stars" who now share their literary fame with the world of consumerism. The demands of the twenty-first-century book market have brought *The Little Prince* into close collaboration with other multimedia goldmines; yet— and this is worth noting—the tale has never been processed by the Hollywood culture. There is no *Little Prince* cartoon. Stacy Schiff tells us that the legendary Orson Welles's business partner "got no rest until he had secured a one-month option [on the book] for Welles. Welles hoped to film the story with some animation but abandoned the project when he was unable to enlist Walt Disney's help" (Schiff 1993, 16). We can only give thanks that the Disney industry declined its chance to refashion Saint-Exupéry's *Little Prince* as it did, for instance, Hans Christian Andersen's classic fairy tale in the 1980s animated film *The Little Mermaid*. It's enough to make one shudder just to think of it!

A film adaptation of *The Little Prince* was made in 1974, however, by Stanley Donen, the American director of *Singing in the Rain*. This surprisingly beautiful and poetic film features a dream cast, with, among other delightful actors, young Steven Warner as an angelic little boy with a sweet British accent. (In an attempt to make the hero more European?) The obvious quality of the cinematography (with, for example, the well-balanced combination of animation and flesh and blood characters that Welles may have envisioned) helps preserve the magic of the book. And yet even this excellent film somehow robs our imagination of the familiar and dependable images created in our mind by Saint-Exupéry. To replace the little prince, the fox, or the snake with real people, even actors of the caliber of Richard Kiley, Gene Wilder, and Bob Fosse, entails a shift from the private realm of the printed page to a world eerily reminiscent of American musicals. If Saint-Exupéry—who also wrote screenplays (such as a script for a film by Raymond Bernard entitled *Anne-Marie*, with Annabella, Tyrone Powers's wife, in the leading role)[12]—could have seen Donen's film, he may have found this interpretation of his tale amusing. He may also have wished that cinema, with all its limitations and distortions, had left him and *The Little Prince* alone. Imagination needs room to flourish, much like two "imperious innocents, whose lives consist of equal parts flight and failed love, who fall to earth," two "exceptional beings" (Perrot 1999, 186) who "are little impressed with what they find here and ultimately disappear without a trace" (Schiff 2004, 11).

REALM OF MEMORY

There is an ironic twist of fate in the fact that *The Little Prince* has stepped beyond the strict confines of his storybook home and gone on to other spheres of being at the moment when Saint-Exupéry's plane, the aviator's physical envelope, was finally found at the bottom of the sea. The discovery of the pilot's watery grave has established a "memory place" for *The Little Prince*, one of the *loci memoriae* that Pierre Nora defines in *Realms of Memory*, the magisterial, multi-volume study of the French cultural heritage created under his direction:

> If the expression *lieu de mémoire* must have an official definition, it should be this: a *lieu de mémoire* is any significant entity, whether material or non-material in nature, which by dint of human will or the work of time has become a symbolic element of the memorial heritage of any community (in this case, the French community). (Nora 1997, xvii)[13]

In the vast spectrum of symbols that Nora's study examines, some of the books used as examples of realms of memory in literature are of particular interest. Antoine Compagnon observes in "Marcel Proust's *Remembrance of Things Past*," for example, that Proust made memory the central theme of a monumental opus which, over time, has become a memory place, too: "We turn certain books, like the *Mémoires d'outre tombe* and *A la recherche du temps perdu* into very special *lieux de mémoire*, and they become essential because they help, because literature helps, us to think of memory in terms other than historical" (Compagnon 1997, 246). Jacques Ozouf and Mona Ozouf's "*Le Tour de la France par deux enfants*: The Little Red Book of the Republic," another contribution to the Nora work, is a remarkable study of G. Bruno's famous tale of the travels of two boys through 1877 France. This best-known book was used in all the public schools of France in the late nineteenth century, at a time when that country was forging a new national identity and instituting important reforms of public education. Today *Le Tour de la France par deux enfants* lives on in the French collective consciousness, where, as noted by the Ozoufs, it found a permanent place "between memory and history." Between 1877 and 1960 the most widely read book in the entire history of French schoolbooks went through 411 different editions! Today this book is firmly fixed in its own realm of memory; indeed, several facsimile of the original edition have been published recently for its most nostalgic fans, the last one by Belin in September 2004.

Like *Le Tour de la France par deux enfants*, *The Little Prince* is about history and memory. The aura of Antoine de Saint-Exupéry and his famous career, spanning two tumultuous world wars that shook the French nation as a whole to its core, permeates the symbolic universe of *The Little Prince*. A colorful banknote worth fifty francs consecrated *The Little Prince* and Saint-Exupéry as a realm of memory. All the signs that identify the aviator, the war hero, and the writer, along with his most famous literary creation, were gathered onto one of the most popular and beloved denominations of currency among the French people, the "Saint-Ex," first printed by the Bank of France in 1992. It symbolized the French Republic's identity for a scant ten years, until the historic moment when, along with eleven other European nations, France adopted the euro. Understandably aware of the powerful image projected by the "Saint-Ex," Geneviève Le Hir wrote about the familiar blue banknote:

> What do you see? A picture of Antoine de Saint-Exupéry, but also a plane and air routes crossing a part of Europe and Africa, and also drawings: the drawing of the little prince on his planet with three volcanoes, the drawing of the elephant-eating boa. All forms of representation of Saint-Exupéry's universe, and as such, symbolic, in the same fashion a baguette of bread or Camembert cheese symbolize France. (Le Hir 2002, 13)

Le Hir's surprising choice of comparisons between the "Saint-Ex" and two staples of French food makes a powerful statement. Antoine de Saint-Exupéry and his *Little Prince* are as essential as bread and cheese; they share the latter's capacity to nourish and their role as French symbols. We should note that the strong symbolic figure of Saint-Exupéry himself as a pioneer of aviation, a war hero, and a celebrated writer had already been institutionalized by the French and many other countries with their national stamps, a recent one having been issued by the Croatian people in celebration of the fiftieth anniversary of the pilot's death. When the Bank of France made the decision to print a last new line of French banknotes in 1992, they chose to emphasize the "great themes that characterize the twentieth century in our collective unconscious." With specific regard to the "Saint-Ex," the bank justified its choice by saying that Saint-Exupéry was universally known and had contributed to France's influence in the world. And for most of us today, what remains the best of Saint-Exupéry in the French collective unconscious is *The Little Prince*. The recent intensification of interest in Saint-Exupéry's extraordinary life, occasioned by the discovery of his final resting place, marks the consecration of his sixty-year-old fictional creation as *un lieu de mémoire*, a part of the heritage of the French nation.

TENDING TO OUR GARDEN

> It is possible that some remote valley of the Alps may one day yield its grim secret to a hardy mountain climber, though even this seems doubtful. Perhaps it is just as well. All of Saint-Exupéry's airmen friends are agreed that the end he met was the one he preferred. Like Mermoz and Guillaumet, no trace of whom was ever found, he carried his final mystery with him to the grave. (Cate 1970, 551)

Today, of course, that "final mystery" stands revealed. But these words, penned by Curtis Cate several decades ago, still retain a certain resonance, intertwining the threads of Saint-Exupéry's biography, the disappearance into thin air of both the author-aviator and his creation, and finally the dramatic discovery in 2004 of Saint-Exupéry's plane beneath the sea near Marseilles. But we still don't know exactly what brought Saint-Exupéry's plane down, and the mystery of the little prince remains completely untouched. His end is only a new beginning. Just as the painter Wang Fô disappeared beyond the horizon on an ocean he created with his paintbrush, carrying his secret along with him, so too did the little prince. Marguerite Yourcenar revived an ancient legend, weaving together age-old themes of love and loss, connection and alienation. Saint-Exupéry, himself a legend, created with the same themes a new tale that would in its turn become legendary. The little prince will never find a resting place; surely he does not belong to a planet inhabited by fools who cannot see that their only concerns are matters of no consequence. Reflecting with a bitter sadness upon the necessities of war and the duties of soldiers, Saint-Exupéry wrote in a letter from Oudjda dated mid-June 1943 addressed to General X, "And if I die in combat, I don't care . . . but if I come back alive from this 'necessary and thankless job,' there will only be one issue: what can we, what must we tell men?" (Saint-Exupéry 1999, vol. 2, 333–34). Indeed, what must we tell men? Perhaps the world should take the discovery of Saint-Exupéry's plane as a much-needed reminder of how far we have drifted from the values of fraternity and responsibility for our fellow creatures that *The Little Prince* espouses. One can only wonder what the world would be like if it were ruled by the little prince's wisdom? Instead, we seem to be hurtling further and further in the wrong direction. "Something irreparable" seems to have happened to the planet briefly visited by the innocent "little fellow" (76).

In the face of human folly, Voltaire's Candide retreated to his garden. Saint-Exupéry had that same yearning deep inside him, though he never came close to tending a garden of his own. A gardener will tame the secluded space of his garden with patience and great care. There, he will douse his special rose with water and unconditional love, always recognizing her among thousands of others. As the fox explained to the little prince, "You become responsible forever for what you've tamed. You're responsible for your rose . . ." (64). It takes at least two to be tamed, but if we reach out to our fellow beings with wisdom, humility, and a sense of responsibility, forging between each other bonds of mutual trust, then the migrating bird will return, roses will bloom, and our garden will flourish.

NOTES

1. Although *The Little Prince* does not appear on the two (essentially identical) lists of the ten best-selling books of all time (http://home.comcast.net/~antaylor1/bestsellingbooks.html and http://www.askmen.com/toys/top_10_60/62_top10_list.html), the *Daily Telegraph* of London asserted on 10 April 2004 that "it is already said to be the third best-selling book in history, after the Bible and *Das Kapital.*"

2. Delphine Lacroix, a member of the editorial board of the website http://www.lepetitprince.com, corresponded with me via e-mail on 1 June 2004

regarding the number of existing translations, and on 8 September 2004 regarding the number of copies of *Le Petit Prince* sold in France since its publication.

3. "Le Petit Prince," http://www.lepetitprince.com/fr/GEO/TraductionsActus.php, accessed 20 July 2004. See Maxwell Smith's *Knight of the Air: The Life and Works of Antoine de Saint-Exupéry*, with its extended bibliography, and also "Saint-Exupéry retrouvé," the special in-depth file compiled by the *Nouvel Observateur* after Saint-Exupéry's name tag had been found in a fisherman's net near Marseilles. In particular see the insert " 'Le Petit Prince,' un mythe en chiffres" (12–18 November 1998, 6). For further references to translations and editions, see the list of works cited at the end of this article.

4. Biagioli's insightful analysis of *The Little Prince* is also the most thorough investigation of the question whether Saint-Exupéry's masterpiece talks to the child or the inner child in the adult. Rather than providing an answer to that question, Biagioli shows how intricately both are linked. The part of the article that investigates how *The Little Prince* helps its adult readership examines the dual nature of the pilot who is "alternatively *Little* when he feels dominated by the elements, and *Prince* when he dominates the earth. He is above all the symbol of those two states of the self" (36).

5. The introduction to the second volume of the Pléiade edition of the complete works of Antoine de Saint-Exupéry (xxxiii) and Michel Autrand's biographical note in that same text (1345) provide invaluable information about the circumstances of Saint-Exupéry's exile in the United States. The pain of that period, the author-aviator's dark night of the soul, was alleviated somewhat thanks to some precious female friendships, for example, with Tyrone Power's French wife, Annabella, who was reading Andersen's tales to a physically and psychologically ailing Saint-Ex; with Elisabeth Reynal and Silvia Reinhard; and, of course, with his ever dramatic wife, Consuelo.

6. Note that Woods's translation of the French sentence "Mais tu es pur et tu viens d'une étoile" is "you are innocent and true and you come from a star" (60), whereas Howard's translation omits "and true" (51).

7. Saint-Exupéry met Werth, an essayist, novelist, and art critic in 1931, and soon he became the closest friend Saint-Exupéry had outside his flying group of Aeropostale. Twenty-two years older than Saint-Exupéry, Werth was an anarchist Jew and a supporter of the Bolsheviks, with a surrealistic writing style. He wrote twelve books and many magazine pieces. Saint-Exupéry dedicated to him *Letter to a Hostage* and *The Little Prince*. At the end of World War II, Leon Werth, who spent the war unobtrusively in Saint-Amour "alone, cold and hungry," said: "Peace, without Tonio [Saint-Exupéry's affectionate nickname] isn't entirely peace." Leon Werth did not see the text of *The Little Prince* until five months after his friend's death. See http://littleprince.8m.com/werth.html, accessed 27 November 2004.

8. "Comment Wang-Fô fut sauvé" is one of only two short stories written for adults that Marguerite Yourcenar revisited for a readership of children (the

other is "Notre-Dame des Hirondelles"). It is the tale of an old painter who is so talented that when he painted a horse, "he always had to paint him tied to a stake or held on a tight rein, otherwise the horse would take off the painting like a shot and never come back." It should be mentioned that Yourcenar added this sentence to her children's version of the tale.

9. See "Books & Things. Books, videos and other neat things related to 'The Little Prince,'" at http://www.b612.net/books-related.htm, accessed 20 November 2004. On the amazon.com website, the "product description" of *A Guide for Grown-ups* reads as follows: "'One sees clearly only with the heart. Anything essential is invisible to the eyes.' For more than sixty years, this insight from *The Little Prince* has been quoted in more than 130 languages by fans around the world. Now, for the first time, quotations from the collected works and letters of Antoine de Saint-Exupéry are presented in a charming gift edition. Six chapters—'Happiness,' 'Friendship,' 'Responsibility,' 'Fortitude,' 'Love,' and 'What Is Essential'—offer inspirational and thought-provoking words about the subjects held most dear by the author. A perfect gift for graduates—or for anyone who wants gentle guidance."

10. See "Books & Things. Books, videos and other neat things related to 'The Little Prince,'" at http://www.b612.net/books-related.htm, accessed 20 November 2004.

11. See http://www.lepetitprince.com/boutique/home_fr.html, accessed 20 November 2004.

12. See Saint-Exupéry 1999, 1091–1183.

13. In his introduction to the English version of Pierre Nora's *Realms of Memory*, Lawrence Kritzman stated that "Nora's *magnum opus* represents the symptomology of a certain form of cultural melancholia as well as the sign of an attempt to construct a symbolic encyclopedia that attests to the values and belief systems of the French nation" (ix).

WORKS CITED

Autrand, Michel. "Le Petit Prince: Notice." In Saint-Exupéry 1999, 1341–55.
Beckett, Sandra. *De grands romanciers écrivent pour les enfants.* Montreal: Les Presses de l'Université de Montréal, 1997.
Biagioli, Nicole. "Le Dialogue avec l'enfance dans Le Petit Prince." *Etudes Littéraires* 33 (2001) 2: 27–42.
Bruno, G. *Le Tour de la France par deux enfants.* 1877. Paris: Librairie Classique Eugène Belin, 2004.
Cate, Curtis. *Antoine de Saint-Exupéry.* New York: G. P. Putnam's Sons, 1970.
Chamberlain, John. "Books of the Times." *New York Times* 1943-04-06.
Compagnon, Antoine. "Marcel Proust's *Remembrance of Things Past.*" In Nora 1997, vol. 2. 210–46.

Fottorino, Eric. "Risques de rupture." *Le Monde* 2004-04-09.

Higgins, James. *The Little Prince: A Reverie of Substance*. New York: Twayne, 1996.

Le Hir, Geneviève. *Saint-Exupéry ou la force des images*. Paris: Imago, 2002.

Mackey, Margaret. "Arthur's Agendas: An Aardvark Avatar Edutains." *Bookbird* 38 (2000) 1: 37–40.

Moore, Anne Carroll. "The Three Owls' Notebook." *The Horn Book*, May–June 1943: 164–66.

Mourier, Anne-Isabelle. *"Le Petit Prince* de Saint-Exupéry: Du conte au mythe." *Etudes littéraires* 33 (2001) 2: 43–53.

Nora, Pierre. Dir. *Realms of Memory: The Construction of the French Past*. 3 vols. Trans. Arthur Goldhammer. New York: Columbia University Press, 1997.

Ozouf, Jacques and Mona. *"Le Tour de la France par deux enfants*: The Little Red Book of the Republic." In Nora 1997, vol. 2.: 124–48.

Perrot, Jean. *Jeux et enjeux du livre d'enfance et de jeunesse*. Paris: Editions du cercle de la librairie, 1999.

Reynal, Thérèse. "La France Libre." *Revue des Livres* 1944-08-15.

Robinson, Joy D. Marie. *Antoine de Saint-Exupéry*. Boston: Twayne, 1984 (Twayne's World Authors Series no 705).

Roy, Jules. "Qu'on lui foute la paix!" *Le Nouvel Observateur* 12–18 November 1998.

Saint-Exupéry, Antoine de. *A Guide for Grown-ups: Essential Wisdom from the Collected Works of Antoine de Saint-Exupéry*. New York: Harcourt, 2002.

———. "A Letter to Young Americans." Trans. Lewis Galantière. *Scholastic* 25–30 May 1942.

———. *The Little Prince*. Trans. Katherine Woods. New York: Reynal and Hitchcock, 1943.

———. *The Little Prince*. Trans. by Richard Howard. New York: Harcourt, 2000.

———. *Night Flight*. Preface by André Gide. Trans. Stuart Gilbert. New York and London : Century, 1932.

———. *Le Petit Prince*. New York: Reynal and Hitchcock, 1943.

———. *Le Petit Prince*. Paris: Gallimard-Folio Junior, 1998.

———. *Oeuvres complètes*. Vol. 1. Paris: Gallimard-Bibliothèque de La Pléiade, 1994.

———. *Oeuvres complètes*. Vol. 2. Paris: Gallimard-Bibliothèque de La Pléiade, 1999.

———. *Southern Mail*. Trans. Curtis Cate. New York: Harcourt Brace Jovanovich, 1971.

———. *Wind, Sand, and Stars*. Trans. Lewis Galantière. New York: Reynal and Hitchcock, 1939.

"Saint-Exupéry." http://www.saint-exupery.org, accessed 13 November 2004.

Schiff, Stacy. "A Grounded Soul: Saint-Exupéry in New York." *New York Times* 1993-05-30.

————. *Saint-Exupéry: A Biography.* New York: Knopf, 1995.

————. "Saint-Exupéry Lands at Last." *New York Times* 2004-04-11.

Sherman, Beatrice. "A Prince of Lonely Space." *New York Times* 1943-04-11.

Smith, Maxwell. *Knight of the Air: The Life and Works of Antoine de Saint-Exupéry.* New York: Pageant Press, 1956.

Vallières, Nathalie des. *Les Plus Beaux Manuscrits de Saint-Exupéry.* Paris: Editions de la Martinière, 2003.

————. *Saint-Exupéry: Art, Writings, and Musings.* Rizolli International Publications, 2004.

Yourcenar, Marguerite. *Comment Wang-Fô Fut Sauvé.* Paris: Gallimard-Folio Cadet, 1984.

————. *Notre-Dame des Hirondelles.* Paris: Gallimard-Enfantimages, 1982.

————. *Nouvelles Orientales.* 1938. Paris: Gallimard-L'Imaginaire, 1978.

————. *Oriental Tales.* Translated by Alberto Manguel. New York: Farrar, Straus, and Giroux, 1985.

3

A Misunderstood Tragedy
Astrid Lindgren's *Pippi Longstocking* Books

Maria Nikolajeva

Pippi Longstocking, the favorite character of Swedish children's literature, Pippi the rebel, Pippi the norm-breaker, has been subjected to serious critical scrutiny in the English-speaking world. Even one of the more subtle evaluations of Pippi uses her to illustrate the essence of children's literature as escape (Moebius 1985). Pippi books are often described in English-language reference works as "comic fantasy" (see also Hoffeld 1977). Pippi herself has been compared to two American characters, the Cat in the Hat (Metcalf 1995, 78f) and Curious George (Moebius 1985); in both cases the anti-authoritarian spirit of Pippi has been recognized, even though the emphasis has been rather on mischief, escape, and compensation. Pippi books have been typically described as "a mock-heroic affirmation of children's autonomy in the face of their powerlessness in the adult world" (Saltman 1987, 83). This is undoubtedly a correct description; indeed, empowering the child is the essence of Pippi stories (see also Nikolajeva 1997). Yet Pippi has also been regarded as sexist (Reeder 1979), basically on the grounds of her suggesting that Annika might wish to join her and Tommy on the high sea adventure to dust the piano! More recent research in Sweden, using as the point of departure Judith Butler's theory of gender performance, presents a considerably more subtle picture of the gender patterns in the Pippi books, also showing that Annika's extremely stereotypical portrayal is a deliberate strategy that allows the author to present Pippi's liberating feminist pathos (Frid 2003). Pippi has also been repeatedly accused of racism, as she is happy to become a "cannibal princess" and even considers painting her face with shoe polish to look black.

Many of Pippi's misadventures in the English-speaking countries come undoubtedly from the extremely deficient translations. Not only have the translators (or the editors?) played down Pippi's defiant tone in her endless parleys with the adults, but both the British and the American translator have liberally omitted most of Pippi's witticism, and her skillful play with language that is absolutely essential to understand both Pippi as a character and the books as an interrogation of authority. In fact, when I used *Pippi Longstocking* in my children's literature classes in the U.S., I discovered, to my frustration, that whenever I wanted to illustrate Pippi's verbal skills by an example I knew from the original, it simply wasn't there in the translated version. As a result, the American film from 1988, directed by Ken Annakin, must chiefly rely on slapstick, because the verbal humor of the Pippi stories is completely gone.

Another important factor affecting the frequent misunderstanding of Pippi is the diverse views on the child and childhood, on children's rights, and on the family. Pippi has been called "the child of the century" (Lundqvist 1979), which alludes to the famous study by the Swedish educator Ellen Key, *The Century of the Child* (1900), maintaining the child's rights to free and harmonious upbringing. Respect for the child has been the dominant pedagogical doctrine in Sweden throughout the twentieth century, and Pippi is an excellent illustration of this spirit, although as the books appeared, they were by no means unanimously appraised. In fact, the initial manuscript of the first *Pippi* book was turned down by the Swedish publisher Bonnier as revolting and totally unsuitable for children, and when the revised book was brought out by another publisher, Rabén & Sjögren, after it won a manuscript competition, a leading Swedish critic condemned it for bad taste and poor literary quality. Nonetheless, the book immediately became a great favorite with young readers, teachers, and parents in Sweden. Yet in countries with a different view on parental authority Pippi can naturally be perceived as too strong a challenge. It is, of course, not totally unimportant to know that Astrid Lindgren, the author of *Pippi*, comes from a country with an early and strong women's rights movement, and that she already had a professional career and was financially independent long before she started writing. Therefore it is quite natural for her to create a strong and independent female character who is also, in many ways, superior to adults.

It does not demand a huge leap of imagination to see the intertextual links between Pippi and another famous red-haired heroine, Anne of Green Gables. In fact, the intertextuality is quite intentional (see Åhmansson 1994). Apart from the archetypal red-hair connection, there is at least one direct reply in *Pippi* to *Anne of Green Gables*, showing clearly not only the distance of almost forty years between the books, but the distance in the authors' attitudes. Like Anne, Pippi is told that children should be seen but not heard. While for Anne, the remark is a reminder to toe the line, Pippi retorts by pointing out that people around her hopefully have ears and well as eyes, and if her looks are joyful to the eye, she would not want the ears to miss the pleasure of listening to her talk (this passage is, incidentally, also lost in the American translation). While Anne hates her red hair and freckles, Pippi loves them and is proud of them. Everything that Anne fails in and gets punished for, Pippi manages effortlessly. Anne has to adapt to the norms and rules of society; by the end of the first novel, she has lost her vivid imagination and her flowery language; she has given up her creativity, and she is also prepared to give up her foremost dream. Pippi is allowed by her author to use her imagination in full scale (although some people, including the prim, well-behaved Annika, call it lying); her language skills get more and more brilliant; and Pippi is definitely not the one who will be stopped from self-fulfillment. In the end, both girls are accepted by society, but for different reasons. Anne has changed and submitted to societal demands. Pippi has changed the society itself, making the people around her accept her exactly as she is, wild, ill-behaved, and uncontrolled. Yet this is only possible because Pippi appears within a different literary mode.

Pippi Longstocking is a complex and multilayered book that invites many different interpretations and, indeed, has been subjected to many, as shown above. In the *Pippi* books we notice the genre convergence that later becomes a characteristic feature of children's literature: elements from high sea adventure, Robinsonnade, treasure seeking, domestic story, and classroom humor—all in intertextual relation to previous works for both children and adults; this is undoubtedly one reason why Lindgren's books are appreciated by readers of all ages.

The limits of this essay only allow me to deal with a few aspects of Pippi. But first of all, it is essential to very briefly put the text in its historical and social context. For a more detailed presentation of the author and her oeuvre, see two excellent studies that complement each other elegantly, Eva-Maria Metcalf's *Astrid Lindgren* (1995) and Vivi Edström's *Astrid Lindgren. A Critical Study* (2000).

THE REMARKABLE GIRL'S
REMARKABLE CREATOR

Pippi's creator, Astrid Lindgren (1907–2002), was the most prominent and famous contemporary children's author in Sweden, winner of the Andersen Medal (1958) and numerous other national and international awards, translated into ninety languages. She was also an outstanding and influential public figure, making substantial contributions to the debates and occasionally even legislation on children's and animals' rights, war and nonviolence, and various cultural issues. In 1976 she contributed to the downfall of the Swedish government with her pungent pamphlet on tax policy.

Born into a family of farmhands in the southern Swedish province of Småland, Astrid Lindgren was educated as a secretary and gave birth to a child out of wedlock at the age of eighteen. She was forced to leave the baby with a foster family in Denmark. There are echoes of this traumatic experience in her poignant portrayal of lonely and abandoned children. She took her son home as soon as her financial and social status was stabilized, and she married Sture Lindgren, a high executive, in 1931, and had other children. Unfortunately, her husband died early, and she remained a widow for the rest of her life. During the years 1946-70, Lindgren worked at the largest children's publisher in Sweden, Rabén & Sjögren, encouraging beginning Swedish writers as well as bringing the best of international children's literature to Sweden.

The appearance of her first books immediately after World War II was prepared by the vast interest in pedagogy and child psychology in Sweden during the 1930s, as well as general awareness about children's rights. Lindgren stands wholly on the child's side, rejecting the early didactic and authoritarian ways of addressing young readers. In the light of the war, earlier idyllic and adventurous children's literature seemed false and superficial, and Lindgren's works took young readers closer to the everyday and offered a more joyous and optimistic tone. Together with such writers as Lennart Hellsing and Tove Jansson, Lindgren radically changed Swedish children's literature and its status in society. Writing in almost every possible genre and style, she consistently broke conventional rules and norms in terms of pedagogical concepts as well as artistic principles.

Contrary to common knowledge, Astrid Lindgren's first book was not *Pippi Longstocking*, but an epistolary girls' novel, *Britt-Mari lättar sitt hjärta* (Britt-Mari opens her heart 1944), in which she transcended the conventions of the popular genre in her use of ironic distance and parody. Yet her internationally best-known book is, without doubt, *Pippi Långstrump* (1945; Engl. *Pippi Longstocking* 1950), featuring the strongest girl in the world, independent and defiant in her confrontation with the world of adults, empowering the child in an unheard-of manner, which caused many educators to see Pippi as offensive.

In the years to come, Lindgren created a vast number of literary figures that are today known and loved all over the world: the children of Noisy Village; the lonely orphan Andy who becomes the valiant prince Mio in Farawayland; the funny man with a propeller on his back, Karlsson-on-the-Roof; the tomboy girl Meg; the little rascal Emil; the faithful brothers Lionheart who fight for freedom and justice; and not least Ronia the Robber's Daughter, the little rebel and feminist who in a way completes the circle that started with Pippi. All Lindgren's characters, whether they appear in realistic or fantastic settings, have common traits with the traditional folktale hero, the youngest son or daughter, the oppressed, the powerless, the underprivileged, gaining material and spiritual wealth during a period of trials. This feature of Lindgren's writing, seldom acknowledged by scholars, has gained her a special appreciation in the former totalitarian states of Eastern Europe, where the rebellious pathos of her children's books and the subversive interrogation of all forms of authorities were recognized.

Astrid Lindgren was an extremely prolific writer with over a hundred books to her credit, including plays, essays, and memoirs. Her novels for children have been turned into stage, radio, and television versions and animated as well as live-action films, both in Sweden and elsewhere. Many of her short stories and fairy tales have been published as picturebooks, illustrated by the most prominent Swedish artists. Her children's verses have been set to music and are regarded as part of the treasury of Swedish children's songs, in some cases substituting, in public function, for traditional church hymns. She was voted the Swede of the Year several times, and was made honorary doctor at three universities. A number of major awards and scholarships have been established in her honor, the most recent the international Astrid Lindgren Memorial Award for Literature, initiated by the Swedish government and comparable in monetary value to the Nobel Prize.

Lindgren holds a unique position in children's literature, and it is difficult to single out any followers in the younger generation of Swedish authors. Her greatest contribution is to have created an extremely favorable climate for children's literature, to have opened avenues for new forms and styles, and thus to have raised the general status of children's literature in Sweden and throughout the world. Her significance as a writer and a national icon in Sweden cannot be overestimated. Much of Pippi's rebellious nature reflects the spirit of her creator.

GETTING TO KNOW PIPPI

As a literary character, Pippi is highly complex and ambivalent. We first learn that Pippi is nine years old and that she does not have a mother or a father. Already the following passage is ambiguous in its voice: "that was of course very nice because there was no one to tell her to go to bed just when she was having the most fun" (*Pippi Long-stocking* 11). Is this Pippi's opinion or an omniscient, didactic narrator's? We are never allowed to enter Pippi's mind, and since only external characterization devices are used, the character can never really become truly round. This does not of course mean that Pippi is deficient as a character; her opacity is part of the design.

The fact that Pippi lives in an "old house" in an "old overgrown garden" characterizes her indirectly, through the setting. The opening itself, "Way out at the end of a tiny little town," alludes to fairy tales and also the famous Swedish picturebook, *The Tale of a Tiny Little Woman* (1897), by Elsa Beskow, which encourages us to view Pippi as a fairy-tale figure. This is important, because if we start applying mimetic criteria to Pippi, that is, if we assess her as a predominantly realistic character, her supernatural strength notwithstanding, we will put demands on the unity and integrity of character that Pippi cannot meet. We must, on the contrary, apply "suspension of disbelief" proposed by J. R. R. Tolkien (1968) in order to judge Pippi properly. A critic's comment on Mary Poppins can just as well concern Pippi:

"Characters in realistic stories are normally supplied with a past: they have parents, have had a childhood, grow up and develop. The figures of myth and fairy-tale, however, most often step out of nothing. They simply *are*" (Bergsten 1978, 27). Pippi can be described as an "alien child," a concept that goes back to a children's novel by E. T. A. Hoffmann and refers to a character—not necessarily a child—who appears from nowhere and occasionally disappears mysteriously in the end. Pippi is thus the same kind of character as Peter Pan and the Little Prince, a character whose ontological status is vague and obscure.

True, we learn very soon that Pippi once had a mother and a father, yet neither fact is very reliable. In the mother, who is up in Heaven, "watching her little girl through a peephole in the sky" (*Pippi Longstocking* 12), we recognize the convention from early sentimental children's books, while the story of the father who disappears in a storm is reminiscent of a sailor's yarn. When we get to know Pippi better, we can suspect that the story of the father is just one of her many tall tales (even though he does make a physical appearance in the end). In *Pippi Goes on Board*, we read: "She really believed it when she said her father was a cannibal king" (10). Pippi's ontological status is therefore different from the heroines of realistic fiction, such as Anne of Green Gables, who must be provided with a background to be plausible.

The plausibility of Pippi's background, that is her life before she came to live in Villa Villekulla, depends on the reader's judgment of the narrator's reliability. We do not believe Pippi's own tall-tales about her experiences in Egypt, Argentina, and Congo, but can we believe the narrator? The first evaluation of Pippi comes from one of the sailors on her father's ship: "A remarkable child" (*Pippi Longstocking* 13). The narrator hurries to confirm this: "He was right. Pippi was indeed a remarkable child" (13), adding that she was extremely strong. We learn that Pippi "had always longed for a horse" (14), which many young readers will empathize with, recognizing their own longing for a pet. The first pages of the novel are thus devoted to a detailed presentation of Pippi, her background, and her most important inner traits.

However, the author waits for quite a while before giving us a description of Pippi's looks, which we receive through Tommy and Annika. The description is, once again, preceded by the statement that she was "the most remarkable girl" they had ever seen (15). The repetition of the word "remarkable" is a powerful device for establishing Pippi's constant epithet. The external description is long and detailed:

Her hair the color of a carrot was braided in two tight braids that stuck right out. Her nose was the shape of a very small potato and was dotted all over with freckles. It must be admitted that the mouth under this nose was a very wide one, with strong white teeth. . . . On her long thin legs she wore a pair of long stockings, one brown and the other black, and she had on a pair of black shoes that were exactly twice as long as her feet. (16)

This description accentuates all Pippi's specific features: hair color, freckles, potato nose, big mouth and her unusual clothes, the features we remember best. Her hair and freckles will later be referred to often, for instance through other people's reaction to them; or through the episode in which Pippi sees an advertisement in a beauty parlor asking: "Do you suffer from freckles?" and responds to it by entering the parlor with a resolute: "No!" (*Pippi Goes on Board* 18). However, this initial description of Pippi is so vivid that it does not need frequent reinforcement, and of course the book is also illustrated, so Pippi's exterior is constantly before the reader. In the beginning of the third sequel, we encounter another description of Pippi, as seen through the eyes of a fine gentleman: "The girl in the middle had lots of freckles on her face and two red pigtails which stuck straight out" (*Pippi in the South Seas* 12). Since the reader is supposed to be familiar with Pippi already, there is really no reason to describe her looks again, but at the beginning of the sequel this description has a didactic function, as a reminder. A similar "estrangement" is used in the chapter about burglars, when Pippi is seen through their eyes. This occasional reinforcement of Pippi's looks is unobtrusive and creates a comic effect.

Everything else we learn about Pippi from the three books is primarily revealed through her speech and actions. The fact that she loves animals and has a way with them speaks in her favor. The narrator never says that Pippi is kind or generous, but we make this inference because she treats Tommy and Annika to nice meals, gives them presents, and so on. Later, she buys sweets for all the children in the town, and comforts children who have failed Miss Rosenblom's examination—the repetition of similar actions amplifies our perception of Pippi as a generous person. However, when we view Pippi all alone in her house in the evenings, her daytime magnanimity acquires a different flavor. She is not merely generous because she is strong and rich, but also because she is lonely, illustrating the well-known phenomenon of a lonely, unhappy child who "buys friendship." Perhaps the difference between the two phenomena is not so extreme. This is merely one of many aspects of Pippi that is seldom discussed by critics, who prefer to see the comic and positive sides of the character rather than her tragic outsider position. The treatment is not unlike the view of Peter Pan as a carefree adventurer rather than a deeply tragic, infantile, self-centered wimp.

Watching Pippi's behavior throughout the books we come to the conclusion that she is brave, independent, and smart (for instance when she figures out how to save the two children from the fire). Yet our assessment depends strongly on our own subjectivity, that is, whether we judge Pippi from a child or an adult subject position. In a child's eyes, Pippi may be liberated, bold, funny, and admirable. From an adult perspective, she is ill-mannered. She lies a lot—or rather tells a lot of imaginative stories. Her ways of cooking or scrubbing the floor are highly original. It is essential to note that Pippi never abuses her strength. In fact, she only uses it against those who are themselves nasty toward the weak: the big boy Bengt, the police officers, Mighty Adolf in the circus, the burglars Thunder-Karlsson and Bloom, or the bandits Jim and Buck. Otherwise she prefers to talk her opponents down. There are practically no negative traits in Pippi. We may perhaps object to Pippi teasing the little girl who is looking for her father in the chapter "Pippi Sits on the Gate and Climbs a Tree," but this episode is so minor in the story, and besides is combined with Pippi's eternal tall tales, that we hardly attach any attention to it. Her lack of manners may, of course, irritate prudish adults, but most young readers find delight in them.

The narrator's comments on Pippi are scarce: "she caught [the eggs] *skillfully* in a bowl" (*Pippi Longstocking*, 20; emphasis added) or "Pippi could work fast, she could" (26). These comments cease completely as the novel unfolds. The other characters' comments on Pippi are also rare. The morning after they have met Pippi, Annika wakes her brother saying: "let's go and see that funny girl with the big shoes" (24). The adults in the little town promptly dislike Pippi. The schoolteacher thinks Pippi is "an unruly and troublesome child" (55), and Miss Rosenblom believes Pippi to be "the most stupid and disagreeable child" she has ever seen (*Pippi in the South Seas* 48). However, most of the adults change their minds on getting to know Pippi better, especially after she has rescued two children in the fire, tamed the escaped tiger, and intimidated the ruffian Laban. The most radical attitude change is noted in Mrs. Settergren, Tommy's and Annika's mother, in the last book. The ladies of the little town wonder whether she, indeed, is considering sending her children to the South Seas with Pippi, and she says: "As long as I've known Pippi she has never done anything that has harmed Tommy and Annika in any way. No one can be kinder to them than she . . . her heart is in the right place" (*Pippi in the South Seas* 66f). The mother has realized that Pippi's inner qualities are more important than her lack of table manners.

Another consistent aspect of Pippi's characterization is her total absence of feelings. The closest we come to an expression of sentiment is when Pippi is "wild with delight" (*Pippi Longstocking* 148) on getting a music box for her birthday. Indirectly, we take part in her feelings when she weeps over a dead bird in *Pippi Goes on Board*. Typically, Pippi herself denies that she is crying, and she also seems to forget about the bird quite soon. She is full of compassion for Countess Aurora during a sentimental theater performance. Sometimes the text will tell us that Pippi is angry, for instance when she sees a man beat his horse. She also cries after the adventure with the shark, but not because Tommy has almost been eaten up, but because "the poor little hungry shark no get breakfast today" (sic! *Pippi in the South Seas* 85). Pippi's statements about herself are not worth much, mostly she just brags: "Grace and charm I have at least" (*Pippi Longstocking* 76), "I do think freckles are so attractive" (80), or "I should imagine I'll be the most stylish person of all at this party" (118). The most decisive of all the actions that characterize Pippi is that she refuses to go away with her father when she sees how upset Tommy and Annika are. Until now, Pippi's generosity did not cost her too much—she has access to an endless supply of gold coins. But to abstain from her own pleasure in order not to upset her friends demands more.

So far, the traits we have discovered in Pippi certainly make her a relatively round and complex character. But what about dynamism? Pippi seems a remarkably static character. The main reason why Pippi cannot evolve as a character is that she already possesses every property desirable for a young reader: she is the strongest girl in the world, she is rich beyond imagination, and she is independent of adult hierarchy, including all rules and laws. In this way, Pippi is placed, from the beginning, in a position of power, which otherwise is the strongest motivation for character development. Consequently, Pippi lacks the desire to grow up—she simply does not have to. The only conceivable change would be to strip Pippi of all her power, which certainly contradicts the author's intention, as well as conventions of children's literature. Thus, if the common dream of many child characters is "to grow up and become strong, rich and admired," Pippi's motto is to be strong, rich and admired, and never have to grow up (cf. my comparison of Pippi and Jacob Two-Two in Nikolajeva 1997).

PUER AETERNUS

Pippi is thus a Swedish variant of the Puer Aeternus theme in children's literature, the child who cannot and is reluctant to grow up—a theme best illustrated in the Anglo-Saxon tradition by Peter Pan, but also tangibly present in a vast number of other children's classics (see Nikolajeva 2000a, 87–123).

In *Pippi* books, adults are presented as ridiculous and hypocritical, including Tommy and Annika's parents and relatives, such as Aunt Laura, the ladies who come to the infamous coffee party, the schoolteacher, the police, the firemen, the circus and theater people, the fine gentleman who wants to buy Pippi's house, and not least the notorious Miss Rosenblom. The author criticizes indiscriminately; respectable citizens and criminals, men and women fall under her ruthless judgment. The message seems to be that adults are inferior to children in intelligence and in every other respect, and therefore adulthood is nothing for children to look forward to. This is naturally what many critics find offensive in the Pippi stories, failing to see the complexity of the issue.

Pippi's extraordinary strength may seem to be her weapon against adults; however, her challenge of adult order is expressed mainly through language, through interrogation of arbitrary linguistic practices presented as unconditional laws. In fact, as already mentioned, Pippi only uses her strength against vile, unfair (and exclusively male) adversaries. In all other situations, Pippi uses her wits, as in the much-quoted interlocution with the schoolteacher:

"Pippi, can you tell me what seven and five are?"

Pippi, astonished and dismayed, looked at her and said, "Well, if you don't know that yourself you needn't think I'm going to tell you."

All the children stared in horror at Pippi, and the teacher explained that one couldn't answer that way in school.

"I beg your pardon," said Pippi contritely. "I didn't know that. I won't do it again."

"No, let's hope not," said the teacher. "And now I will tell you that seven and five are twelve."

"See that!" said Pippi. "You knew it yourself. Why are you asking then?" (*Pippi Longstocking* 54f)

Adults in Pippi can never acknowledge the linguistic genius of a child. Pippi's "deconstruction" of language through her inadequate spelling skills gives child readers a confirmation of their own language proficiency. The arbitrariness of the spelling rules imposed by adults is interrogated. At the question-and-answer bee in *Pippi in the South Seas*, Pippi says: "S-e-e-s-i-k is the way I have always spelled it, and it seems to have worked out just fine" (45). Astrid Lindgren allows her character to defy the dictatorship of norms and conventions, of dull reality, of authority, of structure and order. Pippi demonstrates that adults do not always know best.

Like Peter Pan, Pippi does not want to grow up. However, her reasons are different from Peter Pan's. She does not want to grow into a respectable lady "with a veil and three double chins." Instead, she wants to be a pirate. She does not want to become what the authorities want her to become: ordinary, obedient, and dull. Pippi defies the capriciously prescribed order by doing as she pleases, which includes walking backwards, or sleeping with her feet on her pillow, or watering flowers in the pouring rain. Pippi refuses to accept that children "must have someone to advise them, and . . . go to school to learn the multiplication tables" (*Pippi Longstocking* 40). Pippi's attitude toward authorities is marvelously illustrated by the phrase: "Policemen are the very best things I know. Next to rhubarb pudding" (41).

In the orphanage, Pippi learns, she will not be allowed to keep her horse and her monkey, two attributes which reinforce the child's closeness to nature, maybe even her savagery, "monkeyhood" as Moebius chooses to call it (Moebius 1985, 44). Pippi promptly refuses to go to an orphanage, thus rejecting the order imposed by adults. When Ken Annakin, the director of the American film version, lets Pippi obligingly be taken to a home, dressed in a dull uniform with a pinafore, and have her hair braided neatly, he misinterprets the very concept of Pippi.

The real Pippi promptly refuses to be socialized. She is what every child dreams of being: strong, independent, and free, in confrontation with the world of adults. Unlike the typical underdog character of many children's books, Pippi is secure, self-assured, strong, and rich from the beginning. Everybody wants to be friends with her, and by the end of the first book, when Pippi rescues two small boys from the fire, even adults have to accept her. She can even make "pining away in a dungeon" sound fun, so that Tommy feels enticed to "come down and pine away a little too" (*Pippi Longstocking* 72f).

The plot of the *Pippi* books is the reverse of the most traditional pattern of children's literature: home (boring, but secure)—adventure (exciting, but dangerous)—home (Nodelman and Reimer 2003, 201), which may also be described as order—chaos—order. Pippi comes from chaos to disturb order (cf. Edström 1990), from adventure to home that is boring and therefore must be turned into adventure. Pippi's function in the story is to stir and wake up the old, stale, conservative, slumbering Swedish society, represented by the philistines of the tiny little town. But she herself does not develop, since she is, like Mary Poppins, perfect from the beginning. Instead, she acts as a catalyst.

Pippi's excess in food marks her defiance of any form of limitation. Pippi's role in the stories is to provide food for others, while with her own joyful eating Pippi sets an example for other children. Her tall-tales, often concerning food and eating, have the same purpose. Eva-Maria Metcalf views the function of food in Lindgren's book chiefly as adaptation to the needs of young readers (Metcalf 1995, 40). However, to reduce the function of food in Pippi books to satisfying the readers' desires is to underestimate her totally. Pippi has gigantic proportions both in her cooking ("at least five hundred cookies," *Pippi Longstocking* 25), in her shopping ("thirty-six pounds of candy . . . sixty lollipops and seventy-two packages of caramels," *Pippi Goes on Board* 23), and in her consuming ("She heaped as many cakes as she could onto a plate, threw five lumps of sugar into a coffee cup, emptied half the cream pitcher into her cup," *Pippi Longstocking* 121), and she also eats up a whole cake as if it is nothing (122).

Yet she is just as generous when she invites her friends for a meal, asking Tommy and Annika to have breakfast with her as soon as they meet, serving coffee and cookies both on the porch and up in a tree, or taking them out on a picnic and on a planned shipwreck, not to mention the wonderful travel to the exotic paradise of the South Seas. When shopping, Pippi behaves like a little Robin Hood, taking from the rich (adults) and giving to the poor (children), especially in the magnificently carnivalesque scene in *Pippi Goes on Board* when she extravagantly pours sweets and toys over the town's children.

Pippi's plentiful meals are served incessantly throughout the three books: pancakes, cookies, cakes, buns, caramels, "good sandwiches with meatballs and ham, a whole pile of sugared pancakes, several little brown sausages, and three pineapple puddings" (*Pippi Longstocking* 81), "bread and cheese and butter, ham and cold roast and milk" (112), not to mention soda pop growing in a tree. The symbolical meaning of food as the child's primary need is manifest in children's literature (see Nikolajeva 2000a, 11–16). The abundance of food in Pippi is highly significant. Pippi's numerous tall tales often involve exotic food, for instance, swallow's nests (*Pippi Longstocking* 66). Pippi always turns eating into joy. Even Miss Rosenblom's hateful soup is defied and defeated by Pippi's lofty distribution of sweets. In Sweden, where it is often said that the worst privation during the Second World War was rationed coffee, joking about food was allowed in 1945. Observe, however, that Pippi is never disrespectful about food; pie-throwing in the American film version is totally against her nature. In fact, in *Pippi Goes on Board*, Pippi punishes ruffian Laban who throws sausage on the ground.

Pippi can be generous with food because she has a neverending supply of it. While children in traditional stories seek and occasionally find the source of their individual well-being, Pippi is herself the source of wealth—maybe Astrid Lindgren's early vision of the future Swedish "welfare society"? In Pippi, the primary sense is, her wildness notwithstanding, that of security, home, peace, and harmony. Her role in the story is not that of a desirous child, but of a giving, nurturing Progenitrix, the fertility goddess, a figure which also appears in other Astrid Lindgren's works, the good and nurturing Mother Svea, reflecting the Swedish firm belief in the benevolence of their country. Let us not be deceived by Pippi's childlike appearance; it is merely a disguise.

Pippi has no magic powers and no magic objects to assist her. In the system of characters, whether we prefer Propp's folktale model (Propp 1968), Greimas's actant-model (Greimas 1983), or Campbell's "hero with a thousand faces" (Campbell 1949), Pippi is not a hero, but rather a helper. In fact, she is not even the main character of the story, in the same way that Peter Pan is not, if we accept as the criterion for the main character some form of development or at least a clear focalization (this interpretation of Pippi is not a common assumption, cf. Metcalf 1995, 68). We never share Pippi's point of view. Her role is to set the plot in motion, not to be a primary part of it. Thus, rather than finding herself a helpless victim of evil forces, she stages a shipwreck. She can even turn a fire into a big celebration. In other words, she neither seeks trouble nor shuns it, she is trouble herself.

Of course, Pippi is also the archetypal orphan child, or pretends to be. Her parents, her mother in Heaven, and her father, "formerly the Terror of the Sea, now a cannibal king" (54), may just as well be imaginary. Both the physical appearance of the father and Pippi's wild adventures in the South Seas in the sequels may be just another tall tale (a daring, but not impossible interpretation). Who is Pippi? Where does she come from?

As already mentioned, apart from her unusual strength, Pippi does not possess any magical powers. But at least one habit betrays Pippi's supernatural origin. She can eat toadstools. Any dictionary of myth will tell us that this ability signals belonging to "the other world." Pippi is a witch. She is nice, generous, and beneficial, but she is still a witch. Just as the absence of shadow or mirror reflection reveals a vampire, the witch's eating habits reveal her true nature.

> "What have you got in your basket?" asked Annika. "Is it something good?"
>
> "I wouldn't tell you for a thousand dollars," said Pippi. (*Pippi Longstocking* 79f)

Since Pippi has just eaten a toadstool, Annika's question is not as stupid as it may seem. Pippi has never given them food that has not been good. Annika wonders—subconsciously—whether Pippi is about to initiate them into her witch food, or whether she will once again adjust her witch habits to humans.

Pippi packs the basket while Tommy and Annika run home to ask their mother's permission to go on a picnic with Pippi. The content of the basket is a surprise for them, as it is for the reader. Pippi makes them shut their eyes while she sets out the picnic:

> There were good sandwiches with meatballs and ham, a whole pile of sugared pancakes, several little brown sausages, and three pineapple puddings. For, you see, Pippi had learned cooking from the cook on her father's ship. (*Pippi Longstocking* 81)

We may think that we are just dealing with another of Lindgren's many lavish enumerations of food. However, we see the nice picnic as Tommy and Annika see it when they have opened their eyes. The last statement in the quote above comes from Pippi. As Pippi's background with her life on her father's ship may be just another tall tale, she may have had her cooking lessons anywhere. And why should Tommy and Annika shut their eyes? Maybe Pippi makes the food appear from an empty basket. Maybe she sets the picnic table with witch food—toads, snakes, and toadstools—and casts a spell on it to make it look like delicacies?

On another occasion Pippi betrays herself still more, when she says that she used to shoot an antelope or a llama and eat the meat raw. "Raw or Cooked" is the basic opposition in human culture (as well as the title of Claude Lévi-Strauss's famous study in myth and anthropology; Lévi-Strauss 1983), and Pippi's eating raw meat confirms once again that she belongs to nature, that she is "an alien child," a "non-human."

The very last episode in the *Pippi* trilogy depicts Pippi tempting her friends with a magical device that will prevent them from growing up. The ritual around the chillilug pill recalls the Holy Communion in its solemnity:

> They turned the Christmas tree lights out. . . . They sat down in silence in a circle in the middle of the floor, holding one another by the hands. Pippi gave Tommy and Annika each a chililug pill. Chills ran up the down their spines. Just think, in a second the powerful pill would be down in their stomachs and then they would never have to grow up. How marvelous that would be! (*Pippi in the South Seas* 123)

The Holy Communion, too, promises eternal life. What does Pippi promise Tommy and Annika? Is she in fact a little Mephistopheles inviting the children into her demonic realm? It is quite easy to interpret the chillilug pill in many ways, including drugs. Anyway, it is witch food. According to Pippi, she has been given the pills by an old Indian chieftain (that is, a witch-doctor, a shaman), and we can only hope that their power has worn off. It is time for the children to leave the Nurturing Mother and start coping on their own.

Pippi, on the other hand, chooses—or rather has already chosen before—to conserve herself forever. Liberating the child in the "charming, . . . good, well brought up, and obedient" (*Pippi Longstocking* 16) Tommy and Annika and making at least their mother realize the necessity of this liberation reflects the writer's nostalgic longing for everlasting childhood.

PIPPI AS LINGUIST

As already mentioned, Pippi's foremost asset is her brilliant mastery of language. Together with works such as *Alice in Wonderland* and *Winnie-the-Pooh*, *Pippi* books have sometimes been categorized as nonsense, on the basis of their excessive wordplay. However, Pippi's nonsense is, at closer examination, logical and sensible, as she consistently demonstrates the functions of human language.

One day Pippi "invents" a new word, "spink," and of course as she shares her discovery with her friends, they wonder what the word means. Pippi, however, has invented a signifier without a signified, and, as she says: "The only thing I know is that it doesn't mean vacuum cleaner" (*Pippi in the South Seas* 31). Pippi then tries to find a referent, a signified that would suit the arbitrarily created signifier. She tries to buy some spink in a store, goes to a doctor and complains of acute spink, and so on, finally deciding that the name matches a tiny bug she sees on the path. In doing this, Pippi acts, as she usually does, contrary to the normal course of events. Normally, we seek a suitable word for an object or a concept.

> "Who really decided in the beginning what all the words should mean?" Tommy wondered.
> "Probably a bunch of old professors," said Pippi. (*Pippi in the South Seas*, 31)

Pippi goes right against the bunch of old professors in her handling of language. In an insightful essay, the Swedish scholar Christina Heldner has shown the celebration of a gifted child's language acquisition in Pippi's magnificent play with language (Heldner 1992). Unlike Lewis Carroll, whose nonsensical play with words is often based on phonetics, like puns, Lindgren plays mostly with semantics, with the different meaning of words, as well as with the illogical ways language uses some of them, that is pragmatic rules. Unfortunately, much of Pippi's brilliant word equilibristics is lost in the English translation; yet enough is left to illustrate a few points. Some of Pippi's statements are, for instance, based on the use of incompatible notions. After paying a brief visit to school, Pippi says: "It's so thick with learning in there that you can cut it with a knife" (*Pippi Goes on Board* 31). The sentence is incorrect logically, or rather according to selective rules, which govern how words can be connected semantically. Normally, cutting something with a knife only refers to physical bodies, preferably solid, while "learning" is an abstract noun. However, Pippi uses the combination of words to create a vivid image. When Annika is concerned that Pippi has not dried the floor after scrubbing it, Pippi says: "I don't think it will catch cold so long as it keeps moving" (*Pippi Longstocking* 76). Grammatically it is a correct sentence, but naturally a floor can neither move nor catch cold.

Another example of Pippi's treatment of language is logical contradictions. When Annika asks whether she may eat pancakes with her fingers, Pippi replies that she has no objections, but for her own part she will stick to the good old habit of eating with her mouth. During the question-and-answer-bee, all the children are told to stand in two lines: one for those who have younger brothers or sisters and the other for those without siblings. On arrival, Pippi asks: "In which line should I stand, since I don't have fourteen brothers and sisters of which thirteen are naughty little boys?" (*Pippi in the South Seas* 44). The failing logic of the sentence is obvious: it does not matter how many siblings you *do not* have, and if you do not have any siblings at all, none can be naughty boys. Yet another example of incongruity is: "Even if there are no ghosts, they don't need to go round scaring folks out of their wits." The goal of Pippi's verbal exercises is often to make a fool of the adults and their logic, using analytical truths. An analytical utterance is one that is true independent of the situation, like "medicine is good for sickness." It is something that does not have to be repeated. Therefore, it is pure insult when Pippi replies to the druggist's question about what kind of medicine she needs: "Preferably some that is good for sickness." By breaking the rules of logic, Pippi draws the readers' attention to their existence, showing a powerful verbal creativity typical of children.

Pippi is an excellent illustration of Jacques Lacan's concepts of the Imaginary (preverbal) and Symbolic (verbal) language (Lacan 1977; see also Coats 2004, 110–119). Unlike Freud, Lacan sought the origins of psychological disturbances not in our frustrated sexual desires, but in the inadequacy of human language or, to be more precise, in the discrepancy between the structure of language and the chaos of the unconscious. Young children are always "preverbal" in the sense that they are unable to articulate their emotions to an adult's satisfaction and also in the sense that they have no access to written language. Many children's books depict children who must be socialized, who must adjust to adults' demands and rules, in order to become integrated into the Symbolic. As they do so, they lose their ability to experience the Lacanian Imaginary. One aspect of socialization is learning to read. Thus the use of Lacan's concepts of the Imaginary and the Symbolic can be modified to demonstrate a frequent contradiction in children's fiction, that between the desire to keep the fictional child in the state of natural innocence and ignorance and societal pressure for education (see Nikolajeva 2000b).

In most children's books addressing the issue, the child's ability to use and appreciate the Imaginary language is presented as a deficiency, while the passage into the Symbolic order is hailed as the desirable goal. There are very few children's books in which the value of the Symbolic order is openly interrogated. One of them is, not unexpectedly, *Pippi Longstocking*. Pippi has never attended school, she can barely read, and her spelling leaves much to be desired. The adult authorities naturally try to impose their rules of order on Pippi, since "all children must have someone to advise them, and all children must go to school to learn the multiplication tables" (38). In the chapter "Pippi Goes to School," the teacher shows her a picture of an ibex and the letter "i" (in the Swedish original it is a hedgehog, an image more likely to be familiar to a child than an ibex), while Pippi says, quite reasonably, that she sees a little stick with a fly speck above it (54f). Pippi employs imaginary reading, interpreting the icon and ignoring the conventional aspect of the sign, which is of course what the other children are taught in school. Yet because Pippi is what she is, she not only gets away with it, but can insist on her right to remain at the Imaginary stage. Pippi is, however, one of a kind, and her rule-breaking only emphasizes the existence of rules.

Still, as *Pippi* books are explicitly subversive in their attitude toward the Symbolic, they bring to our attention one of the central dilemmas in writing for children.

WHY DOES PIPPI SLEEP WITH HER FEET ON A PILLOW?

It has been repeatedly pointed out that in *Pippi Longstocking* Astrid Lindgren takes the child's part. In fact, taking the child's part, lending out her voice to the silenced child and similar metaphors of power have been used to emphasize the author's unique position in writing for children. However, an adult author can no better wholly "take the child's part" than a white author can wholly take a black character's part or a male author wholly take a female character's part, and so on, as feminist, postcolonial and queer theories have made us aware of. All these theories focus on power structures, and nowhere are power structures as tangible as in children's literature, the elaborate tool that has for centuries been used to educate, foster, oppress and socialize a specific group of human beings. Children's literature is always, by definition, created by those in power for the powerless. Besides, children's literature shows a constant shift of power relationships: yesterday's children grow up and become oppressors themselves. Or, as Pippi explains to Annika:

> "Of course you have to eat your good cereal. If you don't eat your good cereal, then you won't grow and get big and strong. And if you don't get big and strong, than you won't have the strength to force *your* children, when you have some, to eat their good cereal. . . ." (*Pippi in the South Seas*, 55f; author's emphasis)

Pippi makes it clear that power reproduces itself. Yet it is obvious that Astrid Lindgren assumes that the reader will see through Pippi's statement and recognize its irony. Pippi has been interrogating power in everything she does. Adapting the favorite concept of queer theory, normativity, to the issues of children's literature, we can say that Pippi questions adult normativity. In our society, adults have unlimited power compared to children, who are oppressed and powerless, having no economic resources of their own, no voice in political and social decisions, and who are subject to a large number of laws and rules which adults expect them to obey without interrogation. This is perceived as a norm, in reality as well as in literature. Yet what happens if a literary work, like *Pippi Longstocking*, does not portray adults as the cleverer, richer, and powerful group in the opposition adults—children? What happens if we exchange adult normativity for child normativity?

Pippi sleeps with her feet on a pillow, which is norm-breaking, but only if the norm is sleeping with your head on a pillow and your feet under the blanket. Pippi questions the norms, both through her own behavior and through maintaining that there are other norms in other parts of the world, for instance, that all people walk backwards in Egypt. It may eventually turn out that it is more convenient to sleep with your head on a pillow or walk forward. However, queer theory shows, first, that norms are arbitrary, and second, and perhaps more importantly, that the whole argument concerning norms and deviations gives norms priority over deviations, thus also more power and authority. Yet Pippi, as a true queer theorist, does not wish to supplant one norm by another, but on the contrary shows that all ways and attitudes are equally normal. When Astrid Lindgren makes her ironical comment that all children must "go to school to learn the multiplication tables," she applies queer theory long before the term got into circulation. Pippi's norms appear to be just as good as those set up by adults. In this, Lindgren is indeed far ahead of all childhood utopias that unconditionally substitute one norm for another and thus demonstrate the impossibility of child normativity. The wonderful and sad novel by the famous Polish educator Janusz Korczak, *King Matt the First* (1923), discussed earlier in this volume, depicts children taking power—and failing, mostly because of lack of knowledge and experience. It is highly unlikely that Astrid Lindgren was familiar with *King Matt* when she wrote *Pippi Longstocking*, but in a wider perspective her book poses a dialogical response to the tragedy of child power in Korczak's novel. Pippi does not in any way strive to overthrow adult power, she merely mocks and ridicules it. In the end, the people of the little town are prepared to give Pippi the power, saying that they do not need police or firemen when they have Pippi. Pippi happily participates in the celebration of her courage and wit, but as to seizing power, we have already seen that she is the eternal child, who, like Peter Pan, prefers to play.

Another power-focused theory that has been successfully applied to children's literature (Stephens 1992; Nikolajeva 1996, 2000a) and to *Pippi* books in particular (e.g. Russell 2000) is carnival. Yet much too often carnival is perceived literally, as the expression of the grotesque, the upside-down structures, scatological humor, theater, marketplace, and so on. Naturally, we have plenty of such elements in Pippi, including the circus, the theater, the time-out on the cannibal island, and the truly Rabelaisian gluttony. However, the deeper meaning of the carnival goes beyond these superficial details. It is, in the first place, the issue of temporary power reversal and its subversive effect. Just like the carnival fool, the lowest of the low, was crowned king during the medieval carnival, children are allowed, in fiction written for their enlightenment and enjoyment *by adults*, to become strong, brave, rich, powerful, and independent—on certain conditions and for a limited time. The most important condition is the physical dislocation and the removal, temporary or permanent, of parental protection, allowing the child protagonist to have the freedom to explore the world and test the boundaries of independence. The child may be placed in a number of extraordinary situations, such as war or revolution, exotic, far-away settings, temporary isolation on a desert island, extreme danger (common in mystery novels), and so on. All these conditions empower the fictional child, and even though the protagonist is most frequently brought back to the security of home and parental supervision, the narratives have a subversive effect, showing that the rules imposed on the child by the adults are in fact arbitrary. Fantasy is another common carnivalesque device, as an ordinary child is empowered through transportation to a magical realm, through the possession of a magical agent (object or helper), and through the acquisition of a set of heroic traits or magical force, impossible or at least improbable within the existing order of things (what we normally call the "real world.") Carnival, reversing the existing order, elevates the fictional child to a position superior to adults. Yet, the inevitable reestablishment of order in the end of a carnivalesque children's story brings the characters down to levels at which they are only slightly more powerful than their environment, equal to it or inferior to it.

In view of this, Pippi seems at first sight to be an exception. She is neither bestowed with power in the beginning nor stripped of it in the end. She is rich beyond the imagination of an ordinary child; she has no parents to obey, and she does not obey any other adult who tries to get control over her. Does Pippi then represent carnival made permanent? To address this question we will have to return to the issue that I have already touched upon: that Pippi is in fact not the main character of the books.

The statement may seem ridiculous; by most criteria, Pippi is of course the protagonist: she is the title character, she is introduced first, and she is present in all episodes. Yet, as already stated, she is static and she is almost never used as a focalizer. Whenever we meet Pippi it is either through the omniscient narrator or through Tommy and Annika, as in the first chapter: "Just as they were standing there . . . the gate of Villa Villekulla opened and a little girl stepped out" (15). At the end of each book, Tommy and Annika go home and watch Pippi standing at her window. The perspective is thus detached from her, leaving the reader also observing her from a distance. Tommy and Annika, in contrast, are radically changed through their encounter with Pippi. Among other things, they have learned to interrogate norms. It does not mean that they—or the readers, as vigilant educators have often feared—will sleep with their feet on a pillow, or walk backwards, or misbehave at coffee parties. But they will be alert to arbitrarily set rules, and hopefully they will not force their children to eat the hateful cereal.

The peculiarity of the carnivalesque nature of Pippi Longstocking is thus that Pippi herself is not affected by the carnival, but she is herself the carnival factor (cf. "chaos factor" in Edström 1990) that affects the lives and attitudes of two ordinary children, Tommy and Annika, and through them, the reader. Tommy and Annika, as well as the reader, know that Pippi is one-of-a-kind and that they can never be like her. They are not the strongest in the world, they are not rich, and they are not powerful. The temporality of their carnival implies that they are for a couple of years, supposedly the most formative years of their lives, exposed to the carnival factor represented by Pippi. But, again, is Pippi not a permanent carnival? As I have shown above, I am inclined to interpret the ending of the novel as the affirmation of the necessity of growing up rather than the nostalgic longing back to eternal childhood. Indeed, faith in the magical pill is far from firm in the two children, as the following passage in free indirect discourse shows:

> [Pippi] would always be there. That was a comforting thought. The years would go by, but Pippi and Tommy and Annika would not grow up. *That is, of course, if the strength hadn't gone out of the chililug pill.* There would be new springs and summers, new autumns and winters, but their games would go on. (*Pippi in the South Seas* 124: emphasis added)

The iterative of the passage is reminiscent of the ending of *The House at Pooh Corner*: ". . . the boy and his toy bear will *always* be playing" (emphasis added). The ironic "always" addressed to the adult co-reader is a nostalgic reminder of the impossibility of eternal childhood. But for a young reader—and perhaps for a childlike adult as well—this is also an affirmation of the inner child that can carry her Pippi (or her Peter Pan, or her Little Prince) inside her throughout life.

Unlike Pippi, Tommy and Annika will have to grow up. So will the young readers—and so they have too, several generations of readers all over the world, inspired and enthused by Pippi, but not to misbehave, as many educators have feared, but to be critical, inquisitive, and imaginative. They have learned that social rules and laws are not absolute.

Yet at the end of the third book, Tommy and Annika and the reader have to say farewell to Pippi. The three books are not part of a never-ending series; there can be no sequel to *Pippi in the South Seas*. The end is logical and definitive. Just as they have, against common sense, persuaded themselves that Pippi would always be there, Tommy and Annika watch her through the icy window:

> "If she would only look in this direction we could wave to her," said Tommy.
> But Pippi continued to stare straight ahead with a dreamy look. Then she blew out the light. (*Pippi in the South Seas* 125)

Naturally, this scene can be viewed as a structural closure: after all, a book must have an ending. However, I see it primarily as a psychological closure, as the child's—Tommy's, Annika's, and the reader's—acceptance of the dissolving contact with Pippi, who will of course *always* be there as a memory, but who has played out her role as the active playmate. The carnival is over, but its subversive effect will indeed last forever.

WORKS CITED

Åhmansson, Gabriella. "Mayflowers grow in Sweden too: L. M. Montgomery, Astrid Lindgren and the Swedish literary consciousness." Pp. 14–22 in *Harvesting Thistles: The Textual Garden of L. M. Montgomery* ed. Mary Rubio. Guelph: Canadian Children's Press, 1994.

Bergsten, Staffan. *Mary Poppins and Myth*. Stockholm: Almqvist & Wiksell International, 1978. (Studies Published by the Swedish Institute for Children's Books no 8.)

Campbell, Joseph. *The Hero with a Thousand Faces*. New York: Pantheon, 1949.

Coats, Karen. *Looking Glasses and Neverlands. Lacan, Desire, and Subjectivity in Children's Literature*. Iowa City: Iowa University Press, 2004.

Edström, Vivi. "Pippi Longstocking: chaos and postmodernism." *Swedish Book Review* Supplement 1990: 22–29.

———. *Astrid Lindgren: A Critical Study*. Stockholm, Rabén & Sjögren, 2000.

Frid, Gunnel. "Känner du Annika Settergren?" *Tidskrift för litteraturvetenskap* 32 (2003) 4: 93–104.

Greimas, Algirdas Julien. *Structural Semantics: An Attempt at a Method.* Lincoln, Nebr.: University of Nebraska Press, 1983.

Heldner, Christina. "I gränslandet mellan ingvistik och litteraturvetenskap. En analys av några språkliga drag i böckerna om Pippi Långstrump." Pp. 191–208 in *Modern litteraturteori och metod i barnlitteraturforskningen* ed. Maria Nikolajeva. Stockholm: Centre for the Study of Childhood Culture, 1992.

Hoffeld, Laura. "Pippi Longstocking: The Comedy of the Natural Girl." *The Lion and the Unicorn* 1 (1977) 1: 47–53.

Lacan, Jacques. *Ecrits: A Selection.* New York: Norton, 1977.

Lévi-Strauss, Claude. *The Raw and the Cooked. Introduction to a Science of Mythology.* Chicago: The University of Chicago Press, 1983.

Lindgren, Astrid. *Pippi Longstocking.* Trans. Florence Lamborn. New York: Viking, 1950.

———. *Pippi Goes on Board.* Trans. Florence Lamborn. New York: Viking, 1957.

———. *Pippi in the South Seas.* Trans. Florence Lamborn. New York: Viking, 1959.

Lundqvist, Ulla. *Århundradets barn. Fenomenet Pippi Långstrump och dess förutsättningar.* Stockholm: Rabén & Sjögren, 1979; With a summary in English: The Child of the Century.

Metcalf, Eva-Maria. *Astrid Lindgren.* New York: Twayne, 1995 (Twayne's World Authors Series 851).

Moebius, William. "L'enfant terrible Comes of Age." Pp. 32–50 in *Notebooks in Cultural Analysis* ed. Norman F. Cantor, vol 2. Durham: Duke University Press, 1985.

Nikolajeva, Maria. *Children's Literature Comes of Age. Towards a New Aesthetic.* New York: Garland, 1996.

———. "Two National Heroes: Jacob Two-Two and Pippi Longstocking." *Canadian Children's Literature* 86 (1997): 7–16.

———. *From Mythic to Linear. Time in Children's Literature.* Lanham, Md.: Scarecrow, 2000(a).

———. "Tamed Imagination. A Rereading of Heidi." *Children's Literature Association Quarterly* 25 (2000b) 2: 68–75.

Nodelman, Perry, and Mavis Reimer. *The Pleasures of Children's Literature.* 3rd edition. Boston: Allyn and Bacon, 2003.

Propp, Vladimir. *Morphology of the Folktale.* Austin: University of Texas Press, 1968.

Reeder, Kik. "Pippi Longstocking—a Feminist or Anti-feminist Work?" Pp. 112–117 in *Racism and Sexism in Children's Literature* ed. Judith Stinton. London: Writers and Readers, 1979.

Russell, David L. "Pippi Longstocking and the Subversive Affirmation of Comedy." *Children's Literature in Education* (2000) 3: 167–177.

Saltman, Judith. *Modern Canadian Children's Books*. Toronto: Oxford University Press, 1987.

Stephens, John. *Language and Ideology in Children's Fiction*. London: Longman, 1992.

Tolkien, J. R. R. "On Fairy Stories." Pp. 11–70 in his *Tree and Leaf*. London: Allen & Unwin, 1968.

4

Creating the Eternal Farewell
Tove Jansson's Moomin Novels

Janina Orlov

"Mother, I love you terribly," says Moomintroll, in the closing part of
Trollvinter (1957; Engl. *Moominland Midwinter* 1962). This is the first
Moomin novel in which idyllic childhood and summer adventures,
characteristic of the preceding books, are replaced by winter, cold, and
involuntary solitude. It therefore marks a turning point in the whole
Moomin cycle and thus it serves as a suitable starting point for a discussion of Tove Jansson's Moomin novels. What makes this particular
book so remarkable is the introduction of darkness and change into
the Moomin world. This change happens literally, as well as in a metaphorical sense. As the first of his species ever, Moomintroll wakes up
in the middle of hibernation, unable to go back to sleep. Suddenly, he
is forced to manage in a world that he never knew existed and where
he is an outsider. It takes him several hardships and shortcomings to
realize the essence of his experiences, and eventually he comes to terms
with the order of winter.

> "Now I got everything," Moomintroll said to himself. "I've got the
> whole year. Winter too. I'm the first Moomin to have lived through an
> entire year." (*Moominland Midwinter* 132)

In this distinctive bildungsroman, Tove Jansson unifies the traditional
symbolic meaning ascribed to winter as a time of sleep and death, with

Nordic mythology and concepts, according to which winter is a time
full of life and activity. Furthermore, the setting of the story implies a
process of change. We move from winter and darkness toward spring
and light when nature awakens, with summer not far behind, with play,
adventure, and magic waiting around the corner. The process is personified in Moomintroll himself, whose insight about winter is, in fact,
a sign of enlightenment. It is also the first step in his maturation process. When the story ends, he is not the child he used to be any longer.
Still, he is a child, very relieved when his mother at last wakes up and
takes over. "Mother, I love you terribly."

Like several other Moomin stories, *Moominland Midwinter* also
deals with the process of starting all over. The floods that occasionally
drown the valley as a consequence of comets and volcanoes in the pre-
ceeding books are here replaced by winter, a season traditionally
denied by the Moomins. With their tummies full of pine-needles, they
have crept into their beds sometime in the middle of November only
to wake up again on the first sunny day of April, ready for a new
adventurous summer. The denial of winter confirms the image of
childhood as an eternal summer. Thus, when Moomintroll is wakened
unexpectedly by a streak of moonlight in *Moominland Midwinter*, the
hitherto demarcated and safe world is subjected to change. Its natural
borders are to be removed, and something crucial is bound to happen.
The first sentence reads: "The sky was almost black, but the snow
shone a bright blue in the moonlight" (*Moominland Midwinter* 5).
Everybody is asleep in the house except for the Moomintroll. Silence
dominates the opening; the stage is, so to speak, empty, and as a reader
I cannot avoid the thought that we are dealing with the tellings of a
visual artist. It is therefore hardly surprising that when Moomin
appears in public for the very first time, it is as a drawn image. This
image appeared in April 1943, in the pages of the satirical magazine
Garm, to which Tove Jansson had been a contributor for many years.
At the time, the little figure was called "Snork." It was white with a
long, narrow nose, a long tail, and short, upright ears. As leading Jansson scholar and biographer Boel Westin has shown, the name "Moomin" can be found already at the beginning of the 1930s, although in
different ways, some of which are quite sinister and filled with agony,
referring to the images as "terrifying figures of the subconscious." In
watercolor paintings from the same period, the image is black and,
according to Westin, the pictures "may be seen as early depictions of
the dark mood that, from the beginning, is hidden behind the vision

of the happy Moomin family" (Westin 2002, 155). Finally, there is the caricature of Immanuel Kant, drawn by Tove Jansson on the wall of the outside privy sometime at the beginning of the '30s, which clearly shows the same figure. The name "Moomin" is said to derive from an anecdotal situation. As a young art student in Stockholm, Tove Jansson was living at her uncle's house. Always hungry, she made a habit of sneaking to the kitchen for a little nibble of food on the quiet. Eventually, she was exposed by her uncle, who told her that there are moomintrolls living behind the stove who "blow in your neck" (Tolvanen 2000, 15–25).[1] The episode reappears, slightly modified, in the very first Moomin novel *Småtrollen och den stora översvämningen* (1945; Engl. *The Moomins and the Great Flood* 2005) when Moominmamma tells the Troll about their origin.

> "Did people know about us then?" Moomintroll asked.
> "Some did," said his mother. "They felt us mostly as a cold wind in the neck sometimes—when they were on their own." (*The Moomins and the Great Flood* 18)

The above-mentioned version represents the official pre-history of the Moomins. In what follows I wish to present a reading and exploration of the Moomin novels according to their own version, as told by the omniscient and fickle narrator. Just like Moominpappa, who looks into his very own crystal ball of shining blue glass, "the centre of the garden, of the valley, and of the whole world" in the beginning of *Pappan och havet* (1965; *Moominpappa at Sea* 1967) to watch his family's doings, I intend to look the stories. And just as the Moominsaga itself begins right in the middle of things, an August afternoon, I have set off *in medias res*. The title of my essay refers to an inescapable impression I have of what might be the implied plot of the whole cycle. Maybe it is just the feeling I get while looking into my very own crystal ball reflecting the Moomin universe. Still, it seems to me that Tove Jansson, from the very beginning, is writing herself as well as her characters out of childhood; the narrator of the Moomin stories is constantly, however unconsciously, on the move toward something that inevitably is the end of life. Hence, the concept of the Eternal Farewell.

CONSTRUCTING THE MOOMIN COSMOS

Despite an early start as a writer—Tove Jansson published her first illustrated story at the age of fifteen and her first book at the age of nineteen—she began her professional career by illustrating. "As a child I was constantly drawing," she recalls in an interview (Tolvanen 2000, 12). She studied painting in Stockholm, Helsinki, and Paris, and she always considered herself, first of all, a visual artist. Thus, the constant rebirth we meet in the novels reminds us of the artist, the creator in front of a clean canvas, a blank sheet, or a newly cleaned board, which is to be filled with life, magic signs, and strange figures. Or the traveller who, like Snufkin, leaves again and again for places still unknown. The intensity in the beginning of the movement is not to be mistaken, as shown, for example, in the very beginning of the last novel *Sent i november* (1970; *Moominvalley in November* 1971):

> Breaking camp in this way comes with a hop, skip and a jump! All of a sudden everything is different, and if you're going to move on you're careful to make use of every single minute, you pull up your tent pegs and douse the fire quickly before anyone can stop you or start asking questions, you start running, pulling on your rucksack as you go, and finally you are on your way and suddenly quite calm, like a solitary tree with every single leaf completely still. (*Moominvalley in November* 11)

Evidently, the challenge of the blank page becomes as important as the beginning of a journey, or the first lines in a new chapter. Moominpappa formulates the phenomenon in his own way by a metapoetical statement at the moment of the family's departure for the desert island in *Mooominpappa at Sea*: "Setting out in the right way is just as important as the opening lines in a new book: they determine everything" (22). Movement turns out to be one, if not the main feature within the whole suite of stories. It runs from the very first line of the very first book, *The Moomins and the Great Flood*, which starts off *in medias res*, with the Troll and Mamma coming to the deepest part of the wood, one afternoon at the end of August, until the last line of the last book, *Moominvalley in November*, when we follow little whomper Toft down to the beach and leave him there awaiting the family's eventual return. This perpetual movement is illuminated in a distinct manner in each novel. Altogether they express implicitly an ongoing discussion about the art of growing up and getting old, for which the Eternal Farewell constitutes a metaphor. The process is rendered through the gaze of a child, actually the child within the narrator, who, willingly or not, is part of that very same process. Every single novel tells about a new beginning at the same time as the whole cycle of stories reflects the all embracing, inevitable movement that eventually leads to the departure from the Moomin valley. By repeatedly re-creating the world of the Moomins, Tove Jansson moves, in her writing, from a kind of pastime pleasure and a conventional children's literature toward a more investigative and sophisticated exploration of the psychological development of her characters. Consequently, the movement is explicit and implicit at the same time.

Tove Jansson discusses the essence of art in a highly autobiographical short story entitled "Brev till Konikova" (Letter to Konikova): "I think that every canvas, *nature morte*, landscape, whatever, is deep down a self portrait" (Jansson 1998, 32). The statement is obviously applicable to texts as well, especially in the case of her own. If it was not before, this idea becomes clear in *Moominvalley in November*. Here the symbiotic co-existence of word and image is more striking than ever. In his rich study on Tove Jansson as a painter, Finnish art critic Erik Kruskopf emphasizes the simultaneous development of text and illustration in the Moominbooks (Kruskopf 1992, 192). The more distinct the Moomin world becomes in pictures, the firmer and clearer becomes the content of the tales. Still, we know that when she illustrated her own books, the text was always first. Thus, Tove Jansson's narrative technique is bilingual: it includes both verbal and visual expression in perfect balance. She simultanously elaborates the child perspective, the adult point of view, and the visual image. Readers get the impression of seeing the text and reading the picture. The effect could be described as a kind of double exposure in which the equal co-existence of various means of expression, as well as of experience, does not distort the semantic integrity of the various components involved.

Like many classics for children, the Moomin books were also originally initiated by war. Tove Jansson began to write the first story, *The Moomins and the Great Flood*, in 1939, but it was not published until 1945. The year is generally considered as epoch-making in the history of Swedish children's literature, and Tove Jansson's Moominworld represents the Finno-Swedish contribution in that context. Making use of European and Scandinavian fairy-tale tradition, as well as of the conventions of contemporary children's fiction, Tove Jansson created an imaginary escape from harsh wartime reality into a magical world inhabited by funny looking creatures, eventually named Moomintrolls. In eight more books, three picturebooks, and countless comic strips, she developed a unique universe, one in which, among other pecularities, the traditional struggle between Good and Evil is replaced by the delicate balance between darkness and light. This relationship permeates everything in the Moomimistic universe. Thereby, Moomin lifestyle is determined by an archetypal perception of existence according to which darkness is chaos and light is order. Further on, the dichotomy evidently also refers to the biblical story of creation, according to which light was the first phenomenon that was called into existence. But, instead of fighting dark forces in order to get into the light, the Moomin existence develops into an exploration of the dark, rather than a struggle against it. The process of moving from denial to acceptance, manifested for the first time in *Moominland Midwinter,* emerges gradually to be completed only in *Moominvalley in November,* that constitutes a kind of epilogue. Nevertheless, throughout the books, and regardless of the changing tone and various modes of expression, light always stands for safety and family unity, clearly exemplified, for instance, in *Moominpappa at Sea:*

> The lamp sizzled as it burned. It made everything seem close and safe, a little family circle they all knew and trusted. Outside this circle lay everything that was strange and frightening, and the darkness seemed to reach higher and higher and farther and farther away, right to the end of the world. (*Moominpappa at Sea* 12–13)

The reassuring light is also one of the last things mentioned at the very end of the Moomin suite. In the closing passage of *Moominvalley in November,* on his way down to the beach, little Toft catches sight of the hurricane lamp swaying in the masttop, burning with a steady flame. At this point we realize that the family is returning to the valley and the saga thus ends in harmony.

MORALS AND ETHICS

There is no explicit right or wrong in the Moomin books. If moral or philosophical issues are debated, the debate always occurs by means of parody or seemingly naïve approaches to the question at stake. It seems as if those inviting sympathy are the ones who are moral winners in the long run. Thus, the official law is not necessarily the appropriate one. This idea is the case in the sparkling, Shakespeare-inspired *Farlig midsommar* (1954; *Moominsummer Madness* 1961), in which Snufkin plants hattifattener seeds in a park for orphans and tears down all notices telling people what not to do, in order to rebel against every rule possible that restricts the actions of a free individual. It is an example of constructive anarchy. Since hattifatteners, the enigmatic silent creatures of the Moomin world, are especially electric when newly grown, they make the Park Keeper luminous all over, and he is forced to leave the grounds and abandon the orphans. Snufkin escapes punishment for his act. When he is close to being caught sometime later, Moominmamma interferes by crying (along with the reader): "Flee, the police are here!" (142).

Another hilarious example is given in *Trollkarlens hatt* (1949; *Finn Family Moomintroll* 1965). The Groke, who appears here for the first time, eventually finds herself at court, accused by the small characters Thingumy and Bob of claiming the contents of their suitcase, which turns out to be the King's Ruby. The Groke is actually in the right, but the proceedings turn into a mock trial in which Muskrat, as the Groke's prosecutor, falls asleep, and the Snork, as judge, wears a wig made of wood-wool. Hemulen, as the defence counsel for Thingummy and Bob, tries to vindicate their conduct. At the same time, his pledge is significant for revealing Moomin ideology, as it parodies the whole concept of *juris prudentia*:

> "It's not clear at all!" cried the Hemulen boldly. "The question is not who is the *owner* of the Contents, but who has the greatest *right* to the Contents. The right thing in the right place. You saw the Groke, everybody? Now, I ask you, did she look as if she had a right to the Contents?" (135; italics in the original)

Hardly surprising, it is Moominmamma who eventually comes up with a solution, and everybody, even the Groke, is happy. Hence, ideal justice is based on a secret and unwritten law, which is applied according to the honesty of the feelings and intentions of each character involved.

As mentioned above, there is no evil in this world, and consequently no crucial battles. In fact, the closest one ever gets to evil is irony. This situation is clearly evident in the short story "The Invisible Child" in the collection *Det osynliga barnet* (1962; *Tales from Moominvalley* 1963), in which we meet little Ninni, who, crushed by her aunt's irony, has become invisible. In order to regain her own self and become a normal, playful child again, she is placed in the Moomin family. Little My, as the clear-sighted rationalizer, provides her with a remedy in form of good advice:

"She can't get angry," Little My said. "That's what's wrong with her. Listen, you," My continued, and went close to Ninni with a menacing look. "You'll never have a face of your own until you've learned to fight. Believe me."

"Yes, of course," Ninni replied, cautiously backing away. (*Tales from Moominvalley* 119)

Eventually, the attempts to restore her broken self prove more than successful. When, one gloomy, autumn afternoon, Moominpappa makes a practical joke, pretending he will throw Mamma into the cold water (as he used to do when they were young), Ninni bites him in the tail before he even comes near. He drops his hat into the water, and while reaching for it, topples over and tumbles headfirst into the water. At the same time, Ninni turns visible.

Thus, apart for learning the skills of a normal child, we are also confronted with what is, according to the Moomin ideology, the most negative behaviour, mental abuse of a child, regardless of whether it is a real child or the invisible child we all carry inside us. The notion of the invisible child is not limited to the short story. Gradually, it turns out that visibility and invisibility are significant, not only when it comes to characterization, but also for the narration itself.

THE SEARCH FOR IDENTITY

Since dualism is replaced by the balance between darkness and light, the traditional fairy quests are transformed into mental challenges. For the most part, these occur in the form of more or less conscious searches for identity and approval of one's individualistic "self" that might not coincide with the expected ideal. Moominpappa tries his wings as a playwright in *Moominsummer Madness*, whereas in *Moominpappa at Sea* he imagines himself as a lighthouse keeper and oceanographer. The identity issue is further enlightened in *Moominsummer Madness* through a reflection about the essence of theatre. The old stage rat Emma, tired of the family's ignorance, explains what it is all about:

"A theatre is the most important sort of house in the world, because that's where people are shown what they could be if they wanted, and what they'd like to be if they dared to, and what they really are."

"A reformatory," said Moominmamma astonished. (*Moominsummer Madness* 101f)

Emma's presentation brings forth the theater as a mirror, reflecting both inner and outer reality. Dreams, possibilities, and reality all can be put on stage. Thus embodied, these ideas teach us to see ourselves and others the way we are, but similarly, they prove the meaning of playing roles to apprehend one's own "me," as well as that of others. Misabel has always considered herself a very tragic person, and it is only when she is given the part of tragedienne in Pappa's play that she does herself justice. Only then is she capable of ignoring the comments on her persona. By accepting her own self, she gains self-confidence and becomes completely untouchable. On opening night, the border between play and reality is erased. Suddenly, in the final scene, the audience finds itself on stage witnessing real life action while fully convinced they are watching a play. Thus, real life interferes with art, and *vice versa*. The scene constitutes a metapoetic wink from the author.

Finally, there are Hemulen and Fillyjonk, who desperately try to live up to their imagined versions of Moominmamma and Pappa in *Moominvalley in November*. Sooner or later all the searchers, whether they are aware of it or not, gain the insight that harmony is not to be found until one knows and accepts who one is.

TOPOGRAPHICAL (AND LITERARY) ASPECTS

For a start, life in the paradisical valley, with its eternal summer, play, adventures, and individual freedom, reflects the romantic image of innocent childhood. But instead of denying the inevitable process of maturation, as often is the case in children's literature, the characters change and develop into more complex personalities, which the text also reflects through the depiction of nature and the characters' comprehension of it.

In the first two stories, *The Moomins and the Great Flood* and the apocalyptic adventure story *Kometjakten* (1946; *Comet in Moominland* 1968), where the Moominworld is established, the image of nature is highly influenced by fairy tales, nonsense, and exotism. There are still traces of the exotic in the sequel, *Finn Family Moomintroll*, whereas *Moominsummer Madness*, except for the volcano causing the flood, presents typical scenes of Nordic nature. The settings for the following stories repeat the same pattern, a repetition that has led initiated readers to place the Moomin valley in reality (Björk 2003, 31). However, the maps, which often are enclosed to the Moomin stories, seem to justify localizing the valley somewhere in the Finno-Swedish archipelago. Still, no matter how naturalistic and exact the depiction of nature becomes, we are nevertheless referred to a fictitious world.

The map showing Moomin valley also proves useful in a slightly different context. By including it, Tove Jansson provides us with a metaphorical image of Finno-Swedish literature on the whole. Finland was a part of Sweden until 1809, when it was lost to the Russian Empire, but it stayed close to Sweden during the 19th century. Finland gained independence in 1917 and ever since has had two official languages, Finnish and Swedish, which are unrelated. Today 6% of the population of 5 million have Swedish as their native tongue. The Finno-Swedish language is slightly different from metropolitan Swedish in pronunciation and melody, but more importantly, in vocabulary, not only because of borrowings from Finnish and Russian, but mostly because of several hundred years of independent, parallel evolution (see Nikolajeva and Orlov 2000, 77). The Swedish-speaking minority lives mainly on the southwest coast facing the Baltic Sea, a fact that has clearly influenced its literature. There is a saying that every second Finno-Swede is an author. However untrue, the statement reveals something about the concerns of the minority and the maintenance of a certain identity. Outside of Finland, probably only initiated Jansson readers and literary scholars know that Tove Jansson is actually a Finno-Swedish and not a Swedish writer. The archipelago is a dominating feature in the Finno-Swedish depictions of nature and the Moomin novels are no exception. On the map, the sea is placed in the West. In *Moominpappa at Sea*, it is actually named The Gulf of Finland. In the East, the valley is surrounded by the Lonely Mountains, but, in order to get that far, one has to cross the river, which thereby marks a border. The river symbolizes a passage from one world to another, in this case, from safety to the unknown. We are never told what lies behind the mountains, but they are depicted as threatening.

The similarity between the topography of Mooominvalley and that of southwestern Finland is striking. At the same time this topography represents the abode of Finno-Swedish literature. The Lonely Mountains indicate the threat from the East, but they can also be interpreted as the surrounding Finnish culture. Moominvalley is clearly oriented to the West, with the sea as an opening and possibility. Visits to the mountains are exceptions, whereas sea voyages are frequent because of the Moomins' inherited attraction to this element. The same behaviour is characteristic also for Finno-Swedish literature, whether we are speaking of children's literature or literature in general. This similarity is due to the historical background as well as to the reader population in Sweden, without which Finno-Swedish literature would be quite an isolated phenomenon. However, during the last ten years, the situation has been changing, and the borders between Finno-Swedish and Finnish literature seem to be getting more and more blurred, although the languages still lead separate lives.

In the Moomin world, the ongoing change is not restricted only to the characters' successive understanding of nature mentioned above. It is eventually completed through the altering position of the narrator, who, willingly or not, is forced to leave childhood behind. However, to leave is not to forget, and the exit out of childhood actually confirms its existence as sacred space and untouchable memory.

MOOMINMAMMA AND THE GROKE

When children grow up, something happens to their parents. Tove Jansson carefully chisels out the process in her Moomin novels. The portrait of Moominmamma is probably the most prominent example. We know almost nothing about her background. Still, she is the one who provides us with information about the family's historical origin. Moominpappa, in his memoirs, tells very briefly about their first dramatic encounter. We are told that she, like Venus, comes from the sea. On a windy autumn night, she, "the most delightful of trolls" (*Exploits of Moominpappa* 159), according to romantic, adventurous Pappa, is blown straight into his arms. She is, as always, carrying her indispensable handbag. When the family is split up because of the great flood in the very first book, she is the one who enables the reunion. Moominmamma is the perpetual cornucopia, the ever-willing helping hand, always ready to make another bed for an unexpected guest or to feed yet another mouth at the dinner table. Boundless, never reproaching, constantly there, and sometimes even a bit anarchistic. She is always ready to leave everything for a slice of adventure, or just to follow her husband. She is also the one who encourages him to write, drama as well as memoirs, and thus she becomes his main source of inspiration, muse as well as mother and wife.

In the eyes of a child, she is the ideal and eternal Mother. And since the stories are rendered through a child perspective, the Moomin world turns out to be a matriarchy. Moominmamma is simply the centre of universe. The profundity of motherhood, Mamma's love for her child as well as her unquestionable intuition, is presented in *Finn Family Moomintroll* which contains an episode in which Moomintroll is transformed, without his knowledge, into a strange and monster-like creature. His friends accuse him of having run down and attacked the real troll. Moominmamma hears the noise and interrupts the fight:

> "Isn't there anyone who believes me?" Moomintroll pleaded. "Look carefully at me, mother. You must know your own Moomintroll."
> Moominmamma looked carefully. She looked into his frightened eyes for a very long time, and then she said quietly: "Yes, you are my Moomintroll."
> And at the same moment he began to change.
> . . .
> "It's all right now, my dear," said Moominmamma. "You see, I shall always know you whatever happens." (*Finn Family Moomintroll* 38)

A corresponding event can be found in *Moominland Midwinter*, which Tove Jansson actually dedicated to her own mother. Here Moominmamma is absent in her presence since she sleeps almost throughout the story. But apparently her sleep serves a purpose. It launches Moomintroll's maturation process. All his efforts to wake her up prove in vain: she only mumbles something in her sleep. It is only when he has proved himself capable of managing on his own that she wakes up. Once again she returns to her role as loving, warm, and caretaking Mamma. However, a process of change has begun. Paradoxically, the change is inevitable for the continued existence of the Moominworld.

Little by little, Moominmamma's omnipotence becomes problematic. In *Moominpappa at Sea*, in which the family radically starts all over on a desert island, she is unbalanced for the first time. Her unsuccessful attempt to plant a garden—a reminiscence of the valley—far out in the archipelago, fails. Finally, she escapes symbolically, by painting a mural on the wall of the lighthouse where the family is staying. Just like Wu-tao-tzu and Tolkien's Niggle, she steps right into her own picture:

"I want to go home and leave this terrible, deserted island and the cruel sea . . ." She flung her arms round her apple tree and shut her eyes. The bark felt rough and warm, and the sound of the sea disappeared. Moominmamma was right inside her garden.

. . .

When the kettle boiled for tea, Moominmamma was fast asleep with her head leaning against the apple tree. (*Mooominpappa at Sea* 161–163)

Hiding in her picture, she is invisible to the outside world. Thus, her kinship with Ninni, the invisible child, is obvious. The difference is that Moominmamma's invisibility is her own choice, although it is the consequence of neglect, a conclusion made by Moomintroll while looking for her. "Mamma's vanished," he thought. "She was so lonely, she just disappeared" (*Moominpappa at Sea* 165).

Once we feel neglected, we become invisible. The mysterious character, the Groke, who appears for the first time in *Finn Family Moomintroll*, but whose scary voice is heard already in *Muminpappans bravader* (1950; *Exploits of Moominpappa* 1966) actualizes the dilemma in her own way. The Groke is often referred to as Moominmamma's dark side (Nikolajeva 2000, 247). And it is most significant that Moominmamma and the Groke are the only female characters in the whole suite who are submitted to reconsideration. The Groke's shape resembles Mamma's if seen in profile, and she represents everything Mamma is not, that is, darkness, cold, and loneliness. Her name is occasionally used as a curse or a menace, since she represents the threat against everything that is dear to the Moomins: spirit of community, light, and warmth. In a context where the balancing of darkness and light constitutes the existence of a whole world, the Groke, as embodied darkness, is of major importance. When Moomintroll asks his mother, in *Moominpappa at Sea*, how the Groke has become the way she is, her answer is:

"No one knows," said Moominmamma, drawing her tail out of the water. "It was probably because nobody did anything at all. Nobody bothered about her, I mean. I don't suppose she remembers anyway, and I don't suppose she goes around thinking about either. She's like the rain or the darkness, or a stone you have to walk round if you want to get past. Do you want some coffee? There's some in the thermos in the white basket." (*Moominpappa at Sea* 27–28)

Even in this short passage, Moominmamma's behavior, while she explains, indicates her closeness to the Groke. Her tail has been dipped in water, and she is chilly. In order to enstrange herself from the threatening image of personified darkness and cold, she tries to change the subject by offering the opposite—warmth, represented by something as trivial as coffee.

Moominmamma's description of the Groke comes close to Tove Jansson's statement in her speech in Ljubljana in 1966, after receiving the H. C. Andersen Award: "Worst of all is the fear of darkess, the nameless threat. But this fear can also be apprehended as a magnificent background behind safety, loading it with meaning and making a contrasting effect" (Jansson 1966, 259–261). Thoughts of the nameless threat appear in several of Tove Jansson's rare statements about her writing. However, unaware of their creator's reflections on the "nameless threat," the Moomins do have a name for their own fear, namely The Groke. Consequently, she is the loneliest creature ever, the ultimate outsider, treated as "rain, darkness or a misplaced stone" (*Moominpappa at Sea* 28–29), watching the family from "just outside the circle of light" (*Moominpappa at Sea* 14). Nevertheless, she is constantly reaching for light, and this effort is the reason why she follows the family to the desert island. But there is more to the story than longing for light. The Groke also reflects our inner selves, which explains why she shadows the family. As long as they are not at ease with themselves, the Groke will follow. This recognition brings us to another question that deals directly with her existence. What if she is only the projection of everybody's inner fear? Since the only real threat in the Moomin world consists of darkness, cold, and what could be described in terms of "the Other," the Groke fits all these characteristics very well. But if so, how then are we to explain the relationship between the narrator and the Groke? There are inevitably several occasions when the narrator refers to the doings and thoughts of the Groke, which, of course, would be impossible if she were merely a projection of the Moomins' imagination. This question actualizes the narrator's position within the narration, an issue that will be discussed toward the end of this essay. At this stage there is still one point worth mentioning in connection with the Groke.

In 1968 Tove Jansson published her first book for adults, *Bildhuggarens dotter* (*Sculptor's Daughter* 1969), a childhood story consisting of separate, autonomous episodes without any apparent chronological order. The opening lines introduce us to a child narrator and the autobiographical impact is indisputable. The second chapter is entitled "The Darkness," and it opens with a description of the blocks near the

Jansson family's home, not far from the harbour of Helsinki, and an uncanny feeling of something intangible getting close:

> As soon as it starts to get dark a giant grey creature begins to creep over the harbour. It has not got a face but very distinct hands which cover one island after the other while it creeps on. When there are no islands left, it stretches its arm over the water, it is a very long arm that shakes a little, and it starts to grope for Skatudden. The fingers reach the Russian church and they touch the mountain—ah! A big grey hand!
>
> I know what is the worst of all. It is the skating-rink. . . . When you go down to the ice, the rink is only a small bracelet of light far away in the dark. The harbour is a sea of blue snow and loneliness and sad fresh air. . . . Behind the rink is the creeping creature and it is surrounded by black water. The water is breathing along the ice-edge, it moves slowly, sometimes it rises with a sigh and flows all over the ice. (*Sculptor's Daughter* 14–15)

This passage clearly shows how the fear of the child is shaped by her imagination into that of a a scary, grey creature, whose looks and behavior resemble very closely those of the Groke. The border between fiction and reality is blurred in both cases, although the Moomins have a proper name for their fear. In this particular context, the Groke serves as a kind of metaphoric position of the narrator that unifies the gaze of the child and that of the adult author.

Deep down the Groke wants to be a part of the community. As mentioned above, this is why she follows the family, an action that obviously can be read as the family trying to escape its own inner fear, symbolized by the Groke. Finally, as a part of his own individuation process, Moomintroll unexpectedly comes to her rescue. By lighting the hurricane lamp every night for her on the windy beach, he literally implements her defrostening. In the end, she is just happy to see him, even without a lamp, and the ground under her will never freeze again. Ever. Exit the Groke.

"IT'S SO VERY DIFFICULT BEING A FATHER!"

Step by step, Tove Jansson cautiously dismantles the Moomin world. Placing the nuclear family far out on a naked island in *Moominpappa at Sea*, depriving them of all the facilities in the cosy valley, she forces them to confront themselves with life's essentials. The story can be seen as a variation on the creation myth, in which life is said to have begun on an island in the ocean. The lighthouse would, in that case, be equivalent to the world tree. Thus, the departure from the valley signals the beginning of a new life. This is also the aim of Moominpappa, who initiates the whole enterprise of starting all over. His reason is a feeling of uselessness and loss of authority, a terrifying notion of completion, when there is nothing left to do in life since everything is already done and those for whom you care are fully capable of taking care of themselves.

Despite the fact that two of the novels, *Exploits of Moominpappa* and *Moominpappa at Sea*, and one short story, "Hatifnattarnas hemlighet" ("The Secret of the Hattifatteners" in *Tales from Moominvalley* 1962), are dedicated to his life and adventures, Moominpappa remains remote to the reader, although never indifferent. The distance is also indicated by the dedication in *Moominpappa at Sea*, which reads "To some father." In most of the novels Moominpappa is more or less fully characterized by his black top hat, a clear symbol of dignity and manhood. As is often the case in children's literature, adults play a secondary role, while the children are the focus. This focus is certainly the case within the first Moomin novels; consequently, the doings of the parents remain quite conventional. However, although Moominpappa represents unquestionable authority, he is adventourous, romantic, and childish as well. If we read the novels chronologically, the first notion we ever get of him is that he is lost in the Great Flood. Eventually, we learn that he has saved himself by climbing up in a tree, where he sits waiting for help, helpless and completely unaware of what has happened to his family. Furthermore, the house he built is blown away as well. He is finally rescued by his own family, and they even find the house, stranded in a valley that eventually becomes the Moomin world.

All along one has the feeling that he is parodied and never really taken seriously by the others. They just allow him to play his patriarchal role, because that is the way things ought to be. Interestingly enough, if we cling to the idea of the Moomin books as depictions of childhood, it is only in the fourth book that we find a story that tells explicitly about a child growing up and making his way in life. This account appears in *Exploits of Moominpappa*, a book that differs from the other novels since it is narrated in the first person (Nikolajeva 2003, 109). Moominpappa tells his own story. By giving him a voice, Tove Jansson enables him to follow a well-established tradition within

Finno-Swedish literature, namely autobiographical writing, in this case memoirs. Not only does Moominpappa continue a tradition, but he also comments upon the convention by parodying the whole genre in the style of Benvenuto Cellini (Westin 1988, 191). His memoir writing is mentioned already in *Comet in Moominland* by Moomintroll, but it does not become an issue until two books later. There is a well-known difference between memoirs and autobiography. Memoirs often have a broader focus, the author-narrator usually holds a modest position, whereas the autobiographer seems more self-aware, being author, narrator, and main hero, all three in one. Moominpappa uses both modes of telling without hesitation. He is appropriately humble, especially in the beginning. But at the same time, his high thoughts of his own persona cannot be mistaken. His purpose in writing the memoirs turns out to be a wish to create an ideal image of himself, explicitly for the young generation, but, in fact, he creates his world first of all for himself, the way he wants it to be. Thus, he is a very conscious self-constructor, a feature that becomes problematic in the second novel about him, *Moominpappa at Sea*.

Since he is a foundling, everything is possible; he might even be the son of a king. Born under special stars, he is bound to become something extraordinary. The opening scene provides us with several intertextual references:

> On a gloomy and windy night in August, a long time ago, a simple marketbag was found on the porch of the moomin foundling home. It was no less than me lying in the bag, carelessly wrapped in a newspaper.
>
> How much more romantic would it not have been to place me on moss in a nice little basket! (*Exploits of Moominpappa* 13)

The setting is significant; it refers to the stories of both Moses and Tarzan, which was one of Tove Jansson's favourites, as well as to other leaders-to-be. Moominpappa feels different from the other children. Not only is he a foundling, but he also represents "the alien child," although in a parodical and inverted manner: Instead of expressing wisdom, he constantly asks questions concerning existential matters about dream and reality, thereby repeating the fundamental words, "What when?" and "Who how?" Gradually, he begins to reflect on his own shape:

> I stopped asking questions, instead I was caught in longing to speak about how I felt and thought. But ah, there was nobody, except for myself, who found me interesting. (*Exploits of Moominpappa* 18)

Finally, in his search for his own self, he reaches the moment when life takes a new turn. One windy spring morning, he goes down to the sea, a forbidden place for the children. The water is still frozen, and he looks at his own image reflected in the ice. Enchanted, like Narcissus by his own image, he lies down in order to get a closer look. But the only thing he can see is a green darkness growing deeper and deeper. He himself has disappeared! Strange shadows move around in this other world under the ice. He finds them threatening and tempting at the same time. What if one fell down to these strange shadows? The episode—highly interesting from a psychoanalytical point of view—is suddenly broken by the author's unfailing sense of balance, which never allows situations to get out of hand and become too ceremonial or sentimental. Just like Little My, Tove Jansson punctures the sublime by bringing the young troll back to harsh reality, through the natural consequences of overhasty behavior.

Upset by the occasion, young Moominpappa gets up and stamps his feet until the ice breaks. Suddenly he finds himself lying in the cold, green sea, the clouds sailing above him and the dangerous darkness below. This is truly a moment of birth and entry into a new stage. His life will never be the same again. Shortly afterwards, he runs away from the foundling home, toward a great future, which includes several hilarious adventures in the company of other young and frisky male characters, all of whom, in some way or another, turn out to be parents of or relatives to the central characters who later accompany the Moomin family. The climax and ending of Moominpappa's retellings is the dramatic first encounter with Mamma on a stormy beach at night. Overwhelmed by the emotionally charged situation, Moominpappa chooses to describe his romance "with a light paw" (*The Exploits of Moominpappa* 145), as mentioned in the heading of the chapter. True love is something very private. The few lines dedicated to the subject in Pappa's memoirs prove the point.

As I pointed out earlier, in *Moominpappa at Sea* the family follows the will of Pappa and leaves the valley for a desert island. The opening sentence is almost identical to the opening one in the very first novel. By means of a temporal expression, "An afternoon at the end of August" (3), both the arrival in the valley as well as the departure from it are announced. In fact, the entrance of Mamma and the Troll in the first book is actually initiated by Pappa, or, to be correct, by his absence. He is also the reason for the eventual departure. For him the world is complete; nothing remains to be done; he is simply at a loss:

He had no idea what to do with himself, because it seemed everything there was to be done had already been done or was being done by somebody else. (*Moominpappa at Sea* 3)

His creativity, his strength is connected to self-confidence. Once he feels threatened, as in *Moominpappa at Sea*, where nobody seems to need him or care about his caring for them, he tries desperately to stress his own importance by forcing his family to start all over. His wish is to demonstrate his sense of responsibilty for the family's well-being once more. Or maybe he is simply afraid of aging. The family obeys just as it has always done and sets off on a fake Robinsonade designed by Moominpappa. This time, however, his efforts drive the family apart. Nothing works out according to his expectations. The lighthouse on his desert island is dark, symbolizing his distrust of his own manliness or, rather, the image of it, which he has been nourishing all along. Unfortunately, as it turns out, all his efforts have been in vain. Mamma's efforts to comfort him bring forth an inner confession:

"I don't want to mend anything," thought Moominpappa. "I don't want to pick seaweed. . . . I want to build big things, strong things, I want so terribly much. . . . But I don't know. . . . It's so very difficult being a father!" (*Moominpappa at Sea* 100–101)

The novel tells about a family in crisis, and the disharmony of its members seems to affect nature as well. In the earlier books, nature was indifferent, although causing disasters like floods, volcano eruptions, and comets approaching the earth. But during these events almost nobody has really questioned its behaviour. That is why Moomintroll's premature awakening in *Moominland Midwinter*, and the consequences of it, announces a growing feeling of estrangement from the familiar, which in the Moomins' case is nature. The winter experience introduces knowledge of a new kind. Naïve innocence is infiltrated by rational thoughts about the seasons and changes in the landscape. Thus, the symbiotic co-existence of childhood and eternal summer has definitely come to an end. The increasing gap between the trolls and nature is further emphasized in *Moominpappa at Sea*, where the family members, each in his or her own way, try to reshape and even control it, something they have never tried to do before. And nature responds in its own unpredictable way, which, in fact, reflects the unspoken agony of the family.

Moominmamma seeks to re-create the garden she had in the valley. Assisted by Little My, Moomintroll gets rid of the red ants in his private glade. Finally, there is Pappa, occupied by his frantic oceanographic studies of the unpredictable sea, building a breakwater, or fishing and catching far more than the family is capable of consuming. But nothing works out. Mamma's garden is flushed into the sea by a storm wind, and Moomintroll feels sick when he realizes how Little My has exterminated the ants. Pappa's breakwater is gone. At this stage, Mamma, always constructive, still tries to find an explanation:

"Perhaps one shouldn't try to change things so much on this island," said Moominmamma. "Just leave it as it is. Back home it was easier somehow. . . . But I'm going to try and make a new garden, higher up." (*Moominpappa at Sea* 100)

Nevertheless, things get even worse, and finally, the whole island is on the move, with the trees as well as the sand approaching the dark lighthouse. Once again, the issue of identity, acceptance, and self-knowledge becomes crucial. In their efforts to apply the valley lifestyle to life on the island, the Moomins have gone against its nature as well as violated their own personalities. The result is an all-embracing fear and feeling of uncertainty, grimmer than the frights depicted in earlier novels. When the situation seems to slip totally out of their hands, Moominpappa is the one who restores the balance, and he does so by following his instincts. He lies down and presses his ear to the ground. Deep down he hears the sound of a beating heart, and he realizes that the island is alive and it is afraid:

"Fear is a terrible thing," Moominpappa thought. "It can come suddenly and take hold of everything, and who will protect the little creatures who are in its way?" Moominpappa started to run. (*Moominpappa at Sea* 202)

Metaphorically speaking, one could say that starting all over, as was Pappa's plan, requires a state of *tabula rasa*, since a consciously contrived "rebirth" turns out to be impossible. The insight is never explicitly expressed in the text. However, Pappa's inner dialogue with the sea, "in the spirit of his forefathers," serves the purpose. When he reproaches the sea for its bad behaviour toward the tiny island, for scaring it and showing off, instead of taking care and protecting it, he at the same time implicitly addresses himself and his own previous actions. Finally, he adds: "Now, I'm only saying all this because—well—because I like you" (*Moominpappa at Sea* 203). Thus, the reproach becomes a confession and a plea for reconciliation. Unaware of it himself, Moominpappa, by finally voicing his inner feelings, has solved his own problem. A little later, when walking back from the edge of the water, he turns to look at the island—"*his* island"—only to find out that the lighthouse is working. The balance in nature, inner as well as outer, is restored and a fresh start eventually made possible. Here the book ends but, just as in traditional fairy tales, life goes on. As it turns out, however, it goes on without us, the readers, who previously witnessed the doings of the family. In the final novel, *Moominvalley in November,* the family is absent. One of the main characters, if not the most important one, has been distancing himself already in *Moominpappa at Sea.* Moomintroll is growing up.

CHILD AND NARRATOR

"So long," says Moomintroll when parting from his father near the beach, toward the very end of *Moominpappa at Sea.* Little do we know then that these will remain his last words ever. More or less unnoticeably, he withdraws from the scene.

> It wasn't actually so curious that neither Moominmamma nor Moominpappa noticed what Moomintroll was doing, as they were always thinking of other things. No, he was thinking about the sea-horses. . . . Something had happened to him. He had become quite a different Moomin, with quite different thoughts. He liked being by himself. It was much more exciting to play games in his imagination, too—have thoughts about himself and the sea-horses, about the moonlight; and the Groke's shadow was always in his thoughts too. (*Moominpappa at Sea* 111)

Among many other issues, the novel deals with Moomintroll's coming of age, a process that predicts the end of the Moomin saga. At least, as long as we consider it a story of childhood. From the beginning, Moomintroll, the child, has been the central character of the books, surrounded by his closest friends, just the way things usually are set in traditional children's literature. As we have witnessed, little by little, the atmosphere of the books changes, and the action becomes more introspective, which inevitably affects our understanding of the characters. Thus, Moomintroll's last utterance is only what we are to expect.

But there is even more to come, since, unlike Mamma and Pappa, he is hardly spoken of at all in the last novel, *Moominvalley in November*, not even by his closest friend, Snufkin. The opening chapter tells how Snufkin leaves the valley for winter, as he has always done. While walking along he recalls the Moomin family, and he imagines what Mamma, Pappa, and the Troll are doing at the same time. Suddenly he recalls that he has forgotten to leave his traditional farewell note to Moomintroll in the letter-box. After regretting it for less than a moment, he assures himself that Moomintroll would know the message anyway: "And Snufkin forgot all about Moomintroll as easily as that" (*Moominvalley in November* 16). In fact, nobody in the final story ever mentions Moomintroll. The child is gone for a reason. It is time to grow up, for all of us.

One aspect specific to the Moomin novels is the position of the narrator. As I stated earlier in this essay, I find the stories rendered through the gaze of a child, or, more precisely, the child within the narrator. To begin with, in *The Little Trolls and the Great Flood*, the narrator holds a cautious but conscious position, more or less following the conventions of what a children's book ought to be like. But in the sequel, *Comet in Moominland*, the restrictions are abandoned for the sake of play and imagination. Now the child in the narrator is really on the loose, and gradually the books turn into experimental laboratories where the borders of genre are stretched. Since every single Moomin book represents a dynamic entity in its own right, there is no such thing as a "typical Moomin book." Consequently, we may also deconstruct the myth about the idyllic Moominworld since it exists only in our imagination or as a memory. The same goes for the minor characters in the last novel. The idyll, static by nature, exists only in their memory or imagination, which is enough to lead them to the valley. Longing for the family in *Moominvalley in November*, they take over the scene. Hemulen, Fillyjonk, Grandpa Grumble, and the Mymble gather in the Moomin house only to find it empty. All their efforts to restore the "typical Moomin atmosphere" are in vain. Just like us, the readers, they have to accept that the family is gone, which also implies the acceptance of themselves as fully capable individuals. However, despite the feeling of closure, Tove Jansson remains faithful to her own poetics, according to which "in a children's book there ought to be a road where the author stops and the child walks on. A threat of a spendor which is never explained. A face never revealing itself completely. Questions the child, not the author, will answer. The sacred, the beautiful, the priceless, the surprise, the intimate have to be there" (Jansson 1961, 75–76). The idea of the open ending is carried through by Toft, a small whomper and the only child in the story (the other characters only behave like children but they are, in fact, grown ups). For some unknown reason, little Toft, who is living in the forsaken boat of the Hemulen, has been telling himself the story about the happy Moomin family. Finally, he decides to go and see them. Although he has never visited the valley, he knows the way. He is driven by a dream about Mamma, how she will open the door for him and take him into her arms. But at this point his dream is always interrupted. Toward the end, the idea of Mamma becomes more of a burden:

> Every time he thought about Moominmamma he got a headache. She had grown so perfect, so gentle and consoling that it was unbearable, she was a big, round, smooth balloon without a face. The whole of Moomin valley had somehow become unreal, the house, the garden and the river were nothing but a play of shadows on a screen and Toft no longer knew what was real and what was only in his imagination. (*Moominvalley in November* 172)

The story reaches its climax when Toft is exposed to harsh reality, in this case the insight about Moominmamma being just as weak, sad, and "human" as everybody else:

> Toft saw an entirely new Moominmamma and she seemed natural to him. He suddenly wondered why she had been unhappy and whether there was anything one could do about it. (*Moominvalley in November* 174)

By now, if not before, we realize that Toft is Tove Jansson's alter ego. Because she is always sympathizing with the small "toffles" and "miffles," her choice of representative is characteristic. Toft is the invisible child who cuddles up in a nook, watching life go by. But he is also the one who acts without hesitation, when action is needed.

In an essay on Swedish author and illustrator Elsa Beskow's writing, Tove Jansson describes the device or position of the author in her work: "You often get the feeling that she was working for herself, since she could not resist doing it and that is why her books are convincing and accepted by kids. She made herself so small that she would fit in under a fern and observe safety and danger just like a child does" (Jansson 1959, 420). To my mind, the Beskowian point of view, as described by

Tove Jansson, is exactly the one she uses herself. In the very last scene, we follow Toft through the wood, down to the sea, only to watch the sun set. And then, all of a sudden, we distinguish the hurricane lamp in the masttop. Toft will be there right on time to catch the painter.

Toft, the child, accompanies our path out of the Moomin world of childhood. Luckily, the ending is open, and the movement continues. From the opening sentence in the very first book, "It must have been sometime in the afternoon, some day in the end of August, when Moomintroll and his mother came to the deepest part of the great wood," until the very last line in the very last book, "Toft would be there right on time," the movement never ceases. By refusing to lock up her imaginary world behind the conventional bars of children's literature, Tove Jansson captures the essence of childhood as a complex state of flux. Her stories are inexorable and, at the same time, delicate reflections of herself, as well as of us, her readers. We are all on the move, creating the Eternal Farewell. Tove Jansson has given us the images.

NOTE

1. All translations, other than from Tove Jansson's novels, with the exceptions for *Exploits of Moominpappa* and *Sculptor's Daughter*, are done by me.

WORKS CITED

Björk, Christina. *Tove Jansson mycket mer än Mumin.* Uppsala: Bilda, 2003.

Jansson, Tove. *Moominland Midwinter.* Translated by Thomas Warburton. New York: Walck, 1958 (*Trollvinter* 1957).

———. "Sagan inom verkligheten: Den ärliga Elsa Beskow." *Bonniers Litterära Magasin* (1959) 5: 419–420.

———. *Moominsummer Madness.* Translated by Thomas Warburton. New York: Walck, 1961 (*Farlig midsommar* 1954).

———. "Den lömska barnboksförfattaren." *Horisont* (1961) 2: 8–11.

———. *Tales from Moominvalley.* Translated by Thomas Warburton. New York: Walck, 1963 (*Det osynliga barnet och andra berättelser* 1962).

———. *Finn Family Moomintroll.* Translated by Elizabeth Portch. New York: Walck, 1965 (*Trollkarlens hatt* 1949).

———. *Exploits of Moominpappa.* Translated by Thomas Warburton. New York: Walck, 1966 (*Muminpappans bravader* 1950).

———. "Några ord i Ljubljana." *Nya Argus* (1966) 18: 259–261.

———. *Moominpappa at Sea.* Translated by Kingsley Hart. New York: Walck, 1967 (*Pappan och havet* 1965).

———. *Comet in Moominland.* Translated by Elizabeth Portch. New York: Walck, 1968 (*Kometjakten* 1946).

———. *Sculptor's Daughter.* Translated by Kingsley Hart. London: Benn, 1969 (*Bildhuggarens dotter* 1968).

———. *Moominvalley in November.* Translated by Kingsley Hart. New York: Walck, 1971 (*Sent i november* 1970).

———. *Meddelande. Noveller i urval 1971–1997.* Helsinki: Schildt, 1998.

———. *The Moomins and the Great Flood.* Translated by David McDuff. Helsinki: Schildt, 2005 (*Småtrollen och den stora översvämningen* 1945).

Kruskopf, Erik. *Bildkonstnären Tove Jansson.* Helsinki: Schildt, 1992.

Nikolajeva, Maria. *From Mythic to Linear: Time in Children's Literature.* Lanham, Md.: Scarecrow, 2000.

———. "Den självmedvetna berättaren" Pp. 109–120 in *Kunskapens hugsvalelse. Litteraturvetenskapliga studier tillägnade Clas Zilliacus* edited by Michel Ekman and Roger Holmström. Åbo: Åbo Akademi Press, 2003.

Nikolajeva, Maria, and Janina Orlov. "A Room of One's Own: The Advantages and Dilemmas of Finno-Swedish Children's Literature." Pp. 77–88 in *Text, Culture and National Identity in Children's Literature* edited by Jean Webb. Helsinki: Nordinfo, 2000.

Orlov, Janina. "Mumin on my mind." *Horisont* (1993) 2–3: 25–34.

Tolvanen, Juhani. *Vid min svans! Tove och Lars Janssons tecknade muminserie.* Helsinki: Schildt, 2000.

Westin, Boel. *Familjen i dalen. Tove Janssons muminvärld.* Stockholm: Bonnier, 1988.

———. "Tove Jansson." Pp. 151–166 in *Twentieth-Century Swedish Writers After World War II.* Dictionary of Literary Biography. Volume 257. Edited by Ann-Charlotte Gavel Adams. Detroit: A Bruccoli Clark Layman Book, 2002.

5

Blue Train, Red Flag, Rainbow World

Gianni Rodari's *The Befana's Toyshop*

Ann Lawson Lucas

As the translated English title tells us, Gianni Rodari's *La Freccia Azzurra* (1954; Engl. *The Befana's Toyshop: A Twelfth Night Tale*, 1970) is a story about children's toys. Perhaps that clarity is the reason why the translator, Patrick Creagh, chose radically to change the title from the original Italian, which means "The Blue Arrow." Rodari makes his Italian readers wait until the second chapter to discover that this central, if inanimate, "character" is a toy train with a name that recalls reality (in Europe, for instance, great trains of the past have included "The Blue Train" and "The Golden Arrow"). In his choice of English title, the translator also decided to emphasize the fact, at least for parents and teachers, that the story is set in foreign parts, and he half explains the mysterious Italian word "Befana" in his added sub-title. Such a mystery may be intriguing and attractive, and yet, all in all, these differences from the original make the full title in English a good deal more learned and specialized-sounding than Rodari's simple and traditional "The Blue Arrow." It is likely that for this reason alone the book's circulation in the English-speaking world has been extremely limited by comparison with Italian sales—and much more confined in terms of social class (not what its author would have wished).

RODARI IN CONTEXT

La Freccia Azzurra (pronounced "La fretcha adzoorra," with vowels like those in "fresh" and "wood"), which Patrick Creagh translated in 1970, was one of Rodari's earliest publications. He had already published several volumes of verse for children and a story that is still regarded as both exemplary and typical of his work, as well as being a significant new departure in the children's literature of the period, *Il romanzo di Cipollino* (1951), later *Le avventure di Cipollino* ("The adventures of Little Onion"). Rodari's verse, which he continued to write all his life, constitutes a modern re-invention of the nursery rhyme (in Italian "filastrocca") and employs also some of the techniques of nonsense poetry. Throughout his life, there flowed from Rodari's pen an exuberant tide of children's novels and stories of all lengths, including very short. When the tale of the toy train was first published in Florence in 1954, its title was *Il viaggio della Freccia Azzurra* ("The journey of the Blue Arrow"), but the text was revised and the title modified for re-publication, in Rome, in 1964. Since then it has had numerous reprints and different formats, including a slipcase package with three more works by Rodari in 1971, and at least two school editions (1985 and 1991), as well as appearing in another compendium, with a preface by one of Italy's most eminent literary critics, Alberto Asor Rosa (Rodari 1992).

Gianni Rodari (1920–1980) was one of the most important writers for children in twentieth-century Italy and the dominant figure in the field in the years following World War II, from around 1950 until his death. He was awarded the prestigious Andersen Medal in 1970.[1] Rodari's career was characterized throughout by intense activity in journalism, education, and writing, and it is as an innovator and reformer in all his work that he is remembered. He has not been translated into English as much as his significance at home would warrant; starting with *Telephone Tales* in 1965, a selection of stories from *Favole al telefono* (1962), Patrick Creagh was a pioneer in the field.[2] In Italy, despite a certain *post mortem* forgetfulness by the public, Rodari's books are again in the active process of becoming modern classics, highly regarded as they are by educators, critics, and leading publishers; twenty-five years after his death, the works are still being reissued in new editions. Many illustrators have decorated Rodari's work, including the noted Emanuele Luzzati and Rodari's own daughter, Paola.[3] Bruno Munari's naïve and innovative drawings were among Rodari's own favorites, and these have been reprinted in an important anthology of the best prose and verse, published in Einaudi's de luxe hardback series of (usually adults') classics, *I millenni* (1993). Meantime, new paperback editions, more readily available to children, are coming out with pictures in more painterly styles by recent illustrators, such as Simona Mulazzani's for *La Freccia Azzurra* (2000). From the 1980s onwards a substantial body of highly reputable scholarship and criticism has also been building up; among the leading writers in the field are Pino Boero of Genoa University and the late Carmine De Luca, who established a center for Rodari studies at Orvieto in central Italy.

Rodari's own extraordinarily original (and touching and hilarious) volume of literary analysis and self-assessment, *Grammatica della fantasia* (1973; Engl. *The Grammar of Fantasy*, 1996), identifies in its title the attribute of the children's writer which he held most dear, the imagination. This book seeks both to elucidate his own methods for deploying the imaginative processes and to encourage parents and teachers to emulate him in telling original stories to children. Here, in inimitable fashion, he explains and illuminates his aims. He believed it to be vital to stimulate children's minds through the use of the imagination, not as an end in itself but in order to provide the young with a key to the understanding of reality. Rodari considered that the life of the mind is intimately connected with the imagination and with creativity, supported by play; therefore imagination, creativity, and play are essential elements in education (Cambi 1985, 139). Moreover, the imagination is a "democratic" attribute, common to all, which can be enhanced by education (Cambi 1985, 137). In his *Grammar*, Rodari not only reveals his thinking as a writer for children, but also discusses a number of subjects that are directly relevant to a consideration of *The Befana's Toyshop*. Many of its brief chapters concern aspects of the fairy-tale genre and, after a long sequence of these, one is entitled "The Analysis of the Befana" (Rodari 1996, 53–55); another chapter is devoted to "The Toy as Character" (67–70). Everywhere the book bears witness to the breadth and depth of Rodari's international literary culture and the intense importance this had for him in his work as a writer for children.

THE BEFANA'S TOYSHOP AND THE
ITALIAN LITERARY TRADITION

La Freccia Azzurra/The Befana's Toyshop is a book-length story in prose which, however, is episodic and therefore combines the advantages of an extended narrative with those of a sequence of short stories; Rodari emphasizes the potential separateness of the episodes by not providing chapter numbers, only titles. Therefore, although the narrative engages more sustained attention than a brief tale does on its own, this book is ideal to read in sections, either to a child at bedtime or at intervals with a class.

In terms of literary history, its structure relates to one of the most important devices used in the ancient Italian art of multiple prose narrative. The technique of telling a series of stories held together within a "frame" story is descended from the most famous work of Giovanni Boccaccio who, with Dante and Petrarch, was one of the "Three Crowns" of the earliest period of Italian vernacular literature.[4] *The Decameron* (1349–51) inspired Chaucer's *Canterbury Tales*, and two subsequent Italian writers whose legacy is evident in the history of the literary fairy tale—Gianfrancesco Straparola (d. before 1557) and Giambattista Basile (d. 1632)—followed Boccaccio's example in their collections of linked tall tales and wonder stories; these included the earliest known versions of "Puss in Boots" and "Beauty and the Beast," among other classics of the genre.[5] Possibly like Boccaccio before them, these writers drew material, in varying but sometimes substantial amounts, from popular (oral) story-telling as well as from learned sources. Unlike its negligible role in English literature, the art of the compendium of short stories holds a primary position in Italian literary history and is deeply rooted in Italian literary consciousness.

Italy has a long and influential tradition of the so-called fairy tale, and yet fairies themselves are quite uncommon. Italian fairy tales, whether in popular folklore or in literary versions, tell of magic and spells, metamorphosis, kings, princesses, sorceresses, children, poverty, talking animals, mythical creatures, journeys, murder, treasure, and love. Yet in Italian literature there is no *Faerie Queene* (Edmund Spenser, 1590) and no *Midsummer Night's Dream* (William Shakespeare, 1596). It is true that *The Faerie Queene* was written to outdo Ariosto's *Orlando Furioso* (1532), in which sorceresses such as Alcina and Melissa appear, and that they had some cultural afterlife (in the works of Handel, for example); but the emphasis in Ariosto is on the chivalric, and he does not create a world of faery or fairy figures with the unforgetability of Oberon and Titania. Fairies (some traditional like Morgana, some invented) and enchantment were elevated to a more central role in the plays of Carlo Gozzi (1720–1806), who devised a new genre, the theatrical fairy tale. Nonetheless, it was Carlo Collodi who, as late as the 1880s, created one of the earliest Italian fairies to be individually significant, impressive, and memorable: the Fairy with the Dark Blue Hair in *The Adventures of Pinocchio* (following the original serial, the book version was first published in 1883).[6] The radical nature of Collodi's unique creation is demonstrated by the fact that there is no Fairy in his first, brief version of the tale: the embryo of the character, in its last chapter, is only a "Little Girl" (Collodi 1996, 46).[7] More than half a century later, it was a new idea to write about the Befana, but Rodari's use of this magical being, rather than a proper fairy, can be construed as more in keeping with Italian tradition, both literary and popular.

While Rodari was decidedly an individualist as a writer, it is hard to imagine his works without the prior existence of Collodi's seminal masterpiece; indeed Rodari himself indicated that his own innovations would scarcely have been possible without Collodi's pioneering writing: "The Brothers Grimm, Andersen and Collodi . . . have been among the great liberators of children's literature, freeing it from the pedagogical tasks that were assigned to it . . ." (Rodari 1996, 31). As we shall see, the varied influence of *Pinocchio* can indeed be observed in *The Befana's Toyshop*, as well as in other works by Rodari: he even wrote a verse version of *Pinocchio*, entitled *La filastrocca di Pinocchio*, published as a comic-style picture book in 1974 (Cambi 1985, 143, fig. 60). Repeatedly over the years, Rodari expressed his fascination with the idea of the fairy tale, both in theory and in practice. In 1963 he addressed a letter to the young readers of a new encyclopedia of fairy tales, the *Enciclopedia della fiaba*.[8] In 1970 he wrote a preface for a prestigious new edition of Hans Christian Andersen's fairy tales.[9] In *La grammatica della fantasia* in 1973 he considered extensively the fundamentals of the fairy tale and analyses of it by scholars such as Vladimir Propp.[10] The title of his finest children's novel, *C'era due volte il barone Lamberto* (1978; "Twice upon a time there was the Baron Lambert"), evokes the traditional opening of fairy tales.[11] In 1982 he published an essay on the pros and cons of fairy tales ("Pro e contro la fiaba" in *Il cane di Magonza*),[12] while he himself practiced the art, for example, in 1987 in *Fiabe lungo un sorriso* ("Fairy tales as long as a smile").[13]

AN ITALIAN CHRISTMAS

Rodari's *The Befana's Toyshop*, in common with some of his other narratives, is unquestionably a fairy tale, but, while the leading female character works magic, her species is hard to define; she seems more of a benign witch than a conventional fairy, though she has something in common with the well-known figure of the fairy godmother. This is the "Befana" of the translator's title, whom Rodari does define elsewhere as a "good witch" and whom, using the language of Propp, he classifies as a "donor" (Rodari 1996, 53; Tatar 1999, 386–87). This character, who launches the story, gives us some insight into the author's creative procedures. The Befana was not invented by Rodari; neither is she a traditional denizen of Italian fairy tales: as so often, Rodari has hybridized different branches of culture. The Befana is a figure taken from folklore and popular tradition. Moreover—for we are discussing Italy, the heartland of Roman Catholicism—she provides a pagan dimension during a festival of the Church.[14] Her name is a corruption of the word "Epifania" (Epiphany), the name of the feast-day which falls on 6 January and commemorates the arrival at Jesus' birthplace of the Three Wise Men (or Magi, or Kings) bearing the gifts of gold, frankincense, and myrrh, as recorded in the New Testament of the Bible. This date is the Twelfth Night of Christmas (the end of the festive season), hence the English translator's explanatory subtitle for the book. Father Christmas, the northern pagan figure who brings gifts to children on the night of 24–25 December, the western festival of the Christian Savior's birth, and who derives from the Near Eastern Saint Nicholas, by way of the Dutch Sinta Klaus, is not at home in the Mediterranean land of Italy, except by recent commercial adoption as "Babbo Natale." Instead, presents are delivered to Italian children on the day when, according to the Church, the Baby Jesus received His own more momentous gifts. Nonetheless, this religious exactitude is overlaid, even in Italy, by pagan folk beliefs: there, it is our mythical old woman, the "Befana," whose age, sharp features, and broomstick suggest her kinship with standard witches, who conducts a universal postal service and who, like Father Christmas, flies through the night (on her broomstick) leaving presents in children's bedrooms. Also like

Father Christmas, she may appear in the flesh and in her traditional costume at parties held in the holiday season, and nowadays she, too, is often represented in toy form. As with the popular practice in Northern Europe (and more generally in what Italians call the "Anglosaxon" countries), it is traditional for Italian children to write letters to the magical benefactor asking for the present of their choice, and for parents to enter into the charade by secretly reading the letters and anonymously supplying the presents.

Onto the Christian-*cum*-pagan tradition, Rodari grafts a modern practical-commercial notion: his Befana owns a city toyshop, visible all the year round, where, with the assistance of her equally elderly maid, she stockpiles goods for the following Epiphany, while attracting attention to the toys for sale that are displayed in her shop window. Thus Rodari combines the supernatural with the everyday and, literally, brings it down to earth. In *The Grammar of Fantasy* he illustrates how this process operates: taking an essential attribute of the Befana— her broom—he asks himself what she does with it for the rest of the year. The various answers ("she uses the broom to clean her house") and the questions that they in turn provoke ("where does she live?") can be built into new narratives (Rodari 1996, 53). As in original stories of quality built around Father Christmas or Santa Claus (for example, Raymond Briggs's version),[15] here the author uses the child's familiarity with comfortable and much-loved tradition to settle him or her into a narrative that will prove to be both modern and surprisingly unfamiliar.

Not only will Rodari tell us new things about the Befana, but—in the manner which was to become an established feature of postmodern re-tellings, but which, in 1954, was markedly fresh—he will also subvert the nature, meaning, and atmosphere of the traditional version. Of course, exceptional geniuses of the past had done the same: Collodi had riotously parodied the conventional good child's *bildungsroman* in the picaresque adventures of an irresponsible ne'er-do-well who is not even human. But it was only in the second half of the twentieth century that such subversion of tradition became a literary end in itself. That was not true, or not the whole truth, of Collodi's *Pinocchio*; admittedly Collodi's aims included the intrinsic humor of such a procedure, but were also moral, educational, and political. Though the passage of 70 years had altered public circumstances, exactly the same is true of Rodari. Fantastic invention and humor married to what, in the postwar period, was termed social and political "engagement" or "commitment" form the *sine qua non* of Rodari's work; these characteristics can already be traced in *The Befana's Toyshop*.

THE FIRST SUBVERSION:
PERSONALITY AND EVENTS

In the traditional lore, the Befana is in ultimate control of those elements of human destiny that are in her domain. She gives or does not give. She rewards good behavior and punishes naughtiness. She has the happiness and the desolation of young human beings in her power. In the reality underlying the pretence, the children's parents control these things while hiding behind the mythical figure; indeed it could be said that they exploit the innocent credulity of the young in relation to traditional beliefs in order to reinforce their teaching of their children, and the parents' natural power is thus redoubled and made unarguable by the mysterious enactments of the all-seeing, all-knowing magical being. Through the unchallengeable actions of the Befana, the fallible parent or guardian becomes apparently infallible, wholly just and accurate in his or her judgments. Of course, normally those concerned are entirely benign and generous in their use of the tradition, and the only emotions experienced by both old and young are those joyful ones engendered by the pleasures of giving and receiving, by surprise and delightful excitement. But the potential for manipulation is present and, even in the normal, best scenario, the effect of the Befana's activity is to buttress the inherent power relationship between young and old, by which the old always have the upper hand. Naturally, we find comfort and reliability too in the old tradition which, by definition, lends support to the conventional in life.

Traditionally one cannot and would not question the Befana's actions any more than one can question the festive parent's. Rodari sees things differently. In the very first lines of the story, he indicates the idiosyncrasies and weaknesses of his Befana. She likes to think of herself as aristocratic, or at least as "almost a baroness," and she insists on her hierarchical status in conversation with her maidservant (Rodari 2000, 9). The latter responds with good humor and robust sarcasm, but the Befana is seen to be fundamentally insecure and (therefore) domineering, harmlessly pretentious, flawed, "only human" in fact, and that means that her capacity for dispassionate good judgment is called into question: she is just a querulous old lady, after all. Moreover, she gets wet and cold like the rest of us, and after an exhausting night flying over the city roofs, she is ready for her camomile tea and her account book, but not ready to correct any mistakes or rise to any new demand. In other words, Rodari's Befana is also imperfect in her primary task and does not correct (as one might suppose a good fairy godmother would do) the injustices suffered because of social station and economic hardship. (Think of Cinderella's benefactress.) Therefore the reader cannot help criticizing this latterday Befana, who also has a sharp tongue and no great warmth for her beneficiaries.[16]

Since the traditional Befana of folklore is all-powerful and her actions are supernaturally perfect, there is no call for human beings to be other than passively, nay gladly, accepting what she does. Naturally, the presents themselves are inanimate and inert in the proceedings. Rodari's story, however, hinges on two discrepancies from the traditional, theoretical norm: a deserving small boy has not received any present, and certainly not the one for which he longs; moreover, the toys that inhabit the toyshop window are not only "alive" and capable of speech, but, astonishingly, they rebel against the powerful Befana's decisions and take the enactment of justice into their own hands. Though beset by difficulties and dangers, they do her job better than she does. By the end, the reader perceives the Befana to have been inadequate, and the narrator has done a better justice than hers. However, in the happy ending of the final pages, Rodari's Befana is to a degree redeemed for, unexpectedly, she takes some interest (partly prompted by self-interest) in the poor boy she had previously ignored, and even kindly takes him into her life and work.

THE SECOND SUBVERSION:
(POLITICAL) MORALITY

In the traditional myth, rewards for good conduct and, by inference, the whole moral order are entirely dependent, first, on a single individual who possesses unique power and, second, on a moral system established and supervised autocratically from on high. Normally, of course, this would sound like a preposterously exaggerated and intellectualized description of an innocent festivity designed to add glamor, mystery, and fun to the simple matter of giving pleasure by giving presents. This primary analysis is necessary, however, to an assessment of how Rodari adds further innocent fun and, moreover, subverts the old system by substituting a new one founded on contemporary political theory.

In fairy tales and children's stories, animals and toys regularly come to anthropomorphic life, so the discussions and rebellious action of Rodari's toys are to be seen, initially, as an entertaining extension of this conceit, which is as traditional as the myth of the Befana itself. What makes the toys act, however, is their realization that the Befana has been unjust; she maintains a system of morality based on social class and on wealth or poverty (the parents' ability to buy): her role is commercial, supports capitalism, and therefore exacerbates the division between rich and poor. The trigger for this story's action is the effect of the Befana's system on a good and innocent child, who weeps for lack of a present, the token of approval, a lack which is no fault of his own or his mother's. His dejection causes pity in the "hearts" of the toys and their decision to correct the injustice that has been done to the child. Together they discuss what they have observed and whether a remedy is possible and, if so, "what is to be done?," thus bringing together at nursery level the political system of democracy (or even the collective processes of Communism) and, implicitly in the toys' search for strategies, Lenin's famous question to the community at large. Even though the General at the head of the toy soldiers considers it a revolt, the other toys decide to take collaborative action themselves (instead of relying on an autocrat) and their aim will be the redistribution of presents (if not wealth), a symbol of a better way of ordering society. Not that they will take away from the rich; they will simply give to the poor in the same measure as has already been given to the rich. They will enact a form of egalitarianism. "Being fair" is a concept enthusiastically espoused by children and widespread as a theme in children's literature, but this narrative procedure stemmed, no doubt, from Rodari's fundamental political convictions.

Rodari was twenty-three in 1943, when Mussolini and his Fascist regime fell from power in Italy, and twenty-five when the World War against dictatorships ended two years later. At that time the Italian political pendulum swung from the Far Right toward the Left: both socialism and, notably, Communism now flourished (Italian Communism was gradualist, never revolutionary, and in future years would lead toward western "Euro-Communism" which, similarly, was moderate and democratic). Having qualified and practiced as a teacher, Rodari, like so many Italian intellectuals, committed himself passionately to the achievement of a better world and a fairer society by means of idealistic, utopian Marxism. To this end he plunged into vigorous journalistic activity, throughout his life writing for and editing a number of prominent Communist newspapers and journals; in his early years he founded and edited a children's newspaper and the national paper for young people sponsored by the Italian Communist Party (PCI).[17] He also began to engage in educational experiment and reorganization, based on the Marxist principles of equality and cooperation, so that children and parents became partners with teachers in the development of new educational methods.[18] Naturally, Rodari's writings for children expressed imaginatively the principles in which he believed and which he aimed to apply in his work for the creation of the new egalitarian democracy of postwar Italy. Thus the poor child is to be valued and not neglected, and the efforts to make him equal with the rich will be collective, concerted efforts in which each participant has something of value to offer. Like Collodi in the 1880s, Rodari was seeking through his writing to contribute to the invention of a new and better Italy.

TOYS AS CHARACTERS

In his discussion of "The Toy as Character" (Rodari 1996, 67–70), Rodari's central thesis is that "inventing stories with toys is almost natural" (69). Parents who take the trouble to play with their children, allowing the child to direct the play and following the child's instructions in the handling of the toys, will find themselves involved in a process of storytelling in relation to the toys and their activities; this is storytelling in which the child leads the way (Rodari 1996, 69). A young child will see the toys as having a life and thoughts of their own, and these will be narrated and explained to the parent. In an important sense, then, the independent actions and attitudes of the toys in the Befana's toyshop are the result, for the writer, of children's play and are simply the normal and natural state of affairs for the young reader.

By the time of Rodari's writing, there was already a history, albeit a relatively short one, of toys appearing in Western children's books as anthropomorphic characters; animals did so more frequently, and indeed toys were probably the last major category to join the list of literary heroes typical of children's literature, emerging after animals, supernatural beings, and children themselves. The animals and toys of children's stories have a characteristic in common, for obvious reasons not shared with other categories: they may be represented either anthropomorphically or naturalistically. Anthropomorphic animals have been present in the Aesopic fable tradition ever since Ancient Greek times, with clear consequences for modern children's books. Later on, while many familiar anthropomorphic animals (Puss in Boots) and magical personages (Cinderella's fairy godmother) definitively entered European literature in the late seventeenth and early eighteenth centuries through the medium of fairy tales, whether western (Perrault and followers) or eastern (*The Arabian Nights*), it was not until well into the nineteenth century that toys became established in a similar role. This late appearance, no doubt, had much to do with social attitudes toward children; they had to come to be perceived as a distinctive age-group with unique needs, not just as imperfect or aspiring adults, before the wider, and new, culture now proper to childhood provided trains, teddy bears, and tin soldiers as possible subjects for stories. Moreover, the needs and enthusiasms of very young children had to attract as much attention as those of middle-school children before toys could be widespread literary characters, and this situation did not happen until the twentieth century.

As in so many things, Lewis Carroll in Britain was an essential early innovator in this respect. Admittedly, the *Alice* books (1865 and 1871), devised for a child who was at first only seven, are not populated with Alice's dolls, but they do emphatically re-work much nursery culture and, in the playing cards and chess pieces, they animate and anthropomorphize not toys but games familiar to educated children. Some of the characters in L. Frank Baum's American story *The Wonderful Wizard of Oz* (1900), especially the Tin Man and the Scarecrow, bear an obvious anthropomorphic resemblance to characters in toy stories; the similarity is superficial, however, for these are not toys for children but artefacts possessing something of an allegorical air which comments on the life of adult humans. In Italy a significant step was taken in 1914 in Maria Carrara Lombroso's *Storia di una bambina e di una bambola* ("The story of a little girl and a doll"), while the first Toytown story appeared in Britain in 1925, and *Winnie-the-Pooh*, about a toy bear, was published in 1926.[19]

In addition—and in advance—there had been important European precedents in adult literature for the tale of the "living" toy. Notably, during the Romantic period, bizarre and sinister stories of man-made automata appeared, such as Mary Shelley's seminal *Frankenstein*

(1818) and E. T. A. Hoffman's *Der Sandman* (1816), which gave rise to Delibes' ballet *Coppélia* and other narratives in which a puppet comes to life. It is important to realize, however, that whereas these fantasies no doubt helped to prepare the way for toy stories, they themselves are not about children's playthings. Equally, especially in relation to the country of origin of the adult puppet-theatre version of the *commedia dell'arte*, it is necessary to distinguish between theatrical puppets (for work) and toy puppets (for play). Rodari places three toy marionettes in the window of the Befana's toyshop, but these are distinctively different from Collodi's Pinocchio, who is over three feet tall and was carved by Geppetto to be a theatrical puppet like Harlequin.[20] This purpose sets Pinocchio more in the Romantic tradition of *Der Sandman* than in any literary tradition for children, and indicates the variety of theatrical connections in the book. There is no direct relationship between Collodi's inimitable marionette character (vigorous, contrary, anarchic) and those of *The Befana's Toyshop* (passive, willing, decorative); yet both writers frequently drew on the *commedia dell'arte* tradition, and generally in this story, as in so much of Rodari's work, the spirit (if not the strict genealogy) of Collodi's *Pinocchio* lives on.[21]

In the episode concerning his marionettes, Rodari seems to have had other literary allusions in mind too. He entitles this chapter "Il cuore delle tre marionette," literally meaning "The heart of the three marionettes." Any well-read Italian would be reminded immediately of Collodi's puppet but also, simultaneously, of that other great children's classic of late nineteenth-century Italy, Edmondo De Amicis' *Cuore* (*Heart*), the story of the maturing feelings of a growing boy, his experiences with his family, his schoolfriends and teachers, his awakening to civic awareness.[22] Rodari is engaging here in a little playful intertextuality, teasing his reader with his cross-references to the best-loved works of Italian children's literature (and we shall see how the third major writer of the same period is honored by Rodari in the figure of his toy sea-captain). The episode that brings the three marionettes to prominence is itself vividly symbolic of the human condition in a manner that echoes De Amicis' meaning. In the little blue train on the long journey through the winter's night, the three marionettes get frozen with cold and complain that they do so because they lack a (human) heart to warm them; the red pencil cures their ill by drawing a handsome, fat, red heart-shape onto each marionette's tunic, whereupon warmth suffuses them all and brings comfort.

RODARI'S TOYSHOP

Though the central toy, the electric train, is modeled on an artefact, not
a human being, even it is not depicted literally but takes on a certain life
of its own: above all, the train, without any recourse to the electricity
supply, runs for miles through the snowy city streets at night. It is
worth noting that Rodari chose for his talismanic title, not a living or
anthropomorphic character, but the inanimate vehicle—literal and
metaphorical—for both the journey and the tale. Four other toys are
somewhat similar, being objects or constructs rather than representations of living things. There is a less magical boat with its captain,
which is at home on water, but which has to be towed or mounted on
a goods wagon of the train for most of the journey. There is a tin aeroplane, with its pilot, which has even greater freedom of action than the
train, for which a Meccano set has to provide an emergency bridge in
a flooded street. (The adventures of the toys in the world of humans
are reminiscent of those of Hans Christian Andersen's Tin Soldier,
especially his near-disaster in the flood-water of the drain.) Then there
is a set of coloring crayons, hardly mentioned until a late episode in
which they come to life and demonstrate their skills to the recipient
child, almost like so many "stick-men" (Rodari 2000, 98–105); unlike
the train, the boat, and the aeroplane, which have to be managed and
set in motion by the other toys, even these pencils exhibit a great
degree of anthropomorphism: they move independently and talk, both
to each other and to "their" child, who is awake in bed on the night
of Epiphany. Indeed, these humble playthings perform an important
political role for Rodari, providing a philosophical climax to the story
in its seventeenth chapter, three-quarters of the way through the narrative. Drawing and coloring unaided, the pencils create an "unforgettable night" for the delighted little boy in bed; the last lines of the
chapter describe how they draw flags—the Italian tricolor and the Red
Flag—making the room seem to be full of some national festivity. Each
pencil wanted its flag to be the best, but then they made peace and, all
together, drew a flag incorporating all seven of their colors. In the last
words of the chapter the pencils agree to go ahead together in perfect
harmony. The idea of peaceful and constructive co-operation is evident
to the child reader, while an adult recognizes that, symbolized in the
flag of seven colors, Rodari had in mind either the United Nations or
unity in Europe through the Common Market, or both. Though the
Italian flag and the flag of Communism rank equally in this passage,

the significance of the Red Flag for Rodari is superseded by the ideal of international peace and accord, to which the writer gives primacy. Had he lived to 2003, Rodari would have been delighted to see the Peace flags, with their rainbow colors, flying everywhere in Italy.

Most of the characters in the story are anthropomorphic. There are conventional dolls, including a black one, and toy soldiers, including officers; a station-master, engine-driver, and guard accompany and guide the train; a wonderful old Red Indian chief leads his nation, naturally associated with a group of cowboys; an enterprising pilot flies the plane and a blustering sea-captain sails the boat. Finally, two animals possess totally differing levels of animation: the teddy-bear has none, but the leading activist toy, who sets the moral rebellion in motion, is a nondescript little rag dog who communicates in speech (having forgotten how to bark while sitting in the shop window). Some of these characters are virtually confined to one episode in which they are central; others direct activities and face adventures throughout. The quasi-human toys are presented as caricatures of human (or literary) types. The sailor has a repertoire of exaggerated, baroque swear-words and exclamations uttered as a parody of the best-known maritime adventure heroes of Italian children's literature, those of Emilio Salgari (d. 1911);[23] while eager to swash-buckle, the captain has to be restrained. Equally vocal is the commanding officer of the toy soldiers, who sees enemies everywhere and is always mistaken in his observations, deductions, and plans. Subliminally, Rodari evinces no great admiration for the military, or at least its leaders, and yet he accords the wrong-headed General a scene of unique tragedy and humanity. Like Napoleon, the General meets his Waterloo—or rather, his Moscow—in the snow, and, unlike Napoleon, he there sacrifices himself, becoming a miniature snowman. For him, the meaning has gone out of his efforts because, to lighten the train and help it move, the soldiers have unloaded their cannons and other equipment, saying, moreover, that they are better off without them: Rodari's postwar pacificism prompts the creation of this episode, as it did with the crayons' rainbow flags. By contrast with the tin General, the toy who is always right is the sage, measured, observant old Indian Chief, who sucks his pipe and occasionally utters lapidary phrases in pidgin (a parody, no doubt, of films); his advice is always so wise that the others gladly follow his lead, thus providing a further ethical message, this time with an ethnic connotation.

While Rodari has fun with stereotypical human and literary types in this way, he also draws amusement from the toy condition itself: the pilot, seated in his cockpit, has no need of legs and so has none; the sea-captain is painted on flat tin and so has only half a naval beard. Distinctive features of Rodari's characterization are the freedom with which he combines human and non-human, real and fantasy character-istics, and the mirth which he derives from the bizarre combinations and paradoxes created in this anarchically free-spirited manner. He never blurs the line between the real and the fantastic, but, on the con-trary, specifies clearly the difference: as the cat approaches the train, he emphasizes that it is a real cat, not a toy, creating an encounter between reality and fantasy that is unmistakably his. Certain characteristics and inadequacies of toys are taken for granted by human beings in real everyday life; it is only when those toys "come alive" that the comic or pathetic contradictions come to light. Are these also reflections on the human condition itself? Are we also more imperfect and more inadequate than we normally perceive?

THE SPIRIT OF PINOCCHIO

That same ambivalence created by anthropomorphism had been a vital element in Collodi's masterpiece. Essentially, the story of Collodi's puppet tells how a badly behaved, wild, and self-centered boy learns to be a constructive, kindly, and unselfish member of society and of his family. The story of Rodari's toys recounts how they change from being passive and accepting of the existing order to being questioning and actively seeking to correct the existing order. Pinocchio learns to accommodate himself to live with others; the toys take action to improve the lives of others. These are different processes, and yet something Collodian is present in Rodari.

Collodi's puppet and Rodari's toys have an essential and pre-eminent characteristic in common: they are capable of rebellion, of doing the opposite of what is expected of them. This trait shows a lively and independent spirit, a capacity for unorthodoxy, for behaving unconventionally, all of which is fundamentally admirable, even though the purposes to which this independence is put are wholly opposed: Pinocchio rebels to indulge his own selfish desires; the toys rebel out of moral indignation and public spiritedness. Both Pinocchio and the toys have sympathy and pity for others, but in Pinocchio these are the feelings of a loving, though uncontrolled, nature and are directed toward his close family and friends; thus there is an element of self-centeredness involved. The toys have disinterested and selfless compassion for people they do not or hardly know: the most extreme example is that of the pretty doll who leaves the others to cuddle up to the impoverished old woman dying in a doorway on a snowy night. The toys have the strong desire to help others, a desire that Pinocchio learns only at the end of his tale. However, the lesson for the young reader is exactly the same in Rodari as in Collodi: active concern for others is good.

These two writers married together the telling of an entertaining tale with the communication of some lessons or messages directed to the young readers and also, more unusually, their parents and teachers: both Collodi and Rodari are didactic, though they knew how to disguise this component well. Both sought to encourage sympathy in the young reader for the less fortunate; both sought through the adult reader to promote social justice and political reform. As well as the pervasive pain expressed in response to poverty, both writers included episodes dealing with theft and the police, and references to the importance of education, as well as portrayals of the harmful snobbery of the bourgeoisie.[24] They are writers, then, who have a sense of mission, however cloaked in colorful narrative and humorous exuberance.

Both Collodi and Rodari exhibit high technical skill in organizing their narrative inventiveness. In these stories, the plot is episodic and founded on the idea of a journey, or series of journeys, fraught with adventure and danger, during which the leading characters solve problems and escape from adversity. Many of the episodes narrate passing encounters between the leading figures and minor characters met by chance along the way; in both cases, some of these minor figures are humans naturalistically presented, whereas others are strange and supernatural (like the Green Fisherman in *Pinocchio* and Rodari's talking statue on its monument). In *The Befana's Toyshop*, we find at least one encounter that is directly reminiscent of an episode in *Pinocchio*, or, rather, seems to be an affectionate parody of it. Early in the puppet's acquaintanceship with the deceiving crooks, the Fox and the Cat, a cruel event occurs that should have warned Pinocchio about their true nature. While conversing with a White Blackbird, the Cat suddenly pounces and swallows it to prevent it telling Pinocchio the truth (Collodi 1996, 35). Rodari's cat, an ordinary real-life inhabitant of the town, pounces on a singing canary, only to find that it is a toy fixed to a spring in an ornamental cage; the cat retires wounded by the action of the spring. The main image has been maintained while justice is done in a minor variation: maybe the White Blackbird has even been avenged. Rodari clearly had no illusions about the inherent nature of cats, but an emotional experience in his youth gave him a special affection for them, so that an iconic cat frequently appears in his work, culminating in *Gli affari del signor Gatto* (1972; Engl. *Mr Cat in Business,* 1975).

Amid the journeying of the anthropomorphic puppet and toys, Collodi and Rodari both interweave an important sub-plot concerning a young human boy and the question of just deserts: Pinocchio's naughty schoolfriend ends badly, dying from hard labor in the guise of the donkey he has been turned into (Collodi 1996, 165); by contrast, the toys' young friend, who is good but poor, finds himself rewarded for his hard work, sense of responsibility, and decency. Both narratives are admonitory, but the narrative treatment is different: whereas magic had metamorphosed Collodi's schoolboy, Rodari's is presented entirely realistically. In a way, this good child is the real boy whom Pinocchio longed to become, and did become on the last page of his story.

THE SURVIVAL OF THE FAIRY TALE

The Adventures of Pinocchio and *The Befana's Toyshop* possess a variety of characteristics that link both of them to the traditional fairy tale. While Collodi and Rodari do have fairy-tale magic and the surreal in common, there is a qualitative difference: *The Befana's Toyshop* is set in the real world, where, under cover of darkness, some magic is performed and some surreal occurrences happen against the odds—and against the normal grain of the real life that occupies the landscape of the story; *The Adventures of Pinocchio* is set in an imaginary world where magic and wonderment and impossible creatures and extraordinary events are the norm, but where reality—for instance, in the depiction of the schoolroom and of the policemen—occasionally intrudes. Magic is the stuff of fairy tale and Collodi's story is replete with it. We have observed how the frame story of Rodari's tale concerns a supernatural being, the Befana, who has characteristics akin to those of a fairy godmother or witch, and yet Rodari inserts her into the mundane life of a twentieth-century industrialized town. This is not a fantasy world, but a very recognizable one, with its trams and puddles and petty thieves. Though *The Befana's Toyshop* belongs to the fairy-tale tradition, it clearly illustrates a modern evolution of the genre, which seeks to permit magic and make it visible, but within our own humdrum world. In this evolution, as Jack Zipes has justly observed, Rodari anticipates the "magic realism" of later, especially Latin-American, novelists for adults (Rodari 1996, Introduction xvii); such writers include Gabriel García Márquez and Isabel Allende who, in her *House of the Spirits* (1985), provides a major character, Clara, with green hair, in the tradition of *Pinocchio's* fairy.

In the Collodi and Rodari stories, besides a prominent, if unusual, fairy or witch, and besides magic and the supernatural, some less obvious features repeat those of the ancient tradition. The structure provided by a journey is one of these. Among the defining characteristics of folk tales and their derivative, the fairy tale, is the use of journeys as a central theme and as the means for emphasizing the evolution of a story; this kind of tale lends itself to the inclusion of adventure, danger, and surprise, and is by its nature progressive in the sense that it moves from one situation to another, giving a sense of momentum. The archetypal folk tale, however, presents a circular journey, typically expressed in terms of the hero leaving home, encountering challenges and surviving them, and returning home in some sense a victor. (This kind of leading character is not usually a heroine, though it could be argued that Cinderella provides one such atypical example and that Hansel and Gretel are joint journeying protagonists.)

Collodi's and Rodari's stories both make use of the familiar travelling concept with its episodic structure, but, since these are markedly original writers, there are also significant differences from the model. In *Pinocchio*, the journey is not circular and includes a pattern of inconclusive or contradictory to-ing and fro-ing; on the other hand, not only does the puppet eventually overcome the adversities encountered, but his story reaches its climax and conclusion at home. It is not the impoverished basement room of Geppetto, seen at the beginning, but a quite different, comfortable, and happy home in a new place. The circular device, however, is present metaphorically, for the new home, literally and figuratively far away from the old one, contains the two characters of central importance to Pinocchio who were first encountered in the original home: Geppetto and the Talking Cricket.

In order to consider the various journeys present in the Rodari story, one must take account of extra features not present in *Pinocchio*. Although it appears simple and even artless, Rodari's narrative possesses certain complexities that make it both ancient and modern. First, instead of one protagonist, it seems almost to have several different leading characters, with different roles to play and different journeys to make: the story could not exist without the Befana (a fantastic, magic "person"), who launches and concludes the "frame" story and the book, while the train (a fantastic, magic toy, with no independent "personality") is selected for the title and connects all parts of the book; the *agent provocateur* of the action, however, is the little inconspicuous dog (a fantastic, magic toy, which is fully anthropomorphic), the leader of the toys' convoy, who travels throughout the book and who, more than most, moves with ease between the "frame" story and the enclosed episodes. Despite the importance of the Befana, the train, and the rag dog, Rodari's true hero is, nevertheless, the poor but good young boy (a real human boy who inhabits the real town), who longs to own the beautiful blue train in the Befana's toyshop window; even so, the reader is hardly aware of his narrative status in the early chapters. Eventually one can see that he travels both literally and metaphorically in the course of the tale: he moves to and fro across the city between home, school, toyshop, cinema (where he has evening work), and police-station; by means of these peregrinations he betters himself, finally assuming a new, safer, more congenial work-role. In the new job he is assistant to the Befana in her toyshop, so again we witness the circular journey: at the beginning the boy is outside the toyshop, looking longingly in, and this provokes the whole sequence of adventurous events; at the end the boy has experienced much and is back at the toyshop, but contentedly inside: for him this is a kind of substitute home. Ultimately, the analytical reader perceives that the boy inhabits, in the main, the frame story and is its hero, although he is also the link with the separate episodes of the toys' adventures: after all, the toys' journey is a long search for the boy, which Rodari succeeds in concluding without banality (for the group of toys never finds him). Essentially, the frame story tells the tale of the Befana (mythical), her toyshop (real), and the boy (real).

In a more obvious way than the boy, the toys collectively engage in a truly heroic journey, the connective thread for the whole narrative. Each individual toy is colorful and characterful, and is given prominence at some stage in the context of its own moment of glory. Most of all, however, this variegated group is to be seen collectively as a tiny society which, despite individualisms and disputes, functions constructively and, in the long run, harmoniously to achieve the common goal.

That said, even this non-human group includes a hero, albeit an improbable, rather forlorn hero, or even an anti-hero, the shy, modest rag dog. At the end, Rodari completes another circle, and, like the boy, the little toy dog returns to the Befana's toyshop as the boy's companion, thus weaving together the frame story and the episodic story of the toys. In this way, the frame story's journey describes a circle and the Befana and her maid are observed to travel according to that pattern too (from toyshop to town to toyshop), while the episodic journey of the group of toys is, by contrast, linear and one-way only (toyshop to town). The line of travel for each toy, however, ends at a different stage, each plaything arriving at its own, different future home. Rodari's narrative, then, describes the traditional circle, but this is traversed by an equally important straight line or diameter, with many points of departure punctuating its length.

Within these interlaced narratives, prominent descriptions record the nature of poverty, emphasized by Rodari to provoke empathy and pity and a desire to correct such social injustice. We have observed that the boy hero is too poor to be given a present and that, as well as going to school, he works for money. The unassuming rag dog is a cheap toy, socially inferior to the more elaborate ones (but he nevertheless has the capacity to be a leader). The destinations of the various toys, who seek to give themselves as presents to children who have none, are, by definition, humble and sometimes destitute homes. Rodari's concern for poverty was, of course, a part of his political ideology, and his story embodies his reformist aims. Collodi, like Rodari, had experienced poverty in his youth; seventy years earlier, he had shown similar reformist zeal in the writing of many passages in *Pinocchio*, notably the humorous but graphic description of the hardship evident in Geppetto's basement room. These might seem to be modern, political concerns, and so they are; yet they also belong to the heartland of the folk tradition, which presents the misery of the poor with equal anguish, albeit in ultimately consoling tales of penniless woodcutters (Little Tom Thumb) and exploited scullery servants (Cinderella) whose lives are eventually transformed.

THE DISTINCTIVE GENIUS OF
GIANNI RODARI

What at first appears to be a simple children's tale, concerning toys that come alive, possesses many features and qualities which render it more complex and more distinctive than the average entertainment. Rodari's humor is especially significant because not only does it provide fun, which draws the reader pleasurably into what is, in a sense, a modern moral tale, but also it expresses the writer's humanity. It is never cruel, reductive humor; it is never crudely comic just for the sake of it, because it is always full of human sympathy. Admittedly the humor is often based on caricatures of human types—as in the Sea-Captain, the General, and the Station Master among the toys, and indeed the Befana herself—and yet these are caricatures of already existing stereotypes and are, anyway, gentle, not harsh, and are redeemed by the expression of emotions, such as compassion at some misfortune befalling a character. The tone of the humor, as of the book in general, expresses warmth and kindness.

Rodari's fluency in story-telling is manifest, as is his use of a variety of literary techniques. No doubt his facility for convincing and lively dialogue is among the most important characteristics of the writing, since it occupies more than half the text. The dialogue is easy to read, but it is not simplistic. Through structure, catch-phrases, and *idées fixes*, the dialogue frequently conveys the character of the speaker, and therefore expresses several meanings simultaneously. It is vigorous, natural, modern dialogue which includes exclamations and colloquial expressions, but its standard of quality in the use of language is never compromised. The dialogue lends itself to being read aloud entertainingly and helps to establish a comfortable rapport between listener and author, while its apparent naturalness convinces the child of the apparent reality of the fantastic fiction.

Rodari's characteristic melange of realism and fantasy, developed from the fairy-tale and the Collodian traditions, is sustained in this early work by an already marked formal and technical mastery of his material. Buttressing the technique by which, Rodari juxtaposes, on the one hand, his clear-sighted observation of commonplace reality and, on the other, his contrasting flights of surreal imagination, is the seeming randomness of his interweaving the naturalistic with the fantastic. Since the episodic tale of toys is embraced within a frame story, one might have expected a neat division between reality and the imagination: the fantasy of the talking toys with their social conscience might have been contained strictly within the sequence of episodes telling of their journey, while the frame story might have confined itself to the reality of the busy city, the thieves and the poor boy. But Rodari's book, like life, is not so simple and rejects such a schematic approach, allowing fantasy to interrupt reality and vice versa. Indeed, from the start, the entire premise of the imaginary Befana possessing a mundane city-center shop, is paradoxical. When the Befana and her maid crash-land in the city's trees and observe the journeying toys below, the writer underlines the incongruity by permitting a little structural anarchy in the writing: the frame story is here invading the sequential stories, to mutual benefit, and both of them at this point are dominated by the fantasy. Moreover, each time that one of the toys gives itself to a child living in poverty, the episodic fantasy instead invades the reality of the framing city, and the anthropomorphic toy begins to accommodate itself to real life. The progressive enactment of justice by the kind-hearted toys continues until, in the last couple of chapters, the fantasy world and the real world coalesce. Then, instead of a puppet becoming a real boy, we see a toy dog (which for an illogical moment had wanted to die) becoming a real dog with a bark, and the real boy, Francesco, has found both a new friend and a new home.

Until 1980 Rodari dominated progressive children's literature in Italy, as a lone, individual, and irrepressible voice. The wealth of creative genius now flourishing in Italy in the sphere of children's culture, both in the written word and in the visual media, owes much to his energy, vision, and experimentalism, to his willingness to think differently about children and their stories.

NOTES

1. For readers of Italian who want to know more about Rodari's life and work in general, there is the biography by Marcello Argilli, 1990, and, in his 1996 translation of Rodari's *The Grammar of Fantasy*, Jack Zipes provides a useful biographical outline and other introductory material.

2. At the time of writing, Creagh's translation of *The Befana's Toyshop* is out of print, though available through the library and second-hand networks.

3. Paola Rodari's illustrations were first published in 1971 when she was 14; they appeared in *Tante storie per giocare* ("Lots of stories to play with," 1971). She also illustrated *Novelle fatte a macchina* (1973; *Tales Told by a Machine*, 1976) and a number of other publications by her father. The distinguished illustrator of Italian children's books Emanuele Luzzati worked on various texts by Rodari, starting with *Castello di carte* ("House of cards," 1963).

4. For brief explanations concerning these writers, see for example, Peter Hainsworth and David Robey, eds., *The Oxford Companion to Italian Litera-*

ture (2002), or Peter Bondanella and Julia Conaway Bondanella, eds., *Cassell Dictionary of Italian Literature* (1996).

5. For more information on these writers and stories, see Jack Zipes, ed., *The Oxford Companion to Fairy Tales* (2000), as well as Hainsworth and Robey, *The Oxford Companion to Italian Literature,* and Bondanella and Bondanella, *Cassell Dictionary of Italian Literature.*

6. Note that, whatever the Disney film and some translations say, Collodi's original fairy is not "the Blue Fairy" and that the word he uses for her hair color ("turchino") is not the ordinary Italian word for "blue" ("azzurro," as in the Italian title of the Rodari story under discussion); "turchino" means specifically dark blue, navy blue, indigo. There were precedents in fairy tale for beings with strange hair coloring: Bluebeard is a well-known example from Perrault, whom Collodi had recently translated into Italian (1875).

7. Collodi ended his original serialized version of "The Story of a Puppet" with Chapter XV. He re-started the story only after some months' interval. See Collodi 1996, 178–79, notes 46–49, for further detail.

8. G. Rodari, "Ai ragazzi," in *Enciclopedia della fiaba* (1963).

9. G. Rodari, "Presentazione," in H. C. Andersen, *Fiabe* (1970).

10. In addition to a number of scattered references, Rodari devotes chapter 19, "The Cards of Propp," in *The Grammar of Fantasy* to Propp's ideas on folk and fairy tales (Rodari 1996, 42–49). Maria Tatar provides some useful key extracts from Propp in her volume, *The Classic Fairy Tales* (Tatar 1999, 378–87).

11. G. Rodari, *C'era due volte il barone Lamberto* (1978); it is also included in *I cinque libri* (1993), though as yet not translated into English.

12. G. Rodari, "Pro e contro la fiaba" in *Il cane di Magonza*, ed. C. De Luca, pref. T. De Mauro (1982).

13. G. Rodari, *Fiabe lungo un sorriso*, ed. M. Argilli (1987).

14. Rodari is here concerned exclusively with the folklore and not the religious connotations. In the early postwar period when he was writing, the great opposed power blocs that dominated and polarized Italian social and political life were the Catholic Church and the Communist Party. As an energetic Communist and educational reformer, Rodari was bitterly opposed and condemned by the Church.

15. Father Christmas as we know him dates only from the nineteenth century. L. Frank Baum invented a new life and image for him as early as 1902, in *The Life and Adventures of Santa Claus*. Raymond Briggs's reluctant hero of winter appears in *Father Christmas* (1973), which won a Kate Greenaway medal.

16. This characterization is rather like Raymond Briggs's equally postmodern, but subsequent, Father Christmas, who grumbles about his tasks and the weather.

17. From 1947 Rodari contributed regularly to the official daily newspaper

of the Italian Communist Party, *L'Unità*, and some of his earliest writing for children appeared in it. In 1950 he founded the prominent children's weekly, linked to the PCI, *Il Pioniere*, which he edited until 1953; then he founded and edited *Avanguardia*, the national paper for young Communists. From 1961 until 1977 he also contributed to the long-established (1908), big-circulation, middle-class *Il Corriere dei Piccoli*, the leading national children's newspaper, which was associated with the important Center-Right daily, *Il Corriere della Sera*.

18. In the 1960s Rodari worked with teachers, schoolchildren, and parents, under the auspices of the "Movimento di Cooperazione Educativa" (the movement for educational co-operation).

19. For a more substantial survey of the role of anthropomorphic toys in children's books, see Lois Rostow Kuznets's interesting study, *When Toys Come Alive: Narratives of Animation, Metamorphosis, and Development* (1994).

20. Hence, the mutual brotherly recognition in the episode when Pinocchio visits a traditional Italian puppet-theatre in Chapters X and XI (Collodi 1996, 26–32).

21. Among Rodari's works exhibiting overt inspiration from the *commedia dell'arte* tradition are *Marionette in libertà* (1974, "Puppets at liberty") in verse, and *La gondola fantasma* (1978, "The ghost gondola"), a story, both including such archetypal characters as Harlequin, Columbine, and Pulcinella. For more information on the theatrical roots of *Pinocchio*, see Lawson Lucas 2002.

22. Collodi's masterpiece was published in book form in 1883; De Amicis' classic, *Cuore*, appeared in 1886. This work also had the (overt) ambition of helping to shape the young generation of new Italians in order that the newly unified nation of Italy should succeed, not only politically but morally and socially.

23. Emilio Salgari published around 80 adventure novels in volume form between 1887 and 1913, and added a new dimension to Italian children's literature; with Collodi and De Amicis, he is the third classic writer of the period whose works are still read. His series narrating the adventures of East Indian pirates in the seas around Borneo is dominated by the figures of Sandokan (Bornean) and Yanez (Portuguese); it is the latter, above all, who gives rise to the exotic exclamatory vocabulary that Rodari parodies here.

24. Collodi's real criminals are the Fox and Cat, who steal Pinocchio's gold coins; the puppet pays a heavy price for stealing grapes, but is rewarded for catching the chicken thieves. Rodari's boy-hero is entirely well-intentioned and well-behaved, and intelligently foils the thieves' raid on the toyshop. In both stories the police are depicted as inept: the Carabiniere puts Geppetto in jail when he should have stopped Pinocchio's flight; the police suspect Rodari's innocent child and detain him incorrectly. Both puppet and boy go to school,

even though the boy also has to work for money. The Befana herself is Rodari's snob, while the doctors in *Pinocchio* illustrate dangerous professional snobbery.

WORKS CITED

Argilli, Marcello. *Gianni Rodari: Una biografia.* Torino: Einaudi, 1990.

Cambi, Franco. *Collodi, De Amicis, Rodari: Tre immagini d'infanzia.* Bari: Dedalo, 1985.

Collodi, Carlo. *The Adventures of Pinocchio.* Ed. Ann Lawson Lucas. London: Oxford University Press, 1996.

Kuznets, Lois Rostow. *When Toys Come Alive: Narratives of Animation, Metamorphosis, and Development.* New Haven: Yale University Press, 1994.

Lawson Lucas, Ann. "The Art of Comedy: Theatrical Features and Devices in Collodi's *Pinocchio* and Their 'Retroscena'," in George Talbot and Pamela Williams, eds., *Essays in Italian Literature and History in Honour of Doug Thompson* (Dublin: Four Courts Press, 2002).

Rodari, Gianni. *Gli affari del signor Gatto.* Turin: Einaudi, 1972.

———. *The Befana's Toyshop: A Twelfth Night Tale.* Trans. Patrick Creagh. London: Dent, 1970.

———. *I cinque libri: Storie fantastiche, favole, filastrocche.* With an essay by Pino Boero. Ill. Bruno Munari. Turin: Einaudi, 1993.

———. *Favole al telefono.* Ill. B. Munari. Turin: Einaudi, 1962.

———. *La filastrocca di Pinocchio.* Ill. R. Verdini. Rome: Editori Riuniti, 1974.

———. *La Freccia Azzurra.* Ill. Simona Mulazzani. Rome: Editori Riuniti, 2000.

———. *The Grammar of Fantasy: An Introduction to the Art of Inventing Stories.* Trans. Jack Zipes. New York: Teachers and Writers Collaborative, 1996.

———. *La grammatica della fantasia: Introduzione all'arte di inventare storie.* Turin: Einaudi, 1973.

———. *Le storie.* Ed. C. De Luca. Rome: Editori Riuniti, 1992.

———. *Telephone Tales.* Trans. Patrick Creagh. London: Harrap, 1965.

Tatar, Maria, ed. *The Classic Fairy Tales.* New York: Norton, 1999.

6

Modernism for Children?
Cecil Bødker's *Silas and the Black Mare*

Helene Høyrup

The dramatic adventures of Silas, the self-orphaned protagonist, who has run away from his parents' circus, are set in a mythical landscape framing a radically anti-authoritarian vision of childhood that represented a breakthrough in Danish children's literature. In the opening chapter, resonant of a birth scene, Silas arrives in a small boat, with his magical flute and natural instincts as the guides that will help him claim childhood as a space to be respected by adults. Prefiguring the novel's theme of violent confrontation between child and adult, in the exposition of the novel Silas makes a wager with Bartolin, the inveterate horse-dealer, about the magnificent black mare, which Bartolin promises will become Silas's if he can ride it. Following an intense power game between the two and detailed descriptions of Silas's virtuosity with horses, Bartolin, signifying also the inveterate adult, breaks his promise by refusing to hand over the black mare to a boy. Being, however, not a hero who gives up so easily, Silas uses his magical flute, which can both stir up and calm down listeners, and with its strange music he makes the horses in Bartolin's stable wild and tame by turns. Silas thus wins his first confrontation with adults and sets out into the world on the magnificent black mare, around which the central plot evolves. Riding through an empty, rather hostile landscape, with the fluctuations of the river as his guiding line, Silas gets hungry and makes a stop in a poor, "thievish" village, whose inhabitants are in human decay. It is a socially stratified society, and people's lives are marked by toil, fear, suppression, and a lack of money, which makes them victimize children. In this village, Emmanuel, the peasant, steals the black mare, which could be made into money. The rest of the main plot focuses on the retrieval of the mare, as the central, desired object. In subplots Silas makes friends with child outsiders, such as Maria, the fisherman's daughter, who is so "angry" and traumatized by her environment that she first tries to stab Silas with a knife. The visit to the fisherman's cottage plays out children's different reactions to adult injustice, in the range from passive hostility to active rebellion, and Silas demonstrates that he can also be amoral and irrational, for instance in his cruelty to Maria. In this chapter, adult violence makes him waver between adopting their language of brutality and a feeling of empathy with the victim. On surviving Maria's nocturnal attempt to kill him, only prevented by the magical flute, Silas is again on the run, while trying to collect his energies to confront the thievish village and win back the black mare. Both attracted to the river and to the mare, he makes a stop in the outskirts of the village, where he makes friends with Ben-Godik, the shepherd lad, who is very different from Silas. Contrary to Silas's unconstrained freedom and rebellious nature, it is Ben-Godik's strategy of survival to create secret spaces that adults do not know about. With the help of this new friend, Silas returns to the village to win back his black mare. From a big chestnut tree in Joanna's, Ben-Godik's mother's, garden he sees the village in perspective. The adults are driven by fear and rumors of nearby robbers, and they are involved in different role plays, from bullying, buying and selling to erotic games. The villagers are entertained by a travelling circus that Silas knows very well since it is the one from which he ran away. In a highly dramatic scene, Silas uses his magical flute to stir up emotions and movements in people and animals, and, at the same time, he has a chance to get even with Philip, his stepfather, who would force Silas to swallow swords instead of work with horses in the circus. As a climax of suspense and rodeo-like action, Silas jumps from the chestnut tree onto the back of the black mare and leaves the village and its social patterns behind. He is a not so lonely cowboy, who has successfully attacked adult power structures victimizing children.

A Danish critic once called *Silas og den sorte hoppe* (1967; *Silas and the Black Mare* 1978) a "bull's eye for children," and most readers will probably agree that the novel is children's literature of high quality. In its construction of childhood as instinctual truth it is also a work whose every fibre seems to defy canonical thinking, be it in the shape of adult coercion, as in the first volumes of the *Silas* suite, or, in later volumes, the disciplinary moulding of education by which adults impose a kind of normativity on children, depriving them of their independence and direct access to the world. (Since *Silas and the Black Mare* in a way does not stand alone because its protagonist takes on new aspects in future volumes, or sides that are merely hinted at in the first volume are elaborated on in later ones, I prefer the term "suite" to "series"—a term also indicating the rich intertextuality to Bødker's other works and the novel's exploration of writing for children as a dialogic form in between art and discourse. Moreover, there is a collectivist stance in the *Silas* books, with different volumes focusing on different protagonists and genders.) While being an artistically oriented work, the novel also explores alternative aesthetic approaches to the world, some of which are described as more other-directed and open to the world than others. In the modernist vein, the novel's construction of childhood stresses cultural alterity and a highly oppositional stance to established patterns of thinking, whether they are emerging capitalist (the frequent talk about buying and selling children) or exploitation of children by brute force. In many ways the thinking of child-adult relations along developmental stages, so frequently a cultural master narrative in the twentieth century, is turned upside down. Against adults' negative primitivity, the novel sets up a defence of childhood as a non-traumatized state. *Silas and the Black Mare* is a story about subjectivity: of beginnings, the intensity of childhood, freedom, and its ethical boundaries.

Being initially a lyrical poet, a background that is discernable in the finely chiselled landscape imagery of the novel, Bødker was taken by surprise that the *Silas* universe enabled her to write a saga-like brick of a novel, gradually weaving a multi-perspectival text about growing up in a time when traditions and gender can no longer be inherited, but must be created by the individual, who thereby becomes an artist in his own life. Published in Denmark between 1967 and 2001, the suite now includes 13 volumes, with Silas as the central figure (I hesitate to call him a character, since he rebels against prescribed notions of *bildung*), though later volumes counterbalance the male perspective by including the focalization of girls and women, especially Melissa, Silas's first love, who provides a strong, alternative image for girls into which to read themselves. *Silas and the Black Mare*, however, is primarily a male universe focalizing especially on Silas, its anti-authoritarian hero, in his Rabelaisian encounters with the world and, as the suite develops, his building on Sebastian Mountain of an alternative community of outsiders, including the old, the deaf, the blind, orphans, and even a hermaphrodite.

In terms of critical acclaim, Cecil Bødker is about as big as you can get, in Denmark and in the world. *Silas and the Black Mare* is a "simple" classic in her home country, a work that almost all children know (J. D. Stahl, qtd. in O'Sullivan 2000, 423). Apart from that, it is widely translated, and was turned into a film in Germany in the 1980s. Bødker, very aptly, received the Hans Christian Andersen Medal in 1976, since her novel has been considered a breakthrough for an artistically oriented children's literature in Denmark—a literary tradition going back to Andersen and existing as an undercurrent from Romanticism through the so-called "cultural radicalism" of the 1940s (e.g., Jens Sigsgaard, Egon Mathiesen), and extending beyond Bødker and Ole Lund Kierkegaard to today. Along with Lund Kierkegaard, whose humorous-existentialist novels are reminiscent of Andersen's play with the child perspective to break down the prevailing order, and Ib Spang Olsen's aesthetically fabulous picturebooks, *Silas and the Black Mare* is about as close to being aesthetically canonized as any preceding children's book, excluding those of Andersen, who wrote at a time when the literary system was less bifurcated and readings less segregated (Clark 2003, 48ff.).

Bødker's novel was initially published as the winner of The Danish Academy's first and, to date, only juvenile competition. The jury praised *Silas and the Black Mare* for its literary qualities, almost applying the language of the modernist reading or describing it as a "verbal icon" when commending "the book as a perfect work without aesthetic blemish, written by a poet who plays magically on her instrument" (IBBY 1976, 3). When reading this critical acclaim and its apparently inclusive attitude, I think it is important to contextualize it within the general emphasis on "quality" in the 1960s and '70s. It was a time when the book market and the library system were expanding rapidly,[1] and, in addition, there was a certain cultural animosity or even moral panic triggered by the international "pulp" debate from the mid 1950s. Following the opening of the university to new student groups and the general anti-canon sentiment of 1968, and maybe a change in the function of literature at this time, a more inclusive definition of what might constitute the text of literary studies was introduced. For a time children's literature became a vital field of study at universities in connection with the so-called "ideology critique," and there was a critical focus on the cultural framings of narratives for children. The tension between the jury's description and the contemporary ideology critique indicates the uncertainty of the status of children's literature. Is it an aesthetic or a social/ideological form, or both? How does this question relate to Bødker's novel, we might ask? I think that it is important that writing in a different text form, in many ways the other of Literature, enabled her to develop new ways of addressing the reader, that is, to transcend a type of modernist writer's solipsism that was being culturally transformed by a beginning postmodernist play with genres and seemingly simpler forms of address (Nikolajeva 1996, 115). The breakthrough of *Silas and the Black Mare* meant a cross-fertilization between art and children's literature: this novel was considered a new way of writing for children, but it also changed Bødker's ways of writing for adults. For instance, in *Tænk på Jolande* ("Think about Jolande," 1981), a feminist novel for adults, she builds in elements of paraliterature (pulp fiction romance, comparable to the generic hybridity of *Silas and the Black Mare* and her deconstructions of the adventure novel generally in her children's books). As Beverly Lyon Clark has demonstrated in a recent study, modernism created the segregation between children's literature and Literature, by means of its readings, which single out high and low, serious and popular forms, the very distinctions that postmodernism increasingly questions (Clark 2003).[2]

Cecil Bødker's authorship is impressive in several other senses. A Danish critic once called her mode of telling "dialectical psychology passed on to the youngest audience" (Vinterberg 1982, 225). Her universes strive to keep the world open and unfinished, which is one definition of the function of aesthetics. *Silas and the Black Mare* is a novel that seems to insist on the possibility of a "heterological theory of knowledge" (McGillis 1996, 22). It explores reality and interrogates the status quo. Like critical theory, it alienates clichés and automatic decoding. Slightly derogatory of children's literature as such, Bødker's narration was once described as a "cleansing of children's literature," but this novel does seem to cleanse the senses and make the reader contemplate all the other aspects, underlying or expelled, waiting to be found. Dealing with notions of literary quality is, however, not a simple thing. It involves intricate questions, such as how to describe children's literature as a text and how to envisage the space and agency of the child. Furthermore, given the well-known historic marginalization of children's literature, should it rightly be included in the literary canon—which, however, hardly exists today in terms of a normativity rooted in ideas of *bildung*, since canons have become plural and reflections on quality have been replaced by theoretically informed unravelling of qualities—or would it be better to approach it from a critical-theoretical cultural studies point-of-view? For two angles on the benefits of literary canonization, we may briefly turn to Kümmerling-Meibauer's and McGillis's studies. They share a conviction that it is important to discuss and develop the critical awareness of "quality," and interrogate canons by continually touching the touchstones, but their views of what literature is today seem to differ. And what about children's perspectives? Kümmerling-Meibauer, on the basis of a thorough investigation of the marginalization of children's literature in nineteenth-century Germany, when it was being consecutively defined in the triangle of art, pedagogy, and culture, argues in favour of tentatively setting up descriptive canons of various types and genres of children's literature. McGillis, on the other hand, is keener on qualifying the cultural and institutional readings of children's literature, with theory informing us of "political, cultural, psychoanalytical, and social realities reflected in and impacting on the literature we read" (McGillis 2003, 39). My own position would be that it is important to interrogate institutional readings of children's literature and processes of marginalization, and it may be true that the readings of children's literature and Literature are "merging" in the postmodern paradigm, or even better, cross-fertilizing in new ways of interdisciplinary constructions of text. Theory and cultural studies do not need to validate their readings by a distinction between high and low cultural forms. Cecil Bødker's art for children certainly seems both to transgress the notions of children's literature in Danish in the 1960s and to reflect actively on its shape and function as a text.

CHILDREN'S LITERATURE:
A BYPASS TO THE WORLD?

With its dialogic anticipation of the child reader's response, *Silas and the Black Mare* erupted as a new and playful type of address, in its artistic, yet accessible form, seemingly questioning the bifurcation of readerships. A central idea in Bødker's modernist oeuvre for adults is the perception of there being a "wall to the world" ("Verdensvæg"), which could be taken as her image of writing, as functioning as both a borderline and a kind of encapsulation. Her short story "Det uskabte" ("The uncreated"), from *Øjet* ("The eye," 1961), is a powerful meta-phoric explication of the entropy and encapsulation perceived in mod-ernist discourse to be a crisis in writing: "Everything that existed and everything that once existed was within the globe. . . . Everything that had ever happened, all thoughts conceived and all that had ever stirred emotion. Both that which had been perceived and that which had never hit consciousness. . . . / Death was within the wall to the world" (111).[3] Compared to this image of the writer's solipsism, *Silas and the Black Mare* has been metaphorically described as a "bypass" in her writing. Developing a more dialogic form, she "found a way of opening the closed, almost claustrophobic space [of modernist writing] and the correspondingly hermetic discourse of her earlier books" (Mouritsen 2001, 274). A key to her success as a children's writer is a profound interest in narrative perspective, which is a clear feature both in her early poetry and in *Silas and the Black Mare* (see, for instance, chapters 1–2). In her oeuvre as a whole, which also includes a substantial mod-ernist-cum-realist collection of works for adults, she demonstrates a general interest in seeing from marginalized and other positions, the theorizing of which has been seen as a vital link between children's lit-erature and feminism (Paul 1990; Clark and Higonnet 1999). While being generally interested in gendered perspectives, her focus on reversing cultural notions of center and periphery, for instance, between Africa and Europe, child and adult, "old" societies and modernity, could be seen as a way of coping with notions of cultural change and stability. As a prevalent feature in *Silas and the Black* Mare, her writings often reflect a modern pattern of breaks, beginnings, and confrontations: "She is a modernist addressing pre-modernity; and a pre-modernist addressing modernity with perspectives from an indefinite pre-industrial past or from social outskirts and marginal existences" (Mouritsen 2001, 267).

Silas and the Black Mare was described by one critic as an almost carnivalesque liberation. Her literary development parallels that of Andersen; addressing children made possible another type of voice, more connected to the position of the storyteller, who passes on expe-rience in a dual address dialogue with an audience and herself. It reinvented the possibility of narrative, and transcended what Barthes called the "point zero" of writing into a more popular and subversive form:

> It is as if the Danish Academy competition released a new side of her talent, a hitherto hidden warmth, a burlesque sense of humor, and a sense for grotesque situations, sometimes quite Rabelaisian in character. . . . Her style is brilliant . . . , and her books can be read with equal pleasure by adults and children, and particularly by them together. (IBBY 1976, 3)

Though being more artistically and ethically inclined than overtly political, *Silas and the Black Mare* reflects the principal explosive themes of 1968 and the Youth Rebellion. Shared features are the non-authoritarian stance, the insistence on children's rights, and a focus on the instinctual truths of childhood.[4] Just as the Youth Rebellion coined the slogan "don't trust anybody over 30!" *Silas and the Black Mare* holds a vision of childhood as being, in many ways, more ideal than adulthood, a prevalent way of constructing childhood since Romanticism because it reflects the adult's way of coping with cultural change (a method evident in the profusion of Peter Pan figures around the turn of the nineteenth century). Bødker is especially fascinated by what she calls the "Silas age," around 13, which she reads as a level of personal expansion combined with permeability to the world. From this cardinal point of intersection between egoism and engagement in others, development primarily takes place as existentialism by choice. As a marked feature in *Silas and the Black Mare*, Bødker reflects the general modernist interest in "psychoanalytical myths" of childhood, the existence of which could be interpreted as an attempt to create a modern alternative to the *bildungsroman* (Goodenough 1994, 8). The universe is allegorical, or even mythological. Its "dialectical psychology" is structured as interaction between adults' heavy-handed coercion and children's vigorous revolts. In the composition of the novel, this feature can be seen in the interchange between adult- and child-initiated violence. In all the "even" chapters, Silas initiates violence, whereas in the others it comes about as the result of adults' provocation. The action is laid in a nowhere land undergoing the process of beginning capitalism (marked by the frequent buying and selling of children and horses, actions that most signify for adults exchange value, in contrast to Silas's insistence on the use value of things). It is a rural and weather-beaten society, and the clashes between children and adults are played out in a genre that we might tentatively define as fantastic realism. Additionally, the form is highly dramatic, dialogue-based, and episodic. Resonant of high literary forms such as epics and myth, it also incorporates elements of popular forms, such as fairy tale, adventure story, trickster tale (Nikolajeva 1996, 115). A very important experiential feature is the dramatic unfolding of situations, a feature captured very succinctly by Preben Ramløv, a contemporary Danish critic:

> The stories move rapidly, the plot is of uppermost importance, descriptions are exact and always serve to carry the action forward, and the reflections are so marvellous and earth-bound that children recognize themselves in them. . . . Presto, a situation develops so that the reader bubbles with satisfaction and hurries on, eager to learn what she can make out of *that* (author's emphasis). (IBBY 1976, 12)

The clashes between children's and adults' worlds, such a ubiquitous feature in *Silas and the Black Mare*, are also seen in her writing for younger children, such as *Timmerlis* ("Timandlis" 1969), in which the clash is staged in a humorous form. A more serious play of opposite perspectives is articulated in her ethnic novels, *Leoparden* (1970; *The Leopard*, 1975) and *Dimma Gole* (1971), describing childhood and its circumstances in Ethiopia. Based on several months of field study in a rural village in Ethiopia, *The Leopard* was written at the invitation of a Danish businessman who—not quite in touch with contemporary comparative studies of the instutionalization of children's literature—thought that this project might help to develop a national children's literature in Ethiopia. It was published in Nairobi in 1970, and it is, along with other dimensions, an intense, action-packed story about Tibeso, a boy captured by bandits. As an Ethiopian critic noted, the novel's ethnic other is not trapped as a European projection. The focalization of Tibeso does not tacitly teach the reader to internalize Western values, and the novel avoids subscribing to the logic of the typical adventure story, in which, according to Margery Hourihan, there is a tendency to define "non-white, non-European people as inferior, marginalize women and exploit the natural environment" (back cover). In the Ethiopian critic's opinion:

> It depicts graphically and, except for a few minor details, authentically, life in a small rural Ethiopian village. . . . The book offers a lot of relevant social commentary along the way. Among other things, Bødker succinctly describes the predominant economic and social role women play.

Likewise, the male chauvinism prevalent in the rural society is tersely depicted. . . . The author is to be commended for having captured so well the texture in that area. (Taye Brooks Zerihoun, qtd. in IBBY 1976, 7)

The depiction of male chauvinism in *The Leopard* is, in fact, quite parallel to Bødker's feminist novels for adults that record the same sort of chauvinism in Danish suburbs. This novel also parallels *Silas and the Black Mare* in the focus on strong suspense, a sharp portrayal of childhood as an exposed state, and the recording of images of how the child figure becomes courageous enough to "bounce back," for Tibeso is transposed from being in an almost hypnotic state of passivity into having an urge to create self-affirmative action and social justice.

Turning the perspective around once again—from the "old" world to modernity—*Dimma Gole* was written to show Danish children "the difference between patterns of thinking between two cultures clashing . . ." (Gormsen 1976, 11). It is a collection of short stories about an Ethiopian boy and his first encounter with Europeans and their world of mobility, welfare, education, and abundance. Dimma is portrayed as a many-faceted personality, his circumstances being outlined sharply and counterbalanced by the Danish tourists visiting his village.

As a reflection of her feminist orientation, in the 1970s Bødker set out on a lengthy journey reframing the Western master narratives from a female perspective. Reversing the gender perspectives in Genesis and the New Testament, she retold, for instance, the story of Moses from the point of view of Miriam, his fictitious eleven-year-old sister (*Barnet i sivkurven*, "The Child in the Rush Basket," 1975) and, subsequently, the story of Jesus, focalizing Mary (*Marias barn. Drengen*, "Mary's child. The boy," 1983 and *Marias barn. Manden*, "Mary's child. The man," 1984). Bødker is the author of several other children's novels, such as *Hungerbarnet* ("The hunger child," 1990), another study of social marginality, outsiders, and class structures in rural communities. As in *Silas and the Black Mare*, time and space are mythical coordinates, though a Danish reader would locate them to the meagre Mid-Jutland farmlands around 1800.

There are many orphans in Bødker's oeuvre; Tinke, the eight-year-old "hunger child," has become orphaned because of societal negligence. She is the daughter of two rebels, the farmer's daughter and the red-haired farmhand, who fell in love forgetting about class structures, which relegated them to a harsh life on the fringes of society. Reminiscent of the Scandinavian folk ballads, in which this type of love is also demonized, the novel portrays Tinke's mother as lying dead in a hut without even being given a proper burial. Although the environment appears to be quite tough, the novel is ultimately optimistic. Just as the victimized children in *Silas and the Black Mare* make friends, Tinke bonds with Larus, the eleven-year-old very dynamic shepherd, and she finds a new home on a farm, where they have no daughters of their own.

Whereas not "targeting" children from the point of view that they can understand only a small fraction of the complexity of the world, Bødker does depict writing for children and adults as two parallel authorships, connected, yet distinctly different. She seems to adhere to the conviction of Knud Erik Løgstrup, a contemporary Danish philosopher, that in a children's book there should always be "light at the end of the tunnel," hope being a basic manifestation of life. This assumption, however, does not result in a tunnel vision, since it is transformed into open endings and an invitation to the reader to think: "A children's book does not have to end happily, but I have not yet had the courage to let my books end unhappily. However, one can let problems remain unresolved so that the reader is forced to draw his or her own conclusions" (Jakobsen 2001, 28 ff., my trans.).

Among the best of her works is *Ægget der voksede* ("The egg that grew," 1987), a historic novel set in the period of the abolition of adscription (1789). In lucid and dramatic prose social conditions, the texture of daily life, solidarity, and conflicts between social groups are interwoven. Portraying a universe comparable to that of *Silas and the Black Mare*, it is a story about breaking from old bonds and building a new unprecedented community.

BREAKING DOWN THE WALLS TO THE WORLD: SILAS AS A MODERNIST CONSTRUCTION OF CHILDHOOD

Silas and the Black Mare explores childhood as potentially different from the adult-sanctioned world. A focus on childhood as a time of semiotic play is discernable already in *Luseblomster* ("Flowers of lice," 1955). In this first collection of poems, traditional images of nature and childhood are evoked, but also deconstructed and rebuilt to enter a new modernist unity of vision, reminiscent of Baudelaire's analytical rediscovery of childhood, as "a childhood now possessing, in order to express itself, adult organs and an analytical mind" (Lloyd 1991, 25). Apart from its symbolism, there is a naïve interest in perspectives and positions outside culture, be they cosmological, connected to childhood, or associated with non-cultivated plants, such as dandelions and other weeds. The marginal is seen to possess its own vitality, and there is a general return to childhood and nature as subjectivity returned to at will. The poems' stance of being mythical explorations of human nature parallels the interest in childhood as beginning in *Silas and the Black Mare*. The inaugural poem, titled "Sand," depicts a modernist tension between the proliferation of romantically colored images of childhood as a lost Edenic space and a focus on its reshaping in writing as a condition to which we can return at will. Structured around the color-specter of sand, the first four stanzas present snapshot images of childhood experiences filled with intensity and instinctual appetite: "White sand/ sea and sun/ high wind/ and the hoarse noise of sea birds/ naked brown children/ with sand in sun-bleached hair/ white sand" (7). The fifth and last stanza, however, breaks the production of idyllic images by pointing out the writer's immersion in the process. Just as the children take on colors from the different shades of the sand, the writer is recreating childhood in a parallel artistic exchange, while replacing the Romantic icon of poetry as a blue flower with an image of blue sand: "A goose feather/ and a horn with ink/ written words with sand on them/ blue ink on white paper/ or words written in sand/ writer's sand with ink/ blue sand" (8).

The figure of Silas, in particular, embodies modernist views of childhood. His entry in the novel is endowed with great expectations. Like Moses, he is transported by water, signifying perhaps his potential to integrate opposing principles (water, in a Freudian reading, being a feminine element) and, in its perpetual motion, the capacity to navigate in the light of crisis and change. In the words of Aaron, the otter hunter, in *Silas og flodrøverne* ("Silas and the River Robbers," 1998): "he is just more elastic than other people, there's space in him to think thoughts and do things that other people would not think of doing" (170). Although his introduction is certainly culturally inscribed in its allusion to myth, we also get the impression that Silas is self-possessed and free:

> He came sailing down the river in an odd little broad-nosed boat, not sitting upright like other people and not using the oars, just letting the

current carry him where it wished. He lay in the bottom with, apparently, all the time in the world, for the boat travelled at the river's speed and from a distance looked as if it were empty. (1)

Though "a strange boy in an ownerless boat," he is far from what Ursula Sampath has described as a Kasper Hauser figure, a pure and naïve child of nature on which adults can inscribe their own visions in the Romantic sense (Sampath 1991). His extraordinariness is emphasized as his being very much his own: he is not "other people," but "just myself" (8), and at this point, he is driven by the down-to-earth natural instinct of hunger. In the focalization of Bartolin, the horse-dealer against whom Silas has his first confrontation and wins the central object of the black mare, the novel depicts the adult's gaping surprise at encountering such an anti-authoritarian child. He is "strange and careless" (4) and makes sounds with his flute that "no human being could have made" (3). It is as if Silas is still in the element of water—as with a boat, there is a gliding slowness in the introductory scene before the violent action breaks out.

Bødker frequently contrasts male and female chronotopes (cf. Niko-lajeva 1996, 125f), a traditionally conceived masculine principle of expansion and action that is very prevalent throughout the novel, and a feminine principle of "slowness," signifying beginning and another kind of creation. Arriving in his anti-authoritarian, broad-nosed boat, Silas from the outset contains both orientations. Bartolin, for instance, sees him as "a beanstalk with hair like a girl's" (5), introducing a theme of gender and androgyny played out in the suite as a whole, that is, in the demonized figure of Goat (literally the Horse Crow) whom the reader first meets in *Silas og Ben-Godik* (1968, Engl. *Silas and Ben-Godik*, 1978), in the discussions of gender roles in later volumes, and in dialogues throughout the series. For instance, in *Silas møder Matti* ("Silas meets Matti," 1979) Maria and Ben-Godik have become a couple, and she is afraid that their child will become a hermaphrodite. Perhaps it is also evident in the 13-volume work as a whole, in the tension between action-based confrontation and "slow" descriptions of daily life on Sebastian Mountain. In *Silas and the Black Mare* there is a parallel interaction between a track of violent action and the dwelling on words, situations, and landscape, as in the rendering of calmness after the first violent confrontation with Bartolin:

Silence fell like a box on the ears after the almost deafening noise, but Silas played sweetly and carefully like the voice of friendliness itself. And

Bartolin, that furious, furious man down on the floor of the stable, slowly went to pieces. His wrathful expression collapsed; his shoulders sagged; his mouth fell open. As the horses grew peaceful, Silas played just for him. (29)

Though a handful of adults, notably Anina, Silas's mother, Aaron, and Joanna, are described as positive figures, childhood as alterity and discontinuity to adulthood are stressed. There can be no ideal continuity between a child and an adult brute like Bartolin, whose personality is reduced to exploitation and the bullying of those weaker than himself. Silas is surrounded by children who take on different positions in the novel's discussion of freedom versus victimization. Himself an image of unconstrained freedom and rebellion, the eyeless Maria is a sign of adult traumatization of childhood. Ben-Godik, the shepherd, whose name is literally "Leg-Godik," since he has a limp, takes up a middle position in his successful establishing of a hidden space of freedom that adults do not know about. When learning that Ben-Godik has secretly been apprenticed as a wood carver—wood is another significant element, that is, Silas's flute is made of wood, and the fisherman's "aggressive little beast" of a horse pursues and destroys everything made of wood (148)—Silas ponders:

> "So you are apprenticed to him after all," said Silas, pleased, and at the same time thinking that this was Ben-Godik's way of getting around what the adults had decided for him. He hadn't simply run away from everything like Silas. Ben-Godik had done what he was told and then he did what he wanted on the side—in secret. Silas thought about the difference between them. (89–90)

Silas's immediate, almost allergic reaction to coercion and the portrayal of violence have struck some critics as provocative. Adults' violence is, for instance, made up by their brutality (Bartolin's attempt to fork Silas) and their lack of confidence in children (for example, Emmanuel, the peasant, who finds it totally unbelievable that the horse could belong to a boy). They cheat and deceive those younger than themselves and break their promises, as when Bartolin refuses to give Silas the horse after the wager:

> "The horse is mine," said Silas seriously. We made a wager."
> "I'll be damned if we did," said Bartolin in a loud voice." (25)

Adults' way of administering power constructs children as objects, and there is no humanism counterbalancing this process. Silas reacts by turning the adults' language against them, and he thereby establishes a space of agency for himself and avoids becoming their cipher. In fact, the first chapter, with its dialogic play interchangeably focalizing Bartolin's interpretations of Silas—from the adult's view one close to a Kasper Hauser precept—and Silas exploding of this interpretation is a drama of the child "writing back." The novel certainly does not teach children to take traditions for granted. As one German critic, Suse Liebehart, wrote: "The book's merit lies, above all, in that it allows the reader to apprehend injustice, an injustice which can be untenable as opposed to customary and prevalent, categorical moral conceptions" (IBBY 1976, 4).

The conflation of childhood with intensity is yet another modernist feature in the novel. In her study of the emphasis on childhood in French Symbolism, Rosemary Lloyd has argued that "modernism and the awareness of the intensity of childhood experience and insight are intimately connected" (Lloyd 1998, 53). Again we may hint at the rich intertextuality between Bødker's writings for children and adults, indicating an artistic traffic between these forms that should not be ignored in spite of the modernist segregation of audiences. For instance, the poem "Strawberries" from *Luseblomster* initially evokes images of the texture of childhood, and next renders it as a state of bodily intensity: "Girls with greasy hands/ and sticky hair/ and with strawberries on a straw/ in a ditch.// Strawberries, yes/ to hiccup from tension/ and scurry in hiding/ with an angry man's threats in the neck" (20). In other poems and stories, childhood calls forth the otherness or even anarchy of the marginal, as in the title poem "Luseblomster" ("Flowers of Lice"), in which a girl tells "circular lies" shaped like the "flowers of lice" from a laughing position among dandelions and wild plants. In *Silas and the Black Mare* psychological intensity is a pronounced narrative feature, connected to the focalization of children, as in the scene when Silas first sees Maria's empty eye hollows, eye contact signifying in the novel often human relations or the ability to relate. Seeing her dead eyes creates an impression of unfathomable horror:

> It was too strange and ugly; she had no eyes at all. Only holes. He had never seen a face like that before. It was as if his own eyes began to grow at the thought. They felt much too big and much too hot to be in his head. They had never felt like that before and he had to hold his hands in front of them so they wouldn't fall out or burst. (48)

Strong intensity and shock is sometimes recorded in a language close
to symbolism, as, for example, in its employment of paradox and its
fusion of physical and mental states: "At the narrow kitchen table in
front of the window stood Maria with her back to them, pretending to
peel potatoes. She did not move, but Silas couldn't help noticing how
a thousand eyes grew out of her back. He felt outstared by her blind-
ness" (50). Silas's portrayal as an outsider of necessity and nature
points out several links between childhood and art. In being both a
chosen and a liminal figure, Silas is reminiscent of Bødker's short story
"Ishmael" in *Øjet*, in which she takes up the story of the expelled son
of Abraham and Hagar, the Egyptian slave woman, as a myth of the
modern artist (Genesis 16:15). Ishmael is a visionary figure able to take
in the world and create novelty out of nothing. Contrary to others, he
is able to leave an imprint on the world and make it new: "He came to
them with the improbable stairs of indignation in his mind and the
black rivers of power in his gaze and forced them to remember who he
was" (93).

Silas as a figure seems to share the modernist focus on childhood
as both an individualized state and a capacity to "retain a passionate
relationship with external and internal forces" (Goodenough 1994, 1).
His liminal function is related both to his ability to invert or reorganize
traditional values and to his capacity to strike a balance between personality and other-directedness, as symbolized by the magical flute. Its
"strange," expressive music of nature is an interface between subjectivity and the external world. Sometimes he uses it to distract himself
from circumstances, such as hunger (12) and the appalling sight of
Maria's empty eyes: "Without opening his eyes, he fumbled under his
shirt for his flute and began to play it. He blew all the wildest and most
violent sounds he knew away from him like a howling storm, playing
and playing without thinking where he was . . ." (48).

Playing out his feelings so that they become manageable indicates
that his emotional side is hidden by his overt rebelliousness and apparently quite amoral egoism. The flute also connects Silas to nature: he is
able to calm down horses and move animals and humans because he
listens to nature and expresses it in music. As a material object, the flute
even saves him from being stabbed by Maria. Playing the flute is
described as a nature-bound music or a kind of creativity that could be
either turned into art or channelled more directly into practical life. In
Silas fanger et firspand (1972; Engl. *Silas and the Runaway Coach*,
1978), Silas is introduced to the bourgeois culture of trade, education,

and art. This novel also contains one of the strongest depictions of his virtuosity on the flute. Playing for Karmeol, an immigrant worker, he conjures up visions of his childhood, in a place that might be Venice:

> Silas played softly and dreamingly, he had never seen a city with water in the streets, but he was quietly building it in his inner vision, all that he knew about water and houses and sailing boats and the sun he called forth, and the strong farmhand felt how his heart melted, an almost forgotten childhood in a remote country came back to him, and he also saw how small waves were licking sun-warmed walls. Once there had been a city where people sailed to the doors in the same way as others would drive and pull up their horses. (44)

Being quite a pragmatic and materialist hero, Silas prefers to channel his music into life, as a kind of imagination. In the same novel there is a description of how he senses a certain familiarity with Art, but yet acknowledges that his own playing is different. Listening to a concert in church, he is almost "paralyzed" by its beauty, an effect quite opposite to the workings of the flute:

> And all the while the sound was unfolding in space and becoming music, a greater and more embracing music than Silas had ever heard, he sank paralyzed down on the bench again. There were flutes. . . . The sound came out of all corners and he could hear the migratory birds and the roaring forests and the waves washing from remote skies. (66)

Playing the flute sometimes functions as a way of widening perceptions of the world, as when Silas plays for the peasant family in *Silas and Ben-Godik*:

> They were not used to listening to music, and certainly not to the kind of music Silas pulled out of his instrument, and they stood like glued to the houses, with eyes and mouth wide open they were absorbing it, completely still—as if they expected the flute player to stop if they moved. For them this was the very sound of great happenings of life and connected to festivals and celebration. And yet they were standing here in their own farmyard on a quite ordinary day wearing work clothes and listening. (16)

The sense of his own music being parallel, yet different, to Art is similar to his attitude to institutionalized education in the same volume. Boiling down the use value of middle-class education to literacy, Silas compares himself to Japetus, the merchant's son, and reflects on the difference between independence and socialization: "In a glimpse he understood why Japetus could not do anything on his own, why he could not just go down in the stable, take a horse and ride away. He was not his own, he belonged to his family and was stuck to it as the tip of a finger is stuck to its hand. It was a kind of prison." (54)

When Planke, the merchant who takes Silas in, offers him a formal education so that he can "become someone," he answers that he prefers to be himself, and in *Silas stifter familie* ("Silas Starts a Family," 1976) he chooses to "adopt" an orphan as his little brother, again siding with the ultimate outsider and new beginnings instead of education: "I would rather keep my little brother—and my freedom of movement and independence—I don't need education at the expense of him" (223). In modernism, Romantic views of childhood tended to be replaced by "psychoanalytical myths," literary evocations of childhood retaining, however, a space for childhood as a semiotics containing both subjectivity and culture. In Goodenough's words, "many texts written from a child's viewpoint are brilliantly creative, subversive, or compensatory precisely because children speak from a realm as yet unappropriated, or only partly appropriated, by social or cultural institutionality" (Goodenough 1994, 8; 14). The Silas figure is a good example of this interpretative interface between the literature of childhood and the civilizing process. Furthermore, the novel presents many possible readings, and how we read depends on how our definitions shape the text of children's literature.

CANONICITY AND *SILAS* AND *THE BLACK MARE*

Cecil Bødker's language is a parallel to Silas's flute as a method of play that keeps the world open in an aesthetic form that might be termed "heteronomous."[5] When transposed to the realm of writing, her literary style seems to be insisting that writing for children certainly is an aesthetic form, yet different from the music in the church, in being perhaps more other-directed and related to the interstices between self and other, writing and object. It is difficult not to see Bødker's frequent poetic animation of nature, or even houses, as a parallel to Silas's flute: "The river murmured under the boat and darkness began little by little to creep out of the bushes and the hollow places on the riverbank"

(31), and "Oh God!" keened the women, wringing their hands or trying to cram the children back into the houses, but it was as if the houses
just spewed everything right back out again" (97–98). Her language is
expressive and activating, both analytic and symbolic: "Silas turned his
head just enough to see how their bodies looked like hardening crusts
around their souls" (147) or "More and more heads appeared; his
impression was that all the houses were full to bursting with adults and
children, mostly children. They bumbled out the doors like so many
shaggy balls with eyes . . ." (36).

When analyzing *Silas and the Black Mare* from the viewpoint of the
modernist reading developed by literary studies, one might, for
instance, comment on its mythological complexity and its allusion to
the heritage of Western tradition, that is, its evocation of Moses, Ishmael, Don Quixote and Sancho Panza, Clod-Hans or Pan (for a pastiche of such a "canonically" oriented reading, see McGillis 2003). We
might apply the criteria crystallized in the modernist reading, stressing
its unique autonomy and subtly discriminating it from more ordinary
works. With regard to children's literature, we might perhaps look at
features such as innovation and aesthetic use of language. Is the work
representative of a tradition? Does it relate to children's worlds? Is
there a dialectics between simplicity and complexity? Does it have an
imaginative stance, and is it a work marked by polyvalence, cross-writ-
ing, and intertextuality (Kümmerling-Meibauer 2003, 192 ff.)? It is certainly possible to analyze the novel using criteria inherited and adapted
from the literary institution, but is that way also a good way of describing the qualities of children's literature? After poststructuralism, it is
an extremely complicated task to speak of "imagination" and "relating
to children's worlds." Moreover, there is a danger of transferring the
norms of aesthetic autonomy that have been theoretically abandoned
in literary studies. We would certainly have to reflect on how readings
shape texts.

The reception of Bødker's novel quite unanimously praised its "aesthetic" qualities (IBBY 1976). Several critics commented on its anti-
traditionalism, originality, and novelty of vision, and an Italian critic
stressed its almost Nietzschean attitude:

> The boy Silas is an anti-hero, seen in relation to a certain traditional
> model: instinctive and amoral, gruesome but without hate or cruelty, he
> seems to be a product of a world without social or civil law, where the
> boy's guileless natural instincts are his only guides. Everything else is

secondary.... The most original aspect is the almost heathen atmosphere, which combines fantasy with the most strict realism. Moralizing has been carefully avoided. For example, not a word is used to comment on the fact that a father treats his deformed daughter cruelly. The story takes place in an area where invention dictates its own moral, beyond good and evil. (IBBY 1976, 3)

Seen from the perspective of an adult educated in literary readings, the review captures some of the book's qualities very succinctly, but it also demonstrates some of the problems connected with evaluating the qualities of children's literature. For example, the criterion of innovation is a norm that has been inherited from the literary institution of the nineteenth and twentieth centuries and may be less important in postmodern literature that has abandoned the idea of autonomy or in so-called paraliterature, elements of which also are evident in *Silas and the Black Mare* (Nikolajeva 1996, 115). Moreover, the modernist reading was developed to signify difference. In Beverly Lyon Clark's words, for instance, "New Critical strategies for criticizing a work of literature, strategies that privilege complexity, make it difficult to find anything to say about seemingly 'simple' works" (Clark 2003, 14). This type of reading tends to emphasize text at the cost of its contexts, and it probably would not be able to account for the positive reception and afterlife of *Silas and the Black Mare* as a classic in Denmark. To explore this issue, we would probably have to look into how Silas relates to prevailing pedagogic and cultural constructions of childhood, using works such as A.S. Neill's theory of the child's natural growth or Herbert Marcuse's ideas on subjectivity and aesthetics. Finally, the review does not avoid the modernist belittlement of children's literature by seeing it as a stepping-stone to adult literature, while stressing its difference from most other productions. Clark, for instance, sees a prevalent cultural reification of developmental stage theories, here perhaps spreading its discourse to literary systems.

In Rod McGillis's interpretation, the nature of children's literature works against canonization, in its "overt connection with pedagogical theories and practices," which are not in the need of an aesthetic canon. Secondly, its readership is "unruly," consisting of a dual audience of adult "filters" and children, whose criteria of quality differ, and, finally, the theoretical development in literary studies is replacing ideas of autonomy and canonicity with multi-disciplinary readings (McGillis 2003, 36f); Clark, as previously mentioned, sees a legacy in this respect from feminism. This again refers us to children's literature as a text, whose construction, like all texts, is shaped by readings.

SILAS AND HIS INTERFACES: MYTH AND IMAGES OF PSYCHOLOGY

Silas is a fascinating hero because he plays out beginnings, yet questions received stories of origins and patterns of socialization, all expressed in a seemingly simple form. In Bødker's concept of "walls" to the world, we might see a theme of consciousness becoming too cerebral or specialized, against which she creates the openness of *Silas and the Black Mare*. Reading D. H. Lawrence's modernist experiments with the child perspective as a "visionary blur," Carol Sklenicka and Mark Spilka describe this perception as "the vexed modern issue of hyperconscious awareness" (1994, 165–66). Like the high modernists, Bødker's interest in the child perspective is an artistic, non-disciplinary answer to the challenges of modernity, in which, from the mid to late nineteenth century, there was a clear tendency in art to "above all see the child as a symbol of freedom: freedom from traditional realist writing, from instruction and improvement and from a hypocritic . . . culture" (Boëthius 1998, 6). Bødker's language of freedom was laid out in the form of epic and myth, in which the basic wonders of beginnings can be explored. Flemming Mouritsen, the Danish critic, has described the narrative transition initiated with *Silas and the Black Mare* as a dialogic extroversion:

> Mental spaces . . . have been reformulated to an open landscape, which the eye [i.e., the narrator] is both a part of, can observe and see beyond. This feature illustrates very well the transition from the depiction of encapsulated mental states in her modernist prose, to the space of the *Silas* novels, in which the same thematic field has been transposed to a fictive landscape, to characters and open sequences of action, which are exploratory journeys in landscape. (Mouritsen 2001, 272)

The use of myth is a marked feature in modernism, and in Bødker's oeuvre it has been an element from the beginning, for instance, in *Anadyomene* (1960)—an approach that is nowhere more brilliantly demonstrated than in *Silas and the Black Mare*.

The extroversion of mental scenes in myth allows her to stage and discuss psychology and Silas's interfaces to the world. In the modernist psychoanalysis of Freud, Jung, and Rank, there was a parallel focus on myth, also incorporating the irrational or Dionysian side, which has been frequently commented on in connection with Silas's seemingly amoral behavior. Action, subjectivity, and landscape could be read as an extroversion of mental states. In Otto Rank's interpretation, the hero of the myth is often "a child of noble birth, whose relationships with its family are severed, and who is surrendered to the water and lifted from it (which is a symbolic representation of birth). As in childhood fantasies, the hero endeavors to replace the parents with more distinguished ones" (Tséelon 1995, 1019). As in a myth of psychological creation, Silas is severed from parental figures, notably his mother, Anina, who is a tightrope walker, and Philip, his stepfather and employer at the circus from which he runs away, since Philip wants him to swallow swords instead of work with the horses. As a reflection of the modernity of this myth, however, Silas severs himself from parental bonds and he does not set out on a journey to find worthier parental figures. Anina, in fact, is one of only a handful of positive images of adulthood, and as an ethical counter-point to the expression and extroversion of personality, Silas very soon begins to "parent" the world himself. On Sebastian Mountain he even integrates Goat, the ultimate figure of demonization and marginalization, inasmuch as her monstrosity is shown to stem from a victimization comparable to that of Maria. As in Otto Rank's description of the mythic hero, Silas's personality seems to precede the social level; notice, for instance, the focus on the amoral and irrational side in his cruelty to Maria. His individualism is initially more related to an energetic stance than to having a well-defined ego, the progressive growth of which can be traced in developmental stages. This focus on childhood energies as an interface between subjectivity and the world enables the narrator to express a non-sentimental and non-adult-centered view of childhood, a view in which childhood is valuable in its own right. In fact, many critics have found the energetic intensity of *Silas and the Black Mare* more groundbreaking than the later images of socialization by choice on Sebastian Mountain.[6] Here Bødker seems to be playing out the theme of beginnings without subscribing to developmental ideas of adult rationality as a cohered state and thereby implying the belittlement of childhood.

Focusing on cultural images of "littleness" and historicity that developed in the nineteenth and twentieth centuries, Carolyn Steedman has analysed the burgeoning field of artistic and scientific discourses of childhood (Steedman 1990). Human interiority was thematized in intersections of art, science, and psychology, and the understanding of "interiority" along developmental lines was finally framed and perhaps epitomized by classic psychoanalysis. Compared to disciplinary thinking, literary evocations of childhood sometimes hold other, more playful visions. Bødker, for instance, alludes to various inflections of psychoanalytical myths, yet she refrains from synthesizing these to "child knowledge." In Denmark, Freudian thinking was introduced in the interwar period, and Bødker makes frequent references to the Oedipal myth, e.g., in the limping Ben-Godik and the eyeless Maria. The portrayal of Silas as an "anti-Oedipal" hero is a pointer that literature and critical theory share the function of interrogating stable knowledge and can frequently arrive at similar readings. It has been considered unrealistic that a 13-year-old boy should be as independent of his mother as Silas seems to be. Whereas the numerous battles with male figures could be seen as Oedipally patterned (the black mare being the desired object), the mother seems utterly absent. However, the feminine principle of water, i.e. the river, and, indeed, the mare, are always there as elements to which he keeps returning. Does Silas, taking an anti-Oedipal stance, avoid castration? He seems to run away from it, which is why he confronts the androgynous figure of Goat so violently throughout the series. Although Silas is out of parental touch, he is not out of its range. When he sees Goat forcing the child Jef to slave for her in *Silas and Ben-Godik*, Silas does not protest, though he ran away from the same type of coercion himself when his stepfather tried to force him to follow in his footsteps (his mother implicitly consenting).

One of the multiple significations of Goat is as a focal point of the Oedipal scene, as an image of civilization going wrong. Combating "her" force in the recurring clashes throughout the series, castration is never fulfilled, and the victimization of children and the procreation of sameness avoided. On Sebastian Mountain, Goat is even integrated into the community for a period, but she keeps breaking out, which, in the economy of the novel, provides us with a perpetual villain to be combated. The initial introduction of Goat is in *Silas and Ben-Godik*, in which she observes Silas with the black mare:

> She was a tall, bony woman stretching out to see beyond the others, while clutching a little boy. Her bony, yellow fingers had closed in a firm grip around his upper arm and it was obvious that it hurt.—Bitch, thought Ben-Godik, staring savagely at her, and the more he stared, the more

strange she appeared to him. On her head she had a big broad-rimmed men's hat with a lot of gray wisps of hair sticking out under the brim. This hair certainly had not been combed either today or yesterday. Her long meagre face might as well have sat on a man, Ben-Godik thought, and her heavy floppy skirts reached the tip of a pair of worn-out soldier's boots, whereas on the upper part of her body she wore something that most of all looked like a coachman's cape. A peculiar appearance. (9–10)

The multiple symbol of horses also participates in the discourse of subjectivity and its interfaces. The black mare is certainly the most desired and ideal object in the novel, generating the plot to evolve around its loss and retrieval. In *Fortællinger om Tavs* ("Stories about Tavs," 1971), intertextually close to *Silas and the Black Mare* in its description of the artist, but written for adults, the image of the female centaur describes the interface between art and the libidinal—which in the children's novel is transposed to the theme of personal freedom versus social adjustment to the reality principle. Horses function as interfaces to the world, as psychological extroversions, that is, the black mare is very different from the horse in Maria's family, which is an "incomprehensible little beast" (148). The figure of Goat (the Horse Crow) is, of course, the ultimately liminal figure. Sometimes animals are used to ward off violence, almost as the flute is used in combat from time to time. The human-animal relation being a frequent motif in modernist art, horses in Bødker's oeuvre for children and adults can, for instance, signify fear to be overcome, or they figure as extroversions of mental states, as in the poem called "Fygende heste" ("Drifting Horses," 1956): "Deep down horses drifted/ like a heart throbbing/ a blush/ gone astray over the flank of the rock" (55).

CAN THERE BE MODERNISM FOR CHILDREN?

A few years ago Hans Hauge, a Danish literary critic, set out to demonstrate what he called the "literary turn" in critical theory by applying a modernist, in this case deconstructionist, reading to a "Pixi" book, a commercial series of pocket-size books for the youngest readers that, until this reading, had gone quite unheeded by the literary institution. His point was to clarify, in a humorous form, what he saw as a certain independence of "theory" from its object. It could even be used on this type of book. This reading, arguably, did not meet its objective very well, since it did not reflect on what kind of text it was dealing with and how its reading was, at the same time, constructing its object along lines that are finally political. Today readings of children's literature and literary studies seem to be merging in a critical study of signifying practices, while there is a constant focus on interrogating readings and how they shape their "object." How to define text in relation to context seems to be the challenge of Childhood Studies, and lines between children's literature and "general" literature are being investigated and perhaps redrawn (see Dusinberre 1987; Lloyd 1998; Natov 2003). While the institutional segregation of readings was the cultural work of modernism, Cecil Bødker and countless other artistically oriented writers kept experimenting with discourse and frequently saw children's literature as a way of transgressing systems. Bødker's play with psychoanalytical myths is one example, but we might equally point out her generational reframings of genre. Blending genres could be an expression of the modernist interartistic stance of "making it new." In Lena Kåreland's words about Lennart Hellsing, the Swedish writer for children and adults, "such a form of interartistic aesthetics was . . . characteristic of modernism, where the crossing of borders of different kinds contributed to artistic renewal" (Kåreland 1999, 321). Change, crisis, the dissolution of traditions, and the melting of all that is solid into air are elements in Bødker's "bypass." Her return to the epic mode could be seen as a new return to the possibility of generating and telling experience, in Walter Benjamin's sense of storytelling. Using the epic form connected to oral tradition is, of course, not a simple thing to do in the midst of modern booklore, but telling to children could be seen to radicalize the cultural conditions of narration as such. In Bødker's case, the feature of "return" can be exemplified by her integration of the past when coloring her language with Jutlandish dialect and old-fashioned expressions in the *Silas* books.

Silas and the Black Mare is also generically related to the picaresque novel in its episodic and confrontational structure. It would be worth examing more in depth how its play between the carnivalesque and official culture, and the dialogical versus monological principle could be related to the institutional constraints on authorship. Bødker's "bypass" could be an opening to understanding children's literature as a parallel except for the structural other of her modernist literary language, along the Bakhtinian concept of "heteroglossia." Children's literature became a distinct form of writing concurrently with the development of the novel. In Guillory's interpretation, "the literary language and its other, what Bakhtin called *heteroglossia*, are defined relationally and contextually at the moment of their contact," i.e., children's literature and "general" literature are systemic positions "along a hierarchy of socially marked forms of speech" (Guillory 1994, 66; author's emphasis). In the light of the twentieth-century segregation of readings that followed the previously established idea of art as autonomous, according to Bakhtin, the novel as a genre is itself, interestingly, a "noncanonical" genre welcoming the heteroglossic (Guillory 1994, 67). In terms of the development of the focalization of the child, children's literature is, to a high degree, historically related to the novel. In the 1960s modernism had reached its "point zero" and writing for children helped Bødker to create a new type of aesthetic, blending genres and "high" and "low" forms while negotiating a less solipsist view of language. In conclusion, this indicates that children's literature is not necessarily an anti-modernist form. Spending about the same amount of time writing a children's novel as any other substantial work, Bødker, through her mode of telling and her positioning of the reader as critic, made *Silas and the Black Mare* a contemporary literary work, and she showed an open and critical attitude to modernity by not shielding children from the time in which they live.

NOTES

1. Bettina Kümmerling-Meibauer (2003) points out many such links between discussions of quality and the expansion of the book market in a nineteenth-century German context.

2. Analyzing American material, mainly the reception of children's literature, Clark outlines a movement from the nineteenth century when "children and childhood were less segregated from adults and adulthood . . . , before the split between high culture and low . . ." (Clark 2003, 16)—to a modernist differentiation of readings and audiences. In an American context, this timing could be confirmed by Anne Lundin's (2001) demonstration of a certain fin de siècle ambivalence in the reception of children's literature. Pierre Bourdieu's analysis (1996) of the institution of literature as art and the hierarchization of genres in the nineteenth century sheds further light on this process.

3. All translations in this essay from texts originally published in Danish are mine unless otherwise indicated.

4. Carol Sklenicka and Mark Spilka (1994) analyze this prevalent modernist emphasis on intensity, nature, and the child's vision.

5. Stefan Neuhaus has argued for a more inclusive view of aesthetics, distinguishing between the theorizing of form as autonomous, as in the tradition from Kant, and more "heteronomous" types, i.e., directly addressing an audience or having an ethical relationship to its audience (see also Bourdieu 1996). Children's literature could be seen as an exponent of the latter category, which, until recently, has been marginalized in the institution of literature as Art (Neuhaus 2002).

6. In Sklenicka's and Spilka's portrayal of Lawrence's works, there is a parallel to Bødker: "Lawrence's child . . . loses rather than finds her *self* as she matures, contrary to the model that prevails in much twentieth-century psychology" (1994, 174; author's emphasis). They also record a tendency to establish a personal, artistic view of psychoanalysis.

WORKS CITED

Bødker, Cecil. *Anadyomene*. Aarhus: Arena, 1959.

———. *Barnet i sivkurven*. Copenhagen: Det Danske Bibelselskab, 1975.

———. *Da jorden forsvandt*. Copenhagen: Det Danske Bibelselskab, 1975.

———. *Den lange vandring*. Copenhagen: Gyldendal, 1982.

———. *Den udvalgte*. Copenhagen: Det Danske Bibelselskab, 1977.

———. *Dimma Gole*. Copenhagen: Branner & Korch, 1971.

———. *Evas ekko*. Aarhus: Arena, 1980.

———. *Fortællinger omkring Tavs*. Aarhus: Arena, 1971.

———. *Fygende heste*. Aarhus: Arena, 1956.

———. *Hungerbarnet*. Copenhagen: Gyldendal, 1990.

———. *Leoparden*. Copenhagen: Branner & Korch, 1970 (*The Leopard*. Translated by Solomon Deressa and Gunnar Poulsen. Nairobi: East African Publishing House, 1972. Also New York: Atheneum, 1975).

———. *Luseblomster*. Aarhus: Arena, 1955.

———. *Marias barn. Drengen*. Copenhagen: Gyldendal, 1983.

———. *Marias barn. Manden*. Copenhagen: Gyldendal, 1984.

———. *Silas og den sorte hoppe*. Copenhagen: Branner & Korch, 1967 (*Silas and the Black Mare*. Translated by Sheila La Farge. New York: Delacorte, 1978).

———. *Silas og Ben-Godik*. Copenhagen: Branner & Korch, 1969 (*Silas and Ben-Godik*. Translated by Sheila La Farge. New York: Delacorte, 1978).

———. *Silas fanger et firspand* Copenhagen: Branner & Korch, 1972 (*Silas and the Runaway Coach*. Translated by Sheila La Farge. New York: Delacorte, 1978).

———. *Silas stifter familie*. Aarhus: Arena, 1976.

———. *Silas på Sebastiansbjerget*. Aarhus: Arena, 1977.

———. *Silas og Hestekragen mødes igen*. Aarhus: Arena, 1978.

———. *Silas møder Matti*. Aarhus: Arena, 1979.

————. *Silas—livet i bjergbyen*. Copenhagen: Gyldendal, 1984.

————. *Silas—de blå heste*. Copenhagen: Gyldendal, 1995.

————. *Silas—Sebastians arv*. Copenhagen: Gyldendal, 1986.

————. *Silas—ulverejsen*. Copenhagen: Gyldendal, 1988.

————. *Silas—testamentet*. Copenhagen: Gyldendal, 1992.

————. *Silas og flodrøverne*. Copenhagen: Gyldendal, 1998.

————. *Silas—fortrøstningens tid*. Copenhagen: Gyldendal, 2001.

————. *Timmerlis*. Copenhagen: Branner & Korch, 1969.

————. *Tænk på Jolande*. Copenhagen: Gyldendal, 1981.

————. *Ægget der voksede*. Copenhagen: Gyldendal, 1987.

————. *Øjet*. Aarhus: Arena, 1961.

Boëthius, Ulf, ed. *Modernity, Modernism and Children's Literature*. Stockholm: Center for the Study of Childhood Culture, 1998.

Bourdieu, Pierre. *The Rules of Art*. Oxford: Polity Press, 1996 (1992).

Clark, Beverly Lyon. *Kiddie Lit. The Cultural Construction of Children's Literature in America*. Baltimore: Johns Hopkins University Press, 2003.

Clark, Beverly Lyon, and Margaret R. Higonnet, eds. *Girls, Boys, Books, Toys. Gender in Children's Literature and Culture*. Baltimore: Johns Hopkins University Press, 1999.

Dusinberre, Juliet. *Alice to the Lighthouse. Children's Books and Radical Experiments in Art*. London: Macmillan, 1987.

Goodenough, Elizabeth, Mark A. Heberle, and Naomi Sokoloff, eds. *Infant Tongues. The Voice of the Child in Literature*. Detroit: Wayne State University Press, 1994.

Gormsen, Jakob. *Cecil Bødker*. Copenhagen: Tranehuse, 1976.

Guillory, John. *Cultural Capital. The Problem of Literary Canon Formation*. University of Chicago Press, 1994.

Hourihan, Margery. *Deconstructing the Hero. Literary Theory and Children's Literature*. London: Routledge, 1997.

IBBY, *International Children's Book Service: Cecil Bødker. Nominated by the Danish Section of The International Board on Books for Young People for the Hans Christian Andersen Medal, Author's Award*. Gentofte, 1976.

Jakobsen, Gunnar. *Cecil Bødker*. Copenhagen: Gyldendal, 2001.

Kåreland, Lena. *Modernismen i barnkammaran. Barnlitteraturens 40-tal* ("Modernism in the Nursery. Children's Literature in the 1940s"). Stockholm: Rabén & Sjögren, 1999.

Kümmerling-Meibauer, Bettina. *Kinderlitteratur, Kanonbildung und literarische Wertung*. Stuttgart: J. B. Metzler, 2003.

Lesnik-Oberstein, Karín. *Children's Literature. Criticism and the Fictional Child*. Oxford: Clarendon, 1994.

Lloyd, Rosemary. *The Land of Lost Content. Children and Childhood in Nineteenth-Century French Literature*. Oxford: Clarendon, 1992.

————. "Twenty Thousand Leagues Below Modernism." Pp. 51–74 in *Moder-*

nity, Modernism and Children's Literature ed. Ulf Boëthius. Stockholm: Center for the Study of Childhood Culture, 1998.

Lundin, Anne. *Victorian Horizons. The Reception of the Picture Books of Walter Crane, Randolph Caldecott, and Kate Greenaway*. Lanham, Md.: Scarecrow, 2001.

Lurie, Alison. *Don't Tell the Grown-Ups: The Subversive Power of Children's Literature*. Boston: Little, Brown, 1998 (1990).

McGillis, Roderick. *The Nimble Reader. Literary Theory and Children's Literature*. New York: Twayne, 1996.

McGillis, Roderick. "What Literature Was: The Canon Becomes Ploughshare." Pp. 31–42 in *Canon, Literatura infantil y juvenil otras literaturas* eds. Angel G. Cano Vela and Cristina Perez Valverde. Cuenca: Ediciones de la Universidad de Castilla-La Mancha, 2003.

Mouritsen, Flemming. "Cecil Bødker." Pp. 266–277 in *Danske digtere i det 20. århundrede* ("Danish Authors in the 20th Century"), vol. 2. Copenhagen: GAD, 2001.

———. "Children's Literature." Pp. 609–631 in *A History of Danish Literature* ed. Sven H. Rossel. Lincoln: University of Nebraska Press, 1992.

Natov, Roni. *The Poetics of Childhood*. New York: Routledge, 2003.

Neuhaus, Stefan. *Revision des literarischen Kanons*. Göttingen: Vandenhoeck & Ruprecht, 2002.

Nikolajeva, Maria. *Children's Literature Comes of Age. Toward a New Aesthetic*. New York: Garland, 1996.

O'Sullivan, Emer. *Kinderliterarische Komparatistik*. Heidelberg: C. Winter, 2000.

Paul, Lissa. "Enigma Variations. What Feminist Criticism Knows about Children's Literature." Pp. 148–166 in *Children's Literature. The Development of Criticism* ed. Peter Hunt. London: Routledge & Kegan Paul, 1990.

Rose, Jacqueline. *The Case of Peter Pan—or the Impossibility of Children's Literature*. London: Macmillan, 1984.

Sampath, Ursula. *Kasper Hauser: A Modern Metaphor*. Columbia, S.C.: Camden House, 1991.

Sklenicka, Carol, and Mark Spilka. "A Womb of His Own: Lawrence's Passional/Parental View of Childhood." Pp. 164–183 in *Infant Tongues. The Voice of the Child in Literature* ed. Elizabeth Goodenough et al. Detroit: Wayne State University Press, 1994.

Steedman, Carolyn. *Childhood, Culture and Class in Britain*. New Brunswick, N.J.: Rutgers University Press, 1990.

Tsëelon, Efrat. "The Little Mermaid: An Icon of Woman's Condition in Patriarchy, and the Human Condition of Castration." *The International Journal of Psycho-Analysis* 76 (1995) 1017–1030.

Vinterberg, Søren. "Cecil Bødker." Pp. 219–228 in *Danske digtere i det 20. århundrede* ("Danish Authors in the 20th Century") eds. Torben Brostrøm et al. Copenhagen: GAD, 1982.

7

Michel Tournier Retells the Robinson Crusoe Myth
Friday and Robinson: Life on Speranza Island

Sandra L. Beckett

"Over the past few decades the encounter between Robinson and
Friday has taken on a significance that Daniel Defoe was a thousand leagues from even suspecting."

—Michel Tournier, *The Wind Spirit*

Michel Tournier is one of the best known and most successful contemporary French novelists. Moreover, he is a mainstream writer who has
published extensively and quite successfully for young readers. Many
of his works seem to defy the "boundaries" between adult and children's fiction, crossing them easily without the least concession to
either readership, except for changes of a paratextual nature.[1] The
majority of his "children's books" are actually texts that were originally published for adults. His interest in a cross-audience of adults
and children is evident from the outset of his career. In 1967, Tournier
achieved instant renown when he was awarded the prestigious Grand
Prix du Roman de l'Académie Française for his first novel, a rewriting

of Daniel Defoe's *Robinson Crusoe*, titled *Vendredi ou les limbes du Pacifique* (Friday, or the limbo of the Pacific), which was translated into English as *Friday, or The Other Island* in England and simply as *Friday* in the United States. Four years later, Tournier adapted his award-winning Robinsonade for children, in a version titled *Vendredi ou la vie sauvage* (Friday, or the savage life, 1971), which appeared the following year in English as *Friday and Robinson: Life on Speranza Island.*[2] The so-called "children's version" has become one of France's bestselling children's books, surpassed on Gallimard's list of children's bestsellers only by Antoine de Saint-Exupéry's *The Little Prince.*

A FRENCH CHILDREN'S BEST-SELLER AND ITS FATE ABROAD

Tournier told me that *Friday and Robinson* is "by far his greatest success, in France as well as abroad" (qtd. in Beckett 1997, 274).[3] The novel has sold several million copies in France, where it is well-established on school curricula and read every year by thousands of schoolchildren. For this reason, the author likes to refer to it as a "popular 'classic' " (Tournier 1982, 33). In 1981, *Friday and Robinson* was adapted for French television in a film directed by Gérard Vergez and starring Michael York as Robinson and Gene Antony Ray as Friday. A picture book edition of the work, published by Gallimard/Flammarion in 1981, is illustrated with photographs taken by Pat York during the filming of the movie. Apparently the soundtrack was released in Britain under the title *Robinson Crusoe and Man Friday*. Unfortunately, the film seems to be unobtainable even in France. The popularity of the novel extends well beyond French borders. It has been translated into many languages and is also available in Braille. Tournier is particularly proud of the fact that his novel was chosen to inaugurate a new machine to produce books for the blind at the national public school for blind and amblyopic students in Paris. The successful novel also inspired several pirate editions. Tournier travelled to Tallinn in 1990 to mark the illegal publication of his book when Estonia defied Moscow and began publishing their own foreign books. With regard to a pirate edition published in Baghdad by the Iraqi Ministry of National Education, Tournier jokingly told me that it proved that "the Iraqi government of Saddam Hussein considered that the Iraqi children could no longer do without [his] *Friday*" (Beckett 1997, 265).

In spite of its status as a bestseller, *Friday and Robinson* has not attracted nearly as much critical attention as the version for adults. Unfortunately, this critical indifference to the children's books of even the greatest mainstream authors is quite common in France. In the English-speaking world, only two articles seem to have been devoted entirely to the novel (Lenz 1986; Beckett 1996) and several others examine it briefly (McMahon 1985; Beckett 1994, 1995, 1998, 2002). Tournier laments the fate of *Friday and Robinson* in the United States and in the English-speaking world in general, especially in light of its success in many other countries. According to Tournier, the fault doesn't lie with the excellent American translation by Ralph Manheim, but rather, with the choice of publisher. The version for adults was published in the United States by Doubleday, which has a large children's department, but they were not interested in putting out the children's edition. It eventually appeared with Knopf in 1972, with drawings by David Stone Martin. Tournier blames its lack of success on the fact that Knopf doesn't publish children's books, which meant that *Friday and Robinson* was more of "an intellectual curiosity than a true children's book" in the English-speaking world (Beckett 1997, 265–66). Although it has sold millions of copies in France, where it is constantly being reissued, the modest two thousand copies printed in the United States apparently didn't even sell, and it was out of print for years. Regrettably, this is the fate of most French children's classics, with the notable exception of *The Little Prince*. Tournier's novel has had a brighter fate, however, as it was finally reissued in Britain, in 2003, by Walker Books, under the shortened title *Friday and Robinson*.

When asked why he feels his books haven't had more success in the United States, Tournier replied that he can't reach "[his] major public, which is young people, in foreign countries." According to him, publishers of children's books around the world insist on complete conformity: "And each country has its own kind of conformity. For example, in the United States it's conformity to the Walt Disney model." Even in France, where the author has succeeded in overcoming the obstacles to reach a public of young readers, he says that doesn't prevent conservative magazines from constantly publishing articles "accusing [him] of perverting young people" (Petit 1991, 178–79). Apparently a British publisher was originally to have co-published *Friday and Robinson* with a number of publishers throughout the world, using the illustrations of a Czechoslovakian illustrator, Jan Kudlácek, whom Tournier admired greatly. However, the project was quickly dashed by the great divide that separated the avant-garde world of adult books from the more conservative world of children's books, characterized by its strict, well-defined guidelines and "made-to-measure products." Tournier is convinced that the children's book trade "operates by laws that absolutely ban all genuine literary creativity" (Tournier 1982, 33). He has often bitterly denounced the conservative children's editors, booksellers, press, librarians, and parents, whose censorship prevents many of his texts from reaching a wide juvenile audience. He confesses that the censorship of his children's books is due to the fact that he refuses to avoid subjects considered taboo in children's literature (sex, cruelty, money, politics, etc.), but he insists that "sex, money, and politics are things that children care about" (Petit 1991, 179).

The provocative author who tries to reach a public of all ages often finds himself accused, on the one hand, of perversity by the mediators of children's books and, on the other hand, of bowdlerizing his own books by critics who disapprove of the self-censorship Tournier applies when he rewrites an adult novel for a young audience. Despite Tournier's bitter condemnation of the censorship of sexuality in children's books, the author himself eliminated several passages dealing with sexuality when he rewrote his first Robinsonade. Defoe's silence with regard to Crusoe's sexuality was a particularly "glaring omission in our post-Freudian age" (Roberts 1994, 23), but it certainly facilitated the appropriation of his novel by young readers. Tournier had redressed this omission in his adult novel, but he eliminates from the children's version the scenes depicting Robinson's lovemaking with a tree that has the shape of a woman's body and later with the earth of Speranza. The latter act engenders mandrakes, and Robinson is furious when Friday imitates him and the island bears striped mandrakes. In the pages of *Palimpsests: Literature in the Second Degree* that Gérard Genette devoted to Tournier's Robinsonades, the critic claims to be scandalized by the second *Friday* "mutilated of its erotic dimension" and expresses his shock that Tournier himself would indulge in such an exercise (Genette 1982, 424). Tournier claims that sexuality has not, in fact, been eliminated from the children's version, but has evolved in order to conform better to the needs of children and their diffuse, prepubescent sexuality (Tournier 1971c, 12–13; Beckett 1997, 279). It is not surprising that Tournier shocks North American adults when he provocatively deduces from Freud's theories that children's literature should be "eroticized," perhaps even more than books for adults. In his books published for children, the author attempts to respect the child's vague sense of sexuality that often combines with "affectivity" (Tournier 1971a, 57). The author points to the ambiguous scene, added in the children's Robinsonade, of Friday's intimate relationship with the little she-goat Anda, with whom he sleeps. The author admires the ambiguity of Paul Durand's illustration for the original edition of *Friday and Robinson*, which is reminiscent of the "very daring position" of Leda and the swan in the painting *Leda e il cigno* by Leonardo da Vinci. Whereas this scene would have outraged adults, Tournier claims that it is quite natural to children, who love to have an animal in their bed. The absence of this scene in the adult *Friday* makes it the bowdlerized version, according to the author (Bouloumié and Gandillac 1991, 308). The intimate relationship between Friday and Anda is clearly evident when the she-goat becomes the object of a battle to the death between Friday and his rival, the billy goat Andoar.

FROM CHILDREN'S BOOK TO CROSSOVER BOOK

Tournier's view concerning the status of *Friday and Robinson* has evolved significantly since the novel was first published more than thirty years ago. Originally, he himself called the novel "the children's version" of the first *Friday*. This classification is made quite explicit in the titles of two articles the author wrote at the time of the book's launching in 1971, "When Michel Tournier rewrites his books for children" and "Writing for children." Furthermore, in the only reference the author makes to his children's books in his intellectual autobiography, *Le Vent Paraclet* (1977), published in English in 1988 under the title *The Wind Spirit*, he indicates that *Friday and Robinson* is "a children's version" of *Friday* (WS, 157).[4] The author gradually revised his opinion, however, and now he categorically calls the novel an improved version that can also be read by children, but was not written specifically for them. The author regrets that his bestselling novel is classified as a "children's book," maintaining that there are merely two *Fridays*, one of which is the "rough copy" and the other, the so-called "children's version," the "good copy" (Garcin 1986). In fact, Tournier considers the shorter version to be vastly superior to the longer "adult" version. Few critics and adult readers tend to agree with the author, and *Friday and Robinson* continues to be marketed only as a children's book, despite the fact that many of Tournier's works are published in both adult and children's editions. Tournier actually denies emphatically ever having written deliberately for children. He told a class of students in 1986 that he would be ashamed to write for children, explaining: "I don't like books written for children. It's pseudoliterature" (Tournier 1986, 21). During a conversation in 1993, Tournier once again insisted that his books do not fall within the category of children's literature, even when they are read by children (Beckett 1997, 264–65).

Although the author denies that he writes children's books, he nonetheless seeks first and foremost to please a public of young readers. From the outset of his career, Tournier seems to have had the child reader in mind, for he chose a story with lasting appeal for children as the subject of his first adult novel. In an article published the same year as his Robinsonade for children, Tournier suggests that a book is worth very little "if its author cannot communicate its substance to an audience of ten-year-olds" (Tournier 1971b, 7). He has continued to reiterate this idea throughout his career. Tournier maintains that authors like Shakespeare, Goethe, and Balzac are "marred" by an "unforgivable" defect, the fact that "children cannot read them," and he aspires to join the ranks of the great literary "geniuses" who write so well that they can be read "by everyone, *even children!*"—namely Perrault, La Fontaine, Andersen, Lagerlöf, Kipling, Carroll, and Saint Exupéry (Tournier 1982, 34, author's emphasis). Recounting his own "discovery" of literature at nine years of age, thanks to what he calls his first "literary shock," *The Wonderful Adventures of Nils*, by Selma Lagerlöf, he concludes: "Books that can be read only at twenty are failures" (Payot 1996, 34). The seriousness that Tournier attaches to the task of writing for children is indicated by the title he gives an article published in the *Unesco Courier*: "Writing for Children is No Child's Play." Tournier feels that he has attained the heights of his craft when he is read and appreciated by children: "Sometimes I apply myself so well and have so much talent that what I write can also be read by children. When my pen is less lucky, what it writes is only good enough for adults." In other words, Tournier firmly believes that "a work can be addressed to a young public only if it is perfect" (Tournier 1979b). Because Tournier judges the value of his books according to the minimal age of their readership, he feels that *Friday and Robinson*, which can only be read by nine-year-olds, is not quite as good as his two tales, *Pierrot ou les secrets de la nuit* (Pierrot, or The Secrets of the Night) and *Amandine ou les deux jardins* (Amandine, or The Two Gardens), which can be understood by six-year-old children and therefore constitute the summit of his literary achievement (Payot 1996, 33–34). The author is convinced that his chance of being read by future generations lies with these two short tales and *Friday and Robinson*.

The reflections on his craft that Tournier confided to a class of French students in 1986 clearly reveal that the rewriting of his own works is part of a general evolution of his writing, in which *Friday and Robinson* plays a key role: "When I write, one of three things occurs: in the exceptional case, I am brimming over with talent, with genius, . . . and I write straightaway a work so good that children can read it. Or, I don't carry it off and I write *Friday*, but I have the strength to begin again, and that produces *Friday and Robinson*, which is not at all a version for children but simply a better version. Or I don't pull it off, and the undertaking seems hopeless, beyond saving, and that results in *The Erl-King*" (Tournier 1986, 21). It seems that the "children's version" of the novel had somehow pre-existed the adult version in the author's mind. The year he published the shorter version, Tournier explains this rewriting process in the following terms:

> Translating *Friday* into *Friday and Robinson*, I had the distinct feeling I was taking a path already travelled in the opposite direction . . . in a sense, I was only able to derive a children's novel from an adult novel because the latter had itself in a way been taken from the former in the first place. Aside from the fact, however, that the original novel for children had initially remained unformulated. (Tournier 1971b)

Tournier felt very quickly the need to rewrite his first novel "in a leaner, tauter form," but he claims retrospectively to have been quite surprised to learn on the completion of *Friday and Robinson* that he had written "a children's book" (Tournier 1982, 33). A more disconcerting surprise was the fact that the author couldn't find a publisher for his new book. Gallimard did not yet have a children's department and had no interest whatsoever in the condensed version of Tournier's award-winning adult novel. Several other publishers turned him down before Flammarion finally agreed reluctantly to publish it, predicting gloomily, but accurately, that it would not be a success. Tournier remarks with a note of bitterness that the Flammarion edition was illustrated by an illustrator chosen by the publisher rather than the Czechoslovakian illustrator whom Tournier himself had chosen to illustrate his text (Tournier 1971a, 56). A few years later, the founder of Gallimard's children's department, Pierre Marchand, told the author that *Friday and Robinson* was one of the first books he wanted to publish in the new children's paperback series, "Folio Junior." The book appeared in the series in 1977, with illustrations by Georges Lemoine, a well-known French illustrator who has illustrated many of Gallimard's children's books. Tournier revels in the fact that Gallimard has sold millions of copies of a book that it once refused, a book that is, in fact, a pirate edition, since a contract was never signed with the original publisher (Beckett 1977, 277–78). Regardless of its status in the author's eyes, the publication of *Friday and Robinson* in Gallimard's popular paperback series for children guaranteed its success as a best-selling children's book.

The key to Tournier's ability to appeal to a cross-audience lies in the mythical pre-text that underlies all of his works. A chapter of his autobiography, "The Mythic Dimension," stresses the fundamental importance of this aspect of his writing. When Tournier was forced to renounce what he considered his true vocation as a philosopher to become a novelist, it was myth that provided him with a "bridge from metaphysics to the novel." Defining myth as "a fundamental story" and *"a story that everybody already knows,"* Tournier describes it in terms of "a multistoried structure," which on one level is "a mere child's story," yet on a higher level embodies "a theory of morality, metaphysics, and ontology." He insists that "the child's tale that is the myth's ground floor" is just as important as "its metaphysical summit." Tournier illustrates this belief by describing the pleasure and pride he felt when a technical afterword by Gilles Deleuze was being included in the paperback edition of *Friday,* "while the very same novel was simultaneously being brought out in a children's version and staged as a children's play by Antoine Vitez." Although Tournier is really talking about the two versions as if they were one, his concluding comment clearly shows that in retelling Defoe's well-known story, the author was striving to write a crossover work: "For me, the proof of the novel's success is the response that it was able to elicit from two readers at opposite poles of sophistication: a child at one end of the scale, a metaphysician at the other" (*WS* 156–57, author's emphasis).

THE MYTH OF ROBINSON CRUSOE

The function of the writer, and indeed any artist, according to Tournier, is the renewal of myth. He suggests that the child should be first and foremost in the mind of the writer as he or she fulfills this vocation of reworking myth. In his autobiography, Tournier explains: "The artist's ambition is to add to or at any rate modify the 'murmur' of myth that surrounds the child, the pool of images in which his contemporaries move—in short, the oxygen of the soul" (*WS* 159–60). On numerous occasions, the author describes how he uses the material of myth to make it his own by reinventing a well-known myth, and transmitting it to the reader who then takes charge of it, so that his or her own personal mythology is modified (see Tournier 1994, 35). The example the author most often cites is the myth of Robinson Crusoe. This particular "mythical hero" is "one of the basic constituents of the Western soul" and "the property of all mankind" (*WS* 183). Defoe's hero quickly became the property of children in particular and a major figure in children's literature. A myth that is not continually given new life by successive generations of writers must inevitably die, but a living myth is a very powerful literary vehicle, as the author himself explains: "Myths assure complicity. By manipulating Robinson Crusoe I am manipulating the reader" (Blume 1983, 7). Robinson Crusoe constitutes the example *par excellence* of a myth that has been consistently renewed, reinvented, and retold by successive generations and diverse cultures. "Each new generation, apparently, has felt a need to tell its story through that of Robinson Crusoe," writes the novelist in his autobiography (*WS* 182). The Crusoe myth is therefore "one of the most topical and vital that we possess," one that in fact "possesses us" (*WS* 183). During an interview in 1996, Tournier reiterates his belief that "never has a myth been more living" than that of Robinson Crusoe. He sums up the myth in the following terms: "the desert island, life in nature, the beach, the sun," things that, in our time, evoke "Club Med," at least for the French novelist and his compatriots (Payot 1996, 36). Tournier points out that for contemporary society, the Crusoe myth has come to mean a multitude of things "that were completely unknown to dear old Daniel Defoe." He reflects on this evolution of the myth in a 1990 interview: "Two hundred fifty years earlier, Defoe couldn't have anticipated one one-hundredth of what I saw in it, or what you see in it, because we read it with the eyes of people at the end of the twentieth century, conscious of the problems of the Third World, modern sports, the Club Med" (Petit 1990, 177).

The story of Robinson Crusoe certainly fulfills Tournier's definition of myth as "*a story that everybody already knows*" (*WS* 157, author's emphasis). If you ask almost any child in the Western world if he or she knows the story of Robinson Crusoe, the answer will be an immediate "of course." But if you ask them more pointedly if they have read Defoe's *The Life and Strange Surprising Adventures of Robinson Crusoe of York, Mariner*, they are likely to reply, in a somewhat puzzled manner, that they have seen Robinson Crusoe's adventures on television or read them in a comic book. Very few would be able to name the author of the novel that is nonetheless the most published and translated work in the world, with the exception of the Bible. It is precisely this fact that makes Robinson Crusoe a "mythical hero," as Tournier explains in his autobiography: "He escaped from the work in which he first appeared in order to bring life to many others, and his popularity surpassed and eclipsed that of his author" (*WS* 183). Very few people read the integral version of Defoe's novel, which Tournier claims is "utterly unreadable for children and . . . for a large number of adults as well" (Tournier 1971c, 12). When a child, or even an adult, is asked to summarize Defoe's story, it becomes evident that the universal myth is constructed on a very few facts: a castaway on a desert island struggles to survive by subduing nature and recreating civilization, he acquires a black servant and calls him Man Friday, they are rescued by an English ship. Many will not even be able to recount this very sketchy outline of the story of Crusoe's life on the desert island, which, as Tournier reminds us, makes up only the first third of Defoe's book (*WS* 181).

Tournier is drawn back irresistibly to the myth that launched his career as a writer. After the lengthy adult novel and the shorter children's novel, the author's next Robinsonade was a short story, "La Fin de Robinson" (The End of Robinson Crusoe), which was published unchanged for a dual audience of adults and children, first in *Le Coq de bruyère* (*The Fetishist*, 1978), a collection of short stories for adults, and then in *Sept contes* (*Seven Tales*, 1984), a collection of tales for children. The depressing and cynical story is inspired, not by Defoe's novel, but by Saint-John Perse's *Images à Crusoé*, which is one of the few retellings, according to Tournier, that retains the figure of Friday. Whereas Saint-John Perse tells the story of the degeneration of Friday after their return to London, Tournier recounts the degeneration of Robinson (see Zarader 1995, 214). Furthermore, Tournier's fascination with the Robinson Crusoe myth doesn't reveal itself only in his fiction. An entire chapter of his autobiography *The Wind Spirit*, titled "Friday," is devoted to an examination of the evolution of the myth and its meaning, and Tournier mentions not only Defoe's novel and his own hypertexts, but numerous other retellings as well. Crusoe's privileged status as a mythic hero allows Tournier to engage in a profoundly meaningful meditation on Western man, as had so many of his predecessors. The remarkable thing about Defoe's book, according to Tournier, is the fact that "reading it alone is not enough": "it prompts an irresistible urge to rewrite it" (Tournier 1982, 34). In his reflections on the Crusoe myth, Tournier mentions several retellings by his compatriots, namely Jean Giraudoux, Saint-John Perse, Paul Valéry, and Jules Verne. He dwells at greatest length on Verne's *The Mysterious Island*, which was published for young readers almost a century before Tournier's *Friday and Robinson*. He also mentions several examples of the genre from other countries, notably another Robinsonade for children, Johann David Wyss's *Swiss Family Robinson*. Tournier never seems to tire of reflecting on the Crusoe myth that he claims "shapes *our* fictions," and that certainly shapes *his* fictions (*WS* 184, emphasis added).

INTERTEXTUAL PLAY

Friday and Robinson is a rare example of a rewriting in the second degree, or what the author of *Palimpsests* terms a "hyper-hypertext," because it is a rewriting of *Friday*, which, in turn, is a rewriting of Defoe's novel (Genette 1997, 374). Whereas many Robinsonades for children have very little relationship with the prototype of the genre, and certainly do not require any detailed knowledge of Defoe's text, Tournier's *Friday and Robinson* can be fully appreciated only when it is read in the light of the hypotext or pre-text. In the case of adult readers, they cannot help reading it in the light of Tournier's first Robinsonade as well. I have discussed elsewhere the "double 'reception'" that, according to Genette, the novel receives when it is read on two levels by adults, thus creating what the critic calls "a palimpsest of reading" (Genette 1997, 374; see Beckett 1995, 15). Of all the countless works inspired by Defoe's novel, Tournier insists that his remake respects most closely the model. Tournier's first rewriting of the story was the result of his own close rereading of Defoe's text on the occasion of the publication of a new edition that made the classic once again widely available in France. He, in turn, invites his readers to re-evaluate their past "reading" of the myth and to reread, or read for the first time, Defoe's *Robinson Crusoe*. The resulting intertextual play generates the meaning of the contemporary story. Much of the success of Tournier's book as a school text is no doubt due to the "pedagogical" potential afforded by the confrontation of the modern novel and its model. The reader of the contemporary text is encouraged to re-examine the cultural system and fundamental values upon which the original text is based and to take an active role in reinventing the Crusoe myth.

Tournier has sometimes been accused of not acknowledging his sources, and a reader once rather pointedly asked him why he had not dedicated his first *Friday* to Defoe's memory, thinking that this was the least he could do "to pay [his] respects to Crusoe's creator." The novelist admits that the thought never crossed his mind, "for it seemed obvious that every page of the book paid tribute to its English model" (*WS* 196–97). When the author visits schools, children do not hesitate to ask him outright if he "often copies his books from others" in the same way he did *Friday and Robinson* (Beckett 1997, 276). Tournier reveals a Bloomian "anxiety of influence" (Bloom 1973) in his autobiography, where he describes the intense frustration that often accompanies a writer's admiration for certain masterpieces of which he feels "that he was for all eternity [the] predestined author." The writer who has been "disinherited of what was rightfully his" by being born too late, can reclaim what he considers his birthright by appropriating and rewriting it in such a meaningful way as to establish its authority. The potential charge of plagiarism should not bother the author who has "the strength to invert the chronological order by substituting for it another order of a more profound, more essential kind." In such cases, claims Tournier tongue-in-cheek, it is the original author who should be accused of plagiarism (*WS* 40–41). Tournier admits, however, that he is a "thieving magpie" (Rambures 1970, 163), and he sees the sign of his literary vocation in the fact that already as a child he copied passages of the books he admired in a notebook "to appropriate them" because he felt that he should have been their author. Although Tournier doesn't tell us if he copied passages of Defoe's novel as a child, he admits that by writing *Friday*, he "takes possession of Daniel Defoe's *Robinson Crusoe*" (Delblat 1994, 221).

Robinson Crusoe was based on the real-life experiences of Alexander Selkirk (or Selcraig), a Scotsman who spent over four years of solitary exile on the island of Más a Tierra off the Chilean coast between 1704 and 1709. It is doubtful that Defoe met Selkirk, so the pre-texts for his novel were probably the accounts of Selkirk's adventures found in the memoirs of Captain Woodes Rogers, who rescued him, and in an article published by a friend, Sir Richard Steele (see *WS* 179). Tournier recounts Selkirk's story in *The Wind Spirit* and his novel sometimes refers back beyond Defoe's novel to borrow material from its sources. The most striking example is the episode in which Friday falls over a precipice with his adversary Andoar during their duel, but survives because the king of the goats breaks his fall. Martin's representation of this dramatic scene gives the historical event mythical overtones. This incident is found in the accounts of Selkirk's stay on Más a Tierra by both Rogers and Steele. Defoe transposed the castaway's story from the Pacific Ocean to the Atlantic; Tournier "corrects" Defoe by shifting it back to the Juan Fernández archipelago in the Pacific Ocean, several hundred kilometers off the coast of Chile. Interestingly, the island of Más a Tierra was renamed Robinson Crusoe Island by the Chilean government the year before Tournier published his first Robinsonade. Tournier's hero spends the same length of time on his island as does Defoe's, but he does so exactly a century later, beginning in 1759 rather than 1659, a change that is far from fortuitous. By setting his novel in the Age of Enlightenment, Tournier creates a very different context of reference that allows him to address the subjects being debated by eighteenth-century philosophers, including nature and civilization, the relativity of cultures, colonialism, the re-evaluation of "primitive" peoples, the slave trade, and so forth. The date 1759 is particularly significant because in that year Jean-Jacques Rousseau finished the first version of his pedagogical novel, *Emile, or On Education*, in which he mentions Defoe's novel in terms that clearly demonstrate that Robinson Crusoe already possessed a mythical dimension in Western culture:

> Since we absolutely must have books, there exists one which, to my taste, provides the most felicitous treatise on natural education. This book will be the first that my Emile will read. For a long time it will alone compose his whole library.... What then is this marvellous book? ... It is *Robinson Crusoe*. (Rousseau 1979, 184)

Tournier denies attempting to give new life to Rousseau's myth of the "noble savage," a myth that is nonetheless evoked by the "savage life" in the original title. He insists that for Rousseau, the "noble savage" is not Friday, but Robinson himself, who learns to survive without the society that had corrupted him. Emile would not be allowed to continue reading *Robinson Crusoe* after the introduction of Friday, because his arrival marks the reconstitution of society. When Rousseau "praised Defoe's *Robinson Crusoe* as the only book he would choose for Emile's edification and amusement, he explicitly excluded Friday, a character in whom he saw nothing but the germs of society and domestic slavery," writes Tournier (*WS* 189). The novelist says he had "a nasty fright" when he realized how close Rousseau had come to "pulling the rug out from under him." The author of *Emile* could very easily have had the idea that the arrival of Friday would "turn the relationship upside down in such a way that there was no longer a master and a slave but two equal men." Tongue-in-cheek, Tournier says that "fortunately," the idea didn't occur to "dear old Jean-Jacques," who left "the way clear" for him (Tournier 1986, 24).

SUBVERTING THE MYTH

Tournier claims to have remained "extraordinarily faithful to the rules of the game laid down by Daniel Defoe, except for very small discrepancies that in the end bring about a complete catastrophe" (Tournier 1986, 22). These diversions or deviations nonetheless suffice to turn the model upside down or inside out, in a kind of literary play that inverts, subverts, and perverts the original story. Although the two novels tell "the same story," they are as different as "night and day" (Tournier 1994, 37). Defoe's novel is divided into two complementary parts that Tournier describes as "before Friday and with Friday" (*WS* 193). Only the "before Friday" chapters of Tournier's two Robinsonades in fact reflect the hypotext closely. In the "with Friday" section, which is more important, particularly in the children's version, the two hypotexts begin to diverge significantly from Defoe's. In the contemporary novel, the narrative structure is more complex, because the second section actually consists of two sub-sections, "the first parodying Crusoe's 'education' of Friday from Defoe's novel, the second inverting it (and hence also *Robinson Crusoe*) by depicting Vendredi's initiation of Robinson to the *vie sauvage*" (Roberts 1994, 24).

The fact that Friday replaces Robinson as the eponymous hero of Tournier's novel immediately indicates the author's intention to deconstruct and subvert the myth of Robinson Crusoe. When the novel was translated into English, the publisher or the translator nonetheless saw fit to give Robinson eponymous status as well. In his discussion of Defoe's rewriting of historical fact, Tournier claims that his predecessor's most ingenious embellishment was the invention of Friday. However, he obviously feels that Defoe did not exploit the potential of this find. In the publicity for the French "Castor poche" edition, the author explains the genesis of his novel to young readers. Although his version is a parody of Defoe's novel, it is also a homage to what Tournier calls a "wonderful book." The French novelist is careful to point out that although "parody may descend to pastiche, . . . it can also rise to quintessence" (*WS* 163). His problem with Defoe's novel is the fact that "poor Friday is completely sacrificed." In his comments for the "Castor poche" edition, he explains further: "It is Robinson that possesses all truth because he is white, English, and Christian." It was Tournier's intention to rewrite the story giving Friday "an essential role" (Tournier 1986, 20–21); in other words, his retelling was to be the first "Fridayade."

Tournier points out that almost all of the countless authors who have appropriated *Robinson Crusoe* have "chucked Friday overboard," finding a way to eliminate one of the story's two characters. He marvels that none of his predecessors thought to exploit such a fascinating subject (Tournier 1994, 37). Friday's role is increased in both of Tournier's Robinsonades, but most notably in the children's version, where the Indian is introduced in the seventh of sixteen chapters (as compared to the midpoint in Tournier's adult novel and the two-thirds point in Defoe's novel). Martin's illustrations for the English edition emphasize Friday's importance in the novel. Of the eight full-page drawings, only three occur in the "before Friday" part of the novel, and only two of these are devoted to Robinson. In total, three large drawings represent Robinson, whereas four large drawings and a smaller one are devoted to the Araucanian, who dominates the pictures in the "after Friday" part of the novel. The relationship between Robinson and Friday in Defoe's novel is that of Western colonizer and "savage," Christian evangelist and pagan, master and slave. This relationship may at first seem also to be the case in *Friday and Robinson*, but the reader soon realizes that Tournier's intention is to turn those relationships upside down.

The inversion of the Robinson/Vendredi relationship is symbolized ingenuously within the novel by a game invented by Friday. The two characters re-enact, in reverse, an earlier episode, modelled after the famous scene of Defoe's novel in which Robinson humiliates Friday by placing his foot on the neck of the Indian. Friday disguises himself as "the Robinson of old, master of the slave Friday," and Robinson must play the role of "the Friday of old, the slave of Robinson" (83). This game of role-reversal, which constitutes a form of psychotherapy, allows them subsequently "to consider each other as equals" (Tournier 1971a, 56–57). In a very therapeutic manner, this game permits the companions to come to terms with the negative feelings left over from their previous relationship of master/slave. The scene is rather cleverly represented in the "Folio Junior" edition by Lemoine, who includes two almost identical double portraits of Robinson and Friday facing each other with their noses almost touching. The partial profile of the two characters includes only their chins, noses, and mouths. Although one portrait seems to have a slightly larger nose and fuller lips, and perhaps a slightly darker skin color, they are virtually identical. Both mouths are open and pronounce simultaneously the words "I am Robinson" in the first picture and "I am Friday" in the second (Tournier 1977, 103–4).

Tournier's retelling of Defoe's story, which is meant to transform Friday into a "mythical hero," was rendered possible, according to the author, by Claude Lévi-Strauss and ethnography. Tournier could not help reading or misreading Defoe's novel, which was racist even if unintentionally, in the light of his years of study with Lévi-Strauss at the Musée de l'Homme, Paris's museum of anthropology, from 1962 to 1966, where he had learned that "there are no 'savages,' only men living in civilizations different from our own and most rewarding for us to study" (*WS* 189). These courses obviously had a profound influence on his two Robinsonades published in the years immediately following. The subtitle of his children's version, "or the savage life," is reminiscent of the title of Lévi-Strauss's *The Savage Mind*, published in 1962, the year in which Tournier started writing the adult version. In an important passage of *The Wind Spirit*, the author explains how this transposition of the mythical hero is possible:

> No doubt it was inevitable that at first only Crusoe would achieve the dimension of myth, for it was not until recently that the science of anthropology was developed and the great colonial empires were simultaneously dismantled. What was Friday to Daniel Defoe? Nothing: an animal, at best a creature waiting to receive his humanity from Robinson Crusoe, who as a European was in sole possession of all knowledge and wisdom. . . . The idea that Crusoe might have been able to learn something from Friday would never have occurred to anyone before the age of anthropology. (*WS* 188–89)

Enlightened by what Tournier calls the "age of anthropology," contemporary authors working within the tradition of the Robinsonade generally attempt to redress the racism which prevailed in the relation-ship between Robinson and Friday. Despite his acknowledgement of the importance of his anthropological studies, Tournier admits that in retelling the story of the eighteenth-century Englishman and the Arau-canian Indian, his intention was not really to write "an anthropological novel." In *The Wind Spirit*, he describes the rich subject of the "genu-ine" anthropological novel that remains to be written, that of "the con-frontation and fusion of two civilizations personified by two representative narrators" (*WS* 190).

Readers who expect a "Fridayade" are likely to be disappointed, and many critics have been quick to point out that Tournier's novel fails to deliver what the title promises, so perhaps the English translation of the title of the children's version is ultimately more accurate. Tournier's retelling of Defoe's novel remains focalised, for the most part, on Rob-inson, rather than presenting the European from the point of view of the "savage." As Genette puts it, Robinson remains "the *master* of the narrative, and of a narrative that tells his story, not Friday's." The critic concludes that "the true *Friday*, wherein Robinson would be seen, described, and judged by Friday, has yet to be written" (Genette 1997, 373). Although Friday is not the narrator, the author makes alterations to the narrative voice that reflect his wish to focus more closely on the Indian. Defoe's novel is narrated only in the first person, limiting everything to Robinson's point of view. In Tournier's first Robinso-nade, third-person narration is combined with the first-person narra-tion of a logbook, but in the children's version, he revises the narration more radically by eliminating the logbook entries and leaving only the third-person narrator, thus distancing the reader further from the nov-el's European protagonist. In spite of the title and the elevation of Fri-day to a more active and noble role, Robinson remains the central character of Tournier's story, which traces the initiatory experience of the European. However, the spiritual rebirth of the man of the Old World takes place under the tutorship of the New World Friday, who is introduced much earlier in the novel in order to "annihilate" com-pletely the civilization recreated by Robinson (Tournier 1986, 21).

Ethnography was not the only domain that allowed Tournier to bring new life to the myth of Robinson Crusoe. The author describes his "ground-rules" as being as faithful as possible to his model, while "discreetly and surreptitiously smuggling into it all kinds of modern assumptions in the realms of philosophy, psychoanalysis and ethnog-raphy" (Tournier 1982, 33). He seems to appreciate an American critic's definition of the novel for adults as "Robinson Crusoe written by Freud, Walt Disney, and Claude Lévi-Strauss" (Tournier 1981, 387). Tournier had become a novelist only because his aspirations of a career in philosophy were dashed when he failed the competitive examination for teachers of philosophy. Tournier rewrote his adult Robinsonade because, on later re-reading the novel, he felt the philosophy completely overpowered the narrative. In the version for children, he eliminated the metaphysical meditations, including Robinson's logbook entries. The result is a novel in which the emphasis is on events and action, an important prerequisite of children's books (see Tournier 1971c, 11). Thus the children's version stresses the fundamental adventure-story element of the genre of the juvenile Robinsonade. Tournier states that an author uses "a mythological character," such as Robinson Crusoe, as a "mouthpiece . . . to communicate philosophical ideas through adventure stories" (Worton 1995, 192). This application is not true of most juvenile Robinsonades, but it is certainly the case for Tournier's sophisticated retelling. Although he claims to have rewritten his first *Friday* in order to make it less explicitly philosophical and abstract by weaving the metaphysical speculations into the fabric of the story, he insists that the shorter version retains an important, but implicit, philosophical element. If he had become a philosopher, Tournier says that he would like to have taught philosophy to children. He contends that this is precisely what he is trying to do in *Friday and Robinson* and his other children's books, which he calls "philosophical books for ten-year-old children" (Lapouge 1980, 44).

Several aspects of the Crusoe myth account for the fact that it continues to serve as "a mold into which we pour our modern sensibilities and aspirations," but Tournier attributes this especially to the fact that Robinson Crusoe is first and foremost "a hero of solitude." He feels that "of all the wounds from which contemporary Western man suffers, solitude is the most pernicious." In modern society, loneliness and isolation have been created by barriers that are learned in the civilizing process, and are therefore far more pronounced in Western society than in the so-called "underdeveloped countries," according to Tournier (*WS* 184), who calls loneliness "the dark side of progress" (*WS* 186). The author insists, however, that Robinson Crusoe is "not only the victim of his solitude but also its hero" (*WS* 187). The way most people think of Defoe's hero tells us a great deal about how myth functions, involving us in a process that Tournier calls "autohagiography." He explains this concept in his autobiography: "The mythical hero not only strikes his roots into the heart of every individual, even the most modest and prosaic, but also scales humanity's grandest heights. Paradoxically he is at once everyman's double and a superhuman hero." The solitude that can drive us to despair, suicide, and madness can also become the object of a deep longing. Addressing his contemporary readers, the author of *The Wind Spirit* asks: "Who has not dreamed of running away to a desert island?" (*WS* 188). It was the theme of solitude that inspired the philosopher Gilles Deleuze, a friend of Tournier's, to devote an essay to *Friday*, titled "Michel Tournier and the World Without Others." The philosophical essay was included as an afterword to the revised French paperback edition of the adult novel. The interest for the contemporary novelist, however, lies particularly in the confrontation of the European and the Araucanian, in other words in our relationship with others: "In philosophical terms, this encounter calls into question . . . the status of the relationship with the Other" (Worton 1995, 192).

Robinson's first preoccupation when he regains consciousness after the shipwreck is to find out whether there are other survivors or inhabitants on the island. When he learns that he is all alone on a desert island, he turns his attention to trying to escape by painstakingly building a boat that he optimistically christens the *Escape*, only to discover, ironically, that he cannot launch it because he failed to consider how he would get the heavy boat to the water. Robinson blames this fatal oversight on his frequent reading of the Bible, notably the story of Noah's ark, in which the waters came to the ark. The boat is the object of another very ironic scene later in the novel, when Robinson suddenly remembers it and thinks that with Friday's help, it should be possible to haul it to the beach. Although the hull appears to be intact, the boat has been eaten by termites and disintegrates before their very eyes.

Robinson's initial realization that he will not be found and that he cannot escape brings on a period of hopeless dejection, during which he wallows in the mud like a pig and crawls on all fours. The dog Tenn, the only other survivor of the shipwreck, refuses to have anything to do with this human who has regressed to an animal state. The mudhole period, which does not exist in Defoe's novel, is an ironic commentary on the heroism of the individual so central to the Crusoe myth, but it also seems to symbolize a return to the primordial silt of Genesis, from which a new man will be born on the paradisiacal island of Speranza. The rebirth symbolism is quite transparent in this initiatory novel. During the mud-hole period, Robinson is haunted by visions of his childhood and thinks he is "still a baby in a cradle" (16). On several occasions, Robinson later seeks escape from the onerous chores he has imposed on himself in a hole in the cave, where he finds "the wonderful peace of his childhood" (47). He removes his clothes and rubs himself with milk so that he can slip through a narrow passage in the cave into a warm niche, where his thoughts turn to his mother: "He thought he was in her arms and that she was rocking him and singing softly" (44). The obvious symbolism of this scene as a regression to the womb is very explicit in Martin's full-page drawing of an old man curled up in a foetal position.

Narrowly escaping death during a hallucination, Robinson realizes he is on the verge of insanity and must take his destiny in hand and fight to maintain his humanity in this world "without others," to borrow Deleuze's term. As Robinson himself puts it: "It's hard to live like a human being without anyone to help you" (29). He attempts to do so by unrelentingly "civilizing and putting order into his island" (41), painstakingly reconstructing European civilization in what Tournier calls "the age of administration" (*WS* 194). Robinson's workload becomes increasingly heavy as he domesticates rabbits and goats; plants and harvests grain, rice, and other crops; and constructs a house, church, museum, and even a fortress (after the arrival of warlike Indians). Tournier's exaggerated version of Robinson's "civilization" of the island—anything Defoe's hero can do, it seems Tournier's "can do better, or bigger, or faster," writes critic Martin Roberts (1994, 28)— seems intended, like that of Verne, "to throw down a challenge to Defoe's hero." In *The Wind Spirit*, the author sums up the "dazzling display of inventiveness, discovery, and ingenuity" of Verne's five survivors (who blow glass, build a hydraulic elevator, produce electricity, etc.) in the following terms: "Crusoe and his penned goats are outclassed, outdone, and ridiculed" (*WS* 182). There are five survivors in Verne's novel, however, whereas Tournier's Robinson knows true solitude. In addition to extensive, heavy manual labor, the latter adds many administrative responsibilities, by appointing himself Governor of Speranza Island, assuming the rank of general, and drawing up a constitution and a penal code. In the absence of others to govern and with whom to trade, this maniacal administration of Speranza seems like the folly of a madman, and even Robinson sometimes questions the wisdom and value of the excessive work and official duties. A parenthetical comment by the narrator explains, however, that Robinson hoped that some day "a companion, or perhaps even several companions, would turn up" (50) to justify his elaborate re-creation of a miniature England on a desert island of the Pacific.

Tournier frequently uses irony to subvert the myth. Friday accomplishes good-naturedly even the most absurd tasks because the Indian is eager to please and to show his gratitude to the man who had saved his life when he was about to be sacrificed by his tribe. In Tournier's adult novel, the rescue scene deviates ironically from the model. Robinson actually aims at Friday, thinking it is more prudent to side with the majority, but Tenn bumps his arm, and he accidentally shoots the first of Friday's pursuers. In *Friday and Robinson*, Tournier seems to have self-censured the scene to give a more moralistic slant to the children's version. In any case, that is the view of Genette who condemns the elimination of the egoistic behavior of Robinson in order to "save the moral" (Genette 1982, 424–25). In the children's version, Robinson never intends to kill Friday; he aims at the first pursuer and ends up killing the second. However, the English translation, which is otherwise fairly faithful to the original, rather surprisingly retains the version told in the adult novel. The following scene, in which the narrator describes the Indian's gratitude, thus retains the original irony, which was completely lost in the French children's edition: "The victim was cowering in a clump of dwarf palms. He crawled over to Robinson, touched his head to the ground, and groped for Robinson's foot which he placed on his own neck in token of submission" (51).

It seems that it is the translator, rather than the author, who decides to remain faithful to the adult version. Tournier, on the other hand, had made a conscious decision to offer children a more edifying and didactic version, in which the hero subsequently becomes more sympathetic. The egoism of Robinson's original, callous intent may be shocking, but it merely exaggerates that of Defoe's Robinson, who acts, not out of generosity, but out of self-interest: he saves Man Friday because he wants to have a servant. The manner in which Tournier rewrites this scene for children suggests that the philosopher-novelist assumes for himself a pedagogical role. About a year before the publication of *Friday and Robinson*, Tournier admitted that his literary dilemma was of a "pedagogical nature": how to make clear and agreeable the subtle and difficult things he had to say (Rambures 1970). The pedagogical aspect of his novel is, however, more subtle than that of Wyss's *Swiss Family Robinson*, "in which a father is interested primarily in availing himself of the island's pedagogical resources for the benefit of his children"

(*WS* 181). While he doesn't want to be seen as "teaching" anything in his fiction, but rather as a storyteller whose fiction requires readers to participate actively and "interpret" (Petit 1990, 177), Tournier is nonetheless still obsessed by the teaching career he missed out on. This obsession explains why the author is so anxious to be read in schools. As Tournier himself puts it, the teacher who was chased out the door returns by the window as a story-writer, thanks to *Friday and Robinson*, which "invades schools" (Bureau 1990).

A POSTCOLONIAL NOVEL

When Tournier insists on the actuality of his novel, he generally points to its postcolonial dimension: "The confrontation of the Indian Friday and the Englishman Robinson is a major current events topic . . . when Friday arrives, it is the Third World knocking at the door of the industrial world" (Beckett 1997, 266). The author is convinced that children sense the importance of "the problem of the Third World" that his novel poses, a problem that he formulates in the following very simple question: "What is Robinson going to do faced with the colored outsider who appears before him?" To illustrate children's understanding of this aspect of the novel, Tournier refers to his visits to classrooms where students present theatrical adaptations of *Friday and Robinson*. The role of Friday is inevitably given to a child from the Third World, either a child from black Africa (from Mali or Senegal), an Arab child, or sometimes the child of a Portuguese immigrant (Beckett 1997, 266–67). It seems that a darker skin color is not a prerequisite; it suffices to represent a minority. Tournier had considered dedicating the adult novel to "all of France's immigrant workers, to those silent masses of Fridays shipped to Europe from the Third World—some three million Algerians, Moroccans, Tunisians, Senegalese, and Portuguese on whom our society depends and whom we never see or hear, who have no right to vote, no trade union, and no spokesperson" (*WS* 197). In renewing the Robinson Crusoe myth for the modern world, Tournier seeks to present "the confrontation, through Robinson and Friday, of West and Third World, and that of Frenchman and immigrant workers" (Tournier 1985, 182).

As Tournier explains in his autobiography, "the companion who arrives . . . is of a surprising, totally unexpected, and bitterly disappointing sort, a Negro" rather than "a companion of the sort Crusoe was hoping for—another Englishman, another Robinson Crusoe." The author is quick to point out that such a companion would have been the downfall of the novel, whereas a true "Other" has a potential for "a prodigious renewal of adventure and invention" (*WS* 193–94). The "otherness" of Friday is heightened in Tournier's novel because he is at once both black and Indian, a "difference" that may explain why he has been singled out as the next victim of his fierce tribe's ritual sacrifices. Friday's arrival seems at first to offer a justification of Robinson's monstrous system, providing him with a recruit to fill the various roles—social, political, and economical—prescribed by his colonial system. As Tournier explains in his autobiography: "[Friday] is to be the kingdom's sole 'subject,' General Crusoe's only soldier, and Governor Crusoe's only taxpayer" (*WS* 194–95). Robinson sees Friday only as a servant[5] and a savage "to whom he could teach civilization" (56). This situation seems to reflect the relationship established in Defoe's novel: "Once properly broken in by his master Crusoe, Friday could never aspire to anything more than to be a good servant" (*WS* 188–89). In *Robinson Crusoe* the arrival of the "Other," the "savage," merely confirms Robinson's confidence in the values of the European civilization that he has rebuilt on the island. Man Friday's admiring acceptance of Robinson's lifestyle, value system, religion, and language acknowledges the superiority of the European culture that the latter is reconstructing on the Pacific island. The twentieth-century novelist, on the other hand, points out the need for blacks to question the alien values of Western civilization.

In the early stages of the "with Friday" part, Tournier's novel does not seem to deviate from Defoe's model. The Indian is given the name Friday by Robinson (he can't be given a Christian name until he has been baptized), forced to don pants, and taught enough English to understand his master's orders. In a passage filled with irony, Tournier provides a long inventory of all the skills the "model servant" acquired: "He learned to clear ground, plow, sow, harrow, transplant, hoe, mow, reap, thresh, grind flour, knead dough and bake bread . . . milk the goats, make cheese, gather turtles' eggs and make an omelette out of them, to mend Robinson's clothes and shine his boots." After a very full day's work, Friday dons "servant's livery" to wait on "the governor's table" and warms his master's bed with an iron kettle full of coals. To underscore the contrast between Friday's living conditions and those of his master, Tournier concludes: "Then, his work done, he put down a bundle of straw outside the house door and there he and

Tenn slept" (56). With more than a little irony, the narrator sums up their relationship: "Friday had learned to be a soldier when his master was the general, a choir boy when his master prayed, a mason when he was building, a porter when he went on a journey, and a beater when he hunted; and he had learned to chase the flies away with a palm frond when his master was taking a nap" (56). Robinson's delusions of grandeur are best demonstrated on Sundays, when the "servant" brings the "governor" a kind of cane "which looked like a cross between a king's scepter and a bishop's crozier." Tournier parodies the image of Robinson as he is so often depicted in the plentiful iconography of Defoe's story: "shaded by a goat skin parasol carried by Friday who walked behind him" (57). Robinson would then stride majestically around his domain, inspecting fields, rice paddies, orchards, flocks, and buildings.

In spite of the apparent similarities between Defoe's and Tournier's accounts of Friday's integration into Robinson's "civilized" world, the latter actually begins to deviate significantly from the hypotext as soon as the Araucanian arrives, and his presence will ultimately undermine a system founded on the exploitation of man and nature. As Tournier puts it, Friday's "mere presence is enough to shake the island's organizational structure for it is clear that he understands none of it," not the cultivated fields, domestic animals, or buildings, least of all the rules and ceremonies (*WS* 195). Robinson's explanation that "this was what people did in the civilized countries of Europe" does not convince Friday, who fails to see why "they had to do the same thing on a desert island in the Pacific" (59). Friday's sound reasoning recalls Tournier's comments on the ethnocentricity of Defoe's novel, in which Robinson's attitude toward Friday is both "racist" and "heedless of his own self-interest: "If you must live on an island in the Pacific, hadn't you better learn from a native well versed in methods adapted to local conditions rather than attempt to impose an English way of life on an alien environment?" (*WS* 189). Eventually, Crusoe cannot help seeing himself through Friday's eyes and is forced "to take the measure of his own madness" (*WS* 195). Even prior to Friday's arrival, the seeds of doubt were there, as Robinson often questioned the purpose of working his fingers to the bone. In rewriting Defoe's novel, Tournier intended that Robinson would become aware of "the absurdity of his aim and that this feeling would gnaw away at his construction from the inside" (Tournier 1986, 21). When Robinson discovers the secret camp where Friday continues clandestinely to lead the life of an Indian when his tedious master's back is turned, the European's musings are full of envy: "If the life of a savage could be so amusing what was the use of all his work and all the duties he set himself?" (67–68). Robinson has begun to discern the existence of the "other island" (retained in the title of the American edition for adults), that is to say, of another order radically different from the one imposed on the Pacific island by the European.

Whereas Man Friday accepts his master's cultural system unquestioningly, Tournier's Friday, despite his apparent obedience, instinctively resists assimilation into the colonialist order. The Araucanian begins almost immediately to undermine that order, subverting it merely by his laughter. Seeing Tenn stuck in the mud of the rice paddy, Friday opens the sluice gate, and by so doing ruins one of Robinson's most ambitious projects. The turning point of the novel and the definitive rupture with the old system is marked by a catastrophic explosion that completely destroys all trace of the white civilization Robinson had so laboriously reconstructed over so many years. Rather than be caught smoking his master's forbidden, china-bowl pipe, Friday tosses it into the cave where the kegs of gunpowder are stored, inadvertently provoking an enormous explosion. The motifs of the tobacco, pipe, and gunpowder, borrowed directly from Defoe, thus become the catalysts that precipitate the deviation of the contemporary novel from its model. Robinson realizes that he has failed "to colonize the desert island and civilize Friday" and that to attempt to do so had been a mistake. In *The Wind Spirit*, Tournier describes his aim as being the exact opposite of his predecessor's: "My novel was intended to be both inventive and forward-looking, whereas Defoe's was purely retrospective, confined to describing the restoration of a lost civilization with the means at hand" (191). The explosion leaves Robinson and Friday with a "tabula rasa" on which they can create a new civilization (Tournier 1986, 21).

The explosion marks a reversal of their roles: "From then on, it is Friday who calls the tune and who is going to teach Robinson how one must live in an island of the Pacific" (Tournier 1971b, 7). Henceforth, Friday initiates and teaches, while Robinson observes and imitates his mentor.[6] Robinson is converted to Friday's "savage life" of freedom, innocence, harmony with nature, and communion with the elements. Tournier describes Friday as "an inventor," who "weans Robinson from his slavish reproduction of English civilization and makes him create and invent" (Petit 1990, 185). Together they invent "a new language, a new religion, new arts, new games, a new eroticism" (Tournier

1986, 21). Among Friday's inventions, the author mentions in particular the aeolian harp and the kite, which are made from Andoar's skull
and skin, respectively. On a windy night, Friday uses the inventions to
pay homage to the king of the goats who had saved his life: "The flying
Andoar and the singing Andoar were united in a somber festival"
(103). The author laments the fact that the memorable "kite dance"
was left out of the five hours of filming when *Friday and Robinson* was
adapted for television (Petit 1990, 185). Martin's drawings for the
English edition highlight Friday's creativity. In all the illustrations of
Friday, the Indian's hands are portrayed in a very prominent manner.
Two of the large drawings depict only his hands, busy with one of his
inventions. In the foreground of one drawing, the hands are about to
release from the bow one of the arrows Friday believes will fly forever,
and in another stunning drawing, his large, striking hands are completing the curious aeolian harp made from Andoar's skull.

THE CULT OF THE CHILD

Friday and Robinson gives a particularly important place to the child
and his world. If the novel evokes for adult readers the opposition of
Western man and primitive man, Tournier thinks that young readers
will see instead the relationship between the adult and the child. In the
beginning, Robinson and Friday are very polarized in the children's
version. The severe Robinson, with his beard and goatskins, symbolizes the adult, whereas the playful Friday, with his nudity and giggles,
represents the child. Friday's mysterious games remain incomprehensible to the European, as children's games often do to adults. In one
comical scene, Friday dresses the island's cacti in Robinson's most precious possessions, the magnificent garments and jewels salvaged from
the ship. Friday dances joyfully among the garbed cacti in Martin's
small drawing of this playful scene. In the end, Robinson shaves his
beard, discards his clothes and umbrella, tans his fair skin, and adopts
the carefree lifestyle of Friday, so that they become almost like twin
brothers, indulging in all sorts of games (see Tournier 1971b, 7). In the
version for children, Tournier exploits the "ludic" nature of the child,
developing the games and inventions of the "savage life." According to
Tournier, twenty-five percent of *Friday and Robinson* was new material
that involved fundamental games, like the invention of theatre, music,
poetry, sign language, and so forth (see Tournier 1971c, 11, 13). Le-

moine's illustrations for the French paperback edition include ten drawings of hands using their sign language, which children will enjoy imitating (Tournier 1977, 114–15).

The author claims to owe these new inventions to the collaboration of children to whom he told the Robinsonade for adults. The children's comments and questions engendered a new book that was being written alongside the adult novel by the children (see Tournier 1971a, 56). Tournier endeavored to invent scenes that would meet the desires and aspirations of these young readers. The new games that he claims to have invented with the children pleased the author so much that he integrated some of them into the revised adult paperback edition in 1972. The author mentions in particular the profoundly significant passage concerning the game of the effigies, another ingenious game invented by Friday for psychotherapeutic purposes. He constructs a bamboo and coconut dummy of Robinson, which he beats when Robinson offends him. Robinson follows his example and creates a sand-Friday that he uses for the same purpose. By displacing their anger, they are able to deal positively with their aggressive and hostile emotions, and thus always remain civil to each other. Tournier claims that these appropriations make it difficult to say whether the adult version or the children's version is really the original (Tournier 1971a, 57).

AN OPEN ENDING

As in Defoe's model, a ship arrives toward the end of *Friday and Robinson*, but Tournier's hero sees the *Whitebird* as "a messenger from a civilization to which he had no desire to return" and realizes that he can never go back to England (111). Unfortunately, the English translation cuts short Robinson's reflection on the "destruction and disorder" (112) that the boat and its men had brought to what the French text calls his "ideal life with Friday" (Tournier 1977, 146). The "savage life" on the desert island has become the "ideal life," far superior to life in the "civilized" world, where people behave in a manner that is anything but civilized. Looking forward to many more "long, happy years of solitude" with Friday (112), Robinson is devastated when he learns that the Araucarian has secretly departed on the *Whitebird* during the night. Tournier offers no explanation of this disturbing event in the adult Robinsonade, but the author felt the need to give a partial explanation to young readers. Robinson even seems to have a premonition of events to come when he sadly observes how much happier his companion is than he himself with the arrival of the *Whitebird*. For Friday, the beautiful white sailing ship with its masts rising skyward is "a wonderful wind instrument" (Zarader 1995, 209). Like the arrows, kite, and aeolian harp he himself had made on the island, the ship delights Friday, who, contrary to the "terrestrial" Robinson, is "an aerial, aeolian spirit, an Ariel" (*WS* 195). Friday's departure fills Robinson with dread, as he recalls the mate's gruesome stories about the lucrative slave trade and imagines his free-spirited friend shackled and stowed away in the ship's hold.

Tournier's interest remains focused on the spiritual journey of Robinson in this novel that constitutes yet another Robinsonade. Martin Roberts's accusation that the contemporary novelist's portrayal of Friday is, "in its own way, no less ethnocentric than Defoe's" (Roberts 1994, 23) is no doubt somewhat harsh, but Tournier's representation of the Robinson/Friday relationship does raise some troubling questions. In his essay on "Friday," Tournier uses the following equations to express the formula of the adult novel:

Earth + Air = Sun
Terrestrial Crusoe + Friday = Solar Crusoe (*WS* 195)

When the equation is simplified, even a child can see that the mathematics are faulty: how can Robinson + Friday = Robinson? I have already mentioned elsewhere the problematic ending of *Friday and Robinson* (see Beckett 1996, 124–25). It is the "mythic hero" Friday who naively abandons the savage, ideal life on the island, to which he has initiated the European, in order to adopt inadvertently a life in chains in the "civilized" world that Robinson has renounced. One is justified in questioning Friday's promotion to the role of "mythical hero" in light of his tragic fate. Furthermore, Friday is replaced on the island by another white man, or rather a white boy, the runaway cabin boy from the *Whitebird*, a young, red-haired Estonian by the name of Jaan. There is a striking resemblance between Robinson and Jaan, who is a kind of younger, miniature version of Robinson, a "twin son" or clone.

The principal reason that Robinson decides not to return to the Old World is his fear of aging, after discovering from the crew the actual calendar date and calculating his true age to be exactly fifty years old, "the age of an old man." On Speranza, Robinson seems to have discovered the fountain of youth, as he feels "younger every day," but he has the premonition that he would age suddenly and lose that eternal youthfulness if he left the island (107). That is precisely what happens to the Robinson who returns to England with Friday in the alternative ending Tournier provides in his short story "The End of Robinson Crusoe." Unable to forget his island, Crusoe sets out to look for his Caribbean paradise, but never finds it. Back home, forty years after his shipwreck, he is an aged, broken drunkard who has become part of the local folklore. An old sailor tells Crusoe that he probably sailed past his beloved island ten times without recognizing it, just as his island would not have recognized the old man that he had become. At the end of *Friday and Robinson*, on the other hand, Robinson stands godlike on a pinnacle of the Pacific island, with his newfound miniature double, bathed in the light of the rising sun.

Ultimately, it is Robinson who remains the "mythic hero" of Tournier's novel, not Friday who is in chains in the hold of the English ship and who has already been replaced by the young boy whom Robinson renames Sunday. In the first version, Tournier had named the boy Thursday, because Thursday is "the day of Jupiter, god of the Sky," and because it is "children's Sunday" (Tournier 1972, 254), a reference to the fact that Thursday used to be a school half-holiday for French schoolchildren, before it was later changed to Wednesday. The symbolism of the "golden child," Jupiter's incarnation, is given up in the children's version in favor of the second meaning, so Jaan is renamed Sunday because it is "the day of rest, the day of laughter and games" (118). The open ending of the novel leaves readers free to imagine the "new life" that stretches ahead of Robinson and his newfound companion, apparently the carefree life of playful children.

CONCLUSION

Tournier affectionately calls *Friday and Robinson* his *"livre fétiche"* and considers it one of his best and most important works, superior to all his novels published for adults. That includes novels that earned Tournier the two most prestigious literary prizes in France, his adult *Friday*, which we have already seen received the Grand Prix du Roman de l'Académie Française in 1967, and *Le Roi des Aulnes* (translated as *The Erl-King* in Britain and *The Ogre* in the United States), which was awarded the Prix Goncourt in 1970 and led to Tournier's election to the

Académie Goncourt two years later. In the 1990s, Tournier's publisher, Gallimard, made the ambitious claim that by the year 2000, *Friday and Robinson* would no doubt have been read by every living French person (*Histoire* 1993, 88). In the English-speaking world, however, few people, dead or alive, have read Michel Tournier's "best" novel, although that may change now that it is once again in print. If Tournier is indeed remembered by posterity, not for his adult works, but for his *Friday and Robinson*, as the author himself predicts, that is unlikely to be the case in the English-speaking world. However, Tournier deserves a place of honor among the countless authors who have succumbed to the "irresistible urge to rewrite" Defoe's *Robinson Crusoe* and contributed to the genre of the Robinsonnade. Michel Tournier is perhaps the only author to have offered multiple retellings of Daniel Defoe's famous story in a continued attempt to breathe new life into one of the fundamental myths of our cultural heritage.

NOTES

1. For a detailed examination of Tournier as a crossover writer, see Beckett 1995, 1998, and 2000.

2. Throughout this essay, the title will be abbreviated to *Friday and Robinson*.

3. My book *De grands romanciers écrivent pour les enfants*, which contains a lengthy chapter devoted to Tournier (Beckett 1997, 119–68), also includes two interviews with the author that are quoted extensively throughout this essay (see 264–89). All translations in this essay from texts originally published in French are mine unless otherwise indicated.

4. Because *The Wind Spirit* is quoted frequently throughout this essay, it will be abbreviated as *WS*.

5. He is not so much a slave as a wage-earner, however, because Robinson is now able to justify the capitalist system that he has set up on the island by paying Friday with the coins from the *Virginia* and letting him buy extra food, knickknacks, or a half-day holiday.

6. A similar relationship is set up between the French novelist and a young native boy during one of Tournier's frequent classroom visits. A Chilean boy questioned the author about the araucarias Robinson and Friday climb on Speranza. He suggested that the author must never have seen an araucaria because "nobody can climb an araucaria," not even a monkey, which is why the tree is called "the despair of monkeys" in his country (qtd. in Beckett 1997, 277).

WORKS CITED

Beckett, Sandra. "From the Art of Rewriting to the Art of Crosswriting Child and Adult: the Secret of Michel Tournier's Dual Readership." Pp. 9–34 in *Voices from Far Away: Current Trends in International Children's Literature Research* edited by Maria Nikolajeva. Stockholm: Centre for the Study of Childhood Culture, 1995.

————. "The Meeting of Two Worlds: Michel Tournier's *Friday and Robinson: Life on Speranza Island*." Pp. 110–27 in *Other Worlds, Other Livres: Children's Literature Experiences*. Vol. 2 eds. Myrna Machet, Sandra Olën, and Thomas van der Walt. Pretoria: Unisa Press, 1996.

————. *De grands romanciers écrivent pour les enfants*. Montréal: Les Presses de l'Université de Montréal; Grenoble: Éditions littéraires et linguistiques de l'Université de Grenoble, 1997.

————. "Crossing the Borders: The 'Children's Books' of Michel Tournier and Jean-Marie Gustave Le Clézio." *The Lion and the Unicorn* 22 (1998) 1: 44–69.

————. "Crossing the Boundaries: Michel Tournier's Tales for Children and Adults." Pp. 167–77 in *Children in Literature—Children's Literature* edited by Paul Nebauer. Frankfurt am Main: Peter Lang, 2002.

Bloom, Harold. *The Anxiety of Influence: A Theory of Poetry*. New York: Oxford University Press, 1973.

Blume, Mary. "A Laughing Provocateur is Launched in Britain." *International Herald Tribune* 1983-12-30.

Bouloumié, Arlette, and Maurice de Gandillac, eds. *Images et signes de Michel Tournier*. Paris: Gallimard, 1991.

Brochier, Jean-Jacques. "Dix-huit questions à Michel Tournier." *Le Magazine littéraire* 138 (June 1978): 10–13.

Bureau, Stephan. "Invité Michel Tournier." Television program in the Series "Contact." French Channel of Radio Canada. Montréal/ Trois Rivières: Les Productions de la Tête Chercheuse, 1990.

Delblat, Jean-Luc. "Michel Tournier." Pp. 219–32 in *Le métier d'écrire*. Paris: Le Cherche-midi, 1994.

Garcin, Jérôme. "Interview avec Michel Tournier." *L'Événement du jeudi* 1986-01-15.

Genette, Gérard. *Palimpsests: Literature in the Second Degree*. Trans. Channa Newmann and Claude Doubinsky. Lincoln, NE: University of Nebraska Press, 1997.

Lapouge, Gilles. "Michel Tournier s'explique." *Lire* 64 (December 1980): 28–46.

Histoire du livre de jeunesse d'hier à aujourd'hui, en France et dans le monde. Paris: Gallimard Jeunesse, 1993.

Lenz, Millicent. "The Experience of Time and the Concept of Happiness in

Michel Tournier's *Friday and Robinson: Life on Speranza Island.*" *Children's Literature Quarterly* 11 (1986) 1: 24–29.

Lévi-Strauss, Claude. *La pensée sauvage.* Paris: Plon, 1962.

———. *The Savage Mind.* Chicago, IL: University of Chicago Press, 1962.

McMahon, Joseph H. "Michel Tournier's Texts for Children." *Children's Literature* 13 (1985): 154–68.

Payot, Marianne. "L'Entretien: Michel Tournier." *Lire* (October 1996): 32–40.

Petit, Susan. *Michel Tournier's Metaphysical Fictions.* Amsterdam: John Benjamins: 1991.

Rambures, Jean-Louis. "Michel Tournier: 'Je suis comme la pie voleuse.'" *Le Monde* 1970-11-23.

Roberts, Martin. *Michel Tournier:* Bricolage *and Cultural Mythology.* Saratoga, CA: Anma Libri, 1994.

Rogers, Woodes. *A Cruising Voyage Round the World first to the South-Seas, thence to the East-Indies, and homewards by the Cape of Good Hope begun in 1708, and finish'd in 1711.* London: A. Bell & B. Lintot, 1912 [1712].

Rousseau, Jean-Jacques. *Emile, or On Education.* Trans. Alan Bloom. New York: Basic Books, 1979 [1759].

Saint-Exupéry, Antoine de. *The Little Prince.* Trans. Katherine Woods. New York: Reynal & Hitchcock, 1943.

Steele, Richard. "Steele's Account of Selkirk." *The Englishman* 1713-12-1-3.

Tournier, Michel. *Vendredi ou les limbes du Pacifique.* Paris: Gallimard, 1967.

———. *Friday.* Translated by Norman Denny. Garden City, NY: Doubleday, 1969.

———. *Friday, or the Other Island.* Translated by Norman Denny. London: Collins, 1969.

———. *Le Roi des Aulnes.* Paris: Gallimard, 1970.

———. *Vendredi ou la vie sauvage.* Illus. Paul Durand. Paris: Flammarion, 1971.

———. "Les Enfants dans la bibliothèque." Interview by Jean-François Josselin. *Le Nouvel Observateur* 1971-12-6.

———. "Écrire pour les enfants." Interview by Jean-Marie Magnan. *La Quinzaine littéraire* 12 (1971) 16–31.

———. "Quand Michel Tournier récrit ses livres pour les enfants." *Le Monde* 1971-12-24.

———. *The Erl-King.* Translated by Barbara Bray. London: Collins, 1972.

———. *The Ogre.* Translated by Barbara Bray. Garden City, NY: Doubleday, 1972.

———. *Vendredi ou les limbes du Pacifique.* Paris: Gallimard, 1972 (Folio).

———. *Amandine ou les deux jardins.* Illus. Joëlle Boucher. Paris: Éditions G. P., 1977.

———. *Vendredi ou la vie sauvage.* Paris: Gallimard, 1977.

———. *Le Vent Paraclet.* Paris, Gallimard: 1977.

———. *Le Coq de bruyère*. Paris: Gallimard, 1978.

———. "Écrire pour les enfants." In *Pierrot ou les secrets de la nuit*. Paris: Gallimard, 1979 (Enfantimages).

———. "Michel Tournier: comment écrire pour les enfants." *Le Monde* 1979-12-24.

———. *Vendredi ou la vie sauvage*. Made for TV movie. Dir. Gérard Vergez. 1981.

———. *Le Vol du vampire*. Paris: Gallimard, 1981.

———. "Writing for Children is No Child's Play." *UNESCO Courier* (June 1982): 33–34.

———. *The Fetishist*. Translated by Barbara Wright. New York: Doubleday, 1984.

———. *Sept contes*. Paris: Gallimard, 1984 (Folio Junior).

———. "Pierrot, or The Secrets of the Night." Translated by Margaret Higonnet. *Children's Literature* 13 (1985): 169–72.

———. "Writer devoured by children." Translated by Margaret Higonnet. *Children's Literature* 13 (1985): 180–87.

———. "Michel Tournier face aux lycéens." *Le Magazine littéraire* 226 (January 1986): 20–25.

———. *The Wind Spirit: An Autobiography*. Translated by Arthur Goldhammer. Boston: Beacon Press, 1988.

———. "L'Œil du Bœuf rencontre Michel Tournier," *L'Œil du Bœuf* 3 (February 1994): 19–39.

———. *Friday and Robinson*. London: Walker Books, 2003.

Verne, Jules. *L'île mystérieuse*. Paris: Hetzel, 1874.

———. *The Mysterious Island*. Translated by William Henry Giles Kingston. London: S. Low, Marston, Low and Searle, 1875.

Worton, Michael, ed. *Michel Tournier*. London: Longman, 1995.

Wyss, Johann David. *The Swiss Family Robinson*. Illus. John Gilbert. New York: Hard and Houghton, 1865 [1812].

Zarader, Jean-Pierre. Vendredi ou la vie sauvage *de Michel Tournier: Un parcours philosophique*. Paris: Vinci, 1995.

8

About a Factory-Made Boy
Christine Nöstlinger's Story about Conrad

Sabine Fuchs

The success story of Christine Nöstlinger, born on 13 October 1936 in Vienna, began with her sketches of a plump little girl with flame-colored hair. Soon Nöstlinger came up with an imaginative story for her character, in which the illustrator-turned-author speaks up for the red-headed outsider. *Die feuerrote Friederike* ("Fiery Friederica") was published in 1970 by Jugend & Volk and was immediately praised for its fresh themes and unsentimental tone. The book's illustrations met with rather less enthusiasm, leading Nöstlinger to focus on writing. She went on to become a bestselling author, but stresses that she never intended to become a writer. Instead, she emphasizes the pleasure that she derives from the craft of writing—a pleasure that is evident in her neat turns of phrase, expressive neologisms, and rich use of language. She claims that she is a lazy person who could happily live without writing, but this statement seems hard to believe: in the past thirty years she has published well over one hundred books and countless newspaper articles. Her output includes picturebooks, novels, and plays for children and young adults, poems for adults and children, as well as cookbooks for men and ironic self-help books, not to mention the scripts she wrote for TV dramas, TV series, and radio plays.

The quality of Nöstlinger's books is based on the power of her stories, which are closely observed, linguistically playful, and wonderfully imaginative. Her books feature mothers struggling to emancipate themselves, fathers adjusting to their new roles, young people protesting against authority, and articulate and persuasive children. She writes about the real world, and her social concern is apparent. As she explains, her stories are "stories to make you laugh or cry, to help you get to know the world you live in." They express "something that children are already feeling, but can't put into words."[1] Nöstlinger tells of women and girls trying to break out of their traditional roles and of children struggling to make their needs heard. In *Sowieso und überhaupt* ("Obviously and anyway," 1991) she explains with warm humor how divorce can sometimes be a good thing, if it extends your family circle. And in *Bonsai* (1997) she uses literary allusions and great wit to explore the difficulties experienced by boys finding out what it means to be male.

Nöstlinger's books impress not only readers but also juries. Besides many prizes for different books, she received the Hans Christian Andersen Award in 1984 and, in 1989, the "Österreichischen Würdigungspreis für Kinder- und Jugendliteratur" (Austrian award of recognition for children's and youth literature) for her integral oeuvre. In addition, her commitment against racism and for a more human society earned her the "Nestroy-Ring" from the city of Vienna and the "Großen Österreichischen Staatspreis" (Great Austrian state prize) in 1987, as well as the "Hans-Czermak-Preis" in 1994 (for violence-free education) and the Peace Award of the Austrian Booksellers in 1998.[2]

MASTER OF CONTEMPORARY FANTASY

Artificial or manipulated human beings have populated (children's) literature and other media products for a long time—we meet Golem or Pinocchio in literature and join the adventures of Superman/-woman and Spiderman in comics; laugh with Herman Munster on TV; or get to know AI at the cinema. They are externally manipulated or artificially created characters, with whom we can anticipate a potential future or act out ideal self-perceptions. At the same time, however, these stories may also have a critical undertone.

Conformists or individualists, consumers or reflective persons, obedient citizens or critical intellectuals—these fundamental opposites are not only important in our time but were also crucial in the 1968 student movement. It was in this atmosphere that Christine Nöstlinger wrote a novel about *Conrad: The Hilarious Adventures of a Factory-Made Boy.*[3] In children's books issued in the 1970s, readers found anti-authoritarian ideas, an emancipation from traditional socio-political roles, and a move toward an improved human and tolerant society. Besides Christine Nöstlinger, such authors as Peter Härtling who were writing for children in German-speaking countries revived traditional genres—like the fantastic story and the fairy tale—by adapting them for their purpose. In *Conrad,* Nöstlinger refers to literary genres such as science fiction and to literary characters like Pinocchio or Konrad (well-known as a figure in *Struwwelpeter*) as well as to recent social conditions, not just to criticise education and social objectives, but also to amuse.

In her fantasy stories Nöstlinger skillfully caricatures the society we live in, pushing situations to extremes and making them amusing for both adults and children. In fact, she has much in common with the British writer Edith Nesbit, who also described the realities of childhood in imaginative and humorous ways. In "Teenage Problem Novels," Anthea Bell draws attention to the humor that can convey effectively serious material, and she sees similarities with another author. "I am reminded here, too, of the American writer Katherine Paterson's *The Great Gilly Hopkins*" (Bell 1984, 50). In Christine Nöstlinger's stories there is no sign of the escapism that generally characterizes fantasy literature. In *Wir pfeifen auf den Gurkenkönig* (1972; Engl. *The Cucumber King,* 1984) she satirizes the authoritarianism of some fathers. Her social concern is particularly apparent in *Hugo, das Kind in den besten Jahren* ("Hugo: A child in the prime of life," 1983). In this multilayered story, the author speaks up for children, defending their rights and condemning discrimination, while all the time letting her imagination run riot. Christine Nöstlinger and Hugo call for action: "'You're just being lazy!' yelled Hugo. 'You don't really want to change anything! You have to take action whenever you can! Dreaming won't get you anywhere!" (Nöstlinger 1983).

A STORY TOLD WITHOUT CHAPTERS

The carpenter-artist Berti Bartolotti unexpectedly receives a large parcel. She is not worried much about it because of her weakness for coupons and order forms, Free Offers and Special Offers. In addition, she is a true non-conformist: she smokes cigars, gives herself instructions using "my dear," eats food in unusual combinations, does a dry-cleaning when her bath or shower cubicle are not useable, and paints her face "pink and red and black and brown and green and dark blue" (7). She likes bright colors not only on her face, but also in her clothes and her dresses, which are often inappropriate for the time of the year or the occasion because she always puts on the first outfit she takes out with the color she needs at that moment. She also wants her goldfish to change their environment and puts them in the bath: "After all, thought Mrs Bartolotti, other people go away on holiday, but those fish have to spend their whole time swimming round and round and round in a circular goldfish bowl" (6). The antithesis of a housewife, she dislikes cleaning, is happily divorced, and meets her boyfriend, Thomas, a correct and friendly but also a rather boring drugstore-owner, every Tuesday and Sunday. At least she doesn't care about other people's business and cannot imagine that someone else would.

Wondering what order she has forgotten, she opens the tin can, which was in the parcel, expecting popcorn or corned beef, but finds a little boy nodding to her with "Hullo, Mummy." He is one of the high-quality products, a factory-made boy, introduced by a letter from the factory-manager:

> Our firm has done all in its power to provide you with a satisfactory, promising and good natured child. The rest is up to you! We are sure you will encounter no difficulty, since our goods are particularly easy to handle and control, and, being the products of a highly developed technology, are quite free of those faults or defects which can occur in nature. (17)

This letter indicates that this instant—as well as beautiful and intelligent—child is well behaved, polite, and compliant. In opposition to the usual hierarchy, the mother disobeys educational rules, sings naughty songs to her son, always tells him the truth, and lets him form his own opinions. The model child teaches her the traditional type of correct education, goes to bed even if he is not tired, does not want to eat chocolate right before going to sleep, and asks for work, explaining:

> "I don't know if I enjoy it or not," said Conrad. "But boys of seven are old enough to do those things, and it's their duty to help their mothers by doing little jobs about the house." (28)

He enlightens his mother about what boys are expected to do—like concentrate on one thing or play alone, if it's necessary—and what they are expected not to do—"Boys of seven shouldn't look in the mirror except when they're washing their ears and cleaning their teeth, in case they get vain and conceited" (26). He upholds traditional gender roles when he insists that to play with dolls is no entertainment for boys like him.

Except for his mother, Berti, all adults, beginning with Thomas, whom Conrad has accepted as his father, are impressed by this well-behaved boy, who is an example for all other children. In the classroom he cannot deny teachers' orders and is forced to report all pranks:

> What was more, Conrad knew how to spell everything, he had beautiful writing, he gave the right emphasis to every part of a sentence when he was reading aloud, he sat still at his desk, he didn't chatter, he never ate during lessons, he never chewed gum, and of course he never pulled long strings of gum out of his mouth; he was always looking at Mrs Stone and listening to what she was saying. (83)

It is no wonder that his schoolmates are not interested in his company and jeer at him. Only Kitty, who lives in the flat next to his, likes him and knows about his technological background. She even defends him physically. As in a parody, the factory-made boy behaves helplessly in strange situations and needs explanations for all social skills because his educational program was made for an absolutely authoritarian and perfect society: "Then he asks why some children make fun of other children for no real reason. 'They didn't tell us about that in the factory,' Conrad said" (67). Nöstlinger demonstrates how a perfect child is bound to fail in less-than-perfect reality.

The firm, of course, wants this high-quality, perfect product back, but neither Berti and Thomas nor Conrad and Kitty are willing to give up their situation. In a concerted effort, they start a radical re-education. In a reversal of the normal situation, Conrad gets punished when he is polite—Kitty pricks his arm with a pin—and gets praised, when he is naughty—Kitty kisses him on the cheek. As a highly intelligent boy, Conrad learns quickly to do forbidden things like drawing on walls, shouting loudly, or behaving loutishly. He is no longer the factory-made boy and the property of the factory. With help, he sets himself free, but he wonders:

"Do I have to be like that all the time now?" asked Conrad. "Heaven forbid!" cried Mr Thomas. "Do I have to be the way I was before now?" asked Conrad. "Heaven forbid!" cried Mrs Bartolotti. Kitty put her arm round his shoulders. "Don't worry, Conrad, we'll manage all right!" she said. (125)

In the end, liberty and individuality triumph with humor over strict orders. As Maria Lypp remarks, "the character's conversion from well-behaved to rebellious child causes relieved laughter, which occurs when the tension is relieved" (Lypp 2000, 113). Nöstlinger ties together the idea of technical progress and educational traditions in a marvellous story, and both systems—education and technical progress—subject and collectivize individuals, as Winfried Freund writes (Freund 1982, 179). In her special humoristic way, Nöstlinger criticizes attitudes that attempt to produce idealized and equal humans by eliminating all differences.

AN AMUSING STORY, TOO

"Nöstlinger's books published in the '70s in the context of children's literature, where she sets the tone, are characterized by a talent for humour," Maria Lypp asserts (Lypp 2000, 126). Why do children and adult readers laugh about the story of this factory-made boy? Besides the image of a child sent by post in a tin, a crumpled-up dwarf-like seven-year-old boy, who grows to normal height when you pour a nutrient solution over him, the description of the main characters causes laughter. Extreme positions in attitudes toward work, behavior, cultural traditions, different ways of dealing with other people, and social rules clash in a single family. For example, Conrad doesn't like Punch and Judy shows as Mr Thomas did as a child:

"That crocodile only wanted to have a sleep," said Conrad. "And the person in the red cap woke the poor thing up, shouting and yelling like that!"
"Oh, but the crocodile was creeping up behind him," said Mrs Bartolotti . . .
"I don't think animals know it's wrong to creep up behind someone," said Conrad. "No, but . . ." stammered Mrs Bartolotti.
"And anyway, that person in the red cap oughtn't to be in a wild animal park unless he's driving through it in a car with all the windows

closed," Conrad pointed out. "That would be much safer for him *and* the crocodile." (35–36)

Only the knowledge of the genre, the cultural tradition of these proto-types of good and evil, and the fact that all the characters always come back make it possible to be amused by the show. Conversely, Conrad argues logically, thinking of reality, but with no experience of fictional scenes. Therefore he is unable to understand what is going on and why the other children and Berti Bartolotti enjoy it.

Later, in the so-called "Final Preparation Department," Conrad unintentionally talks about the most important lessons that he should never mention. In these "Guilt Feelings," or lessons, he was prepared to feel guilty if he did something forbidden. When Mr Thomas approves of the result, his authoritarian and traditional thinking is revealed:

> "How appalling!" murmured Mrs Bartolotti. Mr Thomas, however, said, "This is the best boy I've ever met. If all children were like that I'd have had one myself long ago! It's a real treat to find such a well brought up, good, nicely behaved, polite little boy! Only seven, too!" "Tommy, you're a born fool!" said Mrs Bartolotti. (37–38)

Forgetting his own painful childhood, Mr Thomas—as *pars pro toto* for all educational institutions—is only interested in the outcome with-out considering what the Pavlov-like drill means to a young child. Berti—who stands for humanity and tolerance in general—negates this torture and confronts Thomas emotionally. This dialogue makes the dilemma of education clear, but simultaneously, we can be amused by it. Laughter is guaranteed when Mr. Thomas has to praise Conrad dur-ing his re-education by Kitty:

> It was the hardest thing Mr Thomas had ever been asked to do in all his life. But he bent down to Conrad. "How well you say 'Silly old twit,' my boy," he said. "I'm proud of you!" (198)

The inversion of authoritarian education is funny because all children and adults know this routine. Attitudes toward bringing up children are reflected by a distorting mirror in such a way that parents can break into laughter too, even though they recognize parts of themselves.

MORE THAN ONE STORY

In 1975 *Conrad* was published in hardcover by Oetinger in Hamburg, with illustrations by Frantz Wittkamp. In addition, that same year three more books by Nöstlinger were published: Jugend & Volk in Vienna and Munich published *Der liebe Herr Teufel* ("The charming Mr Devil"), with illustrations by Peter Giesel, and *Rüb, rüb, hurra! Was in Oberrübersberg geschah!* ("Rip, rip, hoorrah! What happened in Oberrübersberg!"), with illustrations by Johannes Fessl, both fantastic stories with bizarre ideas and humour, and both offering a re-examination of the values of good and evil, success and failure; Beltz & Gelberg in Basel published the realistic story *Stundenplan* (Engl. *Four Days in the Life of Lisa*, 1977), about school problems, struggles with parents, and first love. These books have recently been made available in Europe in a number of languages, but not readily in English. *Der liebe Herr Teufel* and *Rüb, Rüb, hurra!* were never translated into English—maybe the humor in these books is particularly Austrian and it would be too difficult to translate this specific atmosphere to another culture.[4]

To transfer a story situated in a special location—with all its historical, cultural, and political background—is very difficult. Obviously, translating *Conrad* for an English or American reader was possible because Nöstlinger situated this novel in a vaguely European city, not specifically Austrian or German. Besides, she does not use specific Austrian vocabulary, except the article before names ("die Frau Bartolotti"; "the Mrs Bartolotti"), which is not standard German. Otherwise, the topics of technical progress and different aspects of upbringing are universal questions.

The British translator Anthea Bell[5] knows French, German, and Austrian literature well. She has translated most of Nöstlinger's books for English-speaking readers. Only one year after the German edition, her translation with Andersen Press was released in Great Britain with the same illustrations.[6] The English text is quite faithful to the German—you can hear Nöstlinger's voice in the descriptions of figures and situations, in the dialogs, and in the humorous plot. Anthea Bell guarantees a sensible translation, because she knows that translating literature is more than just translating the language. To translate literature also implies translating that which is different. Children's literature—as well as every literary text—imparts norms, which are transferred by narration at different levels, for example through the characters, the portrayed society, the way authors tell their story, and the emphasis placed on various meanings. To translate literature means also to translate the potentially different norms from another cultural sphere.

Readers familiar with the text will be taken completely by surprise when confronted with the American version, *Konrad*.[7] Although Anthea Bell is cited as the translator, the edition published in 1977 by Watts is a shortened story with new illustrations by Carol Nicklaus. The adaptation of specific words is a common practice—in *Konrad* the English "Mummy" is changed to " Mom," "drawing pins" to "thumb tacks," "carrier bags" to "shopping bags," "parcel" to "package," "raspberry dessert" to "raspberry Jello." An unnecessary, but noteworthy, change is that of the "managing director," who is called the "president of the factory" in the American version. Such changes are necessary to adapt foreign texts to the common target language and mostly do not change the narration or the main issues. To translate meanings may need neologisms or different explanations. In the American *Konrad* the anonymous editor decided to pick a different dirge: "My eyes have seen the glory of the burning of the school . . ." (*Konrad* 122) replaces "Three old ladies got locked in the lavatory . . ." (115). But to tell a story without defined chapters requires a different reading attitude than telling it with chapters, such as one finds in the American *Konrad*. German and English readers can set their own pauses, whereas Americans find eleven already established.

In opposition to the perfect child, Nöstlinger characterizes Berti Bartolotti as a really atypical mother figure, not only in her actions but in the detailed description of her habits in the first pages of the book. Most of these parts have been omitted in the American *Konrad*. The American readers miss the explanation of why Berti is talking to herself, calling herself "my dear." Her mother and her ex-husband always called her "my dear" when they expected her to do something, for example, homework for school or housework and cooking when she was married: "So Mrs Bartolotti was used to getting things done and obeying orders if someone called her 'my dear,' but not otherwise" (5–6). In this part, Nöstlinger criticizes authoritarian education and, at the same time, patriarchal relationships and fixed gender roles.

The American readers will not know what the bathroom looks like—how a clothes-line crossing the window and shower cubicle hinders her from opening the door to the shower, so that Mrs Bartolotti decides on dry-cleaning.

> She put some pink lotion from the big bottle on the cotton wool, and
> then she rubbed the cotton wool all over her face. The cotton wool went
> all sorts of colours: it went pink with her foundation and red with her
> lipstick and black with her mascara and brown with her eyebrow pencil
> and green with her eye-shadow and dark blue with her eye-liner. "How
> pretty!" said Mrs Bartolotti to the piece of cotton wool. (6–7)

And the re-painting of her face is missing, also her polished sky-blue
colored nails. It seems that American children should not be offered
such a person in the role of a positive mother figure.

There is no mention either of her uncontrolled buying: "She was so
hooked on ordering things that she never stopped to think whether she
really needed them or not" (10). A very amusing list of curious things
follows: "an animal encyclopedia in seventeen volumes, a consignment
of gents' grey cotton socks, a plastic tea-set for twenty-four, a sub-
scription to a fish breeders' magazine and another to a nudists' journal.
Also a Turkish coffee mill . . . , ten pairs of outsize angora wool knick-
ers, and nine Buddhist prayer wheels" (10). This list is not just amusing
to read; it is also a satirical criticism of a society where consumption is
one of the important issues. Nöstlinger underscores the fact that consumerism leads to useless purchases by having her main character, the
hand-weaving rug artist, order without reflection "that wickedly
expensive rug, with its ugly flower pattern" (10). Are American children not amused by a satiric introduction to economic issues? With an
ironic tone Nöstlinger describes how business works. Mrs Bartolotti
creates beautiful and brightly colored rugs by hand, but she does not
really get much money, even though the carpet dealers tell their cus-
tomers:

> "Ah, Mrs Bartolotti is a real artist! Her rugs are little masterpieces! That's
> what makes them so expensive!" (The carpet dealers and furnishing stores
> asked their customers three times the price they paid Mrs Bartolotti for
> her rugs; that was what really made them so expensive.) (8–9)

Perhaps Eva-Maria Metcalf is right when she says that these parts are
missing because they do not advance the plot. Apparently the editor of
the American version thinks that American children may not have the
patience to read relatively wordy explanations in marginal notes,
because they are used to consuming "action comedies" (Metcalf 2003,
67). There is, however, more than one explanation possible for the
changes in the American edition. Here are three more worth mention-

ing. First, children's and youth literature and their authors are not treated as seriously as others. For example, Christine Nöstlinger's name is always written as Nostlinger, and neither the translator nor the German editor, nor even the author were informed of the change in the story. Second, in America, Nöstlinger's ideological messages were received as political and provocative, as, for example, in the following: "... don't let anyone preach that an author of children's books should deliberately suppress his political ideas in favor of some 'general humanity'! Whatever someone recognizes as 'human' has always first been passed through the filter of his or her political views. There is nothing 'general' unless one is being stupid or opportunistic" (Nöstlinger 1993, 5). Jeffrey Garrett assumes that the influence of those American critics, who classified Nöstlinger as a political author, could be the reason why Nöstlinger's books were published by second-rate companies (Garrett 2003, 263–64). And third: Eva-Maria Metcalf mentions that "the cultural dominance of America both externally and internally led to a refusal of texts and illustrations which don't fit in with common patterns of reading and culture" (Metcalf 2003, 61). Therefore, texts and illustration were domesticated or changed to an American style.

AMERICAN-STYLE ILLUSTRATION

Frantz Wittkamp illustrated the books published for the German and English-speaking book markets. Ten black-and-white pencil drawings depict the main scenes of the story—Berti looking at the parcel, Berti with her bags, Thomas looking at the sleeping Conrad, Kitty with her mother, the teacher, Conrad playing at Kitty's birthday party, pupils maltreating Conrad, Berti and Kitty carrying a rug hiding Conrad, Thomas praising Conrad, Kitty kissing Conrad. The figures are drawn with clear lines filled in with patterns and situated in vaguely visible spaces without spatial perspective. Furthermore, they cannot be related to a specific time or place. These illustrations remind one of caricatures. That may be the reason why the publisher in America chose a different illustrator. Carol Nicklaus drew ten pictures for the American *Konrad* showing mostly similar situations but with a very different interpretation. Though she, too, draws with pencil, she decided on a dynamic style. Wittkamp's illustrations seem like still pictures, not images in action. Unlike those in Nicklaus's drawings, the figures are not clearly contoured and are situated in a specific place.

In particular, there is one illustration by Nicklaus that I cannot imagine in the German original: Berti is cooking in the foreground and Conrad is eating in the background. In the original text, Berti is characterized as the opposite of a cooking mother. She is, rather, the prototype of a mother with whom to have fun, to do extraordinary things, to fool around, or to have a serious talk. She is a modern woman, emancipated, with plenty of imagination, not fitting in to a success-oriented society but with knowledge of how to be a unique human being. The American drawings, in other words, completely alter her character and meaning.

Incredibly, the American *Konrad* got the Mildred L. Batchelder Award in 1979. This award, established in 1966,

> is a citation awarded to an American publisher for a children's book considered to be the most outstanding of those books originally published in a foreign language in a foreign country, and subsequently translated into English and published in the United States. ALSC [Association for Library Service for Children] gives the award to encourage American publishers to seek out superior children's books abroad and to promote communication among the peoples of the world.[8]

It is incredible that a reduced version of a story, which tells only what is considered appropriate for American children, should be so honored. Promoting communication also has to do with knowing about differences and tolerance of those differences. But how can you learn about differences when the "foreign" elements of stories are removed to make the stories similar to your own? Is it possible that the members of the jury did not know the original, did not know about the changes?

MORE THAN A BOOK

While she was writing *Conrad*, Nöstlinger reworked the story for the theater, and the text was published in Hamburg by Verlag für Kindertheater in the same year as the novel. Since that time the play has been one of the classic examples of contemporary children's drama performed throughout the German-speaking world.[9] In 1982 Claudia Schröder presented her film version of *Conrad*, which is faithful to the novel, though there are modifications caused by the change of media, and *Konrad aus der Konservenbüchse* ("Conrad out of the tin") is part of the repertoire of German children's cinema.

The only film adaptation ever made in a non-German-speaking country to date is a TV-production in the USA based on *Konrad*. First shown as a TV series in 1985, the videocassette *Konrad* was produced by WonderWorks Family Movie. Malcolm Marmorstein wrote the script based on the American award-winning book, but he radically changed the plot. "The book *Konrad* ended at a certain point which I felt was unsatisfactory. I picked up from that point and wrote a whole new ending" (Freyer 1987, 83). After a dramatic hunt through the factory, all the main characters meet in the control room, where Konrad resists a new brainwashing. Because the director unintentionally destroys the whole system, he decides to begin another business; Berti and Thomas get married and adopt Konrad and all the other fabricated children too. In the end, they have a big party—becoming American-like good consumers with hamburgers, fries, ice cream, and cakes. In contrast, the end of the novel presents not only comical but also subversive scenes, such as when Konrad and Kitty throw spinach and raspberry dessert from upstairs right down on the heads of the director and the married couple who have ordered Konrad and want to take him home as their son. The different ending in the American TV-version could be due to something other than subversion. As Metcalf points out: "The film ends with a happy ending which is neither plausible nor credible, that, however, adapts to the format of American children's and entertainment films, with their characteristic expectation patterns, as well as to the wishful imaginations of community togetherness" (Metcalf 2003, 70).

All characters are less extreme than in Nöstlinger's novel. "In the book the doctor was a lesser character. But Max Wright, the actor who played the doctor, was so good that we wanted to give him more scenes" (Freyer 1987, 83). Wright, as Mr Thomas, not only gets more scenes, but his whole character is changed. Mr Thomas is no longer the overly correct and boring drugstore owner. He becomes a musician, who sells instruments and introduces Konrad to the world of music. Berti, on the contrary, is not that extraordinary woman anymore, because "the director did not want to show her as sloppy at all, simply eccentric." Marmorstein realizes that "it's a purely visual decision but it changed the meaning of the story" (Freyer 1987, 83–84). She is transformed into an average woman, weaving average rugs, does not smoke cigars, and her goldfish swim in a bowl. In the American TV production the suspense factor of confronting two extreme positions is missing. Furthermore, Nöstlinger's message is missing, too! There is no critical view of education and society: "Ironically, in the end, the film becomes something that the story of Konrad itself criticized—namely a prepared, clever packaging and easy to consume product, that is not very demanding on the viewers" (Metcalf 2003, 75).

AND NOW

How can a young or adult reader today be attracted by this thirty-year-old novel? Three aspects are particularly worth considering. First, there are the messages that Nöstlinger communicated through this novel. Currently, scientists, medical experts, biologists, and politicians discuss the possibilities and limits of gene-manipulated human embryos or an artificial generation, and arrive at different ethical and legal conclusions depending on national priorities. I have noted that, "In 1975, as *Conrad* was first published, discussions about genetic technology weren't a public theme, but this novel can be read as an ironic description of the unforeseeable effects which will be caused by tailor-made offspring" (Fuchs 2001, 87). Second, the novel may initiate discussions about child rearing, gender roles in society, and tolerance in groups. Last, there are the modifications and reduction of a story published in America—awarded for its smooth translation and its truth about the country and culture of origin—as well as the specific adaptation to TV, which can initiate a discussion about excellence in translation of literary works from different cultures and in different media. In addition, the novel provokes reflection on how children can cope with cultural differences in literature and life.

  Christine Nöstlinger is determined to change and explain things wherever she can, using her texts to champion the rights of children. She has a wonderful sense of humour and a gift for unusual wordplay. Apart from the fantastic novel *Conrad/Konrad*, realistic novels are also available in English (*Girl Missing, Luke and Angela*, and *Marrying off Mother*). Nöstlinger's anti-authoritarian stories are read and loved by children all over the world and would surely appeal to American readers if they were made more available.

  In 2003 the first Astrid Lindgren Memorial Award was given jointly to American writer and illustrator Maurice Sendak and to Christine

Nöstlinger. The jury remarked that Nöstlinger "is a reliably bad child-rearing influence of the caliber of Astrid Lindgren," praising her for her "diversified and highly committed authorship" characterized by "disrespectful humour, clear-sighted solemnity and inconspicuous warmth," and adding that "she is a staunch supporter of children and those living on the margin of society." In this brief characteristic, the essence of Nöstlinger's talent has been expressed.[10]

NOTES

1. Words or phrases in quotation marks are Nöstlinger's. In many interviews Nöstlinger's views about writing children's literature are published (see Fuchs 2001). Further, Nöstlinger reflects not only on her own writing and theories of writing for children but also the place of children's literature in general (Nöstlinger 1996). All translations in this essay from texts originally published in German are mine unless otherwise indicated.

2. For detailed biographic and bibliographic notes, see Fuchs 2001.

3. The first hard-cover edition in English was titled *Conrad: The Hilarious Adventures of a Factory-Made Boy*, but quotations are taken from *Conrad. The Factory-Made Boy*, the English paperback, published as a Beaver Book.

4. I expect that laughing about the troubles of a young devil (*Der liebe Herr Teufel*), who is sent to earth to force a happy couple to become unhappy and bad, but who in the end fails his mission and stays with this family as a cat, does not go without knowing common religious tradition in Austria. Maybe the satirical criticism about tourism by creating nonsense games in skiing-places because of no snow—rolling big cotton balls with a large hair drier down the hills—is difficult to understand for young readers who don't know about the economic needs in alpine regions like Austria.

5. Anthea Bell has not only translated Christine Nöstlinger's stories, but also *Asterix and Obelix*, fairy tales from the Brothers Grimm, and novels and poems by Clemens Brentano, Wilhelm Hauff, and Christian Morgenstern, in addition to modern literature. She has won several prizes—in 2003 the "Österreichische Staatspreis für literarische Übersetzung" (Austrian state prize for literary translation)—and speaks out in favor of more translations of other literature in English-speaking countries.

6. The first edition had the title *Conrad. The Hilarious Adventures of a Factory-Made Boy*.

7. Note that *Conrad* refers to the English edition, whereas *Konrad* refers to the American edition.

8. For information about this award, see http://www.ala.org.

9. The most recent production was at Vienna's Theater der Jugend (Youth theater) during the theater season of 2004–05.

10. The jury's reasons for choosing Christine Nöstlinger for the Astrid Lindgren Memorial Award for Literature 2003 can be found on the Internet at http://www.alma.se.

WORKS CITED

Bell, Anthea. "Christine Nöstlinger introduced by A. B." *Junior Bookshelf*, April 1984: 49–51.
Freund, Winfried. Der fragwürdige Fortschritt. Christine Nöstlinger's 'Konrad'." Pp. 172–183 in *Das zeitgenössische Kinder- und Jugendbuch*. Paderborn: Schöningh, 1982.
Freyer, Ellen. "Adopting Children's Books for Television: Interview with Mary Pleshette Willis and Malcolm Marmorstein." *The Lion and the Unicorn* 11 (1987) 2: 73–86.
Fuchs, Sabine. *Christine Nöstlinger. Eine Monographie*. Wien: Dachs, 2001.
Garrett, Jeffrey. "That Difficult Austrian: Christine Nöstlinger's schwerer Stand in den USA." Pp. 255–270 in . . . *weil die Kinder nicht ernst genommen werden. Zum Werk von Christine Nöstlinger*. Edited by Sabine Fuchs and Ernst Seibert. Wien: Edition Praesens, 2003.
Lypp, Maria. "Zur Komik bei Christine Nöstlinger." Pp. 111–114 in *Vom Kaspar zum König. Studien zur Kinderliteratur*. Edited by Maria Lypp. Frankfurt: Peter Lang, 2000.
Metcalf, Eva-Maria. "Der amerikanische Konrad." Pp. 59–76 in . . . *weil die Kinder nicht ernst genommen werden. Zum Werk von Christine Nöstlinger*. Edited by Sabine Fuchs and Ernst Seibert. Wien: Edition Praesens, 2003.
Nöstlinger, Christine. *Konrad oder das Kind aus der Konservenbüchse*. Ill. Frantz Wittkamp. Hamburg: Oetinger, 1975.
Nostlinger, Christine. *Conrad the Factory-Made Boy*. Ill. Frantz Wittkamp. Trans. Anthea Bell. London: Andersen Press, 1976.
Nostlinger, Christine. *Konrad*. Ill. Carol Nicklaus. Trans. Anthea Bell, New York: Franklin Watts, 1977.
Nöstlinger, Christine. "Doing It But Not Knowing It." *Bookbird* 31 (1993) 2: 5.
Nöstlinger, Chrsitine. *Geplant habe ich gar nichts. Aufsätze, Reden, Interviews*. Wien: Dachs, 1996.
www.ala.org, Mildred L. Batchelder Award.
www.alma.se, Astrid Lindgren Memorial Award.

Films

Konrad aus der Konservenbüchse. BRD 1982. Ottokar Runze Production. Director: Claudia Schröder. Script: S. Bartlich, M. Barden, L. Oschewsky,

M. Sand, B. Wimmer, U. E. Werner-Thilo. 80 min. Release: 07.10.1983 in Germany.

Konrad. USA 1985. Elliot Friedgen Production. Director: Nell Cox. Script: Malcolm Marmorstein. 116 min. Public Media Video. Premiere: TV-Series of WonderWorks Family Movie.

9

A Neverending Success Story?
Michael Ende's Return Trip to Fantastica

Dieter Petzold

The history of Michael Ende's children's books is full of paradoxes. Ende considered himself a playwright first and foremost, but his first great success was a book for children, which he began spontaneously and allowed to grow to such a length that his publishers advised him to issue it in two parts. It was followed by a novel that adopts the narrative style of a children's book but deals with a problem that bothers adults more than children: the shortness of time in modern people's lives. His most famous work owes its international success mainly to a film version that deviates so much from the book that Ende took legal action against it. Even though an excellent English translation was published before the film came out, it has apparently never been widely read in English-speaking countries and even less frequently discussed. In Germany, the original text, *Die unendliche Geschichte*, caused a considerable sensation when it was published in 1979. Hailed as a masterpiece in *feuilletons*, it became quickly both a bestseller and a cult book—only to be frowned upon subsequently by critics of children's literature who complained that it was too hazily romantic and at the same time too didactic and, anyway, not a children's book at all.

It may be true (as some critics have maintained) that *The Neverending Story* is best understood as a product of the 1970s, and its success as a reflection of the mood of the 1980s or even the result of a misunderstanding created by the film version. Yet, twenty-five years after its publication, it is still selling steadily, and we may begin to wonder if it is not on its way to becoming a true classic.

MICHAEL ENDE: THE MAN
AND HIS WORK

It seems as if Michael Ende[1] was predestined for an artistic career. His father, Edgar Ende, was a successful painter with a penchant for fantastic-surrealistic motifs; his mother Luise also had considerable artistic talents (which, however, she subordinated to the task of supporting her family for the larger part of her life). Born on 12 November 1929 in the small town of Garmisch-Partenkirchen in Southern Germany, Michael was to remain their only child. In 1931, the family moved to Munich, where Edgar Ende not only found better opportunities to sell his pictures but also an atmosphere conducive to his artistic development. From early on, young Michael was allowed to be present when his father discussed art, philosophy, religion, and politics with his wife and his artistic friends.

Edgar Ende's career as a painter was stalled, however, when Hitler and his National Socialist Party, after having gained power in 1933, began to persecute artists who would not support their ideology. Edgar Ende's pictures were officially banned from public exhibitions in 1936 as being part of what the Nazis declared to be "degenerate art." In 1941, Michael's father was drafted into military service, and the 12-year-old boy witnessed the bombing of Munich. Eventually, the family survived both the Nazi terror and the war, but obviously the experience left lasting impressions in the young man's soul.

After the war, Michael attended a so-called "Waldorf" school in Stuttgart, a private school conducted after the pedagogical philosophy of Rudolf Steiner (1861–1925). Steiner is best known as the founder of Anthroposophy, a philosophical doctrine he developed from ideas of the German poet Johann Wolfgang von Goethe (1749–1832) and various other sources. While traces of this world-view, which stresses the importance of spirituality, intuition, and life in harmony with nature, can be found in many of Ende's writings, it is really just one of many influences on his thinking. Throughout his life, Ende felt attracted to various thought systems with a magical bias, like Alchemy, Rosicrucianism, and the Kabbala, to the religions and philosophies of the Far East, and to Jungian psychology, while Christian traditions, Romantic literature, and modern fantastic art, form, as it were, the basis of his art.

Michael Ende had been writing poems from an early age, but after graduating from school, it was the theater that attracted him most. While studying acting in Munich, he began to write plays and texts for various political cabaret troupes. In post-war Germany, avant-garde theater was dominated by Bertolt Brecht's plays and theories. Ende, a critic of modern society but never a consistently leftist thinker, struggled with Brecht's concepts of social criticism and didacticism and eventually came to reject them; nevertheless, his writings do carry messages, as critics have been quick to point out.

Ende's first children's book, however, is anything but overtly didactic. The two-part story of Jim Button: *Jim Knopf und Lukas der Loko-motivführer* (1960; Engl. *Jim Button and Luke the Engine Driver*, 1990) and *Jim Knopf und die Wilde 13* (Jim Button and the Wild 13, 1962), is an exuberantly playful fantasy about a black foundling who as a baby was delivered by mail to the minute island of Lummerland. Among its four inhabitants is Luke the Engine Driver, who becomes Jim's fatherly friend and companion on a long journey that takes them to an exotic fairy-tale China, where they rescue the Emperor's little daughter, Li Si, who had been kidnapped by pirates. After many more adventures, Jim is finally revealed to be a prince, married to the princess Li Si, and proclaimed king of an island that has re-emerged from the sea. The charm of the story lies in its abundance of fantastic ideas, its gentleness—there is no violence, and seemingly evil characters are reformed rather than punished—and its apparent naivety tempered with genial irony. The humorous depiction of a miniature world taken straight from the nursery, where technology and magic coexist and characters are allowed their whims and harmless idiosyncrasies, struck a responsive chord in the post-war German audience. The Jim Button novels won several prizes, were dramatized and staged as puppet shows (which, in turn, were immediately televised and proved extremely successful) and subsequently translated into many languages.

For the first time in his life Ende found himself out of financial straits. In 1964 he married his longtime partner, actress Ingeborg Hoffmann; the couple, who remained childless, eventually settled down in a splendid villa in Genzano, a small town south of Rome. Henceforth, Italy remained Ende's abode of choice; it also looms large in his writings. To his mind it represented—just as it had to the Romantic poets and painters—both ancient culture and that "lightness of being" he found deplorably absent in northern countries like Germany.

Characteristically, the setting of his next novel, *Momo* (1972; Engl. 1985), has a distinct Italian flavor; there is a hint that the place of the action may be Rome, but it remains vague, as befits a story that is subtitled "a fairy tale novel." More specifically, it might be described as a satirical dystopian parable with fairy-tale elements. In a basically realistic, contemporary world, mysterious Grey Gentlemen appear who, in the name of rationality and efficiency, steal people's time and make their lives miserable. In the end they are thwarted by a little girl, Momo, apparently an orphan who appeared out of the blue. Although she seems to be doing nothing, she is an instigator of community spirit and artistic inspiration in her friends. She turns out to be impervious to the Grey Gentlemen's coercion because she alone does not regard time as a commodity that, like the money with which it is often equated, can be saved or spent at will. With the help of a mysterious personification of time, Master Hora, and his pet tortoise, Cassiopeia, Momo manages to defeat the Grey Gentlemen with their own weapons. Not only because of this victory, but also because of the mystery of her origins and the softening influence she has on children and adults alike, she may be regarded as a form of the Eternal Child, a type dear to the Romantics (see Ewers 1985, 59–63). Although neither clearly a children's nor an adults' book, *Momo*, illustrated by the author himself, became an immediate success. It was translated into some forty languages, dramatized, turned into an opera, and made the basis for two film versions.[2]

Throughout his artistic career, Ende sought to combine art forms, writing texts for picturebooks, providing illustrations for his books, and, above all, creating or re-working texts for the stage, often with music. Until his death in 1995, he created some 13 picturebooks, 8 plays, 4 opera librettos (among them an adaptation of Lewis Carroll's long nonsense ballad *The Hunting of the Snark*), 4 volumes of stories, 3 volumes of verses, and 3 volumes of essays, interviews, and conversations. In addition to the fantasy novels already mentioned, he published a partly humorous, partly satirical story with the multiple-portmanteau title *Der Satanarchäolügenialkohöllische Wunschpunsch* (1989; Engl. *The Night of Wishes: or The Satanarchaeolidealcohellish Notion Potion,* 1992). None of these publications, however, attained quite the popularity of his longest work, the 428-page novel *The Neverending Story*.

THE NEVERENDING STORY, PART I: FROM GRIPPING YARN TO METAFANTASY

The protagonist of *The Neverending Story* is "a fat little boy of ten or twelve" (5), Bastian Balthazar Bux. He is lonely because his mother is dead, his father is completely withdrawn in his grief, and his schoolmates treat him as an outsider. In the introductory chapter, Bastian, fleeing from his taunting classmates, enters a strange shop of old books and, while the owner is answering the telephone, spontaneously steals the book the owner was just reading, a book to which he feels mysteriously attracted because of its title, *The Neverending Story*. Playing hookey, he hides in the attic of the school and begins to read.

From now on we (the readers of Ende's book) are presented with the text Bastian is reading (which, confusingly, has the same title as the book we are holding in our hands); in addition, we also watch him reading, and responding to, the story. What initially looked like a simple frame story turns out to work on two distinct, but consistently developed levels, which are indicated by different lettering: in the original hardcover versions, Bastian's story is printed in purple ink, the story he is reading, in green. What is even more confusing is the fact that the description of the book fits the actual book that we are reading[3]—at least if we are lucky enough to have a copy of the original hardcover edition; paperback editions in general do not try to reproduce this effect, featuring ordinary covers and using italics to symbolize the purple ink. (Subsequent quotations in this essay will use the same device.)

The story Bastian is reading is about a strange land called Fantastica. It is ruled by a little girl, the Childlike Empress, and peopled with a great many different fantastic creatures. At the beginning of the story, they are in great alarm because, mysteriously, large chunks of the land have begun to disappear recently, and the Childlike Empress in her Ivory Tower is ill. The wisest doctor, Cairon the centaur, is sent to find a hero who is willing to go to find out how the land and its ruler can be saved. This hero is Atreyu, a ten-year-old boy who belongs to a tribe of prairie hunters, the Greenskins (an obvious allusion to, or parody of, the "Redskins" of innumerable adventure stories).

What follows, spread out over ten chapters, is essentially the story of Atreyu's quest, occasionally interrupted by short glimpses (36, to be precise, varying in length between one line and almost two pages) of Bastian reading that story and getting more and more emotionally involved in it. Like the fairy-tale hero that he is in some respects, Atreyu is easy to identify with, especially for Bastian. Strong, brave, and self-confident, Atreyu looks like Bastian's opposite, but their basic situation is alike in that both are, or feel like, orphans, and are dependent on benevolent helpers.

Equipped with AURYN, a magic amulet bestowed by the Childlike Empress, Atreyu sets out on the back of his horse Artax and soon becomes eyewitness of the working of the Nothing, the mysterious negative force that makes the land and all living things that dwell on it disappear. In a dream it is revealed to him that he must consult Morla the Aged One, a giant tortoise who lives in the Swamps of Sadness. Readers who feel reminded here of the "Slough of Despond" in Bunyan's *Pilgrim's Progress* are probably not far off the mark. As we shall see, the book is full of intertextual allusions and borrowings.[4] Regardless of whether Ende knew Bunyan or not, his work certainly betrays a tendency toward Bunyanesque allegory, albeit with very different messages.

Atreyu's horse dies in the swamps, but the boy, protected by AURYN, finds Morla, who turns out to be cynical and tired of life, with a tendency to talk to herself, very much like Tolkien's Gollum. Atreyu refuses to succumb to her nihilism and coaxes her to reveal to him that what the Childlike Empress needs is a new name, which, however, no creature of Fantastica can give her. When pressed to tell him who might be able to give the Empress a new name, she refers him to another creature, "Uyulala in the Southern Oracles."

Plodding on, he crosses the Land of the Dead Mountains, which is haunted by a female monster called Ygramul. She looks, basically, like a giant spider, but is able to shift her shape because she is "made up of innumerable small steel-blue insects which buzzed like angry hornets" (76). When Atreyu stumbles on her she happens to be engaged in a fight with a "luckdragon" who is caught in her web spread over the "Deep Chasm" that runs through the Land of the Dead Mountains. In contrast to ordinary dragons, the narrator tells us, "luckdragons are creatures of air, warmth, and pure joy . . . they swim in the air of heaven as fish swim in water" (75). Apparently Ende borrowed the idea of dragons being beautiful and benevolent from Chinese tradition.

Henceforth, the young luckdragon, whose name is Falkor, is Atreyu's most faithful friend and helper.

At this point Ende hints for the first time at what is to become the ruling idea of the whole book. When Atreyu faces the monster Ygramul, the two worlds, Bastian's "reality" and the fictitious world of Fantastica, connect for a moment: As he reads about the deadly danger of his hero, Bastian cries out in terror, and Ygramul hears his cry. There will soon be more connections of this kind.

The fight with Ygramul shows Atreyu's devotion to his mission. He allows the monster to bite him even though he expects to die of its poison after one hour, because it has the magic property to transport the victim to wherever he wants to be. In this way Atreyu and the luckdragon are able to cover the immense distance to the Southern Oracles in an instant. Of course, they do not die; they are nursed back to health by a motherly female gnome, Urgl, while her husband, Engywook, the caricature of a scientist, instructs the boy about the three gates he has to pass in order to get to the oracle. The first consists of a pair of Sphinxes whose gaze can kill; but Atreyu is allowed to pass them unharmed. At the second, the Magic Mirror Gate, the two worlds connect for the second time: for a short moment Atreyu sees in the mirror Bastian as he is reading the book. After passing the third gate, Atreyu finds himself in a forest of columns. There he hears "Uyulala, the voice of silence," singing in rhymes and telling him that only a human being from the real world outside is able to give the Childlike Empress a new name and thus save Fantastica.

Reading this, Bastian is filled with the desire to enter Fantastica and save it, but he is still convinced (though no longer quite certain) that it is impossible to do so. Atreyu, meanwhile, flies over the land on the luckdragon's back, trying to get to the borders of Fantastica in order to contact a human being, only to learn from Wind Giants that Fantastica has no borders. In the storm raised by the Wind Giants, he falls from Falkor's back into the sea. On shore, he witnesses more inhabitants of Fantastica being drawn into the Nothing. In a deserted town, "Spook City," he meets Gmork the Werewolf, the only creature who is able to wander freely between Fantastica and the world of humans. It is from his mouth that Atreyu, and the reader, get some essential information about Fantastica and its deadly foe, the Nothing:

> "What are you creatures of Fantastica? Dreams, poetic inventions, characters in a neverending story. Do you think you're real? Well yes, here in

your world you are. But when you've been through the Nothing, you won't be real anymore." (151)

Here, at last, it becomes clear that Fantastica needs to be interpreted on more than one level.[5] It certainly is a fantasy world described in a concrete, material piece of text; but Ende has alerted us to the fact that such worlds come alive only through the reader's (or listener's) imagination; their existence depends, as it were, on the reader's ability, and willingness, to "create" it in their minds. In this case, it is Bastian who imagines the world he is reading about so vividly that it becomes "real" to him. In that sense, Fantastica is the product of a cooperation between the anonymous author of the book and his reader, Bastian.

What we learn from Gmork, however, is still a different matter. The existence of Fantastica also depends on the existence of a living tradition of fantasizing in the real world. When that tradition begins to run dry, Fantastica is threatened to fall prey to the Nothing. The implication of this threat is that Fantastica is also symbol, or embodiment, of all fantastic fiction, something like a collective dream of mankind, incorporating all the fantastic inventions to be found in myths, folk tales, and literature. Incidentally, that is why Ende's intertextual allusions and borrowings are more than just an inconsequential game: they are essential for making the point that fantasy fiction, even when written by an individual author, is always also the product of a collective effort because it is constructed out of building blocks created by earlier generations of storytellers.

It is now obvious that Ende's book is not just a fantasy story: it is also a meditation on the essence, and uses, of fantasy stories: in other words, a meta-fantasy.[6] Since it examines not only what fantasy *is* but also what it *does*—for the individual reader and for the general public—it has psychological and political implications. Specifically, what Gmork is talking about is the abuse of fantasy for political reasons. According to him, the Nothing that eats up Fantastica is not only caused by a general disbelief, or lack of interest, in the heritage of myth and fairy tale; it is also the result of active manipulation that seeks to distort, rather than eliminate, the fantastic tradition. To the inhabitants of Fantastica, the Nothing looks simply like non-existence; but, as Gmork goes on to explain, the creatures of Fantastica do not really disappear: they become "lies," that is, they are utilized for specific purposes in the real world:

"If humans believe Fantastica doesn't exist, they won't get the idea of visiting your country. And as long as they don't know you creatures of Fantastica as you really are, the Manipulators do what they like with them. . . . When it comes to controlling human beings there is no better instrument than lies. Because, you see, humans live by beliefs. And beliefs can be manipulated . . .

"When your turn comes to jump into the Nothing, you too will be a nameless servant of power, with no will of your own. Who knows what use they will make of you? Maybe you'll help them persuade people to buy things they don't need, or hate things they know nothing about, or hold beliefs that make them easy to handle, or doubt the truths that might save them." (152)

In other words, there are humans who have a personal interest in making sure that people do not enjoy the *real* pleasures of fantasizing. These "Manipulators" want to fill people's heads with "lies," false dreams—dreams of consumerism or political and religious utopias—that make them easy to manipulate, and thus allow the "Manipulators" to remain in power.[7] Ende does not say who these "Manipulators" are; nevertheless, when Bastian realizes "*that not only was Fantastica sick, but the human world as well*" (153; here and henceforth in quotations author's emphasis), it is important to see that this "sickness" is a metaphor for a specific political situation, not just a general malaise caused by the dominance of abstract attitudes like materialism, skepticism, or rationalism.

Ende does not return to the political message of his allegory except very briefly at the end of the book, when Mr. Coreander intimates that those who, like Bastian, "*go to Fantastica and come back . . . make both worlds well again*" (444). Instead, he focuses on the impact fantasizing has on the individual mind. In order to come to that point, he has first to get Bastian yet more deeply involved in the story he is reading.

Atreyu has done his utmost to bring Bastian into the story. His quest ends after Falkor, the luckdragon, saves him from being swallowed by the Nothing, and takes him to the Childlike Empress. The task of drawing Bastian into the story, however, is not yet accomplished, even though Bastian at this point has a vision of the Childlike Princess and has spontaneously found her new name (Moon Child). Now he learns that all he has to do is call out her new name, but his courage fails him. So in the pivotal twelfth chapter, the Childlike Empress herself sets out on the final quest. Invisible servants carry her to the icy Mountain of Destiny, where she meets the Old Man of Wan-

dering Mountain who lives in a house-sized egg. The Old Man is writing in a book that looks exactly like the book Bastian (and the reader)
is reading, and the words that appear on the page describe exactly what
is happening at that moment. Cause and effect merge in this magic
world and become indistinguishable: "'You write down everything
that happens,' [the Childlike Empress] said. 'Everything that I write
down happens,' was the answer, spoken in the deep, dark voice that
had come to her like an echo of her own voice" (192).

Small wonder that *"Bastian's thoughts were in a whirl. . . . How
could this book exist inside itself?"* (192). When he realizes that *"he,
Bastian, was a character in the book which until now he had thought
he was reading"* (196) and that the Childlike Empress has deliberately
trapped herself (and, by implication, him) in a circular story—giving
its title, *The Neverending Story*, a new grim meaning—he ends this
mind-teasing *mise en abyme* by the only way possible. Flinging himself
into the abyss, as it were, he calls out, "Moon Child, I'm coming"
(199), and he is literally blown into the world of Fantastica.

Things become even more complicated when we pause to consider
the meaning of the two characters the Childlike Empress and the Old
Man of Wandering Mountain. Although dwelling inside Fantastica,
they are not really part of it, being like gods and/or (depending on
one's point of view) allegorical figures. The Childlike Empress seems
to be an incarnation of Fantasy itself, the human power to fantasize, to
invent characters, landscapes, stories—in short, Secondary Worlds. She
is morally neutral because she stands for creation pure and simple:[8]

> She didn't rule, she had never used force or made use of her power. She
> never issued commands and she never judged anyone. . . . In her eyes all
> her subjects were equal.
>
> She was simply there in a special way. She was the center of all life in
> Fantastica.
>
> And every creature, whether good or bad, beautiful or ugly, merry or
> solemn, foolish or wise—all owed their existence to her existence. With-
> out her, nothing could have lived, any more than a human body can live
> if it has lost its heart. (36)

It is no coincidence that she lives, literally, in an Ivory Tower. There is
a nod to the common meaning of the term but its pejorative connotation is rejected. In Ende's theory of Fantasy (just as in Tolkien's) it is
essential that Fantasy offer a haven from the demands of drab reality,

and that it be a place of absolute beauty. The Childlike Empress looks "like an indescribably beautiful girl of no more than ten" (169) but her hair is white, and she is "much older than the oldest inhabitants of Fantastica" (165). As an allegory of the imagination, a basic human faculty, she is as old as mankind; but her image, fittingly, is that of a pre-pubescent child, of an age commonly thought to have the most fertile imagination. At the same time she has something inhuman about her; with her "almond-shaped eyes, the color of dark gold" and "strangely elongated earlobes" (169), she resembles effigies of Indian goddesses or Buddhas. Her title, "Golden-eyed Commander of Wishes," alludes to the Freudian idea that our fantasies are really expressions of our (mostly unconscious) wishes.

Her amulet, AURYN, is but an extension of herself. It bears on one side the ancient symbol of the Ouroboros. In tradition, the Ouroboros is a snake forming a ring by holding its tail in its mouth, symbolizing, among other things, eternity and, in an alchemistic context, ever-changing matter, death, and resurrection. Here the ring is an oval formed by two snakes, one dark and one light, thus suggesting another set of complex meanings, that of yin and yang, the interdependence of light and dark, good and evil.[9] On its reverse side Bastian later discovers the words "Do What You Wish," which again seem to suggest that it is human wishes that inform the Imagination's eternal yet ever-changing power of destruction and re-creation.

Like the Childlike Empress, the Old Man of Wandering Mountain seems to be an allegorical figure who exists on a different level than Fantastica. According to the Childlike Empress, he is like her "because he is [her] opposite in every way" (181). The egg where he dwells is just as remote from reality as the Ivory Tower, and just as full of symbolic meaning. While she represents the infinite possibilities of Fantasy, he is "Fantastica's memory" who "can only look back at what *has* happened" (193). In a sense, what has happened is dead: "By my hand everything becomes fixed and final" (193), the Old Man explains. But the archive of old stories is also the source of new ones, by providing an echo chamber of intertextual references that gives the new stories life and resonance. "Every egg . . . is the beginning of new life" (193).

Having arrived at the middle of the novel, we can see how ambitious, and problematic, it is. What Ende is attempting through his metafictional devices is not just to prove that he can perform inconsequential postmodern sleights of hand. While there is a certain playfulness in his deft juggling of narrative levels, their purpose is not the reader's ironical distancing from the story—after all, what the book advocates is the exact opposite, the reader's total imaginative immersion in this story. Moreover, Ende is also trying to convey messages by giving his story allegorical meanings. The book is thus pulling in three directions at the same time. It tries to be a gripping yarn in which readers can lose themselves. This purpose is undercut, however, by its allegorical nature. The purpose of teaching the reader lessons is, in turn, undercut by its excessive use of metafictional devices that are likely to confuse rather than illuminate the reader.

THE NEVERENDING STORY, PART II: FROM METAFANTASY TO *BILDUNGSROMAN*

If the first part of the book can be read as an allegory of the reception of fantasy fiction—its uses and abuses—the second is an allegory of its creation. Whereas the first twelve chapters describe Atreyu's quest, the hero of the fourteen remaining chapters is Bastian. His adventures are also a kind of quest, but it emerges only gradually.

Bastian's first step into Fantastica is a spontaneous creative act: giving the Childlike Empress a new name. On the allegorical level, the meaning is clear: inventing names is the very core of (literary) creativity, and is therefore a convincing symbol of the creative act as such. (Tolkien and St. John would agree.) What is essential here is Bastian's artistic self-assurance: the name is 'correct' because it feels correct to him. The same applies to the many namings that Bastian performs in the course of his stay in Fantastica. Naming does not bring forth things, but it establishes identities and thus bestows permanence to newly created objects. The creative power as such lies in Bastian's wishes: "Fantastica will be born again from your wishes," the Childlike Empress tells Bastian (204). As a sign of his new power, she gives him her amulet, AURYN. At first, Bastian naively interprets the motto on its reverse side, "Do What You Wish," as a permission, or even order, "to do whatever he pleased" (210). As it turns out, finding what he really wishes is so difficult that the task requires the long and tortuous quest that forms the second part of the book.[10]

One might expect that the idea of Bastian re-creating Fantastica through his wishes would lead to a severe narrative problem: How can there be real danger, and hence suspense, if a simple act of wishing can solve all problems? In actual fact, however, Bastian does not appear as

the master of his wishes; and they are not always automatically fulfilled. If they are formed consciously at all, they remain quite general;
their specific shape seems to be a gift (presumably from the Childlike
Empress, but this is not stated clearly), surprising him as much as the
reader. From the beginning of his stay in Fantastica, when he watches
in wonder as a luscious world of beautiful plants arises from the grain
of sand that the Childlike Empress has given him (all that is left of the
old Fantastica), Bastian experiences himself as a discoverer, rather than
as a creator, of this new world, rarely losing the sense of exploration
and wonder one might have in an elaborate dream. Even his first completely selfish wish, to become handsome and strong, is fulfilled before
he becomes aware of it.

Ende seems to indicate here that creative wishes, like artistic inspira-
tions, arise straight from the unconscious. If this view is correct, the
story implies that the unconscious works on several levels. Firstly, it
must be a repository of visual artistic ideas, because Bastian keeps
"inventing" fantastic landscapes and pieces of architecture. Secondly,
it must also be a repository of characters, images, and motifs gleened
from his readings and, possibly, drawn from a "collective unconscious" since many of Bastian's inventions seem vaguely familiar or can
even be traced to specific literary sources. Thirdly, the unconscious
must be a wise designer of events and symbolic images that have a specific didactic function. Given Ende's knowledge of C. G. Jung, this
interpretation may well be what he has in mind. The impression the
reader gets, however, is rather that there is some unknown guiding
force behind all that happens, just as in genuine fairy tales.

Indeed, the second half of the book turns out to be an elaborate *bildungsroman* whose fantastic events serve to delineate the protagonist's
unconscious search for maturity and autonomy. This search proves
extraordinarily difficult because Bastian does not know what his goal
is, and because with each wish fulfilled he loses a part of his memory
of the real world. As he tries out various models of a new self, he loses
contact with his real self, getting lost in a maze of self-projections that
are merely external role models. While Ende's book is certainly about
the delights of fantasizing, it is also, perhaps even more, about the dangers of abandoning reality in favor of wishful daydreaming, of getting
lost in a homemade fantasy world.

When Bastian awakes after his first night in Fantastica, he wishes to
explore a desert next, and he finds that "Perilin, the Night Forest," the
jungle he had created and named, disappears at dawn, to be replaced

by "Goab, the Desert of Colors." His delight with the sheer beauty of
the place (again, we see Bastian's artistic talent at work) is mingled with
pride at his exploits. By writing his initials in the sand, he tries to send
a message to the outside world: a naive gesture, but an apt symbol of
the artist's wish for prestige and admiration.

Wishing for an adventure to prove his newfound mettle, he next
encounters a huge fire-red lion: "Grograman, Lord of the Desert of
Colors . . . , also known as the Many-Colored Death" (223), who turns
out to be less dangerous (at least to Bastian) than his name suggests.
Grograman is turned to stone every night and re-awakened to life each
morning. To his question why that is so, Bastian answers spontaneously (with a burst of wisdom that seems to come with his gift of creation), "So that Perilin, the Night Forest, can grow in the Desert of
Colors" (232), an explanation that Grograman accepts: "Now I see
that my dying gives life and my living death, and both are good. Now
I understand the meaning of my existence" (232).[11] Later, Grograman
provides Bastian also with a deeper interpretation of AURYN's injunc-
tion, "Do What You Wish": "It means that you must do what you
really and truly want. And nothing is more difficult" (238).

It takes many more adventures before Bastian finds out how difficult
this task really is. His next wish is one that many readers will find
familiar: "to exhibit his talents to others, to be admired and to become
famous" (239). By means of "the Temple of a Thousand Doors," he
leaves Grograman and his desert behind and gets into a world of
Arthurian epic poetry, which is depicted, thankfully, with a few grains
of irony. A tournament is held in the Silver City of Amarganth, situated in the middle of Moru, the Lake of Tears. Here knights from all
over the world fight for the honor of serving the (yet unknown) Savior
of Fantastica. This Savior is no other than Bastian, of course; but he
remains incognito for a while in order to show off his prowess. He
takes part in the contests and, naturally, defeats all the knights hands
down. When his true identity is finally revealed, it is by Atreyu, who
is among the spectators and recognizes him in spite of the drastic
changes in his appearance.

Bastian's long-held wish to be Atreyu's friend is fulfilled, but the
two are far from equal. Not only has Bastian proved himself to be a
super-hero, but he proceeds to dazzle the people of Amarganth even
more by appearing as a master poet and storyteller, whose glory
reaches its climax when he names, and thereby activates, a jewel (Al
Tsahir) that is the magic key to the Library of the Collected Works of

Bastian Balthazar Bux. When Atreyu, after this triumph, suggests that Bastian will now probably want to go back and save his own world as well, his friend agrees only half-heartedly: he has used so many wishes meanwhile that he has completely forgotten who he was before entering Fantastica.

Accompanied by the Heroes Hykrion, Hysbald, and Hydorn, along with Atreyu and Falkor the luckdragon, he sets out again, ostensibly to reach the borders of Fantastica, but really penetrating deeper and deeper into the land in search of new adventures. The following episode can be read as a parable of the responsibilities attached to creatorship. Bastian had created a dragon, Smerg,[12] just to give the Hero Hynreck a chance to prove himself and rescue his lady, the Princess Oglamar. Smitten with remorse, he decides that "he had no wish to go down in the history of Fantastica as a creator of monsters and horrors. How much finer it would be to become famous for his unselfish goodness . . ." (285). The wish, of course, is anything but unselfish, and Bastian fails miserably when he tries to change the lot of the Acharis, hideous worm-like creatures who are superb artisans, but so unhappy about their ugliness that they are constantly weeping. He turns them into "Shlamoofs, the Everlasting Laughers" (291), who prove to be silly clowns in the shape of butterflies, with no sense of beauty, dignity, or respect.[13]

After going in circles for a while, Bastian discovers that where he really wants to go is to the Ivory Tower where the Childlike Empress dwells. Gradually, a host of grotesque creatures joins the party, all ardent fans of the Savior of Fantastica (and manifestations of the fecundity of Bastian's—or rather, Ende's—imagination). Impervious to Atreyu's warnings, Bastian becomes prouder and prouder. He willfully approaches the castle of "Xayide, the wickedest and most powerful sorceress in all Fantastica" (316). With the help of his friends, he enters her castle in a daring rush and takes her prisoner, only to succumb subsequently to her sex-appeal[14] and her flatteries and feigned humility.

The next episode may be regarded as a comical interlude with serious implications. Bastian is invited by the Monks of Knowledge, who live in the Star Cloister of Ghigam, a kind of philosophical academy, to answer the question "What is Fantastica?" Bastian's enigmatic (and circular) answer is: "Fantastica is the Neverending Story" (347). Asked for an explanation, he uses the magic stone Al Tsahir to open a window to the outside world, revealing, for a short moment, the attic of his old school where the book is still lying. The Three Deep Thinkers are much too self-centered and vain to draw any real illumination from the revelation, while it has cost Bastian dearly: he has lost not only a valuable magic tool but also all memory of his past life outside Fantastica.

The nadir of his moral degeneration, however, is reached when Bastian and his host of followers reach the Ivory Tower and discover that the Childlike Empress is gone. Using Xayide's gift, a magic belt of invisibility, to spy on his friends, Bastian learns that Atreyu plans to take AURYN from him. He bans Atreyu and the luckdragon and prepares to have himself crowned Childlike Emperor. In the ensuing battle Bastian wounds Atreyu, and the Ivory Tower is destroyed.

This Pyrrhic victory is the turning point in his moral career. His magic-mechanical horse (another gift of Xayide's) is shattered during his mad pursuit of Atreyu, and Bastian finds himself alone in a dilapidated city full of zombie-like madmen and madwomen. A cynical monkey informs him that they were all once Emperors, or would-be Emperors, of Fantastica, who have lost their memories and, consequently, their ability to have wishes. The only way to avoid the same destiny is to find a wish that will take him back to his own world, but his power of wishing is running out, and he has only very few wishes left.

The rest of the book is concerned with Bastian's goal of finding a way back to the human world. Ende is here giving yet another twist to an age-old motif that can be traced all the way through literature to myth and folklore. The motif of humans being held captive in, or otherwise unable to leave, fairy-land or a similar retreat, is well-nigh ubiquitous. In folklore, it is often connected with the changeling motif and with the motif of humans being seduced into following some alluring fairy into her realm.[15] Among the best-known examples are the Circe episode in the *Odyssey*, the folk ballads "Tam Lin" and "Thomas Rhymer," the Middle English verse romance *King Orfeo* and the medieval story of the Tannhäuser (best known through Richard Wagner's opera), James Hogg's long ballad "Kilmenny" (1813), Keats's "La Belle Dame Sans Merci" (1819), and Tennyson's "The Lotos Eaters" (1832). George MacDonald used the motif in his fairy tale "The Carasoyn" (1866–71); it informs J. M. Barrie's *Peter Pan* (1901) and even—in ironic guise—Thomas Mann's realistic novel *The Magic Mountain* (*Der Zauberberg*, 1924). What these widely different texts have in common is the ambivalence of the Otherworld: it is both alluring and dangerous, making it a perfect metaphor for poetic rapture, wishful daydreaming, sexual bondage, drug addiction, or any combination of these and other impairments of rationality and freedom of will.

The next, and final, episodes are even more like parables: so much so that they need little explanation. Since he feels lonely, Bastian unconsciously wishes "to belong to some sort of community, to be taken into a group" (386), and he soon reaches a floating city in The Sea of Mist, where the Yskalnari dwell, a people who live together harmoniously because they have no sense of individuality at all. After a while Bastian understands that what is lacking in this state of perfect communism is love. His desire to be loved just as he is (instead of being admired for conforming to some extrinsic ideal) takes him to the House of Change and its mistress, the Dame Eyola. Her house, and even her body, abound with delicious, nourishing fruits. In her presence Bastian feels like a little child, absolutely trusting and loving, and he is treated accordingly (even by the house, whose furniture becomes so large that Bastian appears quite small). Telling him his own story, she makes him realize that "he had always wanted to be someone other than he was, but he didn't want to change" (402). But he need not feel guilty, because all his errors belong to the way he has to go in order to get to "the fountain from which springs the Water of Life" (409), whence he will be able to return to the human world.

The figure of Eyola is reminiscent of George MacDonald's Grand-Mothers; but she is less spiritual and more motherly, making Bastian regress to the state of infancy, from which he can start to reconstruct his true personality. Her house is a house of healing as much as a house of change. Bastian is ready to leave it when he has discovered his true wish, which marks his maturity: not to be loved, but to be able to love. But, paradoxically, this wish has cost him the memory of the one person he needs to love: his father. To regain it, he has to work as an apprentice for Yor, a blind miner who excavates "paper-thin sheets of colored, transparent isinglass" (418), that bear pictures representing "forgotten dreams from the human world" (419).[16] After being pampered by motherly Dame Eyola, Bastian has to work hard for the stern, taciturn, "fatherly" Yor, who symbolizes the artist who is also a guide to the unconscious. After a long and laborious search in the mines (of his unconscious), Bastian finds his own forgotten dream: the picture of his father, "shut up in a transparent but impenetrable block of ice" (423). His longing to help that strange man break free of the block of ice is his last wish. Embracing it, he forgets the last thing he remembered: his own name.

Once more he has to face his shameful past when the Shlamoofs, the butterfly clowns he had created, persecute him; but although his father's picture is broken in the ensuing scuffle, he is saved, for he next meets Atreyu and Falkor, the luckdragon, who are still his true friends. He is now able to fulfill Atreyu's wish and give up AURYN. As he places the amulet on the ground, it is transformed into a gigantic dome of light that houses the fountain of the Water of Life, encircled by the two snakes depicted on the amulet, now grown to gigantic size.

There is no need to unfold the multiple meanings of this universal symbol, the Water of Life, since Ende is quite explicit about what the ensuing scene of baptism does to Bastian. He is given his former real-world shape, bathes in the water, and is

> newborn. And the best part of it was that he was now the very person he wanted to be. . . . Because now he knew that there were thousands and thousands of forms of joy in the world, but that all were essentially one and the same, namely, the joy of being able to love. (434)

He takes leave of his friends, the snakes open a gate for him, which he passes to find himself back in the real world where, to his surprise, only a few hours have elapsed. The Water of Life that Bastian had tried to bring to his father is spilled, but it is not really needed. Bastian's story is enough to release his father from his stupor of grief: for the first time since the death of his wife, he is able to weep and to hug his son.

The next day, Bastian goes to Mr Coreander to tell him that the book he had stolen from him has disappeared. He learns that the bookseller never owned such a book, but that he, too, had been to Fantastica. Bastian won't be able to visit Moon Child a second time, Mr Coreander tells him; *"but if you can give her a new name, you'll see her again. And however often you manage to do that, it will be the first and only time"* (445). The experience he has gone through in Fantastica has given Bastian self-confidence and the ability to care for others instead of avoiding the outside world by retreating into the shell of his own fantasies. And, as Mr Coreander (surely Ende's mouthpiece) intimates, it may have opened the way for Bastian to find his real profession as a teller of stories from which readers, and thus society, will benefit: *"If I'm not mistaken, you will show many others the way to Fantastica, and they will bring us the Water of Life"* (445).

THE RECEPTION OF *THE NEVERENDING STORY*
(with a Glance at the Film by Wolfgang Petersen)

The Neverending Story took Ende about two years to write, and he was by no means certain about its success when it finally appeared in November 1979. Reviews, however, were enthusiastic, and within six months the book began to occupy top ranks in the charts. Although the book was comparatively expensive—for a long time, Ende vetoed paperback editions because he wanted the book to be beautiful and to look exactly like the book Bastian steals from Mr Coreander—some 200,000 copies were sold in the first year; within four years, the figure had risen to over one million copies. Translations began to be published as early as 1981; the English version, prepared by the renowned translator Ralph Manheim, came out in 1983, simultaneously in England and America.

Having won no less than ten international prizes within the first four years of its publication, *The Neverending Story* has been selling steadily ever since. All in all, 7.7 million copies of *The Neverending Story* have been sold worldwide: 3.2 million in Germany, the rest abroad, translated into a total of 36 languages.[17] Apart from Germany, Ende's books were particularly successful in Japan. As early as 1982 *The Neverending Story* won the Japanese prize of the best translation of contemporary literature; more than two million copies of *Momo* and *The Neverending Story* were sold in Japan before 1993 (Hocke/Kraft 1997, 129).

A decade after his death, Michael Ende remains something like a cult author in Germany. A Michael Ende Museum was opened in 1997 at the International Youth Library in Munich; the *Jim Button* stories were turned into a musical in 1999, and as recently as April 2004 an opera based on *The Neverending Story* premiered in two German theaters at the same time and to much critical acclaim.[18] In 2003 and 2004, five books that are all set in Fantastica were published, commissioned by a German publishing company as a kind of homage to Ende (and, one suspects, a publicity stunt) and written by some of the best-known German authors of fantasy fiction.[19]

The fact that *The Neverending Story* is not easy to classify, least of all as a children's book pure and simple, has apparently never been an impediment at the sales counter. According to booksellers interviewed by Pfau, the book appealed particularly to the age group between eigh-

teen and thirty-five (Pfau 1984, 92); although children liked it, too, it
was the group of young adults who turned it into a cult book. Pfau's
sampling of fan mail suggests that readers sought, and relished, the
"enchantment" of the story, the multiple suggestiveness of its images
and fairy-tale motifs; they endorsed its opposition to the "cold rationalism" and "materialism" of everyday life, and felt personally
touched and strengthened by the optimistic message implied in its
story of healing through symbolic self-exploration.

Not only most of the reviews in newspapers and magazines, but also
some academic criticism that began to appear in the 1980s tended to
endorse such readings. Relying heavily on Jungian depth psychology,
Wilfried Kuckartz (1984) praises *The Neverending Story* for being an
"educational fairy tale" ("ein Bildungsmärchen"); Helmut Gronemann's *Phantásien—das Reich des Unbewußten* (Fantastica—the
Realm of the Unconscious, 1985) is an even more consistent Jungian
interpretation that identifies each and every detail of the story (including Atreyu) as an archetype or symbol that helps Bastian achieve his
individuation. Claudia Ludwig's doctoral dissertation (1988) is less
outspoken in that respect, concentrating instead on Ende's literary
sources and intertextual allusions; but it does regard the richness of
Ende's romantic symbolism as the great asset that explains its success.[20]

The very aspects that were applauded by these critics were a source
of irritation for others. On the one hand, the book came under attack
from the extreme religious right who claimed that "the so-called fairy
tales of *The Neverending Story* are nothing but magic and occultism in
its purest form"[21] and denounced the book as an insidious temptation
to lure readers away from orthodox Christianity.

On the other side of the spectrum, some members of the liberal left
eyed Ende's romantic anti-rationalism with considerable uneasiness.
While they welcomed his criticism of modern Western society in principle, they felt doubtful about the solutions his books seemed to offer,
which they regarded as a form of escapism (see, for instance, Kaminski
1992, 92; Prondzynsky 1983, 88). Ende became enmeshed in a larger
debate among the left that pitched "materialist" (largely Marxist) positions advocating an intellectually rigorous analysis of the power structure of society against an "idealist" position that called for new
attitudes toward work, money, and lifestyle—in other words, a change
of heart. In that light, Ende's success seems to be due to a swing of the
pendulum of public opinion, away from the political revolutionary
spirit of the 1970s, to what was termed, in German, "die Neue Inner-

lichkeit" of the 1980s, a return to the romantic heritage privileging feeling over thought, "interior" matters like emotions and the imagination over "exterior" matters like politics and daily life.

Other critics have deplored Ende's stereotypical treatment of female characters, his cumbersome prose style, and his lack of humor and irony (see Aschenberg 1991, 126–129; Kaminski 1992, 90 and 112). Most serious, perhaps, is the complaint about inconsistencies and contradictions in Ende's work, including *The Neverending Story*. Ende, it has been said, distrusts politics, yet tries to influence political thinking (Doderer 1998, 261); he advocates spontaneity and playfulness, but is unable to camouflage the effort he has put into the construction of his parables (Tabbert 1996, 30); he speaks out against literature being used to convey messages, but cannot contain his urge to preach (Hetmann 1984, 114; Kaminski 1992, 90)—in short, he is a Romantic trying to treat the public to his own brand of enlightenment.

I trust my analysis in this essay has shown that such criticism is not unfounded. Apart from the question of whether one agrees with Ende's messages or not, one could argue that the book is groaning under the load the author has put on its back: by means of a fiction that is extremely complicated, operating on several levels and featuring a protagonist who is the reader, the hero, and the quasi-author of one and the same story, he tries to philosophize about the nature of fantasy and, at the same time, to teach about the social importance of fantasy. He employs metafictional devices to demonstrate that each reader creates his own story, and asserts his authorship by designing a parabolic narrative calculated to show the therapeutic uses of fantasizing for the individual and to suggest, moreover, that society could be healed the same way. One could also point out that the book carries conflicting messages in that it is a celebration of fantasizing and at the same time a warning against fantasizing. On the other hand, there is the irrefutable evidence of the book's lasting success, which seems to point to the possibility that Ende's story affects its readers on more than one level.

For support of this hypothesis, I propose to look at some of the material manifestations of this success, in particular the 1984 film version that popularized *The Neverending Story* on the international stage. It was followed by two sequels (*The Neverending Story II: The Next Chapter*, directed by George Miller, USA/Germany, date given variously as 1989 or 1990, and *The Neverending Story III*, directed by Peter MacDonald, USA/Germany 1994); a Canadian-French-German Cartoon TV series, "Die unendliche Geschichte," directed by Mike

Fallows (1996), and a Canadian TV series, "Tales from the Neverending Story," directed by Giles Walker and Adam Weissman (2001).[22] All of these films take great liberties with Ende's book. Due to lack of space, we shall consider here only the one product that is comparatively faithful to the text and, moreover, has made the biggest contribution to the proliferation of Ende's story: the 1984 film version by Wolfgang Petersen.

The production of the 1984 film version is a gripping tale in its own right that can be told here only in an abbreviated version.[23] As early as May 1980, Ende and his publisher agreed to sell the film rights to the German producer Dieter Geissler, who subsequently, after an abortive attempt to get the production started, re-sold the rights to Bernd Eichinger. Ende had agreed to the filming on the understanding that every effort should be made to keep the film as close to the book as possible, including its metafictional trappings, which proved to be next to impossible. From the sale of the rights in 1980 to the completion of the film in 1984, two directors (Helmut Dietl and Wolfgang Petersen) and no fewer than six scriptwriters (Hans W. Geissendörfer, Christian Schneider, Helmut Dietl, Herman Weigel, Wolfgang Petersen, and John Hill as a "ghostwriter") tried their hands at the intractable story, partly in close cooperation with Ende. The final version of the script exasperated Ende so much that he tried (in vain) to take legal action against it. In a press release he stated that the script had nothing in common with his novel: "The difficult problems of converting the novel into a film were solved by simply eliminating the causes of the problems. The end result is exactly what I decidedly tried to avoid all along: a film that is spectacular and perfectly fashioned, but without individuality, made after the well-tried American pattern."[24]

In part, the thus deplored "Americanization" of the story had very material reasons: the production cost had skyrocketed from an initially estimated 7–8 million DM to an unprecedented 60 million, making it not only necessary to draw in American investors but to streamline the film for the taste of the lucrative American market. In addition, there were, of course, intrinsic reasons for substantial changes, as in all dramatizations of long novels, the most drastic being the sacrifice of the second half of the novel that describes Bastian's sojourn in Fantastica.

Important modifications of the story, however, set in right at the beginning of the film. Bastian is a handsome American boy, by no means fat or gauche; his father is a little stiff and formal, but well-meaning and certainly not wrapped in a cocoon of grief. Bastian is drastically bullied by three classmates; at the end of his encounter with Mr Coreander he does not steal the book but leaves a note that he will bring it back. Bastian is thus much easier to identify with, and the film avoids all risks of being thought to disseminate doubtful role models.

The novel's moving back and forth between two fictional levels is, as it were, a cinematographic device as such and is quite faithfully reproduced by dint of cuts. As in the book, nevertheless, it is Fantastica and Atreyu's adventures that form the emotional center of the story. The first scene—various creatures meeting on their way to the Childlike Empress—is given, comparatively, a great deal of space, providing the special effects department of the film crew with ample opportunity to display their skill and allowing the viewers to get emotionally involved, especially with Pyornkrachzark the rock-chewer, who is turned into a specimen of that well-tried Hollywood type, the Amiable Monster. Having invited the viewers to like these characters, it is only consistent that they re-appear at various stages of the story (in contrast to the book version), which also makes economic sense. (It is interesting to note that the rock-chewer seems to be featured in most of the sequels of the film as well.)

In Atreyu's quest, the most striking departures from the book are the sacrifice of the Ygramul and the Wind Giant episodes (both made dispensable by transferring the essential pieces of information that they provide to other episodes), the depiction of the workings of the Nothing, and the additional dramatic weight given to Gmork the Werewolf. Atreyu's loss of his horse, Artax, in the Swamps of Sadness is an emotional climax that eclipses the encounter with Morla, the giant tortoise, whose morose nihilism appears in a rather humorous light in the film. So do (with better right) Falkor the luckdragon and the gnome couple, Urgl and Endywuck, who prepare Atreyu for his passage through the gates to the Southern Oracles. The passage is dangerous in both versions, but it is characteristic that in the film the Sphinxes' eyes send out laser-like flashes of light that burn up their victims, whereas in the book the person who is caught between their gazes "freezes to the spot, unable to move until he has solved all the riddles of the world" (98). In Ende's story, the Sphinxes simply shut their eyes, thus indicating their approval of Atreyu's mission, while he has to run for his life in the film version.

The Gmork episode, too, makes Atreyu more like a conventional hero than he is in Ende's story. Whereas Ende gives only a few hints that the monster is pursuing Atreyu, the film uses its visual effects to make the pursuit dramatic, with Falkor the luckdragon coming to Atreyu's last-minute rescue. Even more significantly, in the film Atreyu has to fight and kill the monstrous werewolf when he meets him again in Spook City, thus showing his prowess in a violent, heroic action. In the book, Gmork is unable to harm Atreyu, being chained and so weak as to be close to his death. Thus, the episode has a completely different function in the original story: it provides an opportunity for Atreyu to display not his prowess but, rather, his capacity to pity his foe and for Gmork to give far more substantial information about the meaning of the Nothing.

The depiction of the Nothing is another instance of how the film distorts important details by dramatizing them. Ende goes out of his way to describe in visual terms an idea that is essentially abstract, non-sensual. Early in the story, Atreyu climbs a tree to see that

> the tops of the trees nearest him were still green, but the leaves of those farther away seemed to have lost all color; they were grey. A little farther on, the foliage seemed to become strangely transparent, misty, or, better still, unreal. And farther still there was nothing, absolutely nothing. Not a bare stretch, not darkness, not some lighter color; no, it was something the eyes could not bear, something that made you feel you had gone blind. For no eye can bear the sight of utter nothingness. (58)

Surely this must be the ultimate cinematographer's nightmare. To visualize, and dramatize, the Nothing that threatens Fantastica's existence, Petersen could not possibly adopt the author's description; instead, he chose to present it by showing buildings tumbling down and, later, as a gigantic storm that literally tears the land asunder, until all that remains is isolated chunks of dead matter that drift through the air like disintegrated spaceships. If this representation does not go beyond the conventional imagery developed in countless B movies of world destruction, it has the virtue of reminding us that it may well be the similarity to the time-honored vision of the apocalypse that gives the motif its emotional impact, irrespective of the philosophical twist the author has provided.

Skipping the episode of the Old Man of Wandering Mountain, the film next presents a dramatic tug-of-war between Atreyu's urging and Bastian's hesitation (realized by a rapid series of cuts) that ends with Bastian shouting the Childlike Empress's new name and being wafted to her throne. Having instantaneously restored Fantastica in its old shape, Bastian is seen triumphantly riding on Falkor's back through the air, straight to his home town where he uses his newfound air power to chase the bullies who had previously pursued him. In the end, the narrator's voice declares that Bastian would return home after having had many more adventures in Fantastica, ending with Ende's favorite tag, "but that is another story and shall be told another time."

Small wonder that Ende complained in his press release that the film abandoned "the most important interior aspects of the novel, the real meaning of *The Neverending Story*, for the sake of exterior effects created for the general public."[25] It seems, indeed, that in the film little is left of what Ende tried to convey in his novel. On the other hand, the film does realize the central idea—a reader literally entering a fiction—and it does follow the storyline fairly faithfully. Could it be that its success is due (apart from its technical brilliance) to the fact that it realizes the heroic pattern, the wishful daydream inherent in the story's deep structure, more clearly than the book?

Reinbert Tabbert may well be right when he proposes that the book's success lies in its mixture of exuberant fantasizing and philosophical "depth" (Tabbert 1996, 31). One could also point out that the reader is always free to disregard the story's pedagogical and philosophical freight. If he does, what remains is the description of a colorful and vividly presented Secondary World, and a "gripping yarn" that conforms, as Maria Nikolajeva has demonstrated, with the time-honored formulas and motifs of the fairy tale (see Nikolajeva 1990, 37). Interestingly, the plot also resembles Jerry Griswold's description of the master plot of classic American children's books: it is the story of an orphan (for all practical purposes, since his father all but physically absents himself) who feels neglected until he embarks on a (metaphorical) journey that gets him into contact with surrogate parents and magical helpers. In the end, he emerges from his journey to the other world as a person who has found his true identity and his role as a savior of others, and is able to accommodate the "two lives" he has experienced (see Griswold 1992, 4–9). The only significant way Ende's novel deviates from Griswold's pattern is the absence of a same-sex antagonist. Interestingly, it is precisely in this point that the film differs from the book. Whereas in Ende's book both heroes, Atreyu and Bastian, lack a striking male adversary (both Ygramul and Xayide being female), the film recognizes the symbolic potential inherent in the figure of Gmork when it has Atreyu actually fight, and kill, the monster.[26]

Thus, while the intricate metafictional structure of the book, and its concomitant philosophical freight, are certainly dear to Ende's heart, and will certainly continue to intrigue the cognoscenti, it seems possible that it is the deep structure of the story, along with the sheer imaginative exuberance of the book, that has been, and will be, at the bottom of the long, if not neverending, success of *The Neverending Story* among readers of all ages.

APPENDIX: A NOTE ON THE
ENGLISH TRANSLATION

Considering what translators, and their publishers, often do to children's books, Ralph Manheim's English version of *Die unendliche Geschichte* must be considered a happy exception to a sad rule, for it is, on the whole, remarkably accurate. Omissions of whole sentences or paragraphs do occur, but they are very rare and do not distort meanings. Ende's style, in general, is not overly demanding. Manheim is particularly conscientious in faithfully reproducing Ende's circumstantial descriptions; when it comes to his dialogs, there is a tendency to smooth out idiosyncracies, for instance, in the speech of Morla the Aged One, in the dialogs of the gnome couple, Endywook and Urgl, and in Xayide's stately, slightly old-fashioned style of speech that she uses when she wants to flatter Bastian. On the whole, Manheim's style strikes me as tending more to the colloquial than Ende's, but only very slightly.

Among the stylistic features that often constitute considerable—in some cases insurmountable—difficulties for translators are verses, word-play, and names. Ende uses verses occasionally, in particular in chapter 7. They are not exactly sublime poetry, but they do scan and, when intended, rhyme. Manheim tries to reproduce the effect, but he does not hesitate to sacrifice both meter (for instance, in the "old song" about Ygramul, 65) and rhyme (see Uyulala's lines, 114–116) to accuracy of sense.

Word-play is even rarer in *The Neverending Story*. In one conspicuous instance Manheim proves to be up to the mark: Ende's title of chapter 5 is "Die Zweisiedler," a (not too subtle) play on the German word *Einsiedler*, "hermit." Manheim replaces Ende's neologism by a portmanteau word, "Gnomics," formed out of "gnome" and "comic," which is exactly what Engywook and Urgl are. In another case, Manheim is less fortunate: as I have already indicated, his "Fantastica" does not quite reproduce the pun contained in the German name of the land, Phantásien (see note 5).

Names, of course, play an enormous role in *The Neverending Story*. Taking a leaf out of Tolkien's book, Ende acts on the same maxim that rules Bastian's creativity: worlds are created by inventing names. The book abounds with strange names, both for places and for persons. Most place names, and some personal names, are created by combining common words to form a poetic-sounding compound, and are easy to translate: Swamps of Sadness, Dead Mountains, Deep Chasm, etc. Manheim's translation of the place where Morla the Aged One lives is less happy. While "Hornberg" contains only an obscure allusion to the true nature of that mountain (the giant tortoise's shell), the English version, "Tortoise Shell Mountain," gives the riddle away. The Childlike Empress, too, could not be brought unscathed through the translation process: she lost the alliteration Ende gave her when he named her the "Kindliche Kaiserin."

Some place names and most names of persons, in contrast, are opaque, having no recognizable intrinsic meaning. Their sounds, however, are meant to be suggestive, which is one reason why they cannot automatically be adopted unchanged in a foreign-language version. English and German are sufficiently alike to allow names like Artax, Gmork, Morla, and Urgl to remain as they are. In many other cases the translator (or his editors) have thought it advisable to simplify the spelling of names, and sometimes the sound, too, ignoring (for no apparent reason other than saving expenses) Ende's penchant for accents. Thus, the German version has, for instance, Amargánth, Aiuóla (Manheim's Eyola), Atréju, Caíron, Graógramán (in English, Grograman), Hýkrion, Oglamár, and Xayíde. Where sounds seem to indicate the person's nature, efforts are usually made to preserve the effect, as in the names of the creatures that appear in chapter 1: Blubb the will-o'-the wisp, Gluckuk the tiny (in German, Ückück der Winzling), Vooshvazool (Wúschwusul) the night-hob, and Pyornkrachzark (Pjörnrachzarck) the rock-chewer. Only the luckdragon was allowed to enjoy the privilege of the Childlike Empress, i.e., to receive a new name. It seems that his original name, Fuchur, was felt to sound too much like "future" to an English-speaking person, so it was change to "Falkor."

NOTES

1. The following information is based mainly on the biography by Hocke and Kraft.

2. Ende himself wrote the libretto for the opera, which was set to music by the composer Mark Lothar and first staged in 1979. There is a film version by the renowned German director Johannes Schaaf (1986) and a cartoon film made in 2001 by the Italian director Enzo d'Alò.

3. The narrator even mentions that "the book [Bastian was reading] was printed in two colors" (10), which seems to imply that it contains not only the story of Fantastica, but also his own story. That, however, is not stated clearly, doubtlessly to spare the reader, at least at this early stage, the giddy feeling caused by this fiendish *mise en abyme*.

4. A great many (though not all) of them are listed in Ludwig's dissertation.

5. The double meaning of Fantastica is particularly clear in its German name, Phantásien. When the phonetic stress is on the second syllable (as the accent indicates) it sounds like a place name; without the accent, the word means "fantasies."

6. For the term, cf. Petzold 1999, 91. Other fantasy stories about fantasizing are Lewis Carroll's *Alice* books, J. M. Barrie's *Peter Pan*, J. R. R. Tolkien's *Smith of Wootton Major*, Peter Beagle's *The Last Unicorn*, and Salman Rushdie's *Haroun and the Sea of Stories*.

7. There is a striking similarity here with what the Cultmaster Khattam-Shud says in Salman Rushdie's *Haroun and the Sea of Stories*: "Inside every single story, inside every Stream in the Ocean, there lies a world, a story-world, that I cannot Rule at all" (161). Cf. Petzold 1999, 100.

8. Cf. Filmer, who recognizes a similar allegorical meaning of the Childlike Empress: "She symbolizes, perhaps, the realm of the subconscious mind, where archetypal images and shapes are manifested and from which the Imagination springs" (Filmer 1991, 61).

9. Filmer is right in pointing out that Ursula Le Guin's fantasy novels advocate the same worldview, derived in both cases from Taoism (cf. Filmer 1991, 62; also Ludwig 1988, 30–35).

10. The inscription harks back to "Fay ce que voudras," the motto of the utopian society of Thélème described in the second book of François Rabelais's fantastic novel *Gargantua et Pantagruel* (1532–64). In contradistinction to Rabelais's optimistic belief in the intrinsic nobility of human wishes, Ende appears more skeptical about people's ability to find out what they really want.

11. The idea of the cyclical interdependence of life and death permeates the whole book as a minor theme. Ende is likely to have adopted it through his studies of Goethe, of anthroposophism, and of Far Eastern philosophies. Cf. Ludwig 1988, 36–40. For psychoanalytical readings that focus on Bastian's task of coping with his mother's death cf. Bosmajian 1988; Weenolsen 1988.

12. The similarity of his name to that of Tolkien's dragon in *The Hobbit*, Smaug, is hardly a coincidence. For more traces of Tolkien in *The Neverending Story*, cf. Ludwig 1988, 130–137.

13. There is a possible connection here to the cliché-quoting butterfly in Peter Beagle's *The Last Unicorn* (1968), a book that influenced Ende in several ways. Cf. Ludwig 1988, 121–130.

14. Critics have accused Ende of excluding all hints of sexuality from his books (cf. Kaminski 1992, 111), but Xayide, with her "long gown of violet silk," her "flaming red hair," her "long thin hands . . . as pale as marble," and her "long lashes" that hide eyes "of different colors, one green, one red" (328) does have the trappings of a *femme fatale*. It is hardly a coincidence that the moment he falls into her sway, Bastian rejects Atreyu's friendship, and his "memory of having been a child in his world [is] effaced" (331).

15. Cf. F 320 ("Fairies carry people away to fairyland") and F 370 ("Visit to fairyland") in Thompson's *Motif-Index of Folk-Literature*.

16. Ende gives some specific examples that suggest that not all of these dreams are quite forgotten, for they are pictures by such well-known fantastic painters as Bosch, Goya, Dalí, de Chirico, and Arcimboldo.

17. According to information provided by Ende's publishers, Thienemann Verlag, Stuttgart.

18. The opera, by Anton Perrey (libretto) and Siegfried Matthus (composer), premiered on 10 April 2004 in Weimar and Trier.

19. They are: Wolfram Fleischhauer, *Die Verschwörung der Engel*; Peter Freund, *Die Stadt der vergessenen Träume*; Ralf Isau, *Die geheime Bibliothek des Thaddäus Tillmann Trutz*; Tanja Kinkel, *Der König der Narren*; Ulrike Schweikert, *Die Seele der Nacht*, all Droemer-Knaur Verlag, Munich.

20. In one of the few articles on *The Neverending Story* in English, Kath Filmer arrives at similar results, approvingly pointing out Ende's indebtedness to Romanticism (including latter-day romantics like George MacDonald and C. S. Lewis) and suggesting a Jungian interpretation of characters like Atreyu, Xayide, and Dame Eyola.

21. "Die angeblichen Märchen der 'Unendlichen Geschichte' sind nichts anderes als Magie und Okkultismus in reinster Form" (Berger 1985, 94). The similarity to more recent attacks on the *Harry Potter* books by Christian fundamentalists is striking

22. Information on these various film versions can be accessed via "The Neverending Story Webpage." Most reviews of the sequels to the 1984 movie seem to range from negative to devastating, except for *The Neverending Story, Part II*, which has occasionally found some approval because it follows, to some extent, the second part of Ende's book.

23. In the train of the film, two books describing its making were published. For more details, cf. Eyssen 1984 and Pfau 1984.

24. "Man hat die schwierigen Probleme der Umsetzung des Romans in

einen Film dadurch gelöst, daß man die Ursachen der Probleme ganz einfach weggelassen hat. Es ist nun ganz genau das daraus geworden, was ich . . . von allem Anfang an mit allem Nachdruck zu verhindern suchte: ein spektakulärer, perfekt gemachter, aber wesenloser Fantasy-Film nach bewährtem amerikanischem Muster" (qtd. in Pfau 1984, 161; my translation).

25. "Es müßte eigentlich jedem klar sein, daß damit die wichtigsten inneren Aspekte des Romans, der eigentliche Sinn der 'Unendlichen Geschichte', zugunsten einer äußerlichen Publikumswirksamkeit aufgegeben worden sind" (qtd. in Pfau 1984, 161–162; my translation).

26. One might speculate that Ende avoids the creation of strong male adversaries because he shies away from the implication that such adversaries are symbolic father figures in the context of the oedipal conflict. It is interesting to note that in the book Gmork is presented as the victim of an evil *femme fatale*, the Dark Princess, which makes him, in a way, an *alter ego* of Bastian, like him a traveler between worlds, and a creature that deserves Atreyu's pity. Equally interesting is the fact that Xayide's role is considerably enhanced in the film *The Neverending Story, Part II*, which thereby acknowledges the dramatic potential, and unconscious significance, of the female evil character as a major adversary.

WORKS CITED

Aschenberg, Heidi. *Eigennamen im Kinderbuch: Eine textlinguistische Studie.* Tübingen: Narr, 1991.

Berger, Klaus. *Michael Ende: Heilung durch magische Phantásien.* Wuppertal: Verlag und Schriftenmission der Evangelischen Gesellschaft für Deutschland, 1985.

Bosmajian, Hamida. "Grief and Its Displacement through Fantasy in Michael Ende's *The Neverending Story.*" Pp.120–123 in *Proceedings of the Thirteenth Annual Conference of The Children's Literature Association,* edited by Susan R. Gannon and Ruth Anne Thompson. West Lafayette: Purdue University, 1988.

Doderer, Klaus. "Michael Ende—Der weite Weg in Momos Heimat." Pp. 252–262 in *Reisen in erdachtes Land: Literarische Spurensuche vor Ort—Essays.* München: Iudicium, 1998.

Ende, Michael. *Die unendliche Geschichte.* Von A bis Z mit Buchstaben und Bildern versehen von Roswitha Quadflieg. Stuttgart: Thienemann, 1979.

———. *Momo.* Translated by J. Maxwell Brownjohn. Garden City, NY: Doubleday, 1985.

———. *Jim Button and Luke the Engine Driver.* Woodstock, NY: Overlook Press, 1990.

———. *The Night of Wishes: or The Satanarchaeolidealcohellish Notion*

Potion. Translated by Heike Schwarzbauer and Rick Takvorian. New York: Farrar, Straus and Giroux, 1992.

———. *The Neverending Story.* Translated by Ralph Manheim (1983). New York: Penguin, 1997.

Ewers, Hans-Heino. "Kinder, die nicht erwachsen werden: die Geniusgestalt des ewigen Kindes bei Goethe, Tieck, E.T.A. Hoffmann, J.M. Barrie, Ende und Nöstlinger." Pp. 42–70 in *Kinderwelten: Kinder und Kindheit in der neueren Literatur.* Weinheim: Beltz, 1985.

Eyssen, Remy. *Der Film Die unendliche Geschichte: Story—Dreharbeiten—Hintergrundbericht.* München: Heyne, 1984.

Filmer, Kath. "Religion and Romanticism in Michael Ende's *The Neverending Story.*" *Mythlore* 18 (1991): 59–64.

Griswold, Jerry. *Audacious Kids: Coming of Age in America's Classic Children's Books.* New York: Oxford University Press, 1992.

Gronemann, Helmut. *Phantásien—Das Reich des Unbewußten: "Die unendliche Geschichte" von Michael Ende aus der Sicht der Tiefenpsychologie.* Zürich: Spiegel, 1985.

Hetmann, Frederik. *Die Freuden der Fantasy: Von Tolkien bis Ende.* Frankfurt: Ullstein, 1984.

Hocke, Roman, und Thomas Kraft. *Michael Ende und seine phantastische Welt: Die Suche nach dem Zauberwort.* Stuttgart: Weitbrecht, 1997.

Kaminski, Winfred. *Antizipation und Erinnerung: Studien zur Kinder- und Jugendliteratur in pädagogischer Absicht.* Stuttgart: M&P Verlag für Wissenschaft und Forschung, 1992.

Kuckartz, Wilfried. *Michael Ende "Die unendliche Geschichte": Ein Bildungsmärchen.* Essen: Verlag Die blaue Eule, 1984.

Ludwig, Claudia. *Was du ererbt von deinen Vätern hast . . . Michael Endes Phantásien—Symbolik und literarische Quellen.* Frankfurt: Lang, 1988.

Nikolajeva, Maria. "How Fantasy is Made: Patterns and Structures in *The Neverending Story.*" *Merveilles & Contes* 4 (1990): 34–42.

Petzold, Dieter. "Taking Games Seriously: Romantic Irony in Modern Fantasy for Children of All Ages." Pp. 87–104 in *Literature and the Child: Romantic Continuations, Postmodern Contestations,* edited by James Holt McGavran. Iowa City: University of Iowa Press, 1999.

Pfau, Ulli. *Phantásien in Halle 4/5: Michael Endes 'Unendliche Geschichte' und ihre Verfilmung.* München: Deutscher Taschenbuch Verlag, 1984.

Prondzynsky, Andreas von. *Die unendliche Sehnsucht nach sich selbst: Auf den Spuren eines neuen Mythos. Versuch über eine "Unendliche Geschichte."* Frankfurt: dipa, 1983.

Rushdie, Salman. *Haroun and the Sea of Stories.* London: Granta, 1991.

Tabbert, Reinbert. "Zwischen Kinderzimmer und literarischem Salon: Nachdenken über Michael Ende." *Beiträge Jugendliteratur und Medien,* 48 (1996): 26–34.

"The Neverending Story Webpage," http://www.fantasien.net/tnes/books/,
    accessed 15 June 2004.
Thompson, Stith. *Motif-Index of Folk-Literature*. Revised and enlarged edi-
    tion. Vol. 3. Bloomington: Indiana University Press, 1956.
Weenolsen, Patricia. "The Influence of Parental Death on Identity Formation."
    Pp. 124–128 in *Proceedings of the Thirteenth Annual Conference of The
    Children's Literature Association* edited by Susan R. Gannon and Ruth
    Anne Thompson. West Lafayette: Purdue University, 1988.

10

"We Were a Pair"
Peter Pohl's *Johnny, My Friend*

Roberta Seelinger Trites

An early postmodern novel published in Sweden by Peter Pohl, *Janne, min vän* (1985; Engl. *Johnny, My Friend* 1991), illustrates how an author can rely on readers' narrative expectations to transform them. Johnny makes great friends with a twelve-year-old named Chris Nordberg; Chris narrates the story of how two very different people become emotionally intertwined. Johnny is a trickster on a bicycle who is not above punching anyone who deserves it. Chris is a compulsive cataloguer of facts. Late in the novel, he even admits that he has preferred the statistics he compiles about cars and the citizens of Sweden to interacting with real people, but that has been "*A pretty boring way to live, cos life is replaced by data, figures, facts on cards. Then you turned up, Johnny, and turned everything upside down, cos I never got any data from you, no facts to collect*" (241; author's emphasis). The plot is initiated by a police officer asking Chris to identify some of Johnny's personal effects: pants, shoes, bicycle, a bracelet. Johnny has gone missing, and Chris's efforts to help the police lead him also to understand, finally, his friend's identity.

The elegance of *Johnny, My Friend* can be understood in light of literary critic Susan Stewart's theories about authors' deviation from standard genre forms in a process she calls "estrangement" (Stewart

2000, 95–97). Estrangement is the process by which texts alienate read-ers so that readers can potentially reflect on the text with greater objec-tivity (see also Stephens 1992, 70–71). Pohl relies on two techniques of narrative estrangement throughout *Johnny, My Friend*: shifting narra-tees and subverting the reader's ideological expectations. These two techniques highlight Chris's confusion, and they also force readers' expectations to be upended. Thus, in a fascinating process of reversals, Pohl is able to communicate his ideology of social protest by estrang-ing the reader. The political message works because of the narrative feats Pohl works; they are feats worthy of Johnny's tricks on a bicycle.

NARRATIVE TECHNIQUE

In "Beyond the Grammar of Story," Maria Nikolajeva urges critics of children's literature to use narrative theory to analyze "how" chil-dren's stories function (Nikolajeva 2003, 6). The aspect of her grammar most germane to my reading of *Johnny, My Friend* is her distinction between the narrative voice and the point of view: "we must discern between the narrative voice we hear and the point of view, that is, through whose eyes we see the events" (11). In *Johnny, My Friend*, the ideologies that are communicated are more sophisticated than the nar-rator's. Pohl relies on this distinction to destabilize the reader. Chris serves as the focalizer, the persona whose perspective focuses the read-er's attention (Stephens 1992, 27). But his story also requires narratees. The perspective of the narratee, the character to whom the story is told, also affects how the reader interprets the story (Chatman 1978, 151). As Gerald Prince notes, narratees can come in four forms: invisi-ble narratees who occur in novels with no clearly articulated narratees, who are a clear presence in the novel and to whom the narrator speaks but who are not characters; narratees who are characters; and narratees whose presence determines the resolution of the plot (Prince 1980, 17–19). *Johnny, My Friend* switches among multiple narratees.

Initially, and in the beginning of many new sections in the novel, the police officer who is questioning Chris about Johnny's whereabouts serves as a character-narratee: Chris tells the cop facts that help in the manhunt for his friend. Occasionally, the police officer asks questions that remind readers that his narrative presence is the activating circum-stance creating the need for Chris's monologue. Sometimes, Chris answers him directly, as when the cop asks for a physical description of Johnny:

> The cop's interested in that front tooth, in that gap. Asking right or left. Notes down right, but changes it to left when I add, From where I am.
>   Part of the tooth, or all of it?
>   Half the tooth is missing, as stated above: the lower half to be more precise, in the upper right front molar. From where I am. (11)

Chris's insistence that *his* perspective is the one that matters, with the reiteration of "from where I am," draws the reader's attention from the narratee to him as a focalizer. But frequently, the cop's questions send Chris into a reverie in which he responds with an internal monologue that focalizes the reader on Johnny, rather than on the narrator or the narratee:

> Have I forgotten Johnny? Asks the cop.
>   No way. You don't forget Johnny. You force yourself to stop thinking about him, once you've realized there's nothing you can do about his mysterious absence and silence. . . . But nothing helps really: you can't forget Johnny even so. (180)

In this case, the narratee appears to be the type of invisible narratee that Prince refers to as the "zero-degree narratee" (Prince 1980, 9); the zero-degree narratee has no personality traits and understands the narrator's language, logic, and rules of narrative but must be told all aspects of the story in order to understand it, so the zero-degree narratee is clearly not an actor in the plot (9–11). In other words, the zero-degree narratee is so invisible that the actual reader can, as a general rule, forget that the text even contains a narratee.

Chris dispenses with the convention of the zero-degree narratee, for example, when he is feeling most intense. At those times, his interior monologue is italicized, emphasizing to the reader his extreme emotion, and he generally addresses Johnny as a character-narratee:

> The cop holds up Johnny's bracelet. . . .
>   *Johnny! Now I k n o w something awful's happened!*
>   *Warning bells were ringing in the background. Look out! Look out! Deep down inside me at first. They were getting louder every time the cop produced your most intimate belongings, one after another. And the questions! Watch out! Watch out! The leading questions, the images they*

*conjured up. Warning! Warning! Details I hadn't noticed before. And now
your bracelet. Now the sirens are screeching. Something awful's happened!
Somewhere or other something awful's happened!* (189; author's emphasis
and spacing)

Chris's emotional outburst to Johnny as a narratee focalizes the reader's attention on Johnny even more than Chris's descriptions have.
Chris's shifting to the use of Johnny as a second character-narratee is
an unusual strategy in adolescent literature.

The majority of the novel, however, is written in a direct address
from Chris to an invisible narratee who eventually melds seamlessly
with the implied reader. While Chris narrates the year and a half he
gets to know Johnny better—while Chris narrates how he came to
understand the poverty, abuse, and lack of parental love that has led
Johnny to be so secretive—the actual reader can, for many long passages of the story, forget the narrative convenience that a police officer
is listening to the story. Indeed, much of the story is private thoughts
that are clearly not articulated for the cop, as when Chris responds to
the police officer about Johnny's missing tooth:

How did he lose that then?
    Johnny's own version is, I bit it off when some old bloke made a grab
at my dick.
    But I don't try that fairy tale on the cop. Partly cos I never believed it
myself, partly cos it would give a false picture of Johnny to kick off by
describing him like that.
    That was the only time Johnny ever mentioned the word dick, in fact.
(12)

As Chris says, "And what I do know [about Johnny] might not be
suitable for cop's ears" (85).

One effect of multiple shifting narratees is the possibility of the
actual reader's estrangement. One moment in *Johnny, My Friend*, the
narrator is talking directly to a zero-degree narratee whose subject
position the implied reader shares comfortably; the next, the narrator
is talking directly to a cop or apostrophically to Johnny. If the actual
reader assumes even temporarily the subject position of the implied
reader, the sudden shift away from the narrator's direct address has an
unsettling effect: "Hey, I thought Chris was talking to *me*." But the
shifting estrangement serves Pohl's intentions well, since his ultimate

purpose seems to unsettle many of the conventions that readers bring to books.

SEX AND EXPECTATIONS

For example, Pohl relies on the generic conventions of the "buddy novel," in which two acquaintances become best friends. John Knowles's *A Separate Peace* (1959) and S.E. Hinton's *The Outsiders* (1967) are two notable examples of this genre. When sexuality is an element in such novels, it tends to be sublimated or homoeroticized (see McGavran 2002; Tribunella 2002.) Johnny and Chris are clearly attracted to one another, and their passion ultimately leads them to spend a romantic night nestled in one another's arms. The scenes in which the two wrestle are described in homoerotic terms:

> It was great, wrestling with Johnny. . . . You realized he wasn't really all that strong. He noticed that himself as well, but as long as it was in secret, just between the two of us, he didn't mind being the underdog. When he was hopelessly beaten, he'd give up by tickling me till I had to let him go. . . . We used to lie there fighting on the floor, choking our laughter in each other's stomachs. (81)

Later, Chris says, "Johnny meant an awful lot to me, but don't ask me what" (87) and is grateful that his friend "clung to me" (86). "We were a pair," Chris asserts (85), and he cries at the moments in their friend-ship when he worries about losing his friend (65, 118, 139, 207). In the last of these scenes, Johnny consoles Chris by giving him "a whopper of a kiss" (207), and Chris describes their physical gestures lovingly: "Johnny leant over towards me and rested his red head on my shoul-der" (135). When Johnny disappears for the summer, Chris mentions repeatedly that he misses his friend "so much I was ill" (154, 156, 157, 163, 165, 177, 182). As Chris puts it, "I like him so much it hurts" (192).

Two memorable scenes depict Chris and Johnny's tenderness. As they are bicycling out of Stockholm to go camping one night, Chris describes the experience of riding together on one bicycle in poetic sex-ual imagery:

> I was pedaling faster and faster, my thighs were rubbing up and down along Johnny's hips . . . so my knees went backwards and forwards like

pistons along Johnny's side . . . and his shirt work[s] its way up, so after a bit his back was all bare, all white and naked, it had never seen the sun, and I had my face buried in a knot of a shirt smelling of tar and pine needles . . . Johnny pressed hard against my body, jammed between my legs as I pedaled away, . . . cos in that world we both had the same body, his arms, my legs, his legs, my arms, and the same thoughts. (197–98)

As they are camping that night, they share one blanket because Johnny has not brought anything with him, preferring to be a "free man" (195, 208). They lie with their arms around one another:

The warmth came back again, though now my back was cold, and the tar and pine needles swept over me and I was whisked away into that other world again and I could feel my dick hardening and growing. I'd been afraid of that all the time, ever since Johnny had started talking about spending the night together, but now that it was happening, I didn't mind. Johnny must have noticed, but he didn't say anything. . . . Anyway, he didn't react in the same way now, or I'd have noticed, of course. . . . I just lay in another world and couldn't care less that my dick was pressing up against him. (209)

Although Chris and Johnny never consummate their passion, their story is nonetheless one that equates a sexual awakening with maturation. Notably, all of the details of their shared sexuality happen in direct narration addressed to the zero-degree, invisible narratee. The police officer—the alleged narratee of the story—would undoubtedly be unnerved by such details.

The effect of shifting the narratee throughout the novel, however, adds several layers of complexity to *Johnny, My Friend*. Just as Chris is trying to determine both Johnny's identity and current whereabouts, the reader is trying to determine who Johnny is and what Chris understands about his friend's identity. With a series of narrative clues that become more apparent after the reader has finished the novel the first time, Chris's focalization describes Johnny quite aptly. But because Chris's expectations of social roles are as solidly fixed as most readers', some readers may initially miss some clues that seem obvious after the first read. For example, the first time Chris meets Johnny, Chris is impressed with Johnny's bicycle tricks—and Chris assumes Johnny is a girl: "What precision! . . . Though when I saw the rider's fizzog, that grin, my heart fell back into place. It was a girl" (10). But when the bike rider says, "Hiya! My name's Johnny" (10), Chris thinks, "I kept on saying nothing, cos if life has taught me one thing it's that if a boy looks like a girl, he doesn't want to go on about what he looks like" (10). In subsequent narration, Chris describes his own or other people's perception of Johnny as having a "girlish face" (18, 24, 62, 211), as being a "poof" (21), as being like a "young lady" (44), as throwing a ball "like a tart" (55), as being "that little poppet" (137) and "prettier" (182) and "lovely" (201, 211) and "very skinny" (210) and "soft and cat-like" (211). Twice, Chris makes intertextual references comparing Johnny to that most famous of all Swedish children's literary characters, Pippi Longstocking, not only because of Johnny's red hair, but also because of Johnny's anti-authoritarian attitudes and unwillingness to grow up (10, 90; see Nikolajeva 2000, 208–10). Like Johnny, Pippi lives "in her own house with no parents, more or less, and outside all rules"; Chris considers Johnny and Pippi "two of a kind" (90). Moreover, Johnny refuses to swim with the gang and has a marked modesty about undergarments that the boys in Chris's gang mock. When he wonders about Johnny's identity, Chris speculates either in terms of social class or science fiction, thinking that Johnny might be either desperately poor or a refugee from an alternative world. Only in the final pages of the novel, when Chris has seen his missing friend's naked body murdered, does he understand that Johnny is a girl. The narrative estrangement is dramatic because Pohl has relied so thoroughly on readers' fixed sense of gender identity.

IDEOLOGY AND ESTRANGEMENT

Two reversals of expectations may shock the first-time reader of *Johnny, My Friend*. The generic expectations of adolescent literature can lend themselves to a certain optimism, although Pohl prepares the reader for a disastrous ending. Chris's recognition of Johnny's body, murdered by a sexual predator, provides the confirmation that all is not right in the world:

> But I have time to see . . . through the hole . . . where the door should have been . . . something light . . . What the light thing is . . . I can only guess . . . but the nightmare . . . fills in, . . . adds to, . . . joins together . . . to make a picture . . . from which I'll . . . never be free. *I'll see it, over and over again."* (249; author's bold and emphasis)

Chris's life is shattered because his friend has died, and he also needs to reverse completely his self-narrative. He has not been a boy loving his best mate; he has been a boy in love with his first girl. The shock of discovering Johnny's gender is lessened only by discovering simultaneously that s/he is dead.

Maria Nikolajeva reads *Johnny, My Friend* mythically, rather than mimetically (Nikolajeva 2000, 210). In her interpretation, Johnny is the mythic guide who leads Chris to maturity (210–15). The maturation that occurs, however, is articulated in terms of Christian allegory. That is, Chris depicts the maturation that occurs because of his sexual awakening to Johnny in terms of a fall. In his last italicized interior monologue to Johnny, he laments:

> *Now you've fallen even so, far down into the gaping black hole with crumbling edges and no railings . . . and the worthy gents, who were your mates for a year a long time ago, the school year 54–55, will remember you with admiration, but not me, cos when you fall, I fall as well, I'll follow you as soon as tonight, I'll go there tonight, I'll climb over the rail, and close my eyes, cos I'm frightened, Johnny, I'm so frightened, close my eyes and fall, and we'll meet somewhere in the Alternative World, somewhere far, far away from all this.* (252)

Four times in their friendship, Chris has felt a great fear of Johnny falling. The first time occurs at their initial meeting, when Johnny accepts a challenge to ride down sixty-two steps along the side of the school-yard (which Johnny does successfully). Another time, Johnny proves that he can walk along a six centimeter-wide handrail over a viaduct that is twenty meters over a ravine. While this stunt is going on, Chris says, "But I won't be there in that future, cos when Johnny falls, I fall as well. It doesn't take much!" (64). In a third scene, set underground in the basements and passages beneath Stockholm, Chris becomes frightened when Johnny runs off because "there were black holes in two of the passages, crumbling round the edges and with no protective barriers" (135). When Johnny asks where they lead, Chris answers, "Right down into hell" (136). Chris is referring to these holes-that-lead-to-hell when he discovers that Johnny is dead and threatens to throw himself into "*the gaping black hole with crumbling edges*" (252). In the fourth instance that Chris fears Johnny falling, Johnny contemplates climbing over the rooftops and ridgepoles of the houses in Stockholm that lead to Maria Magdalena Church. To stop his friend, Chris yells: "Johnny, please Johnny, for God's sake, don't leave me on my own! I'll die, Johnny!" (139). Four times, Chris perceives himself as having almost witnessed Johnny's fall into death; three of those times Chris connects falling to his own death.

During the summer that Johnny disappears, Chris indicates that he has more awareness of Johnny's situation than his subconscious has allowed him to believe. He speculates that Johnny has slipped into an "alternative world" in which circus performers are stolen as children and later become the "assaulted, murdered little girls" whom he keeps reading about in the Stockholm newspapers (162). Johnny is, indeed, a circus performer; she is billed as "Miss Juvenile" and rides her bicycle in a high-wire act—another site from which she might fall. Indeed, the manager of the circus where she serves almost as slave labor argues that "safety nets weren't a good thing at all, cos if there was a safety net the artistes would relax and get careless" and fall (159). Lissa Paul identifies the circus in *Johnny, My Friend* as functioning like the transgressive carnivalesque described in Bakhtinian theory; the circus provides a moral opposite to the conservatism of Stockholm (Paul 1997, 1). It is, indeed, the type of place where the possibility of children falling is met with unconcern. The police officer gives Chris a carnivalesque picture of Miss Juvenile (although he does not recognize it as Johnny at the time):

> The photo is taken from below; focused on the lace panties she's wearing, and her face is bathed in spotlights. The little panties are the most important feature, that's obvious. The whole set-up reminds you of Sten's dirty magazines with flabby tarts and legs apart, showing all they've got, and you follow their legs up till you arrive at something that seems to have got there by accident, and the tart and the photographer would both have loved to show you a bit more, if only. . . . The photo was designed to attract old men who like looking up girls' skirts. (143)

The imagery of a virginal girl falling from innocence is strong.

Although Johnny never literally falls, s/he does save Chris from plunging into shallow water at the beach when Chris is unaware that the diving boards have been moved closer to shore for the winter (220–21). Immediately following that scene, Johnny offers to tell Chris a secret, the truth about her identity. Johnny struggles to find the right words, taking several deep breaths: "He worked hard on how to begin, which word he was going to start with, and it was, Well . . . , and that was all. And I could see the black chasm widening, saw the darkness inside there" (223). Chris grows too uncomfortable to hear the truth, and jumps up, shouting, "I'll *die* if you go on like this!" (223; author's emphasis). Deciding to spare Chris's pain, Johnny never tells the secret of the life s/he lives, and so s/he dies instead. Although s/he has died to protect Chris's innocence, he falls from grace anyway. He can no longer exist in the Edenic, prelapsarian world he typifies as "innocent" because it is comprised solely of the "lads" who are his friends (176).

Chris's family lives in the parish of Maria Magdalena. Johnny, it turns out, is more Mary Magdalene than Christ-figure, the fallen woman, the victim, the objectified body of male lust. As Nikolajeva indicates, Johnny sacrifices herself (Nikolajeva 2000, 214), but no one is saved through her death. Nevertheless, it is through her death that Pohl comes to the theme of the exploited female, the exploited child, and his ideological intentions become clearest. Pohl's novel is an angry indictment of the failure of the welfare state, so his characters make overt comments to this effect. For instance, Chris refuses to use the government's official name for a local street, efficiently renamed in 1949, Södergatan, which means "Street of Söder" (Söder is the part of Stockholm in which the story is set). Instead, Chris refers to the street by its traditional and more interesting name, Repslagargatan, which means "Street of the Rope-makers." His rebellion is a small one, but it is communicated as an anti-authoritarian stance when Chris refuses to tell a police officer why he still uses the traditional name for the street:

> We were playing gratey on Repslagargatan. The chance of the ball bouncing right down to Södergatan added a bit of extra spice to the game.
> Repslagargatan? says the cop. It's six years since it was called that.
> One of these days, I'll explain why we, the front line troops representing adults and kids in the parish of Maria Magdalena, insist on calling the eastern end of Södergatan Repslagargatan. Another time, another time, can't muck about now! (238)

Chris uses language here to resist the government.

In an ideological articulation that is more germane to Pohl's agenda of social critique, Chris ironically comments on recent reforms in Sweden: "Not for nothing were we renowned as a welfare state, where the worst of the injustices had been reformed and banished. There was no exploitation of children here" (144). The passage is one of the clearest examples in the book of the adult ideology of the author creating a separate narrative voice from the point of view of the adolescent focalizer. Chris doesn't understand when his mother recognizes Johnny as one such child in some of the book's most explicit ideological commentary:

> What kind of a poor kid is Johnny then?
> Johnny's the kind of poor kid lots of other poor kids are all over the world, who are exploited for all kinds . . . all kinds of . . . purposes. But in the ideal homes of the welfare society young kids like that are reformed out of existence according to official information to obey. They don't exist. And if some slip through the great welfare security net even so, the public just put up with the claim that they *don't* exist.
> The Swedish people applaud the boasts of the politicians and pay up. Pay up fantastic good taxes, so they don't get their impressions clouded by proof that need really does exist. Everybody helps to keep the painful truth under the covers. (187–88; author's emphasis)

Chris is disturbed when he learns that Johnny has no parents and lives with a man who pays him for "what should you call it? . . . his little favours" (231). But Johnny is even more exploited than Chris realizes at that juncture.

Some of Chris's inability to recognize Johnny's identity and exploitation resides in his own innocence. He is sincere in expressing his inability to understand molestation: "I just couldn't work out what could tempt some old bloke into 'outrageous behaviour,' which is what the papers claimed they did" (158); "Summer is the . . . time for missing, assaulted, murdered little girls. The warmer it is, the more of them there are" (162). He also worries about what happens to women in circuses who get too old to perform: "I was moved to tears. All these tragic fates for those poor women!" (163). *Johnny, My Friend* is a poetic elegy for the body of the exploited female child.

Chris's fall from innocence results in his eventual ability to understand Johnny's condition: "It's only afterwards, when you've been through all that happened like this, that you realize how blind you were then, when it was all going on," Chris comments to the police officer as his narratee (85). He makes a similar statement later in the novel, directly to the implied reader as narratee: "Cos this straightforward, uncomplicated world I had all around me isn't all there is, I knew that even then" (137). Chris is—as Robyn McCallum notes—subject to the ideological constructions of childhood, adolescence, and adulthood that his culture promulgates (McCallum 1999, 9). That it is physical violence moving him from one stage to the next has ideological impli-

cations for his identity: neither he nor the reader can believe in a
Romantic construction of innocent childhood.

Trying to console Chris in the novel's denouement, the police officer
says, "But you knew Johnny. . . . You know the truth" (250). The cop's
comment leads Chris back into his interior monologue: "I know the
truth? I, who knew Johnny? I know the truth, I knew Johnny. Too late!
I got to know Johnny too late" (251). Chris's ultimate self-condemna-
tion comes, not surprisingly, in the italicized interior monologue that
reflects his most emotional moments:

> *But didn't you understand, Johnny, that I was just a child. I was a child
> until an hour ago. I c o u l d n' t see and hear. I had to have everything
> spelt out. . . . I was a child, and I didn't even realize there was anything
> to see.* (253; author's italics and spacing)

Although the truth might have set Johnny free had Chris known it
before her death, there is nothing freeing about the truth after her
death.

As so often happens in adolescent literature, the adolescent's fall
from innocence is linked to both sex and death (see Nikolajeva 2000,
212). Johnny and Chris share an idealized sexual moment, and within
a matter of days, Johnny is killed by someone who, it is implied, has
treated her sexuality with far less innocence than Chris has. I have written elsewhere about the connection between sexuality and death in
adolescent literature, as has Nikolajeva; inspired by Mircea Eliade,
however, she adds an important third aspect of initiation to her analysis: the sacred (Trites 2000, 122; Nikolajeva 2000, 6). Sexuality and
death are the two aspects of carnality that lead many adolescent characters to understand maturation; they are the "steps into initiation" in
this novel (Nikolajeva 2000, 212). In *Johnny, My Friend*, the narrator's
anagnorisis in the face of death assumes tragic proportions, and the
reader's estrangement is complete. How can this happen? How can a
child be so exploited? How can evil be let to flourish so freely? And
how can our understanding, our recognition, of this evil be so well-
hidden by a simple matter of (wrongly) assuming that someone's gender protects him?

CONCLUSION

Pohl's postmodern triumph at the end of *Johnny, My Friend* is to have
subverted not only his narrator's expectations but also his readers'.

Chris understands that Johnny is male; so do all but the most discerning of first-time readers. Chris thinks of Johnny as a "free man" because Johnny describes himself that way (195, 208, 228), and the reader's recognition that Johnny is neither "free" nor a "man" can take almost as long to fully develop as Chris's recognition does. Chris talks to Johnny, so the reader assumes for a good measure of the narrative that Johnny will return to engage in his part of the conversation. Chris understands that children are exploited, but believes that his mates—even one boy who has a drunken father—are safe, so readers can believe the same for much of the narrative. Chris believes that Christianity is so pervasive that he cannot comprehend how Johnny has never heard of saying grace or Jesus or God (126–29), so readers may expect a Christian redemption at the end of this narrative, instead of Chris's falling from grace. In short, all of the ideologies that shape the innocence of Chris's childhood are stripped from him, and the reader is left to condemn a brutal world.

Pohl has been systematic in his use of estrangement to communicate his ideology (see Stewart 2004, 129–43). He relies on our understanding of narrative address only to shift the subject position of the reader time and time again, so that the implied reader is repeatedly estranged from the narratee. Pohl relies on our understanding of the conventions of genre—and the conventions of gender—to subvert the reader's expectations of the buddy tale. In the process, he estranges the readers from their notions of what it means to be gendered in a stable and specific way. And Pohl relies on the reader's understanding of Christianity to depict a fall from grace that is a failure of the social welfare state in an ideology that critiques the dominant culture. Although *Johnny, My Friend* appears to be an ambiguous novel as it unfolds, by the end, its ideologies come together neatly through a series of narrative estrangements that allow the author to criticize the dominant culture in a powerful indictment.

WORKS CITED

Chatman, Seymour. *Story and Discourse: Narrative Structure in Fiction and Film*. Ithaca, NY: Cornell University Press, 1978.

Eliade, Mircea. *The Sacred and the Profane*. New York: Harper and Row, 1961.

McCallum, Robyn. *Ideologies of Identity in Adolescent Fiction: The Dialogic Construction of Subjectivity*. New York: Garland, 1999.

McGavran, James Holt. "Fear's Echo and Unhinged Joy: Crossing Homosocial Boundaries in *A Separate Peace*." *Children's Literature* 30 (2002): 67–80.

Nikolajeva, Maria. *From Mythic to Linear: Time in Children's Literature*. Lanham, MD: Scarecrow, 2000.

———. "Beyond the Grammar of Story, or How Can Children's Literature Criticism Benefit from Narrative Theory?" *Children's Literature Association Quarterly* 28 (2003): 5–16.

Paul, Lissa. "Bike Dreams." Review of *Dance on my Grave*, by Aidan Chambers, and *Johnny, My Friend*, by Peter Pohl. *American Book Review* (Nov.–Dec. 1997): 1, 5.

Pohl, Peter. *Johnny, My Friend*. Translated by Laurie Thompson. Stroud, Glos.: Turton and Chambers, 1991.

Prince, Gerald. "Introduction to the Study of the Narratee." Pp. 7–25 in *Reader-Response Criticism* edited by Jane Tompkins. Baltimore: The Johns Hopkins University Press, 1980.

Stephens, John. *Language and Ideology in Children's Fiction*. New York: Longman, 1992.

Stewart, Susan. *Genre, Ideology, and Children's Literature*. Illinois State University, 2004 (Diss).

Tribunella, Eric L. "Refusing the Queer Potential: John Knowles's *A Separate Peace*." *Children's Literature* 30 (2002): 81–95.

Trites, Roberta Seelinger. *Disturbing the Universe: Power and Repression in Adolescent Literature*. Iowa City: University of Iowa Press, 2000.

11

Philosophical Homework or Universal Amazement?
Jostein Gaarder's *Sophie's World*

Harald Bache-Wiig

In the house where I grew up, one of the walls in our best sitting-room was covered by an enormous world map. On this map could be seen a huge number of pictures showing selected scenes from world history: a discus-thrower from Athens, three ships on their way to America, a Paris guillotine, a convoy of tractors heading for Siberia (as a part of Stalin's five-year plans). Above it all, there was a little boy in a flying suitcase. In this manner the Danish author H. C. Andersen provided the logo ("The Flying Suitcase") for this rather original piece of visual didactics. I have never stopped believing in the possibility of combining fact and fiction so as to obtain power and world conquest.

Jostein Gaarder has succeeded in conquering an entire world by means of his philosophical-historical fable about the Norwegian girl Sophie. It is quite amazing, although perhaps not more so than the fact that Selma Lagerlöf achieved similar fame by publishing *The Wonderful Adventures of Nils* in 1907–08.[1] Like *Sophie's World* this was also a novel amalgamating textbook, fantasy story, and *bildungsroman*. This book was even a didactic fable whose purpose was purely national in character. Selma Lagerlöf wrote for the Swedish primary school, with

255

the aim of making children identify with Sweden through knowledge of the country, its people, and its history. Nils Holgersson did cross the borders of Sweden, however, no doubt because of a poetic and human quality that enabled children all over the world to fly high.

The goose that carries Nils Holgersson on his back on his journey across Sweden also picks up Sophie in *Sofies verden* (1991; Engl. *Sophie's World*, 1994), but the goose admits that he hardly was the most apt means of transport in the textbook in which Sophie, quite unwillingly, has been involved. New ages call for new didactic means of imparting knowledge. At the time when Selma Lagerlöf wrote her book, airplanes had just recently made the movable bird's-eye view a human option. Sophie has to fight for attention in a world where children float in the staggering cyberspace on a daily basis. Sophie's world is a bit like that too: a kind of historical-philosophical space odyssey in a universe where there are no firm boundaries between the simulated and the real, between that which is thought and that which is actually experienced.

MEDIUM AS MESSAGE

At the outset nobody saw the incredible potential of the book—least of all Gaarder himself; he thought that he had written an enjoyable textbook aimed at a relatively small audience. Instead, it turned out to be a blockbuster, signaling a forceful cultural desire of our time, until then totally ignored by the institution of literature for young people. It was a book that seemingly could be regarded as marginal within the system of children's literature, yet it exploded in the epicenter of the same system. Ideas of what kind of literature might be worth attention and marketing changed rapidly.

It has long been outdated to regard children's literature as part of the pedagogical institution. Answering the question whether books for children and young people should be didactical or free fiction, a number of experts have asserted that worthy pedagogical intentions can provide little legitimacy if not integrated into an independent, artistically redeemed text. In order for us to take children's literature seriously and for such literature to emancipate itself, it must be interesting in its own right, not just by way of its intention, be it ever so pedagogical.[2] Even the claim that it should be adapted to the way a child reads and understands has become suspicious. Despite this change, *Sophie's*

World had considerable impact on the world. And it makes no secret of its didactical mission in the subtitle, *A Novel about the History of Philosophy*. As such, it is provocatively old-fashioned. But it is also astonishingly modern—even to the brink of being postmodern—in its way of sweetening the pill, of making the material relevant to the reader. Directing patterns of conflict in a novel as a struggle between fiction and reality, and questioning the reality status of the fictional universe by means of metafictional devices, has almost become conventional in postmodern literature. M. C. Escher's famous image of the two hands that are at the same time both writing and being written has become an emblem of postmodernist writing and its theory. In a comment on three of Gaarder's most important books, *Kabalmysteriet* (1990; Engl. *The Solitaire Mystery*, 1996), *Sophie's World*, and *Julemysteriet* (1992; Engl. *The Christmas Mystery*, 1996), Boel Westin points out that such metafiction may trace its roots right back to the Renaissance (Westin 1998, 109–123). The postmodern aspects logically become the mirror of the premodern aspects. In *Sophie's World*, the book's fictional author, Albert Knag, the UN major, uses romantic irony as an echo wall for his disrespectful treatment of his characters. Alberto Knox and Sophie Amundsen gradually bang their heads against the wall of the fictional parallel world in which he has trapped them.

On one occasion Albert Knag fancies a book that might make people better able to think: "Perhaps the best remedy against violence would be a short course in philosophy. What about 'The UN's little philosophy book'—which all new citizens of the world could be given a copy of in their own language. I'll propose the idea to the UN General Secretary" (184). Looking back on the popularity of *Sophie's World*, we can see that this quotation may be interpreted as an instance of romantic irony. Gaarder's novel turned out to be the realization of such a project. It has been translated into more than fifty languages and has become a compulsory gift to young people all over the world. This popularity, however, probably cannot be accounted for only by referring to the educational value that has been ascribed to *Sophie's World*. It is also a novel that, to a very significant extent, has succeeded in making the medium the message, making aesthetical experience and philosophical knowledge—material and form—two sides of a coin. Art and knowledge serve one another. I will try to show what I mean by this statement in the following analysis, and I will also indicate the limitation in Gaarder's project as regards the philosophical actualization of the material in the book.

PHILOSOPHY IN NORWAY
(AND DENMARK)

The didactic situation presented in the novel is most likely quite astonishing to the majority of young readers outside Norway: an ordinary teenage girl is admitted to an intensive course in Western philosophy. An enthusiastic teacher provides her with material, written as well as oral, prescribes exercises, and encourages self-reflection. It is likewise obvious that the course enables her to reflect independently on her regular school subjects. She has somehow added a dimension of reflection and criticism that help make these subjects something more than just homework and curriculum; they appear as something useful for the future.

Such a pedagogical angle is far from curious in a Norwegian context. If Sophie were real, she would in all probability have begun studying at a Norwegian university four years later, and the compulsory introductory course she would have to take at university level would be almost identical to the one given to her by Alberto, and it would be delivered by a similar, enthusiastic, professional philosophy teacher. It is a peculiar custom in Norway that university students have to pass a so-called "preparation course of philosophy." In Sweden it was never introduced, whereas Denmark once had it, but abolished it about 1970. Gaarder himself has an academic background, and he has taught philosophy at a non-academic college institution ("folkehøyskole"), where most students are around twenty years old.

The belief in philosophy as a major and basic knowledge goes back a long way in Norwegian history, as far back as 1814, when Norway was established as a nation state of its own. This independence was reinforced by a new bourgeois elite that brought with them German ideas of "*bildung*." To an educated individual with knowledge and insight into the weal and woe of the community, philosophy was regarded as the basic subject. The idea of an ennobled humanity, with its roots in antique heritage and philosophy, was likewise accepted by the new popularly based power elite, which gradually gained a strong influence. The idea of a democratic, humanistic universalism was kept alive and did not give in to the partial glorification of people and the nation. "The popular element was not mobilized to strengthen a dictatorship," says the Norwegian historian Rune Slagstad, "but to deepen democracy" (Slagstad 1998, 130). The traditional schools that provide a general education for young people ("folkehøyskole") of the kind at which Gaarder has been teaching,[3] have been meeting-places for democratic popular ideas and the European bourgeois educational tradition.

It should be added that it was the Danish vicar and poet Nikolai S. Grundtvig (1783–1872) who established the Scandinavian "folkehøyskole." Here young people from the provinces could acquire a nationally rooted supply of cultural knowledge as an alternative to the classical heritage dominant in the bourgeois-academic system. A personally acquired spiritual life in the service of people and religion was likewise a goal for each individual. Knowledge was dead unless it was conveyed through "the living word," that is to say, by the oral presentation of an exuberant teacher. This presentation is exactly one of the tricks that is being used pedagogically in *Sophie's World*: it simulates an oral narrator's situation, taking the material out of the textbook and putting it into the mouth of a passionate mediator.[4]

The fact that the learning material, as well as the educational situation, are both directed toward the entire personality is in line with the ideals of German academic tradition of *"bildung."* The introductory course in philosophy required for academic studies in Norway is a particularly Norwegian variant of this tradition. It is supposed to open up a world for the individual, and open up the individual for a world. Still, it ought to be said that, despite all the enthusiasm and pedagogical invention that philosophy teacher Alberto Knox shows in Gaarder's novel and despite the oral presentation, the learning situation in *Sophie's World* is extremely authoritarian. By her standard answer "I see," Sophie's task is to confirm knowledge, not to challenge or develop it. There is a curious tension between the monological and omniscient learning situation in *Sophie's World* and the essence of the basic philosophical attitude that Knox—and Gaarder himself—tries to impart.

COUNTERPOINT

Norwegian scholar Sissel Veggeland has found an interesting parallel between Mikhail Bakhtin's famous thesis on polyphony in modern novels and Gaarder's treatment of the author's point of view in *The*

Solitaire Mystery and *Sophie's World* (Veggeland 2004).[5] In *The Solitaire Mystery* we meet a creator, a man stranded on a desert island, who has provided a pack of cards with life and created his own universe where the various cards appear as individuals in a thoroughly organized society. They do not realize their lack of freedom, however, until the Joker reveals to them that they are created artificially to constitute a comfort for the stranded and to be pieces in a story that is also told in the book that the reader is reading. The Joker calls for rebellion, and chaos and destruction follow. This development may be read as a postmodern fable, or as the fictional characters' rebellion against their narrator. The Joker, who reflects his own creator, finds his own voice and lives on as a modern, homeless, and roaming spirit, a sort of ghost in the machine.

Veggeland points out that the major-narrator in *Sophie's World* himself reveals his role to the fictional characters Sophie and Alberto, albeit without risk, since both of them exist in a different reality (Veggeland 2004, 50). But there is a kind of rebellion to be found here as well; Sophie and Alberto apparently escape the major's didactic arrangements. Toward the end, they both appear in a story that is not included in the book written by the major for his daughter Hilde. And here they overhear a conversation on the subject of counterpoint:

> Contrapunctual form operates on two dimensions, horizontally, or melodically, and vertically, harmonically. . . . The melodies combine in such a way that they develop as much as possible, independently of how they sound against each other. But they have to be concordant. Actually, it's note against note. (405)

The Solitaire Mystery and *Sophie's World* both have a built-in critical reflection on their fictional creator as a monological dictator in his self-created universe. Gaarder tries to achieve the effect of a counterpoint polyphony, in which different voices are opposed to each other. He questions above all the right of a narrator to rule his characters unrestrictedly. In *Sophie's World* the major-narrator gradually stands out as a somewhat presumptuous tyrant who rather capriciously plays cat and mouse with his fictional characters. His daughter, Hilde, eventually makes him taste his own medicine in an ever so little daughter's rebellion against her father. Correspondingly, there is a questioning of the teacher figure's overriding of his student. Sophie, the studious philosophy student, gradually resents submitting to Alberto Knox's many instructions. In a review of the book appearing in *Newsweek*, we read: "Gaarder develops his mostly passive heroine into a feisty little cosmic thinker, far more combative than the Yes-I-agree-Socrates stooges in Plato's dialogues" (Sullivan 1994). Eventually, Sophie and Alberto act together as equal partners in breaking away from the major. Veggeland concludes: "Sophie turns into an active and strong conversation partner and she has a say in what is going to happen" (Veggeland 2004, 83).

Thus there is a movement toward communication free of domination in these two novels by Gaarder. There is, of course, a superior narrator who has assembled these multileveled stories, but the plots thematize and question this superior, or immanent, narrator's right to have the last word, and the ball is played into the reader's hands. From this perspective, we see the element of anti-pedagogy even in a pedagogically constructed work like *Sophie's World*.

CHINESE BOXES

As already mentioned, the various fictional universes of the book are inter-constructed like Chinese boxes. On the outside there is the interchange between the actual reader and the actual author that occurs when a reader finds himself reading *Sophie's World*. Sophie, too, finds a book with the same title in the bookstore and takes it home with her (390). Once we have entered the universe of the book itself, we encounter the director of it all, the implicit narrator and the mastermind, who appeals to the bright and interested implicit reader—possibly a young woman not inclined to take kindly to a male's know-it-all attitude. Then we have the frame story of the writing father, his particular birthday present, and his daughter who has a passion for reading. Embedded within this text, its author, the writing father, Albert Knag, has passed the task of philosophy teacher to his alter ego, Alberto Knox, and he has replaced in the role of earnest and clever student his daughter, Hilde, with Sophie. The stories act as mirrors for each other, and simultaneously the girls establish an uncanny, almost telepathic contact beyond the major's arrangements. one obviously moulded on the relation between the goddess of wisdom Sofia and the great medieval scholar Hildegard von Bingen.

In the inner box there is the story of Alberto and Sophie, who have to admit that they have been stranded in a children's Neverland of literature in the company of other great immortal, albeit imagined, characters. Even this part of the novel appears strangely prophetic; Alberto and Sophie seem to have gained a neverending access to the sort of celebrity parties they experience on midsummer's eve in the café called Cinderella. However, before the two of them withdraw to enjoy their place as newly lit stars in the heaven of classical children's literature, they succeed in playing a practical joke, a tiny earthquake in the reality from which they are abolished. By a joint effort, they manage to free the Colonel's boat, a rowboat which is moored in the real world: the impossible is made possible. This act indicates that we apply to *Sophie's World* a concept from *The Solitaire Mystery* in which Chinese boxes put within each other are characterized as follows: "the inner box wraps up the outer at the same time as the outer box wraps up the inner" (Gaarder 1996, 286).

This Escher-like logic may, I think, shed light on the connection between philosophical knowledge and the book's fictional arrangement. Thus, we have come to the point at which we need to ask about the book's perspective on the two basic questions posed by philosophy throughout time: "Who am I? Where do I come from?" Is it correct to assert that this book represents the history of philosophy, and thus the attempt to formulate answers to these questions, in the form of a story, with a basic conflict, the building up to a climax, and a possible crisis?

THE STORY OF THE HISTORY
OF PHILOSOPHY

Jostein Gaarder is convinced that children and philosophers have one basic, mutual characteristic, the ability to be amazed: "to pose existential questions is not something we learn, it is something we forget when we grow up. The great philosophers have retained the amazement of the child, they have stayed children" (Fransson 1993, 11). The existence of a world is just as amazing as the fact that a magician is able to draw a huge white rabbit from his hat. Gaarder makes use of a parable in which he sees the child as a being born on the outer edge of one of the rabbit's hairs, looking out to most of the rabbit's body and thus made to ask himself what strange sort of world he inhabits. Gradually, as the child grows up, he sinks down into the rabbit's fur and begins to take his everyday life for granted, life becomes a habit.

In *Sophie's World* the major tries to refresh Sophie's child-like look of marvel in the company of the great philosophers. Every one of them has had one thing in common with the great Socrates, no matter what they have thought of him generally: they have admitted that they know nothing of the world in which they have been placed and that this situation calls for further investigation. Sophie becomes involved in the results of these investigations, always presented in a loyal, clarifying fashion by Alberto, and always in such a way that Sophie's questions along the way give Alberto the opportunity to explain rather than criticize.

There is a double meaning, a contradiction in this situation. It touches a dilemma in what we might call "the philosophical project," but the book itself does not overtly thematize this relationship. The aim of all this doubt and amazement is surely to gain a kind of knowledge or cognition that appears true and certain. It is an attempt to find an Archimedian point, within or without the human being, that renders life less arbitrary, capricious, and odd. In this walk through the history of philosophy, each philosopher serves as a supporting cane. Critical questions and contradictions of predecessors keep coming up, but always with the hope of a new kind of truth. Philosophers are far from all being rationalists, philosophically speaking, but they do agree on the basic belief that thinking may lead to a solution in the struggle to make life more transparent and less bizarre.

Now it might seem as if all this thinking somewhere between outright amazement, on the one hand, and traditional systematic pondering, on the other, could lead to even more profound and positive results through history. Further on in history, Alberto may, after all, gradually make his material more accessible by presenting it as a continuance of philosophical traditions through dialogue and critical comments. He mentions Hegel's main point, the idea that a world reason comes to terms with itself. As a teacher, Alberto has the aim of making Sophie the heir to this grand and glorious Western tradition of thinking, of giving her privileged access to a well of wisdom, an accumulated, consolidated capital of knowledge. Although this track of wisdom is more obscure than Hegel would have imagined in his dialectical form of reason, the well-trained Sophie would soon be able to find her way into a world that is more familiar, more thoroughly explored than the one opened up by the initial questions of philosophy. To write out a history that eventually would turn its reader into a wise child carrying a bourgeois mental ballast of traditional philosophical thinking would, however, be far from Gaarder's vision of the great amazement of the world. Nevertheless, at the outset he wanted to write a pure and simple book of philosophy for young readers. "I wanted to write a factual book, but it turned out extremely dry. But then the thought of Sophie struck me" (Senje 1995).

Central to "the thought of Sophie" is no doubt the connection between philosophical knowledge and a meta-novel about two characters who gradually realize that they are appearing in a textbook. By means of this idea, Gaarder has also discovered how to make the text dynamic, thus avoiding a progressive accumulation of steadily new names and new thoughts. It all tends toward a crisis, a downfall. In one of her practical tasks, Sophie touches a profound ambiguity in the development of the philosophical tradition. She recapitulates Alberto's picture of the created world: a rabbit drawn out of the hat by the Great Magician. Sophie comments:

> Philosophers try to climb up one of the fine hairs of the rabbit's fur and stare straight into the eyes of the Great Magician. Whether they will ever succeed is an open question. But if each philosopher climbed onto another one's back they would get even higher up in the rabbit's fur, and then, in my opinion, there would be a chance that they would make it some day. (104)

Would such an omniscient observation point be a happy and desirable result of the philosophers' collective contemplation? Is Sophie's philosophy course intended to move her closer to such an insight? If so, such a victory for philosophical amazement would make the amazement itself redundant; it would even remove the basis for pursuing the mysteries of the world, the most noble of all pursuits in the literary universe of Jostein Gaarder. Sophie, thoughtful girl that she is, adds a postscript, however. She reminds us of the Bible and its story about the Tower of Babel, which God crushes on the grounds that "he didn't want the tiny human insects to crawl up that high out of the white rabbit he had just created" (n.p.).

Elements of such a breakdown of the trust that philosophy has in its own project may also be seen in Alberto Knox's own story of philosophy. The fact is that the philosophers have not become more certain of their true knowledge just because they have placed themselves on the shoulders of their predecessors. Plato and Aristotle were safe enough, and Augustine and Thomas Aquinas secured their faith with the support of these two authorities. For one thousand years, philosophers thought that they could see God. During the Renaissance and the

Baroque period, however, this idea starts crumbling, and the idea that the wonder of life is just a dream comes to the surface. Only by means of the utmost effort could a certain substance of reason be found by Descartes or a small piece of freedom be detected by Spinoza. With Hume, everything we can possibly know is reduced to pure sensory impressions.

The knowledge that the philosophers have fought for grows steadily harder to reach. In the dramaturgy of the novel, George Berkeley appears to be the crisis. Even Alberto himself has problems with him when it comes to presenting his philosophical views. Alberto explains that Berkeley is of the opinion that we do not have access to a world outside our own consciousness. The world exists exactly as we experience it: *"esse est percipi."* If things are not experienced by anyone, they do not exist. In a world without objective existence, categories such as "room" and "time" also disappear. The fact that we still imagine that there is a physical, well-structured world must be due to a spiritual force, "God," whose power it is to maintain this idea in our human consciousness. Berkeley makes use of his power of thought to show that human consciousness cannot capture anything outside itself. Skeptical empiricism moves him over to pious belief in God. Man is made very small so that his dependence on God shall loom large; God is the one, the only certainty. Berkeley was made a bishop.

This more or less desperate solution to the tension between philosophical, wondering doubt and the need for certainty is paired with the important realization made halfway through *Sophie's World*. Sophie is forced to "realise that life is only a dream" (237) the day she reaches fifteen. Alberto and Sophie are thus captives in a fictional world where they find themselves subject to the whims of an almighty God, just like the human being in Berkeley's world of pure consciousness. On a fictional level, they seem to have gained a cruel, final insight into who they are and where they have come from, which ought to prevent every need to continue their amazement.

It is, however, the major who has forced this situation on them. In my opinion, this move halfway through the book functions as a correction to philosophy's need to free itself from nervous amazement by replacing it with definite given knowledge and insight. The major gets presumptuous in his superposition as a teacher of philosophy, and Hilde (as well as Sophie and the reader) is easily oppressed by his capricious know-it-all attitude. The tension in the rest of the book is found in the ability of Alberto and Sophie to oppose him, to complete their wondering philosophical project without being distracted by the fact that the major is using them as toys. They simply refuse to accept the conditions for their existence given to them by the major. Eventually they succeed in reaching a form of existence outside the consciousness of the major, and once more there is an "objective" world in which they can search for their own relation to things. Thus Berkeley is contradicted. Finally, they win what appears to be a tiny victory, but which in reality is a huge one: undoing the mooring of the major's boat, they disturb the seemingly subordinate relationship of fiction and fantasy to reality.[6] Consciousness and imagination may exert power to disturb the familiar world that constitutes human limits. Once more Berkeley is contradicted.

The major's daughter, Hilde, carries out her own rebellion against her father's self-proclaimed right to decide what is reality and what is fiction, or a "subordinate world" made by himself. In the same way that Sophie has been terrorized by strange postcards, the major is afflicted by the written messages Hilde placed at Copenhagen airport. He is made to feel what it is like to be reduced to a fictional character in a play directed by an omniscient narrator: he is being placed in a "secondary world." "I can see you wherever you are, Dad," Hilde writes (413).

This protest against "the major's world," which makes Alberto, Sophie, and Hilde true heroes at the closing of the book, thus counteracts the tendency to pedagogical overruling. It also creates, however, a framework around the teaching situation that is reminiscent of the critical conditions confronting philosophy since the rise of modernity. Berkeley's philosophy contained human weakness and triumphant conviction; in the book, this division is mirrored by the casting of the major and his two fictional characters: Sophie and Alberto can no longer trust their perception of reality; the major is presiding as their God. Later in history, philosophy is treated with a similar kind of ambiguity, though in a way turned upside down. God is dismissed as the guarantee for absolute truth beyond human consciousness. In his place science is installed as the Archimedic point of knowledge. But insight into all sorts of orderliness in nature, biology, and history makes humans powerful and vulnerable. Hegel turns out to be the last creator of systems; in his wake there is thinking and science that give man a rather insecure, contingent place in the created world. Knowledge about all kinds of governing forces outside of human consciousness makes thinking about the conditions of freedom the central idea.

It makes sense that the existential philosophers are granted the last word in the book. The *angst* of Kierkegaard and Sartre's blind faith in freedom beyond all claims of the "nature" of things both provide a meaningful backdrop for Alberto and Sophie when they break away from the "philosophical garden party" that the major directs toward chaos. Man's opportunity for freedom is found in not accepting reality as something given, as the other guests at the party seem to do, no matter what the results. Sharing the collective amazement of the philosophers toward the world in which they have been placed, Alberto and Sophie are able to break loose from the mock world the major constructed and in which he has imprisoned them.

In a recently published dissertation on *Sophie's World* by Ellen Steinsland (2001), the main view is that the author systematically creates uncertainty as to where to draw the line between reality and imagination. She illustrates this uncertainty by pointing out that the relationship between what is the primary world and the secondary world is turned upside down halfway through the book. In the first part, it is Hilde and her world that has a ghost-like existence for Sophie, whereas in the latter part, for Hilde, it is Sophie who gets this magical glow of reality. In the same manner, the facts of philosophy blend with the fictional situation: "The textbook part is interwoven in the story and seeps through it in such a way that the two aspects become inseparable" (Steinsland 2001, 82–83). As I have previously implied, it is, to say the least, conspicuous that the problems of the philosophers are clearly mirrored in the existential problems of the protagonists, problems that arise because they do not trust their own status in the real world. The basic questions of life and death become their personal questions.

THE VICTORY OF PHILOSOPHY
OR ITS RUIN?

When Sophie and Hilde both have completed the material provided by Albert and Alberto, they are not in for a syllabus review and a subsequent exam. On the contrary, we then go back to the original situation of philosophical amazement. With Sophie and Alberto as the invisible audience, Albert and Hilde just sit there, side by side, staring into the starlit cosmic infinity. There is no talk of providing knowledge, but of making the teacher share man's complete lack of certainty about the

very origin of the universe: is the universe something that has been created in a moment of time and is then expanding in the direction of
death and emptiness, or is the cosmos a cyclic *perpetuum mobile*? In
more romantic terms: "a cosmic heart that beats and beats and
beats . . ." (423). Both are "equally inconceivable and equally exciting"
(n.p.), according to Sophie.

There is little doubt that Gaarder supports the latter theory. In his
"novel of the history of philosophy," he does not intend to impart a
huge amount of knowledge. He aims to show that philosophy is a
source for perpetual amazement, to which you keep coming back with
the same basic questions, such as "was everything created in the Big
Bang?" or "has the world always been there?"—be it in a state of permanence or of cyclic change. If philosophy and science were to reach
their apparent goals, this arrival would be the end of the primary condition of man: the ability to be amazed. Gaarder's project is to make
use of philosophy to strengthen this ability. Or, as he says in his novel
I et speil, i en gåte (1993; Engl. *Through a Glass, Darkly* 1998): "man's
ability to look up from the page on which they have been created."

Hilde seems afraid to find the final solution to the riddles. In the
chapter "The Age of Reason," she ponders: "As soon as Sophie and
Alberto 'knew' how everything hung together, they were in a way at
the end of the road" (253). The quest for truth has led them to a fatal
dead-end street. And Hilde's subsequent reflections make her even
more uptight. What if this problem also belongs to her nonfictional
world?

> People had progressed steadily in their understanding of natural laws.
> Could history simply continue to all eternity once the last piece of the
> jigsaw puzzle of philosophy and science had fallen into place? Wasn't
> there a connection between the development of ideas and science on the
> one hand, and the greenhouse effect and deforestation on the other?
> Maybe it was not so crazy to call man's thirst for knowledge a fall from
> grace? (254)

Is it possible that the need to look at God's cards has misled man into
a self-destructive, presumptuous Babel-project? Hilde is confident that
she will find the answer by continuing to read the book her father gave
on her birthday. But she does not, and neither does the reader, get any
clear answer by further reading of the major's book. It ends by the
destructive chaos of the garden party, which constitutes the final turn-

ing point of the novel. There is, on the other hand, some comfort to be found in the last two chapters, of which the first is titled "Counterpoint." Here we find Hilde's "realistic" world and, gradually, also Sophie's "fantastic" world side by side. They are kept apart, each with its own tune, and they touch one another in beautifully attuned harmony. And they are played out against each other in a way that shows us that the major's picture of the world has no eternal validity. The philosophical human being will always have the possibility to find a new, life-giving opening, a new view to replace old truths. There is no such thing as one privileged melody, "God's voice," nor one eye, "God's eye," but rather, myriads of possible voices and a number of different eyes looking at the world. Still, we may perceive a harmony in the polyphonic universe of the book and of philosophy.

There is hardly any reason to define polyphony as the equal validity of all voices. In "The Catalogue," one of the short stories in Gaarder's first book, *Diagnosen og andre noveller* ("The Diagnosis and Other Short Stories," 1986), the narrator combines the concept of God's eye and the Hindu concept of the universal soul: " we are all parts of the same consciousness, impulses of the same soul or facets of the same eye . . . God's eye" (Gaarder 1986, 248). This is a theory that pairs with Berkeley's philosophy, which is clearly contradicted in *Sophie's World*, and the narrator in "The Catalogue" is an outright pessimist who cannot be mistaken for the author's mouthpiece. Meaningful discussion presupposes case circumstances, that is: a world out there beyond the individual consciousness, which the discussion is intended to reveal. If such is not the case, all conversation will be ostensible, like a cacophony of monologues. When Sophie and Alberto with great effort succeed in unmooring the major's boat, they have planted a prolific doubt with respect to the difference between reality and fiction, between "things" and "consciousness," but that is all. The discussion can continue.

Boel Westin sees the introduction of a dramatized narrator, the major, as a way of rendering visible an implicit author as the originator of the novel. She interprets the fact that this major eventually is outmanouvered by his two constructed fictional characters as an attack on the concept of such an authoritative narrator's voice in a novel: "One may assume that Gaarder's novels set aside the theory of an implicit author" (Westin 1998, 121). She also claims, however, that Alberto and Sophie are given no chance to "look into the third and superior level that constitutes the entirety in the construction called *Sophie's World*"

(Westin 1998, 122). It is left open whether she thinks that the entire novel is the major's work or whether he is responsible only for the parts that Hilde is able to read within the framework of the fictional universe. The latter is the most likely. But if so, it is hardly right to interpret the character of the major as an attack on the implicit author theory. A more likely interpretation would be that Gaarder, the teacher of philosophy and novelist, wants to drop his readers a hint that even the "world" that he presents in his novel should be met with the reader's philosophical doubt. He is doubting his own authority, so to speak.

FOUR POINTS

In my opinion, the main project of *Sophie's World* is not to "draw on three thousand years," as Goethe claims in the novel's epigraph,[7] neither is it to make the reader feel "a little less ordinary" (137), as Sophie feels it after "she knew her historical roots" (n.p.).[8] Above all, the project is to strenghten the ability to adopt an enquiring and open-minded attitude to life without letting oneself be subdued by learned authority and seemingly ready-made solutions. That is why it was not sufficient to write a textbook; that is why the knowledge had to be incorporated into an ingenious metanovel. Thus, I entirely disagree with Reynold Jones, who, from a professional philosopher's point of view claims that "however successful the story is in persuading people to read *Sophie's World* . . . it adds nothing to the book's philosophical content and sheds no light on any of the problems it deals with" (Jones 1996, 25). In my opinion, the fictional setting of *Sophie's World* is a very decisive and integral part of the philosophical message, one that is not all about "content," but about attitude. Expanding on my opinion, I could sum up the attitude the book creates in four points.

One: The ultimate aim of philosophy must never be to search for world knowledge of eternal validity. The concept of philosophy, the quest for truth as a *final* project is bound to end in a hubris followed by fatal consequences. This situation is exactly the one that threatens the world today in the areas of the natural sciences. Hegel, too, thought he was close to the final insight: the absolute world reason. In the novel, the danger of such a final way of thinking is demonstrated by depicting Berkeley's idea that he can finally prove that no truth can be found beyond man's consciousness, by showing the consequences of this philosophy for Sophie and Alberto.

Two: Teaching philosophical knowledge cannot take place with any success if it is regarded as a *vertical* impartment of knowledge from a knowing teacher to an ignorant student. With insignificant exceptions,[9] the novel's many philosophical lessons involve a hierarchical role distribution between teacher and student, with Alberto in the safe position of authority and Sophie in the role of model student, clever and willing to learn. Through his metafictional move, however, the major efficiently undermines Alberto's authority. Alberto is exposed and humiliated. Sophie shows more independence. They are made equal by the common state of (un)reality in the major's world. In a similar way, the bottom also falls out of the major's own position as the superior narrator. Hilde humiliates him, and both of them become victims of a practical joke directed by another narrator beyond the world known by the two. No reality, no master mind has been given the last word. That is left to the reader.

Three: Philosophy, the discussion of the nature of the world and man's place in it, cannot be presented as an omniscient monologue. What is conveyed by Alberto all along are the answers of the philosophers, not their amazement. Each philosopher presents a view of the world that claims to be valid by virtue of the authority of thought and logic—this claim also goes for those who are skeptical of philosophy. The monologue incorporated into the didactic aim of the book in both its content and form is counteracted strongly by the fictional framework of the novel. Inside the Chinese box composition, a number of worlds are played polyphonically against each other: the world of philosophy, the world of Sophie and Alberto, the world of the major, the world of the novel in the book *Sophie's World*. The book's metafable makes the implicit author of the novel point to his fiction as something created, something haphazard, without final validity, having a reality status that is just as insecure as that of the reader. It is, of course, eventually the reader's view of reality that the novel wants to stir; it aims at challenging readers to think for themselves, to go beyond the familiar scope of ideas.

Four: Philosophy cannot eliminate freedom as an inevitable dimension of human existence merely by pondering about it as an impossibility, even though attempts to do so have been made. Pondering on the enigma of life is in itself an expression of this very freedom. Acknowledgement of frameworks for human life, such as in nature, science, and society, does not necessarily lead to a view of man as governed and subjugated, but, instead, opens up man's possibility to influence the framework of his existence. In the novel, Sophie and Alberto manage to change the apparently impenetrable limits of their fictional lives. They gain access to the major's "primary world," and they make their "secondary" world felt. There is room for movement in the field of tension between the known reality and the imagined one.

It is by virtue of the various metafictional and fantastic devices of the book that Sophie, as well as the reader, is efficiently prevented from depositing the many philosophical lessons as dead capital and knowledge. As Ellen Steinsland has pointed out, the basic insecurity of what is real and what is fiction is constantly renewed. She thinks that "reflection or amazement in the implicit reader . . . is a result of the inversion and the convergence between the two levels, and the infinite doubling of these levels" (Steinsland 2001, 83). Gaarder's text disconcerts the reader again and again; new rabbits are drawn out of the hat, just as philosophers have kept doing for centuries, and the act of doing so stimulates us to renewed doubt and reflection. Gaarder's rabbit metaphor is clearly drawing on the world's most famous children's book with a philosophical content, Lewis Carroll's *Alice in Wonderland*. The rabbit in Carroll's book never rests, but always runs on in an unstable, steadily altered world, anxious to avoid being late for the garden party at the Queen's, which turns out to be just as chaotic as the garden party in *Sophie's World*.

CONCLUSION

Throughout this essay, I have focused on the positive aspects of the fact that the protagonist of the novel learns to question her existence and eventually to challenge the apparently absolute limits of her life, her ontological status. Gaarder himself often appears to be enthusiastically promoting the message of permanent, childish, ground-breaking amazement: "Children's literature is important for adults in order to give them back their questions and feelings. Children relate more adequately to the world, they ask questions all the time" (Fransson 1993, 11). Still, there is ambiguity toward the end of *Sophie's World* which I will finally investigate, supported by an article written by Bettina Kümmerling-Meibauer (1995), to date the most stimulating and clever article on the book.

It is, after all, a fact that the novel has two female protagonists, both celebrating their fifteenth birthday in the course of the plot. Within the realm of Christian culture, this age is the time for initiation into adulthood, ritually staged by confirmation. Both females share the wish to become grown-ups. And both of them do grow up somewhat in the course of the book. Hilde even reaches a mature composure by the end of the novel, where she watches the sky with her father as a friend. The changes in Sophie are far more profound. In the garden party she has been evicted from the green garden of childhood (the first chapter is titled "Out of Eden") to undergo a symbolic death, then to be resurrected, apparently alive but not visible to the living, in the world of Hilde and the major. She has become an inhabitant of a Never-Neverland where all the other eternal characters of children's literature live: Peter Pan, Pippi Longstocking, the many heroes of fairytales. Instead of growing up, she has become an eternal child, a representative of "the mysterious people," a relative of "the alien child" that lives separately from the adult world.

There is a strange melancholic note in this situation which, toward the end, lets itself be heard like a dark counterpoint to the novel's preaching of the blessings of eternal world amazement. In the no-man's-land where Sophie has ended up, between fiction and reality, she reminds us of the Joker in *The Solitaire Mystery*, the one who revealed that the inhabitants on the island were nothing but cards, and therefore roams restlessly around the world forever as a sort of Ahasverus. The Joker is the utmost image of philosophy which dares to pose the ultimate questions. Obviously, philosophy is something that renders the world eternally new and wonderful, as it appears to children at all times, but it is also bottomless and unfathomable.

This rather frightening perspective may be the reason why Gaarder chooses to end his history of philosophy with Sartre and refrains from continuing into a modern world where one of the most important trends has been to mistrust language itself, a trend initiated by Wittgenstein (who was influenced by Berkeley). Curiously enough, Wittgenstein is on the sleeve of the Norwegian pocket edition of the novel, but he is not mentioned in the book. "I am concerned with the opposite of deconstruction: to put the puzzle together," says Gaarder (Fransson 1993, 12). As I have tried to focus on throughout this article, however, there is a strong contradiction imbedded in the very philosophical project. Philosophers are driven by an impulse to find the final answer, the truth, while, at the same time, finding such a thing would be the death of philosophy. It is a blessing and a curse that there is room for steadily renewed amazement. In *Sophie's World* Gaarder makes sure that our sense of the mysterious is renewed and stimulated. But the book does not conceal that the heritage of philosophy is the unhappy consciousness of modernity, a Joker existence that is unable to find peace.

The novel ends on a midsummer's eve. In Scandinavia this cyclic turning point in the rhythm of nature contains a lot of magic and mystery. In *Sophie's World* we may say that midsummer's eve marks the transition to a new kind of existence for Sophie and Alberto. Their pseudo-lives as didactic constructions in a textbook of philosophy is over. But by this nocturnal bonfire they join the party of fabled characters to which literature has given immortality.

One might ask: is it true that Jostein Gaarder has created in *Sophie's World* a magical work of art that will secure Alberto and Sophie eternal residential right in such famous company? If they do achieve this status, it will not be because of their role as entertaining constructions serving pedagogy. It will more likely be because they manage to question the place they have been given, because they succeed in looking up from the pages on which their lives are moored, and because they look their creator in the eye, and through this look they gain disquieting eye contact with bodies outside the text: both Gaarder himself and the reader of the book. The philosophical regard is not something that can be had through teaching and knowledge. But it may be stirred up by an author who knows how to make magic with rabbits and hats, who can play with worlds within worlds and make the reader dizzy. Perhaps the essence of the knowledge that Sophie is made to share is this: all the drafts of the world made by philosophers can never be anything but "a pack of cards," reshuffled for a game of solitaire that can never be won, but which it is paramount to play, again and again.

NOTES

1. Bettina Kümmerling-Meibauer draws the same parallel (Kümmerling-Meibauer 1995). She also mentions that Lagerlöf created a pattern that was later used by others, also in Norway. The same goes for Gaarder.
2. Hans-Heino Ewers has asserted, however, that the dichotomy between pedagogy and art is no longer relevant for modern literary criticism of children's literature: "The overall question in children's literature concerning ped-

agogy and art has been removed; now we concentrate on each genre of children's literature, so as to be able to explore the genre specific areas of function" (Ewers 2001, 194). But to which genre does *Sophie's World* belong?

3. The first school of this kind was established in Norway in 1868.

4. The Norwegian scholar Eva Brobjerg asserts that the fictionalizing of the teacher figure is a pedagogical move that gives the student "inspiration and vigor" (Brobjerg 1994, 49). But Knox, himself created as an instrument of learning, is more of a pedagogical technician. There are other arrangements in the book that are more important in the development of Sophie's "vigor."

5. See also her unpublished thesis, "52 stemmer summet samtidig i noen få sekunder. Dialog mellom personer og virkeligheter i Jostein Gaarders *Kabalmysteriet, Sofies verden* og *I et speil i en gåte*" (52 voices hummed constantly for a few seconds—a dialogue between persons and realities in Jostein Gaarder's *The Solitaire Mystery, Sophie's World,* and *Through a Glass, Darkly*), Universitet i Oslo, 1995, especially pp. 7–87.

6. This is a main point in Boel Westin's article. Imagination is granted a relative independence in the fictional universe of Jostein Gaarder. Still, it has a limited scope within a superior, minutely calculated authorial direction. See Westin 1998, 122.

7. J. W. Goethe: "He who cannot draw on three thousand years is living from hand to mouth."

8. In a critical comment to Gaarder's books Åse Kristine Tveit asserts that "the joy of new [philosophical] insight may contribute to legitimise contempt for those who lack such insight" (Tveit 1996, 47). For Sophie, however, philosophical knowledge becomes more like an accompaniment to the feeling of being at somebody's mercy in a dark capricious world, randomly created by an author-God.

9. Sissel Veggeland points out that Sophie at one time breaks off a lesson before Alberto has finished his lecture, and at another point she forces him to elaborate on a problem that he had intended to leave out (Veggeland 1995, 81).

WORKS CITED

Brobjerg, Eva. "Mærk Sofies verden. En analyse af samspillet mellem fag og fantasi." *Dansk* (1994) 4: 49–59.

Ewers, Hans-Heino: "Børne-og ungdomslitteratur—litteratur i pædagogikkens tjeneste eller selvstændig digtekunst?" Pp. 177–197 in *Nedslag i børnelitteraturforskningen 2.* Frederiksberg, Denmark: Roskilde University Press, 2001.

Fransson, Birgitta. "Han drivs av förundran över att finnas till." *Opsis Kalopsis* (1993)2: 43–47.

Gaarder, Jostein. *Diagnosen og andre noveller.* Oslo: Aschehoug, 1986.

————. *Kabalmysteriet.* Oslo: Aschehoug, 1990.

————. *Sofies verden.* Oslo: Aschehoug, 1991.

————. *Julemysteriet.* Oslo: Aschehoug, 1992.

————. *I et speil, i en gåte,* Oslo: Aschehoug, 1993.

————. *Sophie's World.* Translated by Paulette Møller. New York: Farrar, Straus and Giroux, 1994.

————. *The Christmas Mystery.* Translated by Elizabeth Rokkan. New York: Farrar, Straus and Giroux, 1996.

————. *The Solitaire Mystery.* Translated by Sarah Jane Hails. New York: Farrar, Straus and Giroux, 1996.

————. *Through a Glass, Darkly.* Translated by Elizabeth Rokkan. London: Phoenix, 1998.

Jones, Reynold. "Sophie or Sophistry?" *Books for Keeps* (1996) 99: 25.

Kümmerling-Meibauer, Bettina. "Philosophie in 'Sofies Welt'. Der Welterfolg von Jostein Gaarder." *JuLit* (1995) 3: 23–37.

Senje, Cathrine. "Jostein Gaarder—et dikterportrett." Oslo: Biblioteksentralen, 1995.

Slagstad, Rune. *De nasjonale strateger.* Oslo: Pax, 1998.

Steinsland, Ellen. *Mellom fiksjon og virkelighet—diktning i refleksjonens vold. En narratologisk analyse av Jostein Gaarder Sofies verden.* Kristiansand: Agder University College, 2001.

Sullivan, Scott. "Have Some Spinoza, My Dear?" *Newsweek* June 1994.

Tveit, Åse Kristine. "Forundring fryder: et blikk på Jostein Gaarders forfatterskap." *Norsklæraren* (1966) 1: 43–47.

Veggeland, Sissel. "Samtaler mellom barn og voksne i *Kabalmysteriet* og i *Sofies Verden.* Pp. 45–55 in *Årboka. Litteratur for barn og unge.* Oslo: Det Norske Samlaget, 2004.

————. 52 stemmer summet samtidig i noen få sekunder. Dialog Mellom personer og virkeligheter i Jostein Gaarders *Kabalmysteriet, Sofies verden* og *I et speil i en gåte.* Unpublished thesis, Oslo University, 1995.

Westin, Boel. "Filosofi och fiktion i Jostein Gaarders romaner." Pp. 109–123 in *Årboka. Litteratur for barn og unge.* Oslo: Det Norske Samlaget, 1998.

12

What Do We Translate When We Translate Children's Literature?

Maria Nikolajeva

Children's literature is an international phenomenon in the sense that the most outstanding and successful children's books usually get translated into other languages. The *Harry Potter* books are a recent and convincing example, as they have already been translated into more than fifty languages. *Alice in Wonderland*, universally considered a major children's classic, has been translated into many languages, as has *Winnie-the-Pooh* (including Latin and Esperanto), and Astrid Lindgren's books are available in more than eighty languages.

However, there is no universal agreement among the scholars of children's literature, or even more specifically, among the scholars of translation of children's literature, concerning what a translation is, what a "good" translation is, whether there is any difference in translating books for children and for adults, and not least, whether and why translated children's literature is a valuable part of any child's reading.

Concerning the last question, much effort has been taken in the English-speaking world to introduce international children's classics and modern works, and these endeavors stress the importance of making, for instance, North American children aware of the existence of other countries and cultures (see, e.g., Tomlinson 1998; Stan 2002). In the academic area, many empirical studies focus on the reception of children's books from a certain country in another country or even the reception of a particular author or book (for an excellent overview of children's literature translation studies see Tabbert 2002). There is, however, considerably less research into translation itself, into the issues of what it means for a children's book to appear in a different language and start functioning in a new cultural context, of what strategies there are to make this transposition as graceful and successful as possible.

The art of translation is perhaps as old as literature itself, and the most important translations in the Western world have been the translations of the Bible. Because the Bible was supposed to be the true words of God, great importance has been always attributed to the "correct" translation, and the debates of what exactly is the most correct translation have occupied learned men throughout the centuries. Since words in any language are polysemantic (have several different meanings or shades of meaning), the process of translation does not simply imply substitution of one word for another—which is what some people not involved in translation occasionally believe. A translator is faced with the necessity of choosing between several meanings of a word in the source language (the language of the original text) and finding the adequate word in the target language (the language of the translated text). Further, translation implies not only conveying denotation (the literal, dictionary meaning of words), but also connotation, that is, contextual meaning that may change from text to text. It is often in this contextual area that translation for children becomes different from translation for adults. Adult readers can be assumed to be familiar with the phenomena of foreign cultures or at least accept that names, places, ways, and habits can be different if a book they read comes from another country. Young readers may lack both the knowledge and the tolerance; in fact, some reader-oriented research shows that children are considerably less tolerant toward alien elements in their reading. We may as adults try to encourage children to learn more about foreign countries and cultures, as part of their multicultural education, but we should be aware of the risks of translated literature being rejected by readers as too "strange" (see Nikolajeva 1996, 34–38).

APPROACHES TO TRANSLATION

Among the few existing theoretical studies two radically different approaches to translation of children's literature emerge. One of them, represented by the widely known study by the Swedish scholar Göte Klingberg, *Children's Fiction in the Hands of the Translators* (1986) and his many followers, propagates equivalence, that is, a maximal approximation of the target text to the source text. A translation, in this view, should be "faithful" to the original, and no liberties are to be taken.

The opposite view suggests that the translator should take into consideration the target audience, whereupon changes may not only be legitimate, but imperative, if the translated text in its specific context is to function somewhat similarly to the way in which the original functions in its initial situation. This view, represented by the internationally acclaimed Finnish scholar Riitta Oittinen in her *Translating for Children* (2000), can be called dialogical, after Mikhail Bakhtin's dialogical theory, since it presupposes an active dialogue, or interaction, between the target text and its readers. The key question in dialogical translation is "For whom?" unlike the question "What?" in the equivalence theory.

The universal success of the *Harry Potter* books offers an excellent illustration of these two strategies. The translators of *Harry Potter* throughout the world—much like their predecessors with *Alice in Wonderland*—have grappled with the dilemma of either remaining true to the original and thus robbing their readers of much of the pleasure the English-speaking readers are getting, or substituting new connotations for names, objects, and phenomena to suit the target audience. The existing *Harry Potter* translations display a variety of solutions. In an essay, the Norwegian translator has revealed his professional secrets and also accused his Swedish colleague of denying the Swedish readers the joys of the text (Bugge Høverstad 2002). In Russian, several translations exist already, some on the Internet, also illustrating different approaches. Note that we are not dealing with the question of poor or good translations, but the basic principles of what it means to translate a children's book.

The two views, elaborated in general translation theory, apparently acquire special significance in connection with children's fiction, and both have been ardently defended by their respective advocates. Some of the premises lie undoubtedly in the general approach to children's literature reflecting the pedagogical versus the aesthetic view. It is not accidental that Klingberg is a pedagogue while Oittinen is a literary critic. The views of the "Klingberg school" are normative, perhaps even prescriptive. Oittinen's theory is based on the relationship between the text, the translator, and the implied audience, and as such is more flexible.

Further, the categorical attitude of the Klingberg school has very much to do with the practice of translating children's books, which in some essential ways differs from the practice of translating general literature. First of all, children's books have, to a considerably high extent, been subjected to adaptation when translated, something that is seldom if ever done with books for adults. Adaptation means that a text is adjusted to what the translator believes to be the needs of the target audience, and it can include deletions, additions, explanations, purification, simplification, modernization, and a number of other interventions. The purpose is ostensibly to make the text more accessible for the target audience—naturally based on the dominant pedagogical ideas of what exactly is "more accessible." The strategies do not differ radically from adaptations within the same language, which has also been discussed thoroughly (see, e.g., Hunt 1991, 26–36). All such adaptations are based on the assumptions—often arbitrary—about young readers' needs and interests.

Both Klingberg himself and many of his adepts have indiscriminately expressed indignation over all such intrusions. True, in many cases they indicate lack of respect for children's literature that, much more often than general literature, gets into the hands of less talented, occasionally totally unqualified translators. However, even the most skillful translators frequently resort to some of the above-mentioned practices, therefore there are serious reasons to subject them to a closer examination.

Daniel Defoe's *Robinson Crusoe*, the text perhaps most often subjected to adaptation, which is about 500 pages in the original, has been cut down to 24 pages in some adaptations. The incentive has naturally been to make the book more accessible to young readers. The nature of the cuts has varied; most frequently, the self-reflexive and religious passages have been removed from this particular book. In the shortest versions, of course, only the very gist of the storyline remains. Quite a few classics, including *Alice in Wonderland*, have been subjected to similar surgery. A frequent interference implies periphrasis (retelling), abridgement, and text compressions. Rather than merely cutting out pieces of text, the translator retells the story, often turning direct speech into summaries, focusing on the central episodes, omitting characterization, and other more complex dimensions of the original.

The practice of additions would seem to contradict the drive to make the story shorter and thus more suitable for children, but in some cases, translators have added passages explaining the characters' actions and other aspects of the source text. In one of the most famous adaptations of *Robinson Crusoe*, done by the German pedagogue Joachim Heinrich Campe, a frame story is added, in which a father is telling Robinson's story to his children. This enables the narrator to explain, comment, and pass judgment, in accordance with the didactic purpose of the adaptation.

Alterations can include such instances as changing the ending to suit the target audience. In many translations, the end of Hans Christian Andersen's *The Little Match Girl* has been changed from the character's death to her finding a good and loving family. The happy ending of *The Little Mermaid* in many American editions is another similar example. Omissions and alterations for political, cultural, or religious reasons are called purification: the text is purified from passages that are perceived as offensive (another term is bowdlerization, after the 19th-century British clergyman Thomas Bowdler who produced *Family Shakespeare* fit to be read in the presence of ladies). It may be the matter of abusive language, the mention of bodily functions viewed as inappropriate in a children's book, or an expression of ideology unacceptable by the target culture. While in the original of the Swedish children's classic *The Wonderful Adventures of Nils* by Selma Lagerlöf, the protagonist's parents go to a church, in the Russian translation they go to a market. Churches and religion were not supposed to appear in children's books published in the Soviet Union. One can, of course, feel indignation about the intervention, but it demonstrates the strategy of adapting the target text to its audience. Most translations (as well as English-language abridgements) of Jonathan Swift's *Gulliver's Travels* omit the episode in which Gulliver extinguishes the fire in the royal palace of Lilliput by passing water. Both the British and the American translations of *Pippi Longstocking* have changed Pippi's imaginative mention of Negroes, her father the Negro King, and her own future as the Negro princess into—less offensive?—cannibals. Similarly, in one of Pippi's many tall-tales, a Negro girl is changed into a girl with "very dark complexion." In the American translation of the nonsense verse by the Swedish poet Lennart Hellsing, *The Pirate Book*, a striptease dancer—introduced solely for the sake of a funny rhyme—has been changed into a "smashing lady" in the text, and in the picture she has been given a proper black dress (in the original she is, of course, nude). In another Swedish picturebook, *Else-Marie and Her Seven Little*

Daddies, by Pija Lindenbaum, the American publisher opposed the illustration in which the protagonist was depicted in a bathtub together with her mother and her imaginary daddies. By agreement with the author/illustrator, a different picture was provided, with the family reading in an armchair. All these examples say a lot about the view on children and children's literature in the target cultures.

Simplification implies that a foreign notion is supplanted by something less specific, for instance when a particular dish is simply translated as "food" or the title of a newspaper is changed into the general "newspaper." In *Pippi Longstocking*, her little pet Mr Nilsson is in Swedish referred to as a guenon, a specific kind of monkey. In the American translation it is simply "a monkey," and in the British version the sentence is omitted altogether. In another episode, when Pippi mentions "radio police" in the original, the translation simplifies it to merely "police." In Ottfrid Preussler's *The Satanic Mill*, the girl who finally saves Krabat from the bond with the devil is referred to in the original as Kantorka, which means Singer in Sorbish, the local language of the area where the novel takes place. In the English translation she is consistently called "the girl." Of course, the appearance of a Slavic word in the original German text is in itself a problem, since not all German readers will know the meaning. Yet supplanting the generic "girl" for something that has a specific meaning in the text is a typical case of simplification. Incidentally, the Swedish translator of *The Satanic Mill* misunderstood Kantorka for a personal name, which does not make sense in the story, as Krabat cannot possibly know the name of the girl he has only seen at a distance.

Rewording means that a metaphor or some other figure of speech, nonexistent in the target language, is rendered by a circumscription. Both English translations of Astrid Lindgren's *Pippi Longstocking* abound in rewording, apparently because the translators gave up. The result is, of course, a considerably more meager language. In fact, most of Pippi's witticisms, puns, and other verbal games are completely lost in the English versions, which makes Pippi essentially a different character. A frequent argument from less skillful translators (as well as most laymen), "wordplay is not translatable," is a myth, and consistent omission of Pippi's linguistic proficiency has contributed to a catastrophic misunderstanding of this figure in the English-speaking world.

Modernization means bringing everyday details, objects, and concepts up to date in translation, including changing or deleting what may be perceived as offensive, such as racism and sexism. Also, purely linguistic modernization is frequent, when, for instance, 19th-century fiction is translated into more modern idiom. This can be feasible if the translated text sounds obsolete; yet a skillful translator may employ minor stylization to indicate the time period, but still use the language adapted to the modern audience. This can be important in translating young adult novels with a strong flavor of youth jargon. For instance, the 1953 Swedish translation of *The Catcher in the Rye* is completely unreadable today because of its outmoded slang, and a later translation brought the language more up to date.

Harmonization may include, for instance, changes in children's behavior, if considered improper in the target culture. The infamous example is the first French translation of *Pippi Longstocking*, where three most "offensive" chapters have been omitted altogether: "Pippi Plays Tag with Some Policemen," "Pippi Entertains Two Burglars," and "Pippi Goes to a Coffee Party"—chapters in which Pippi clearly shows her superiority over the adults. Apart from these omissions, every occasion in which Pippi is impolite or in some way interrogates adult authority is played down in this translation. Moreover, on several occasions the translator adds a few sentences in which Pippi regrets her bad behavior and apologizes (Heldner 1992). The result is, of course, that the French Pippi is considerably more tame and compliant than the original, which clearly reflects the attitude toward children and the relationship between children and adults in the target society. It is also one of the most ridiculous facts in the history of children's literature translation that the French publisher asked Astrid Lindgren's permission to change Pippi's horse into a pony, commenting that perhaps Swedish children who have not been affected by the war could believe that a girl can lift a horse, but not the French children. Ostensibly, on granting the permission, Lindgren in passing asked the publisher to send her a photo of a French girl lifting a pony.

In many theoretical discussions of children's literature, all these practices are unconditionally condemned, since they are perceived as censorship. While we may indeed interrogate the intentions, the practice itself is merely an extreme form of the dialogical approach to translation mentioned above, the one that takes into consideration the target audience. In fact, the use of foul language can be less offensive in some cultures than in others, and the attitude toward nakedness varies substantially between countries and epochs. The practice of adaptation of target texts is then in no way radically different from adapting originals to what authors (or publishers) believe to be the needs and interests of the young audience, which, in its turn, depends on the views on childhood and education. Putting a dress on the striptease dancer is no different from pasting underpants on Mickey in Sendak's *In the Night Kitchen*, an infamous case of censorship in American children's literature history. Taming the translated Pippi is no different from "updating" *The Tale of Peter Rabbit* (see Hunt 1991, 26ff).

FAMILIAR OR EXOTIC?

All the described interventions reflect the fact that translators of children's books have to deal with elements of source texts that may be unfamiliar or offensive to the target audience and thus may be assumed to hamper understanding. However, in each case it can be argued whether the changes are reasonable and justified. Two possible strategies of dealing with strange elements are domestication and foreignization. In domesticating a translated text, the translator substitutes familiar phenomena and concepts for what may be perceived as strange and hard to understand. Even in "translation" of the *Harry Potter* books from British into American English, some domesticating changes have been made, as is the common practice when pounds and pence are changed into dollars and cents and so on. It is not uncommon in translations of children's books to change foreign food, weights and measures, currency, flora and fauna, customs and traditions, to something that the target readers will more easily understand. In the American *Pippi Longstocking*, dollars, quarters, and cents are mentioned, while the British version features pence. The British translation has substituted ginger beer for the original soda. In the English translation of *Johnny, My Friend* by the Swedish Peter Pohl, a novel that very deliberately abounds in concrete details reflecting the time of action, most elements have been domesticated: the brand names of sodas and candy, other food brands, and so on. The distance measures have remained intact, though, apparently because the translation was published in the UK, where metric system has won more ground than in the United States.

Localization implies a form of domestication through changing the setting of a book to a more familiar one. For instance, the German translations of Enid Blyton's adventure novels are set in Germany. We can laugh at this, dismissing the intervention easily in the case of what is commonly labeled formulaic fiction, but we will perhaps be more disturbed by a similar change in a quality novel, for instance, when the initial setting of Astrid Lindgren's fantasy novel *Mio, My Son* is moved from Stockholm to Copenhagen in the Danish translation (see Steffensen 2003) and to Helsinki in the Finnish translation. In assessing domestication and localization (universally condemned by the adherents of the equivalence theory), we should ask ourselves what the translator's motivation might have been. This is obviously not a mistake, but a conscious alteration that would never occur in a novel for adults. Can you imagine *Ulysses* taking place in Berlin in a German translation or Paris in a French translation? Again we are dealing with the adult assumptions about children's cognitive capacity. When a novel for adults is translated, the target audience may be expected to understand that certain objects and concepts are different in a foreign culture. Young readers have less knowledge of foreign countries and cultures. Children are seldom aware that the book they are reading is a translation, and as already pointed out, tolerance for strangeness is usually lower in children's texts than in literature for adults. While transposing the setting of a British novel to Germany may be an unnecessary interference, some other changes may be fully justified, to make the text more accessible to the target audience. If the Swedish setting of *Mio, My Son* is perceived as a hindrance for the young Danish or Finnish audience, is it worth the sacrifice? On the other hand, will we also accept moving the American version to New York and the Chinese version to Beijing? After all, Stockholm, Copenhagen, Helsinki, New York, and Beijing are equally unfamiliar to a child living in the countryside who has never been to any of these cities. The alternative is to skip the place name altogether, which is simplification that is again condemned by many translation scholars.

Most American translators of children's books have a strong tendency toward domestication. It can be something less significant, but still amazing, for instance when the characters at the end of Sven Nordqvist's *Pancake Pie* play "The Star-Spangled Banner" on the gramophone when, in the original, they play Viennese waltzes. More disputable are the liberties the translator has taken with Jostein Gaarder's *Sophie's World*. This is a very complicated novel that, among other things, abounds in quotations and allusions. The novel cannot be accused of being overloaded with Norwegian facts, since the author focuses in the first place on world philosophy, yet he does include some references to Norwegian literature that the translator changes into something she obviously believes to be better known. Thus the Nobel Prize winner Knut Hamsun's novel *Victoria* is replaced by another Nobel Prize winner John Steinbeck's *Of Mice and Men*. Byron and Shelley are substituted for the Norwegian Romantic poets, and since some facts do not really match the rest of the argument, the translator supplies a completely new text about Byron. A poem by the Norwegian classic Bjørnstierne Bjørnsson becomes a poem by Thomas Hardy that in no way expresses the same idea. The characters from medieval Scandinavian ballads and the infamous Norwegian trolls are changed into Joan of Arc and the Pied Piper. To crown it all, in one place the mention of Norway itself is omitted and replaced by France. It can be argued that these changes are so minor that they do not affect the general message of the novel. However, they very clearly demonstrate the general attitude toward translation, especially translation for a young audience. Obviously the rationale behind the changes was sparing the target readers redundant information. All the more remarkable given the fact that the novel is educational by definition and quite intentionally encourages its readers to enrich their knowledge.

The opposite of domestication is foreignization. If a translated text is foreignized, the translator may decide to keep some words untranslated, in order to preserve the foreign flavor. The proponents of this approach maintain that it is essential that young readers become aware of cultural differences as they read translated books. Admirable as it is, the approach may sometimes be stretched too far. In the American translation of *Pippi Longstocking*, Pippi is shown "busy making *pepparkakor*—a kind of Swedish cookie" (translator's emphasis). The motivation behind this translation is apparently to show the American readers that Sweden is a different country with a different sort of cookies. The cookies are, however, nothing more exotic than the universally known gingerbread. By using a foreign word in the English text, the translator focuses the readers' attention on the cookies, thus creating a different effect than is the case with source-text readers. Further, the phrase "a kind of Swedish cookie" is, of course, an addition, the translator's explanation of the foreign word, which is unnecessary in the source text, and which would have been superfluous if the word had been translated as "gingerbread." Incidentally, the British translation features "ginger snaps." On the other hand, if Pippi were indeed making a cookie that completely lacked a correspondence in the target language (which is more likely with a translation into Chinese or Swahili), would it be motivated to supplant the exotic *pepparkakor* with something more familiar? After all, Swedish readers do not experience a sense of foreignness and exoticism when encountering this word in a text. Similarly, the British translation of Pippi (quite inconsistently, since pence were mentioned earlier) refers to "some of the shiny Swedish coins called crowns." Some translators of *Pippi* and other Swedish children's books have been confronted with the difficulty of translating the common practice of children drinking coffee, which is acceptable in Sweden, but less so in other cultures. Retaining coffee naturally makes the situation more deviant and attracts the target-text readers' attention to details that the source-text reader will not even notice. Many translators, including the British, have substituted tea or some other drink for coffee, without in any way distorting the meaning of the text. The question in each individual case is whether the cultural detail is indeed significant. A notorious example of an over-conscientious Swedish translator concerns the phrase: "He wished he were a hundred miles under ground," whereupon the translator added a footnote: "English miles, of which 6 correspond to one Swedish."

In a dialogic translation, the goal is to approximate the response of the source-text readers, and substituting a familiar notion for a foreign one would be considered more appropriate. A famous example can be gathered in the Bible translations: in translating the phrase "God's lamb" into Inuit, the translator changed it into "God's seal cub," since a lamb is an animal unknown to the Inuit. In fact, in a Swahili translation of Astrid Lindgren's *Noisy Village*, spring was changed into the rainy season, because spring is an unknown concept for the target audience, and the Noisy Village children's joyful anticipation of spring had to be translated into a similar experience.

Even when a concept in itself is not perceived as foreign, too specific a word in the target text can create a foreignization effect. In a recent English translation of *Pinocchio*, the Blue-Haired Fairy has been changed into Indigo-Haired Fairy, with the motivation that the correct translation for the Italian word used in the original is "indigo" rather than "blue." This may sound reasonable, yet there are some possible counter-arguments. Indigo feels more exotic in English than the neutral blue, and it is unlikely that the author's intention was to be exotic. Further, the character is already known in English as the Blue-Haired Fairy, and whatever the reason might have been for a new translation, it is not desirable to change an established character name, even if the new translation shows greater fidelity to the original. In a recent translation the name of Hans Christian Andersen's tiny heroine was changed from Thumbelina to Inchelina, which is not only a worse solution, but also confusing to a reader already familiar with the character.

NAMES AND PLACES

Personal and geographic names in translation present a special dilemma, as Yvonne Bertills has shown (Bertills 2003). The equivalent theory prescribes that names should always be retained as they are in the original. The voluntary change of Norwegian names Jorunn and Jørgen in *Sophie's World* into neutral-English Joanne and Jeremy is merely a part of the overall domestication of the text. Similarly, turning Mr Nilsson into Mr Nelson and Malin into Martha in *Pippi Longstocking*, or changing Swedish names into the English Johnny, Chris, Harold, and Bobby in *Johnny, My Friend* is typical domestication, perhaps motivated, perhaps not. On the other hand, as the narrator in the latter novel is playing with the last name of one of his schoolmates, calling him subsequently Greenwood, Greenland, Greenwoodland, Greengreen, Greenfrog, and Greenwotsit, the adaptation is of course not only plausible, but necessary.

There may, however, be several reasons why names are changed. First, the sound of the name may give undesirable associations in the target language. The name Pippi, for instance, in a number of languages suggests urinating. The character is therefore renamed Fifi in French, Pippa in Spanish (which, by the way, sounds obscene in Swedish), and Peppi in Russian. In the translation of Astrid Lindgren's *Mio, My Son*, the protagonist's name was changed from Bo Wilhelm Olsson to Karl Andrew Nilsson, seemingly without reason. However, the last name "Olsson" carries comic connotations for English-speaking readers, which is highly objectionable in Lindgren's text. Another reason may be that the name in the target language is already firmly connected with a famous literary character. The hero of Astrid Lindgren's *Emil's Pranks* has been renamed Mickel in the German translation, since the name Emil is associated with the protagonist of the German classic *Emil and the Detectives* by Erich Kästner. Although this particular case has been discussed in several studies (e.g., Stolt 1978), newcomers to the field keep wondering, often with a good deal of indignation, why it has been done. A popular Swedish character Max, in a picturebook series by Barbro Lindgren and Eva Eriksson, is renamed Sam in the

American translation, obviously to distance him from Max in Maurice Sendak's *Where the Wild Things Are.* In contrast, when the name of the title character in Lindgren's *Ronia, the Robber's Daughter* is changed to Kirsti in the British version, the only motivation seems to be foreignization, since Ronia is just as much a nonexistent name in Swedish as in English, or was, before the novel was written. Interestingly enough, in the American edition that uses the same translation, the name is changed back to Ronia.

Further, when a name is changed in translation, some subtle shade of meaning can be lost. In the German translation of the Swedish Ulf Stark's "comedy of errors" *Loonies and Phonies,* the heroine's name Simone and the male name it is confused with, Simon, is changed into Paula and Paul, respectively. Not only is this completely unmotivated—is indeed Simone more exotic for a German ear than Paula?—in the novel the name has a clear allusion to Simone de Beauvoir, which prompts a feminist interpretation. Paula does not, of course, carry any similar connotation. This example especially shows that the translator should not only know the source language, but be sensitive to the connotations of the source culture.

Yet another problem may arise if a name has a specific sound in the source language that gives some associations for the source-text readers. The name Eeyore is of course an example of onomatopoeia (sound imitation) referring to a donkey's neigh. In most translations, it has been changed to match the corresponding sound in the target language. Many names in the *Harry Potter* books carry associations that critics have tried to interpret: Dumbledore, Malfoy, Lupin, and especially Voldemort. The translators around the world have either retained the names, thus losing the association (equivalent solution), or invented new names with similar associations in the target language (dialogic solution). Some translators have even considered—and rejected—changing Harry's last name, to stress its plainness, into a corresponding last name in the target language, meaning "the maker of ceramic vessels."

Yvonne Bertills has, in her above-mentioned study, discussed the translation of names in *Winnie-the-Pooh* into Swedish and Finnish and the names in Tove Jansson's *Moomin* novels into English and Finnish. She tries to account for the associations that the Moomin names evoke in a native Swedish speaker (also taking into consideration the specific version of the Swedish language spoken in Finland, the land of origin of the Moomins) in order to see whether the possible connotations have been retained in translation. It can be argued whether all Bertills's interpretations are tenable, but it is obvious that the translators have attempted in some cases and given up in others. While the names such as Snufkin, Fillyjunk, and Groke perhaps evoke the same feelings in the target audience as in the source audience, the exciting connotation of the Hemulen is lost. Moreover, the word "hemulen" in Swedish already has a definite article ("-en" in postposition), the indefinite form being "hemul," so the English form "the Hemulen" is grammatically redundant. There seems to be no reason for this solution. The names of the two tiny creatures in *Finn Family Moomintroll*, Thingummy and Bob, may seem a good choice, unless you know that the original names Tofslan and Vifslan, refer to actual people, one of which is Tove Jansson herself. This may seem insignificant, but still it shows how important the names can be in a literary text and how careful a translator should be in rendering them in the new context.

In *Johnny, My Friend*, the translator has chosen to translate some place names, such as South Side Grammar School, but left others as they are, for instance "Medis," which, in Swedish, is a popular name for Medborgarhuset, Civic Center. Instead of translating the strange word into something familiar, the translator adds an explanation, "the indoor pool." When the narrator of the story refers to Medis in Swedish, it reflects the colloquial style of his narration, which is, of course, lost in translation.

TRANSLATING CULTURE

Some examples of foreignization of culturally dependent phenomena are, in fact, connected to the practice of explanatory additions, strongly questioned by the equivalent theory. For instance, for a Swedish reader, the connotation of "the blue and yellow flag" is as clear as "stars and stripes" for an American reader. In two different Russian translations of *The Wonderful Adventures of Nils*, two strategies have been employed. The equivalent translator has chosen to write "the blue and yellow flag," providing a footnote with the explanation that the colors of the Swedish flag are blue and yellow. While the solution may seem fortunate, using footnotes in fiction, especially children's fiction, is definitely undesirable. Another translator has circumvented the problem by adding one single word: "the blue and yellow Swedish flag." Much more dubious is the opening of the British translation of

Pippi Longstocking. While the American version follows the original, saying: "Way out at the end of a tiny little town was an old overgrown garden," the British translation adds a specification: "At the end of a little Swedish town lay an old, overgrown orchard." Unlike the example of the Swedish flag, the indication that the town is Swedish is not prompted by the original text. Although the description of the town and its inhabitants renders them indeed unmistakably recognizable for someone familiar with Sweden and for the Swedes themselves, the absence of the adjective "Swedish" in the original makes the story more universal, while the British version immediately creates a sense of foreignness.

Many children's novels contain allusions and other literary and extra-literary references. In translation, it is, of course, pointless to retain the allusion to a text that is completely unknown to the target readers. Dialogic translators may choose to delete the reference or, if it works, to provide another reference that will create a similar effect. The translators of *Alice in Wonderland* into different languages have either translated all parodies on well-known poems exactly as they are and thus lost the allusions or written new parodies on well-known poems in the target language (see, e.g., Weaver 1964; O'Sullivan 2001). In the latter case, the target audience gets the adequate associations. The same strategies have been employed by the different translators of *Winnie-the-Pooh*.

Naturally, if the text alludes to another text widely known in the target language, this available translation should preferably be used, even if the translator judges it to be poor. For instance, the title of Philip Pullman's trilogy *His Dark Materials* is translated literally into Swedish, ignoring the fact that the Milton quotation to which the title alludes is rendered in Swedish as "the dark element." The readers of the target text have no chance to make the connection between the title and the poem it alludes to.

NARRATIVE CHANGES

Some more fundamental alterations, motivated as well as unmotivated, include the shift from personal to impersonal narration (as in the many abridged versions of *Robinson Crusoe* retold in the third person); the change of tense, sometimes resulting in a more distanced narration or occasionally depriving the readers of guidelines when complex temporal switches are involved; and forced changes of the characters' gender (usually only possible with animal and inanimate object characters), resulting in distorted gender relationships between the characters in the story.

Shel Silverstein's *The Giving Tree* starts: "Once there was a tree, and *she* loved a little boy" (emphasis added). By ascribing the inanimate character a gender, the author provides the reader with an interpretative strategy. The tree may be viewed either as a caring mother or as the boy's sweetheart; in both cases, the story is about a self-sacrificial female and a self-absorbed, extremely egoistic male. In the Swedish translation, the first sentence of the story goes, back to English: "Once there was a tree, and *it* loved a little boy" (emphasis added). The character is deprived of her gender, and the relationship between the tree and the boy becomes much less poignant. The genderless tree becomes more like a typical fairytale helper, and the psychological tension between the agents is subdued. The translator has thus robbed the young readers of an essential support in reading the story.

Gender does not always work in translations, since different languages have different systems of grammatical gender. The Finnish language, for instance, does not have any grammatical distinction between feminine and masculine. The feminine nature of Tove Jansson's Groke is lost in the Finnish translation (the originals are in Swedish), which also eliminates the natural connection between this character and the Moominmamma. Silverstein's text would not be easily translated into German, French, Russian, or Finnish. In each case, a skilful translator would have to find an adequate solution. In the case of Swedish, however, the shift in meaning seems to be a result of translator's negligence.

The tense system is different in different languages, and translators often face the necessity to compensate the difference by other means, lexical rather than grammatical. Russian, for instance, lacks both the perfect ("has done," "had done") and continuous ("is doing," "was doing") forms, and translators from English into Russian have to convey them with the help of adverbs. More important is the semantic and stylistic difference in tenses in different languages. Modern Swedish children's literature is often written in the narrative present tense. When the whole text is narrated in the present tense, it is sometimes impossible to discern between narrator's discourse and character's discourse. Maria Gripe's *Elvis and His Secret* and its sequels are a good example. In English translations, the past tense is used. This implies that the border between narration and Elvis's thoughts, rendered through free indirect discourse, has been made more clear-cut. I think this is against the writer's intentions.

While the translator's choice of tense in *Elvis and His Secret* can, at least with some reservations, be justified by the implied readers' presumed expectations, the arbitrary change of tenses in the translation *Johnny, My Friend* completely disrupts the interpretation. In the Swedish original, the recurrent shifts between present and past tense assist the reader in deciding on whether the narration is simultaneous (Chris is telling about something happening right in front of our eyes) or detached (Chris is recollecting events that happened more than a year ago). Compare the existing translation:

> The cop *noted* down this freckles business as well . . . Johnny's girlish face *hovered* there in front of us: freckles dotted evenly all over, apart from his chin.
>
> Not his chin? Neck? Forehead?
>
> The cop *wanted* to know exactly. (24)

with the original, in a more accurate translation:

> The cop *notes* down this freckles business as well . . . Johnny's girlish face *hovers* there in front of us: freckles dotted evenly all over, apart from his chin.
>
> Not his chin? Neck? Forehead?
>
> The cop *wants* to know exactly.

The disastrous effect of the existing translation is obvious. The reader is left without further indication of the temporal shifts, which to a great extent facilitates the understanding of this extremely complex narrative. The immediacy and intensity of Chris's account, established in the opening passage, is lost. Both temporal levels are now detached from the narrator. Instead of the intricate alternation of extradiegetic and intradiegetic narration, two equally extradiegetic narrative perspectives are used, for both the primary story (the interrogation) and the flashback. The device of the novel is, however, that at the moment of narration, Chris does not know the outcome of his conversation with the police officer; his memories of his year with Johnny parallel the painful ongoing process of insight when he understands, step by step, what he has in fact experienced. In the present-tense passages, Chris's mental transformation is unfolding in front of our eyes. By using the past tense for the narrative present, the translator distances this process, making it, by definition, an accomplished fact.

UNTRANSLATABLE?

There are, of course, many other difficulties that translators may
encounter. One is how to deal with puns and other linguistic games
often found in children's books. Some critics claim that certain texts
are "untranslatable." It is indeed a challenge to translate a title such as
War and Peas by Michael Foreman into any language in which the pun
will not be possible. Yet a skillful translator can resort to something
called compensatory translation, which implies adding a different pun
or word play to compensate for the lost one. As already noted, the
American translator of *Pippi Longstocking* has basically lost all puns
and Pippi's witty comments, either because of incompetence or
because dialogical translation, including compensatory, was believed to
be disadvantageous.

So what is the conclusion of this longish argument? What is a translation as opposed to adaptation or retelling? Why are adaptations and
retellings more acceptable in children's literature than in adult literature? What is a good translation? It is obviously a matter closely connected with the general views on what is "good" children's literature.
Is a faithful translation best? Personally, I find dialogic translation
strategies more adequate. They may be less faithful to the source text,
but instead more loyal toward the target audience. And, most relevant
to the theme of the present volume: what do we translate when we
translate children's literature? Is it merely the plot or do we want the
target audience to take part in the foreign culture? Are European
books too strange and exotic for the American young readers so that
they must necessarily be domesticated? Or is at least some form of
domestication inevitable if foreign books are to become a natural part
of any given culture? There are still more questions than answers. After
all, a decision on an appropriate translation strategy must naturally be
taken in each individual case.

WORKS CITED

Bertills, Yvonne. *Beyond Identification. Proper Names in Children's Literature*. Åbo: Åbo Akademi University Press, 2003.
Bugge Høverstad, Torstein. "Å oversette et fenomen. Harry Potter." Pp. 59-
69 in *Litteratur for barn og unge. Årboka 2002* edited by Per Olav Kaldestad
and Karin Beate Vold. Oslo: Det Norske Samlaget, 2002.

Heldner, Christina. "Une anarchiste de camisol de force: Fifi Brindacier ou la métamorphose française de 'Pippi Långstrump'." *La revue des livres pour enfants* 145 (1992), 65–71.

Hunt, Peter. *Criticism, Theory and Children's Literature.* London: Blackwell, 1991.

Klingberg, Göte. *Children's Fiction in the Hands of the Translators.* Lund: Gleerup, 1986.

Nikolajeva, Maria. *Children's Literature Comes of Age. Towards a New Aesthetic.* New York: Garland, 1996.

Oittinen, Riitta. *Translating for Children.* New York: Garland, 2000. Previously published as *I Am Me—I Am Other. On the Dialogics of Translating for Children.* Tampere: University of Tampere, 1993.

O'Sullivan, Emer. "Alice in Different Wonderlands: Varying Approaches in the German Translations of an English Children's Classic." Pp. 11–21 in *Children's Literature and National Identity* edited by Margaret Meek. Stoke-on-Trent: Trentham Books, 2001.

Stan, Susan, ed. *The World Through Children's Books.* Lanham, Md.: Scarecrow, 2002.

Steffensen, Anette. "Den samme fortælling i to versioner—Om Astrid Lindgrens *Mio, min Mio* på svensk og dansk." Pp. 161–187 in *Nedslag i børnelitteraturforskningen,* vol. 4, edited by Torben Weinreich et al. Frederiksberg: Roskilde University Press, 2003.

Stolt, Birgit. "How Emil Becomes Michel. On the Translation of Children's Books." Pp. 130–146 in *Children's Books in Translation. The Situation and the Problems* edited by Göte Klingberg et al. Stockholm: Almqvist & Wiksell International, 1978.

Tabbert, Reinbert. "Approaches to the Translation of Children's Literature. A Review of Critical Studies Since 1960." *Target* 14 (2002): 2, 303–351.

Tomlinson, Carl M. *Children's Books from Other Countries.* Lanham, Md.: Scarecrow, 1998.

Weaver, Warren. *Alice in Many Tongues: The Translations of Alice in Wonderland.* Madison, Wis.: University of Wisconsin Press, 1964.

Note: For a comprehensive bibliography, see Reinbert Tabbert's essay (in the above list).

CHILDREN'S BOOKS DISCUSSED

Andersen, Hans Christian. *The Complete Fairy Tales and Stories.* Translated by Erik Christian Haugaard. New York: Doubleday, 1974.

Carroll, Lewis. *Alice's Adventures in Wonderland* (1865). In: *The Penguin Complete Lewis Carroll.* Harmonsworth: Penguin, 1982.

Collodi, Carlo. *The Adventures of Pinocchio* (1881). Translated by Ann Lawson Lucas. Oxford: Oxford University Press, 1996.

Foreman, Michael. *War and Peas*. London: Hamish Hamilton, 1974.

Gaarder, Jostein. *Sophie's World* (1991). Translated by Paulette Møller. New York: Farrar, Straus & Giroux, 1994.

Gripe, Maria. *Elvis and His Secret* (1972). Translated by Sheila La Farge. New York: Delacorte, 1976.

Hellsing, Lennart. *The Pirate Book* (1965). Freely adapted from the Swedish by William Jay Smith. New York: Delacorte, 1972.

Jansson, Tove. *Finn Family Moomintroll* (1949). Translated by Elizabeth Portch. New York: Walck, 1965.

Kästner, Erich. *Emil and the Detectives* (1928). Translated by May Massee. New York: Doubleday, 1930.

Lagerlöf, Selma. *The Wonderful Adventures of Nils* (1906–07). Translated by Velma Swanston Howard. New York: Dover, 1995.

Lindenbaum, Pija. *Else-Marie and Her Seven Little Daddies* (1990). Adapted by Gabriella Charbonnet. New York: Holt, 1991.

Lindgren, Astrid. *Pippi Longstocking* (1945). Translated by Florence Lamborn. New York: Viking, 1950.

———. *Pippi Longstocking* (1945). Translated by Edna Hurup. London: Oxford University Press, 1954.

———. *Mio, My Son* (1954). Translated by Marianne Turner. New York: Viking, 1956.

———. *The Children of Noisy Village* (1947). Translated by Florence Lamborn. New York: Viking, 1962.

———. *Emil's Pranks* (1963). Translated by Michael Heron. Chicago: Follett, 1971.

———. *Ronia, the Robber's Daughter* (1981). Translated by Patricia Crampton. New York: Viking, 1983.

———. *The Robber's Daughter* (1981). Translated by Patricia Crampton. London: Methuen, 1983.

Lindgren, Barbro, and Eva Eriksson. *Sam's Ball* (1982). New York: Morrow, 1983.

Milne, A. A. *Winnie-the-Pooh*. London: Methuen, 1926.

Nordqvist, Sven. *Pancake Pie*. New York: Morrow, 1985.

Pohl, Peter. *Johnny My Friend* (1985). Translated by Larry Thompson. London: Turton & Chambers, 1991.

Preussler, Ottfrid. *The Satanic Mill* (1971). Translated by Anthea Bell. New York: Macmillan, 1976.

Pullman, Philip. *Northern Lights*. London: Scholastic, 1995 (the first part of *His Dark Materials* trilogy).

Rowling, J. K. *Harry Potter and the Philosopher's Stone*. London: Bloomsbury, 1997 (the first of the Harry Potter series).

Salinger, Jerome D. *The Catcher in the Rye.* Boston: Little, Brown, 1951.
Sendak, Maurice. *In the Night Kitchen.* New York: Harper, 1970.
————. *Where the Wild Things Are.* New York: Harper, 1963.
Silverstein, Shel. *The Giving Tree.* New York: Harper & Row, 1964.
Stark, Ulf. *Dårfinkar och dönickar.* Stockholm: Bonnier, 1984.

Selected Bibliography of European Children's Literature Studies

The bibliography includes a selection of publications in English devoted to classic and contemporary West European children's literature. Interested scholars will find more information in the international journal *Bookbird*. For country surveys, see *The International Companion Encyclopedia of Children's Literature* edited by Peter Hunt.

Åhmansson, Gabriella. "Mayflowers Grow in Sweden Too: L. M. Montgomery, Astrid Lindgren and the Swedish Literary Consciousness." Pp. 14–22 in *Harvesting Thistles: The Textual Garden of L. M. Montgomery* edited by Mary Rubio. Guelph: Canadian Children's Press, 1994.

Alfano, Christine. "How Swedish picture books changed my life." *Riverbank Review* (1999) 4: 4–6.

Asplund Carlson, Maj. "Gummy Tarzan in the School Library." *Para*doxa* 2 (1996) 3/4: 393–98.

Baumgarten-Lindberg, Marianne von. *Swedish Children's Books*. Stockholm: Swedish Institute, 2003.

Beckett, Sandra L. "From the Art of Rewriting to the Art of Crosswriting Child and Adult: the Secret of Michel Tournier's Dual Readership." Pp. 9–34 in *Voices from Far Away: Current Trends in International Children's Literature Research* edited by Maria Nikolajeva. Stockholm: Centre for the Study of Childhood Culture, 1995.

———. "The Meeting of Two Worlds: Michel Tournier's *Friday and Robinson: Life on Speranza Island*." Pp. 110–27 in *Other Worlds, Other Livres: Children's Literature Experiences* edited by Myrna Machet et al. Pretoria: UNISA Press, 1996, vol 2.

———. "Crossing the Borders: The 'Children's Books' of Michel Tournier and Jean-Marie Gustave Le Clézio." *The Lion and the Unicorn* 22 (1998) 1: 44–69.

———. "Crossing Child and Adult in France: Children's Fiction for Adults? Adult Fiction for Children? Fiction for all Ages?" Pp. 31–62 in in *Transcending Boundaries. Writing for a Dual Audience of Children and Adults* edited by Sandra L. Beckett. New York: Garland, 1999.

———. "Parodic Play with Paintings in Picture Books." *Children's Literature* 29 (2001): 175–95.

———. "Crossing the Boundaries: Michel Tournier's Tales for Children and Adults." Pp. 167–77 in *Children in Literature—Children's Literature* edited by Paul Nebauer. Frankfurt am Main: Peter Lang, 2002.

———. *Recycling Red Riding Hood.* New York: Routledge, 2002.

———. "Artists' Books for a Cross-Audience." Pp. 162–69 in *Studies in Children's Literature 1500–2000* edited by Celia Keenan and Mary Shine Thompson. Dublin: Four Courts Press, 2004.

Bell, Anthea. "Children's Books in Translation." *Signal* 28 (1979): 47–53.

———. "Children's Literature and International Identity? A Translator's Viewpoint." Pp. 23–30 in *Children's Literature and National Identity* edited by Margaret Meek. Stoke-on-Trent: Trentham Books, 2001.

Blockeel, Francesca. "History and Collective Memory in Contemporary Portuguese Literature for the Young." Pp. 53–59 in *The Presence of the Past in Children's Literature* edited by Ann Lawson Lucas. Westport, CT: Greenwood, 2003.

Bosmajian, Hamida. "Grief and Its Displacement through Fantasy in Michael Ende's *The Neverending Story.*" Pp. 120–23 in *Proceedings of the Thirteenth Annual Conference of The Children's Literature Association,* edited by Susan R. Gannon and Ruth Anne Thompson. West Lafayette, IN: Purdue University, 1988.

Bredsdorff, Elias. *Hans Christian Andersen: The Story of His Life and Work.* London: Phaidon, 1975.

Camton, Glauco. "Pinocchio and Problems of Children's Literature." *Children's Literature* 2 (1973): 50–60.

Capasso, Ruth Carver. "Philanthropy in Nineteenth-Century French Children's Literature: The Example of La Bibliothèque Rose." *Children's Literature* 29 (2001): 18–33.

Cate, Curtis. *Antoine de Saint-Exupéry.* New York: Putnam, 1970.

Cevela, Inge. "Looking for the Absent Father in Contemporary German-Language Children's Books." *Bookbird* 39 (2001) 2: 39–42.

Christensen, Nina. "Teaching Tolerance. A Comparative Reading of Two Danish Picture Books." *Bookbird* 37 (1999) 4: 11–16.

———. "An Attempt to Create an International Identity. The Picture Book in a Literary, Didactic and Historical Perspective." Pp. 109–23 in *Text, Culture and National Identity in Children's Literature* edited by Jean Webb. Helsinki: Nordinfo, 2000.

Coats, Karen. *Looking Glasses and Neverlands. Lacan, Desire, and Subjectivity in Children's Literature*. Iowa City: Iowa University Press, 2004.

Colin, Mariella. "Children's Literature in France and Italy in the Nineteenth Century: Influences and Exchanges." Pp. 77–88 in *Aspects and Issues in the History of Children's Literature* edited by Maria Nikolajeva. Westport, CT: Greenwood, 1995.

Cotton, Penni. "The Europeaness of Picture Books." Pp. 111–20 in *Children's Literature and National Identity* edited by Margaret Meek. London: Trentham, 2001.

———. "An Analysis of Settings in Selected European Picture Books." *Bookbird* 40 (2002) 2: 6–13.

———. "Adult Challenges from the European Picture Book: The European Picture Books Collection and the European School Education Training Course." Pp. 53–67 in *Books and Boundaries: Writers and Their Audience* edited by Pat Pinsent. Lichfield: Pied Piper, 2004.

———, ed. *Picture Books Sans Frontièrs*. London: Trentham, 2000.

Detti, Emmanno. "The Difficult Art of Making People Laugh: Comic Children's Literature in Italy." *The Lion and the Unicorn* 26 (2002) 2: 150–68.

Doderer, Klaus. "Change and Renewal of a Famous German Classic." Pp. 183–88 in *Change and Renewal in Children's Literature* edited by Thomas van der Walt. Westport, CT: Greenwood, 2004.

Edström, Vivi. *Selma Lagerlöf*. Boston: Twayne, 1984.

———. *Astrid Lindgren: A Critical Study*. Stockholm: Rabén & Sjögren, 2000.

Ewers, Hans-Heino. "Changing Functions of Children's Literature: New Book Genres and Literary Functions." *Bookbird* 38 (2000) 1: 6–11.

Fernández Lopez, Marisa. "Translation Studies in Contemporary Children's Literature: A Comparison of Intercultural Ideological Factors." *Children's Literature Association Quarterly* 25 (2000) 1: 29–37.

Filmer, Kath. "Religion and Romanticism in Michael Ende's *The Neverending Story*." *Mythlore* 18 (1991): 59–64.

Fransson, Birgitta. *Once Upon a Time . . . Swedish Children's Books—Then and Now*. Stockholm: Swedish Institute, 1990.

Franz, Marie Loiuse von. *Puer Aeternus. A Psychological Study of the Adult Struggle with the Paradise of Childhood*. 2nd ed. Santa Monica: Sigo, 1981.

Freund, Winfried. *German Literature for Children and Young People Today: Themes, Structures, Analyses*. Bonn: Inter Nationes, 1987.

Fouts, Elizabeth. "Spain: Literatura infantil: A Brief History of Spanish Children's Literature." *Bookbird* 37 (1999) 3: 47–51.

Gagnon, Laurence. "Webs of Concern. The Little Prince and Charlotte's Web." Pp. 66–71 in *Reflections on Literature for Children* edited by Francelia Butler and Richard Rotert. Hamden, CT: Library Professional Publications, 1984: 66–71.

Grenz, Dagmar. "Literature for Young People and the Novel of Adolescence." Pp. 173–82 in *Aspects and Issues in the History of Children's Literature* edited by Maria Nikolajeva. Westport, CT: Greenwood, 1995.

———. "Realistic Stories for Children in the Federal Republic of Germany, 1970–1994: Features and Tendencies." Pp. 141–51 in *Reflections of Change: Children's Literature Since 1945* edited by Sandra L. Beckett. Westport, CT: Greenwood, 1997.

Grønbech, Bo. *Hans Christian Andersen.* New York: Twayne, 1980.

Hannesdóttir, Sigrún Klara. "Children's Literature as the Basis for Cultural Identity: The Case of Iceland." Pp. 209–33 in in *Text, Culture and National Identity in Children's Literature* edited by Jean Webb. Helsinki: Nordinfo, 2000.

Happonen, Sirke. " 'Never Lonely, Always on the Go': The Merry-Go-Round as Kinetic Metonym, in Text and Illustration, in Tove Jansson's Short Story, 'The Hemulen Who Loved Silence.' " Pp. 141–57 in *Change and Renewal in Children's Literature* edited by Thomas van der Walt. Westport, CT: Greenwood, 2004.

Heisig, Fr. James. "Pinocchio: Archetype of the Motherless Child." *Children's Literature* 3 (1974): 23–35.

Hendrickson, Linnea. "Lessons from Linnea: *Linnea in Monet's Garden* as a Prototype of Radical Change in Informational Books for Children." *Children's Literature in Education* 30 (1999) 1: 35–45.

Higgins, James E. *The Little Prince. A Reverie of Substance.* New York: Twayne, 1996.

Higonnet, Margaret R. "Marguerite Yourcenar and Michel Tournier : The Arts of the Heart." Pp. 151–58 in *Triumphs of the Spirit in Children's Literature* eds. Francelia Butler and Richard Rotert. Hamden, CT: Library Professional Publications, 1986.

———. "War Games." *The Lion and the Unicorn* 22 (1998) 1: 1–17.

Hildebrand, Ann Meinzen. *Jean and Laurent de Brunhoff: The Legacy of Babar.* New York: Twayne, 1991.

Hoffeld, Laura. "Pippi Longstocking: The Comedy of the Natural Girl." *The Lion and the Unicorn* 1 (1977) 1: 47–53.

Hunt, Peter, ed. *The International Companion Encyclopedia of Children's Literature.* Vol 1–2. 2nd revised edition. London: Routledge, 2004.

Hürlimann, Bettina. *Three Centuries of Childrens Books in Europe.* Translated and edited by Brian W. Alderson. London: Oxford University Press, 1967.

———. *Picture-Book World.* Translated and edited by Brian W. Alderson. London: Oxford University Press, 1968.

Jan, Isabelle. *On Children's Literature.* London: Allen Lane, 1973.

Jones, W. Glyn. *Tove Jansson.* Boston: Twayne, 1984.

Kamenetsky, Christa. *Children's Literature in Hitler's Germany: The Cultural Policy of National Socialism.* Athens: Ohio University Press, 1984.

Kampp, Bodil. "Generations in Dialog. The Literary and Pedagogical Potential of Modern Danish Literature of Youth." *CREArTA* 3 (2003) 2: 34–45.

Kåreland, Lena. "Two Crosswriting Authors: Carl Sandburg and Lennart Hellsing." Pp. 215–37 in *Transcending Boundaries. Writing for a Dual Audience of Children and Adults* edited by Sandra L. Beckett. New York: Garland, 1999.

Klingberg, Göte. *Children's Fiction in the Hands of the Translators*. Lund: Gleerup, 1986

Klingberg, Göte, et al., eds. *Children's Books in Translation. The Situation and the Problems*. Stockholm: Almqvist & Wiksell International, 1978.

Kohl, Herbert. *Should We Burn Babar? Essays on Children's Literature and the Power of Stories*. New York: New Press, 1995.

Kümmerling-Meibauer, Bettina. "Comparing Children's Literature." *Compar(a)ison* (1995) 2: 5–18.

———. "Crosswriting as a Criterion for Canonicity: The Case of Erich Kästner." Pp. 13–30 in *Transcending Boundaries. Writing for a Dual Audience of Children and Adults* edited by Sandra L. Beckett. New York: Garland, 1999.

Kunze, Horst J. *German Children's Literature from its Beginning to the Nineteenth Century*. Chicago: American Library Association, 1990.

Lawson Lucas, Ann. "Decadence for Kids: Salgari's Corsaro Nero in Context." Pp. 81–90 in *Children's Literature and the Fin de Siècle* edited by Roderick McGillis. Westport, CT: Greenwood, 2003.

Lenz, Millicent. "The Experience of Time and the Concept of Happiness in Michel Tournier's *Friday and Robinson: Life on Speranza Island*." *Children's Literature Quarterly* 11 (1986) 1: 24–29.

Lierop-Debrauer, Helma van. "Crossing the Border: Authors Do It, but Do Critics? The Reception of Dual-Readership Authors in the Netherlands." Pp. 3–12 in *Transcending Boundaries. Writing for a Dual Audience of Children and Adults* edited by Sandra L. Beckett. New York: Garland, 1999.

Linders-Nouwens, Joke, and Marita De Sterck. *Behind the Story: Children's Book Authors in Flanders and The Netherlands*. Antwerpen: Ministerie van de Vlaamse Gemeenschap, 1996.

Lloyd, Rosemary. *The Land of Lost Content. Children and Childhood in Nineteenth-Century French Literature*. Oxford: Clarendon, 1992.

Lundqvist, Ulla. "Some Portraits of Teenagers in Modern Junior Novels in Sweden." Pp. 117–24 in *The Portrayal of the Child in Children's Literature* edited by Denise Escarpit. München: Saur, 1985.

Lurie, Alison. *Boys and Girls Forever. Children's Classics from Cinderella to Harry Potter*, pp. 79–90. New York: Penguin, 2003.

Malarte-Feldman, Claire-Lise. "The French Fairy-Tale Conspiracy." *The Lion and the Unicorn* 12 (1988) 2: 88–96.

———. "Editor's Introduction." *The Lion and the Unicorn*, special issue on "French Children's Literature" 22 (1998)1: v–xii.

Malarte-Feldman, Claire-Lise, and Jack Yeager. "Babar and the French Connection: Teaching the Politics of Superiority and Exclusion." Pp. 69–77 in *Critical Perspectives on Postcolonial African Children's and Young Adult Literature* edited by Meena Khorana. Westport, CT: Greenwood, 1998.

McMahon, Joseph H. "Michel Tournier's Texts for Children." *Children's Literature* 13 (1985): 154–68.

Meek, Margaret, ed. *Children's Literature and National Identity*. Stoke-on-Trent: Trentham, 2001.

Metcalf, Eva-Maria. "The Invisible Child in the Works of Tormod Haugen." *Barnboken* (1992) 1: 15–23.

———. *Astrid Lindgren*. New York: Twayne, 1995.

———. "Leap of Faith in Astrid Lindgren's Brothers Lionheart." *Children's Literature* 23 (1995): 165–78.

———. "The Changing Status of Children and Children's Literature." Pp. 49–56 in *Reflections of Change: Children's Literature Since 1945* edited by Sandra L. Beckett. Westport, CT: Greenwood, 1997.

———. "Stairways to History: The Novels of Torill Thorstad Hauger." *Bookbird* 37 (1999) 4: 31–33.

———. "Life is Crazy: Ulf Stark's Stories for Children." *Bookbird* 37 (1999) 4: 35–37.

———. "A Tribute to Erich Kästner (1899–1974)." *Bookbird* 37 (1999) 4: 62–63.

———. "First Astrid Lindgren Memorial Award for Christine Nöstlinger and Maurice Sendak." *Bookbird* 41 (2003) 4: 51–57.

———. "Fostering Controlled Dissent: Democratic Values and Children's Literature." Pp. 79–87 in *Change and Renewal in Children's Literature* edited by Thomas van der Walt. Westport, CT: Praeger, 2004.

Mjør, Ingeborg. "Tradition and Modernity in Prose and Picture Books: Trends in Norwegian Children's Literature 1991–97." *The Norseman* (1998) 4/5: 4–13.

Moebius, William. "L'enfant terrible Comes of Age." Pp. 32–50 in *Notebooks in Cultural Analysis* edited by Norman F. Cantor, vol 2. Durham: Duke University Press, 1985.

Mouritsen, Flemming. "Children's Literature." Pp. 609–31 in *A History of Danish Literature* edited by Sven H. Rossel. Lincoln: University of Nebraska Press, 1992.

Morrissey, Thomas J., and Richard Wunderlich. "Death and Rebirth in Pinocchio." *Children's Literature* 11 (1983): 64–75.

Mylius, Johan de. *The Voice of Nature in Hans Christian Andersen's Fairy Tales*. Odense: Odense University Press, 1989.

Mylius, Johan de, et al., eds. *Hans Christian Andersen. A Poet in Time*. Odense: Odense University Press, 1999.

Nières-Chevrel, Isabelle. "In and Out of History: *Jeanne d'Arc* by Maurice

Boutet de Monvel." Pp. 33–39 in *The Presence of the Past in Children's Literature* edited by Ann Lawson Lucas. Westport, CT: Greenwood, 2003.

Nikolajeva, Maria. "How Fantasy is Made: Patterns and Structures in *The Neverending Story*." *Merveilles & Contes* 4 (1990): 34–42.

Nikolajeva, Maria. *Children's Literature Comes of Age. Toward a New Aesthetic*. New York, Garland, 1995.

———. "Pigs Aren't Meant to Have Fun: The Swedishness of Swedish Children's Literature." Pp. 14–33 in *Other Worlds, Other Lives* edited by Myrna Machett et al. Pretoria: UNISA Press, 1996.

———. "Literature for Children and Young People." Pp. 495–512 in *The History of Swedish Literature* edited by Lars Warme. Lincoln: University of Nebraska Press, 1996.

———. "Two National Heroes: Jacob Two-Two and Pippi Longstocking." *Canadian Children's Literature* 86 (1997): 7–16.

———. "National Identity in Minority Literature for Children: The Case of Swedish-language Literature in Finland." Pp. 7–14 in *Gunpowder and Sealing-Wax: Nationhood in Children's Literature* edited by Ann Lawson Lucas. Hull, Troubador, 1997.

———. "Exit Children's Literature?" *The Lion and the Unicorn* 22 (1998) 2: 221–36.

———. "Similar but Separate. National Features in Scandinavian Children's Literature." *Bookbird* 37 (1999) 4: 6–10.

———. "Children's, Adult, Human . . . ?" Pp. 63–80 in in *Transcending Boundaries. Writing for a Dual Audience of Children and Adults* edited by Sandra L. Beckett. New York: Garland, 1999.

———. *From Mythic to Linear. Time in Children's Literature*. Lanham, MD: Scarecrow, 2000.

———. "Tamed Imagination. A Rereading of Heidi." *Children's Literature Association Quarterly* 25 (2000) 2: 68–75.

Nikolajeva, Maria, ed. *Aspects and Issues in the History of Children's Literature*. Westport, CT: Greenwood, 1995.

Nikolajeva, Maria, and Carole Scott. *How Picturebooks Work*. New York: Garland, 2001.

Nodelman, Perry, ed. *Touchstones: Reflections on the Best in Children's Literature*. 3 vols. West Lafayette, IN: Children's Literature Association, 1985–89.

O'Sullivan, Emer. *Comparative Children's Literature*. London: Routledge, 2005.

Ommundsen, Åse Marie. "Girl Stuck in the Wall: Narrative Changes in Norwegian Children's Literature Exemplified by the Picture Book 'Snill'." *Bookbird* 42 (2004) 1: 24–26.

Orlov, Janina. "'Nobody is Perfect': Some Thoughts Concerning Gender in Finnish and Finland-Swedish Children's Literature." Pp. 61–70 in *Female/Male. Gender in Children's Literature* edited by Lena Pasternak. Visby: Baltic Centre for Writers and Translators, 1999.

Österlund, Mia. "Girls in Disguise: Gender Transgression in Swedish Young Adult Fiction of the 1980s." Pp. 175–85 in *Text, Culture and National Identity in Children's Literature* edited by Jean Webb. Helsinki: Nordinfo, 2000.

———. "Gender and Beyond: Ulf Stark's Conservative Rebellion." Pp. 177–200 in *Children's Literature as Communication* edited by Roger D. Sell. Amsterdam: John Benjamins, 2002.

Pálsdóttir, Ágústa. "Children's Literature in Iceland." Pp. 224–36 in *Text, Culture and National Identity in Children's Literature* edited by Jean Webb. Helsinki: Nordinfo, 2000.

Pálsdóttir, Anna Heida. "Rolling Hills and Rocky Crags: The Role of Landscape in English and Icelandic Literature for Children." Pp. 64–76 in *Text, Culture and National Identity in Children's Literature* edited by Jean Webb. Helsinki: Nordinfo, 2000.

Perrot, Jean. "Pan and Puer Aeternus: Aestheticism and the Spirit of the Age." *Poetics Today* 13 (1992) 1: 155–67.

———. "Revolution and Reverence: French Children's Literature Collections." *Signal* 87 (1998): 187–92.

———. "A 'Little Tour' of the USA in Contemporary French Children's Literature." *The Lion and the Unicorn* 22 (1998) 1: 70–91.

Perrot, Jean, ed. *Tomi Ungerer.* Paris: In press editions, 1998.

———. *Europe: A Dream in Pictures?* Paris: L'Harmattan, 2000.

Petit, Susan. *Michel Tournier's Metaphysical Fictions.* Amsterdam: John Benjamins: 1991.

Petzold, Dieter. "Taking Games Seriously: Romantic Irony in Modern Fantasy for Children of All Ages." Pp. 87–104 in *Literature and the Child. Romantic Continuations, Postmodern Contestations* edited by James Holt McGavran. Iowa City: University of Iowa Press, 1999.

Poeti, Alida. "Crossing Borders: Calvino in the Footprints of Collodi." Pp. 201–14 in *Transcending Boundaries. Writing for a Dual Audience of Children and Adults* edited by Sandra L. Beckett. New York: Garland, 1999.

Proud, Judith K. *Children and Propaganda : il était une fois . . . : Fiction and Fairy Tale in Vichy France.* Oxford: Intellect, 1995.

———. "Occupying the Imagination: Fairy Stories and Propaganda in Vichy France." *The Lion and the Unicorn* 22 (1998) 1: 18–43.

Purdy, Anthony. "From Defoe's 'Crusoe' to Tournier's 'Vendredi'": The Metamorphosis of a Myth." *Canadian Review of Comparative Literature* (June 1984): 216–35.

Rahn, Suzanne. "The Boy and the Wild Geese: Selma Lagerlöf's Nils." Pp. 39–50 in her *Rediscoveries in Children's Literature.* New York: Garland, 1995.

Rättyä, Kaisu. "The Image of Finland in Finnish Children's Literature." Pp. 79–86 in *Europe: A Dream in Pictures?* edited by Jean Perrot. Paris: L'Harmattan, 2000.

————. "Intertextualities: Subtexts in Jukka Parkkinen's Suvi kinos novels." Pp. 55–70 in *Children's Literature as Communication* edited by Roger D. Sell. Amsterdam: John Benjamins, 2002.

Reeder, Kik. "Pippi Longstocking—a Feminist or Anti-feminist Work?" Pp. 112–17 in *Racism and Sexism in Children's Literature* edited by Judith Stinton. London: Writers and Readers, 1979.

Renonciat, Annie, ed. *The Changing Face of Children's Literature in France.* Paris: Hachette-Livre, 1998.

Richter, Gudlaug, and Idunn Steinsdottir. "Iceland" *Bookbird* 37 (1999) 4: 48–52.

Roberts, Martin. *Michel Tournier:* Bricolage *and Cultural Mythology.* Saratoga, CA: Anma Libri, 1994.

Robinson, Joy D. Marie. *Antoine de Saint-Exupéry.* Boston: Twayne, 1984.

Rodari, Gianni. *The Grammar of Fantasy: An Introduction to the Art of Inventing Stories.* Translated with an Introduction by Jack Zipes. New York: Teachers and Writers Collaborative, 1996.

Romøren, Rolf. "From Literary Text to Literary Field: Boys' Fiction in Norway between the Two World Wars; a Re-reading." Pp. 13–21 in *The Presence of the Past in Children's Literature* edited by Ann Lawson Lucas. Westport CT: Greenwood, 2003.

Romøren, Rolf, and John Stephens, "Representing Masculinity in Norwegian and Australian Young Adult Fiction: A Comparative Study." Pp. 216–33 in *Ways of Being Male: Representing Masculinities in Children's Literature and Film* edited by John Stephens. New York: Routledge, 2002.

Rossel, Sven H., ed. *Hans Christian Andersen: Danish Writer and Citizen of the World.* Amsterdam: Rodopi, 1986.

Russell, David L. "Pinocchio and the Child-Hero Quest." *Children's Literature in Education* (1989) 4: 203–13.

————. "Pippi Longstocking and the Subversive Affirmation of Comedy." *Children's Literature in Education* (2000) 3: 167–77.

Salstad, Louise M. "Female Protagonists in Lazarillo Prize-winning Fiction in the Context of Spanish Children's Literature Today. *Bookbird* 37 (1999) 3: 52–56.

————. "A Question of Distance: Three Spanish Civil War Narratives for Children." *Bookbird* 39 (2001) 3: 30–36.

————. "Narratee and Implied Readers in the Manolito Gafotas Series: A Case of Triple Addresses." *Children's Literature Association Quarterly* 28 (2003) 4: 219–29.

Salvadori, Maria Luisa. "Apologizing to the Ancient Fable: Gianni Rodari and His Influence on Italian Children's Literature." *The Lion and the Unicorn* 26 (2002) 2: 169–202.

Schiff, Stacy. *Saint-Exupéry: A Biography.* New York: Knopf, 1995.

Schwarcz, Joseph H. *Ways of the Illustrator: Visual Communication in Children's Literature.* Chicago: American Library Association, 1982.

Schwarcz, Joseph, and Chava Schwarcz. *The Picture Book Comes of Age*. Chicago: American Library Association, 1991.

Senje, Catherine. "'No Mercy on the Population' (Adolf Hitler, October 28, 1944): Childhood Memories of War in Children's Literature from Norway. *Bookbird* 41 (2003) 4: 28–32.

Smith, Maxwell. *Knight of the Air: The Life and Works of Antoine de Saint-Exupéry*. New York: Pageant Press, 1956.

Sollat, Kate. "The Boundaries of Fantasy in German Children's Literature." *Bookbird* 35 (1997) 4: 6–11.

Springman, Luke. *Comrades, Friends and Companions: Utopian Projections and Social Action in German Literature For Young People, 1926–1934*. New York: Lang, 1989.

Stan, Susan, ed. *The World Through Children's Books*. Lanham, MD: Scarecrow, 2002.

Svensen, Åsfried. "From Grand Narratives to Small Stories: New Narrative Structures in Recent Scandinavian Children's Literature. Pp 59–63 in *Reflections of Change: Children's Literature Since 1945* edited by Sandra L. Beckett. Westport, CT: Greenwood, 1997.

Tabbert, Reinbert. "National Myth in Three Classical Picture Books." Pp. 151–63 in *Aspects and Issues in the History of Children's Literature* edited by Maria Nikolajeva. Westport, CT: Greenwood, 1995.

Tebbutt, Susan. *Gudrun Pausewang in Context. Socially Critical 'Jugendliteratur', Gudrun Pausewang and the Search for Utopia*. Frankfurt: Peter Lang, 1994.

———. "Voices of Protest: One Hundred Years of German Pacifist Children's Literature." Pp. 41–50 in *Children's Literature and the Fin de Siècle* edited by Roderick McGillis. Westport, CT: Greenwood, 2003.

Thaler, Danielle. "Fiction Versus History: History's Ghosts." Pp. 3–11 in *The Presence of the Past in Children's Literature* edited by Ann Lawson Lucas. Westport, CT: Greenwood, 2003.

Thomson-Wohlgemut, Gabriele. "Children's Literature in Translation from East to West." Pp. 119–28 in *New Voices in Children's Literature Criticism* edited by Sebastien Chapleau. Lichfield, UK: Pied Piper, 2004.

Tomlinson, Carl M. *Children's Books from Other Countries*. Lanham, MD: Scarecrow, 1998.

Usrey, Malcolm. "Johanna Spyri's *Heidi*: The Conversion of a Byronic Hero." Pp. 232–42 in *Touchstones: Reflections on the Best in Children's Literature* edited by Perry Nodelman. West Lafayette, IN: Children's Literature Association, 1985, vol. 3.

Vold, Karin Beate. "Golden Ages" at the Turns of a Century: Norwegian Writing for Children and Young People." *Bookbird* 37 (1999) 4: 22–27.

Vries, Anne de. "Literature for All Ages? Literary Emancipation and the Borders of Children's Literature." Pp. 43–47 in *Reflections of Change: Chil-*

dren's Literature Since 1945 edited by Sandra L. Beckett. Westport, CT: Greenwood, 1997.

———. "The Century of the Child: Dutch Children's Poetry in the Twentieth Century." Pp. 23–30 in *Children's Literature and the Fin de Siècle* edited by Roderick McGillis. Westport, CT: Greenwood, 2003.

Vrooland-Löb, Truusje, and Annelies Fontijne. *Dutch Oranges; Fifty Illustrators from Holland*. Zwolle: Waanders, 2001.

Webb, Jean, ed. *Text, Culture and National Identity in Children's Literature*. Helsinki: Nordinfo, 2000.

Weber, Nicholas Fox. *The Art of Babar: The Works of Jean and Laurent de Brunhoff*. New York: Abrams, 1989.

Weinkauff, Gina. "Between Village Mentality and Cultural Hybridity: Mapping the Immigrant Self in German Children's Literature." *Bookbird* 39 (2001) 4: 17–24.

Weinreich, Torben. *Children's Literature: Art or Pedagogy?* Roskilde: Roskilde University Press, 2000.

Westin, Boel. "The Androgynous Female (or Orlando Inverted)—Examples from Gripe, Stark, Wahl, Pohl." Pp. 91–102 in *Female/Male. Gender in Children's Literature* edited by Lena Pasternak. Visby: Baltic Centre for Writers and Translators, 1999.

Worton, Michael, ed. *Michel Tournier*. London: Longman, 1995.

Wullschläger, Jackie. *Hans Christian Andersen: The Life of a Storyteller*. New York: Knopf, 2001.

Wunderlich, Richard, and Thomas J. Morrissey. "Carlo Collodi's The Adventures of Pinocchio: A Classic Book of Choices." Pp. 53–64 in *Touchstones: Reflections of the Best in Children's Literature* edited by Perry Nodelman. West Lafayette, IN: Children's Literature Association, 1985, vol. 1.

———. *Pinocchio Goes Postmodern: Perils of a Puppet in the United States*. New York: Routledge, 2002.

Zipes, Jack. "Down with Heidi, Down with Struwwelpeter, Three Cheers for the Revolution." *Children's Literature* 5 (1976): 162–80.

———. *Happily Ever After: Fairy Tales, Children and the Culture Industry*. New York: Routledge, 1997.

———. *When Dreams Came True. Classical Fairy Tales and Their Tradition*. New York: Routledge, 1999.

———. *Sticks and Stones. The Troublesome Success of Children's Literature from Slovenly Peter to Harry Potter*. New York: Routledge, 2001.

Zipes, Jack, ed. *The Oxford Companion to Fairy Tales*. Oxford: Oxford University Press, 2000.

———. *The Oxford Encyclopedia of Children's Literature*. Vols. 1–4. New York: Oxford University Press, 2006.

Index

About the Contributors

Harald Bache-Wiig is professor of Scandinavian literature at the University of Oslo. He has published two books on children's literature: *Lek på alvor. Norsk barnelitteratur—glimt gjennom 100 år* (1996) and *Frisetting av barndommen. Radsmus Løland som barnebokforfatter* (2000). From 1996 to 2000 he managed a research project called "Establishing Norwegian Childhood." He has edited three anthologies about children's literature and he also has published numerous articles on this topic. Most of his research and publications are not related to the field of children's literature and encompass many literary themes and periods.

Sandra L. Beckett is a professor in the Department of Modern Languages, Literatures, and Cultures at Brock University in Canada. She is the author of numerous books, including *Recycling Red Riding Hood* (Routledge, 2002) and *De grands romanciers écrivent pour les enfants* (PUM, 1997), and she has edited several other books on children's literature and Francophone literature, including *Transcending Boundaries: Writing for a Dual Audience of Children and Adults* (Garland, 1999) and *Reflections of Change: Children's Literature Since 1945* (1997). She is currently completing a book titled *Crosswriting Red Riding Hood* and working on another on crossover literature. She serves on the editorial boards of several children's literature journals. She is a member of the ChLA International Committee and a former president of the International Research Society for Children's Literature (1999–2003).

Sabine Fuchs was involved for seven years in a research project about "Austrian Literature in National Socialism" at the German Institute in the Karl-Franzens-University in Graz. Her main interest is children's literature and media. She was a founding member of the Austrian Research Society for Children's and Youth Literature and she is Liason Officer of IBBY Austria. She is the author of *Christine Nöstlinger. Eine Monographie* (2001) and the co-editor of *Macht Literatur Krieg* (1998), *Der vergessene Klassiker—Karl Bruckner* (2002), and . . . *weil die Kinder nicht ernst genommen werden. Zum Werk von Christine Nöstlinger* (2003). She has also published articles in books and journals about children's literature and film.

Helene Høyrup is associate professor at The Royal School of Library and Information Science, Denmark. She teaches children's literature and culture, and her research focuses on children's literature in a cultural perspective. Currently, she is doing research on the shaping of children's literature as a field, with an emphasis on the period from Romanticism to today. She studies children's literature as a domain of knowledge shaped by intersecting ideas of childhood and literature and is interested in the historic positioning of children's literature between the literary canon and cultural contexts. Her work on children's literature has appeared in Denmark and internationally, for instance in Thomas van der Walt et al. (eds.) *Change and Renewal in Children's Literature* (2004), and in *Scandinavian Studies*.

Ann Lawson Lucas was senior lecturer in Italian at the University of Hull, UK, and subsequently visiting research fellow at the Institute for Advanced Studies in the Humanities, University of Edinburgh. Her publications on nineteenth-century Italian children's literature include the Oxford World's Classics edition of Collodi's *The Adventures of Pinocchio* and several volumes, published in Italy, on the adventure novelist Emilio Salgari. She edited a volume of essays, *The Presence of the Past in Children's Literature* (2003), and is an advisory editor for the *Oxford Encyclopedia of Children's Literature*.

Claire L. Malarte-Feldman is professor of French at the University of New Hampshire, Durham, where she teaches courses in French language, culture, and literature. Her research interests lie in the field of French children's literature, particularly contemporary rewrites and illustrations of French literary tales and folktales. She contributed articles to the *Oxford Encyclopedia of Children's Literature*, as well as essays and reviews to journals such as *The Lion and the Unicorn*, *The Children's Literature Association Quarterly*, *Cahiers Robinson*, and *Children's Literature*, among others. She has been an active member of the Children's Literature Association in the past twenty years, and she is currently a member of its International Committee.

Maria Nikolajeva is a professor of comparative literature at Stockholm University, Sweden. She is the author and editor of several books on children's literature, among them *Children's Literature Comes of Age: Toward the New Aesthetic* (Garland, 1996), *From Mythic to Linear: Time in Children's Literature* (Scarecrow, 2000), and *The Rhetoric of Character in Children's Literature* (Scarecrow, 2002). She has also published a large number of articles in professional journals and essay collections. She was the president of the International Research Society for Children's Literature, 1993–97.

Janina Orlov holds a Ph.D. in Russian language and literature from Åbo Akademi University. She works as senior lecturer in children's literature at Stockholm University and Mälardalen University. She has guest-lectured in many countries and published several articles and reviews on children's literary history, Finland-Swedish and Finnish children's literature, as well as on Russian literature. Her current research work focuses on Soviet orphan stories and depictions of nature in Soviet books for children. She is also involved in writing a major history of Finland-Swedish children's literature. Janina Orlov also works as translator and columnist.

Dieter Petzold is an associate professor of English at the University of Erlangen-Nuremberg, Germany. He has also taught at the Universities of St. Andrews (Scotland), North Carolina (U.S.), and British Columbia (Canada). He is the author of books on Victorian nonsense literature (1972), J. R. R. Tolkien (1980, rev. ed. 2003), nineteenth-century literary fairy tales (1981), and Robinson Crusoe (1982), and the editor of several collections of essays, in particular on popular literature and fantasy fiction. Since 1996, he has also been the editor of *Inklings—Jahrbuch für Literatur und Ästhetik*, the yearbook of the German Inklings Society. He has published numerous articles, mainly in his major fields of interest: late Victorian literature, in particular Kipling;

non-mimetic fiction; and children's literature, both in English and in German, of the 19th and 20th centuries and the present.

Lilia Ratcheva-Stratieva was born in Bulgaria but has lived and worked in Austria since 1996. She graduated from the Sofia University "St. Kliment Ohridski" with an MA in literature and linguistics and specialized in children's literature in Poland, Germany, and the U.S. She has worked as a publisher and editor, a presenter of a TV program on children's books, and a university teacher in Bulgaria. She was coeditor of *Bookbird*, 2001–2004, and international coordinator of the EU Comenius Network BARFIE (Books and Reading for Intercultural Education), 2002–2005. She is the author of four books for children and numerous articles, published in journals or in book form in Austria, Bulgaria, Poland, France, China, Slovenia, UK, and other countries. She has served as a member of the international Andersen Jury (1996, 1998) and president of the Janusz Korczak International Jury (1987, 1990, 1998, and 2000).

Roberta Seelinger Trites is a professor of English at Illinois State University, where she teaches children's and adolescent literature. She is the author of *Waking Sleeping Beauty: Feminist Voices in Children's Books* (U of Iowa P, 1997) and *Disturbing the Universe: Power and Repression in Adolescent Literature* (U of Iowa P, 2000). She served as editor of the *Children's Literature Association Quarterly*, 2000–2004, and president of the Children's Literature Association during the 2006–2007 academic year.